Worship in the Letter
to the Hebrews

Worship in the Letter to the Hebrews

John Paul Heil

CASCADE *Books* • Eugene, Oregon

WORSHIP IN THE LETTER TO THE HEBREWS

Copyright © 2011 John Paul Heil. All rights reserved. Except for brief quotations in critical publications or reviews, no part of this book may be reproduced in any manner without prior written permission from the publisher. Write: Permissions, Wipf and Stock Publishers, 199 W. 8th Ave., Suite 3, Eugene, OR 97401.

Cascade Books
An Imprint of Wipf and Stock Publishers
199 W. 8th Ave., Suite 3
Eugene, OR 97401

www.wipfandstock.com

ISBN 13: 978-1-60899-947-7

Cataloging-in-Publication data:

Heil, John Paul.

    Worship in the Letter to the Hebrews / John Paul Heil.

    viii + 318 p. ; 23 cm. Includes bibliographical references and indexes.

    ISBN 13: 978-1-60899-947-7

    1. Bible. N.T. Hebrews—Criticism, interpretation, etc. 2. Worship—Biblical teaching. I. Title.

BS2775.2 H45 2011

Manufactured in the U.S.A.

Contents

Abbreviations • vii

Introduction • 1

1 Hebrews 1:1—2:18 • 15

2 Hebrews 3:1—5:10 • 50

3 Hebrews 5:11—7:28 • 88

4 Hebrews 8:1—9:28 • 119

5 Hebrews 10:1—11:19 • 163

6 Hebrews 11:20—13:25 • 207

Conclusion • 275

Bibliography • 289

Scripture Index • 299

Author Index • 315

Abbreviations

AB	Anchor Bible
ABD	*Anchor Bible Dictionary*, edited by D. N. Freedman, 6 vols. (New York, 1992)
AsTJ	*Asbury Theological Journal*
AUSS	*Andrews University Seminary Studies*
BBR	*Bulletin for Biblical Research*
BDAG	Bauer, W., F. W. Danker, W. F. Arndt, and F. W. Gingrich, *Greek-English Lexicon of the New Testament and Other Early Christian Literature*, 3rd ed. (Chicago, 1999)
Bib	*Biblica*
BIS	Biblical Interpretation Series
BR	*Biblical Research*
BRev	*Bible Review*
BSac	*Bibliotheca Sacra*
BT	*The Bible Translator*
BZ	*Biblische Zeitschrift*
BZNW	Beihefte zur Zeitschrift für die neutestamentliche Wissenschaft
CBQ	*Catholic Biblical Quarterly*
CBQMS	Catholic Biblical Quarterly Monograph Series
CTQ	*Concordia Theological Quarterly*
EDNT	*Exegetical Dictionary of the New Testament*, ed. H. Balz, G. Schneider (Grand Rapids, 1990-1993)
ETR	*Etudes théologiques et religieuses*
EvQ	*Evangelical Quarterly*
ExpTim	*Expository Times*
IBS	*Irish Biblical Studies*
Int	*Interpretation*

	JBL	*Journal of Biblical Literature*
	JETS	*Journal of the Evangelical Theological Society*
	JOTT	*Journal of Translation and Textlinguistics*
	JSNT	*Journal for the Study of the New Testament*
	JSNTSup	Journal for the Study of the New Testament: Supplement Series
	LNTS	Library of New Testament Studies
	Neot	*Neotestamentica*
	NICNT	New International Commentary on the New Testament
	NIGTC	New International Greek Testament Commentary
	NovT	*Novum Testamentum*
	NovTSup	Supplements to Novum Testamentum
	NRTh	*La nouvelle revue théologique*
	NTAbh	Neutestamentliche Abhandlungen
	NTL	New Testament Library
	NTS	*New Testament Studies*
	NTOA	Novum Testamentum et Orbis Antiquus
	ResQ	*Restoration Quarterly*
	SP	Sacra pagina
	SBLAbib	Society of Biblical Literature Academia Biblica
	SBLDS	Society of Biblical Literature Dissertation Series
	SBLMS	Society of Biblical Literature Monograph Series
	SNTSMS	Society for New Testament Studies Monograph Series
	STDJ	Studies on the Texts of the Desert of Judah
	TJ	*Trinity Journal*
	TLNT	*Theological Lexicon of the New Testament*, C. Spicq, tr. and ed. J. D. Ernest, 3 vols. (Peabody, MA, 1994)
	TynBul	*Tyndale Bulletin*
	WBC	Word Biblical Commentary
	WTJ	*Westminster Theological Journal*
	WUNT	Wissenschaftliche Untersuchungen zum Neuen Testament

Introduction: Worship in the Letter to the Hebrews

A DUAL PURPOSE INSPIRES AND drives my writing of this book. First, I seek a more comprehensive understanding and appreciation of the New Testament document known as the letter to the Hebrews by examining it from the viewpoint of its prominent theme of worship. With this book I assert and aim to demonstrate that the topic of worship in all of its rich and varied dimensions provides the major concern and thrust that embraces Hebrews from start to finish. The author of Hebrews encourages his audience to hold on to the letter he has written to them as "the word of the encouragement" (13:22). In a very carefully concerted and masterfully artistic way, the letter persistently encourages the members of its audience with regard to their worship. Indeed, Hebrews was intended to be presented orally in a public performance as a liturgical or homiletic letter, an act of worship in itself, heard by its audience gathered together as a worshiping assembly. Hebrews exhorts the members of its audience not only with regard to their liturgical worship in which they engage during their communal gatherings, but also with regard to their ethical or moral worship in which they engage by the way they conduct themselves outside of their communal gatherings.

Secondly, this close examination of Hebrews through the lens of worship is intended to inform and enrich the worship of Christians today.[1] In this book I will answer the question of what Hebrews tells us about not only the eucharistic dimensions of Christian worship but its other dimensions as well, such as listening and responding to the word of God, professing faith, seeking divine intercession and assistance, celebrating

---

1. Peterson, *Engaging with God*, 228: "Hebrews presents the most complete and fully integrated theology of worship in the New Testament."

and receiving the divine grace of forgiveness, praying, teaching, offering sacrifices of praise, sharing fellowship, etc.[2] Hebrews presents important and unique points about worship not found in any other New Testament writing. My goal is to illustrate and illuminate these points for the benefit of those who desire to deepen their worship as Christians by deepening their understanding of the magnificent literary masterpiece that the poetically lively letter to the Hebrews articulates for all Christians.

Worship in the New Testament

Before we begin our investigation of the theme of worship in the letter to the Hebrews, we need to consider the topic of worship more generally. Worship can be defined as

> those actions by which people express and reaffirm their devotional stance toward, and relationship to, a deity . . . worship more typically involves expressions of praise and adoration and also appeals directed to a deity, the devotee(s) usually expressing subordination to and/or dependence on the intended recipient of worship while also affirming a positive relationship with the recipient. In the NT—and in Christian tradition generally—although prayer and praise can be offered by individuals privately, Christian worship is more characteristically set in the gathered *ekklēsia*, the church.[3]

The praise and thanksgiving of Christian worship centers around the person, life, death, and resurrection of Jesus Christ. He is not only the one through whom and with whom Christians worship God, but also the object of worship himself along with God.[4] Christian worship is directed toward the risen Jesus now exalted at the authoritative and powerful right hand of God in heaven. The worship of Christians thus places them in contact with heavenly realities and the worship believed to be taking place in heaven. In and through their communal worship, Christians not

---

2. Among those who have argued for and stressed a eucharistic dimension to Hebrews are: Andriessen, "L'Eucharistie"; Swetnam, "Christology and the Eucharist"; Backhaus, *Neue Bund*, 228–32; Just, "Entering Holiness." See also Farkasfalvy, "Eucharistic Provenance."

3. Hurtado, "Worship," 910–11.

4. Powell, "Worship," 1392: "The most distinctive theological characteristic of NT worship is the centrality of Christ as its rationale, mediator, and ultimate object." See also Hurtado, *Origins of Christian Worship*; idem, *Lord Jesus Christ*; idem, *How on Earth*.

only commemorate and thus make present the past salvific activity God has accomplished in the life, death, and resurrection of Jesus, but anticipate and eagerly look forward to his final coming in glory to bring God's creative and redemptive activity to its ultimate completion.[5]

Presuppositions for Worship in Hebrews

Although we do not find evidence in the New Testament for many of the more exact details regarding the rituals involved in early Christian communal worship, we can point to some of the key elements that were most probably included, in one way or another, when Christians gathered as a liturgical assembly. We can assume that, in general, "Christians gathered to eat together (i.e., to celebrate the Lord's Supper), to baptize new members, to read Scripture, to listen to God speak to them through other Christians, to experience healing, to pray and sing hymns of praise and thanksgiving to God."[6]

The Acts of the Apostles describes what took place in the regular communal gatherings of the early Christians in Jerusalem in the following way: "They were devoting themselves to the teaching (*didachē*) of the apostles and to the fellowship (*koinōnia*), to the breaking of the bread (*klasei tou artou*) and to the prayers (*proseuchais*)" (Acts 2:42).[7] The author of Hebrews seems to presuppose that the members of his audience are familiar with these basic elements of Christian worship. As part of their communal worship they hear the "teaching" (*didachēs*) of the living word of God (Heb 6:2); they share in the "fellowship" (*koinōnias*) of professing their faith (13:15–16); they are to "pray" (*proseuchesthe*) as a community (13:18) with psalms (13:6); and they share in the eucharis-

---

5. Hurtado, "Worship," 911: "Christians ascribed a high meaning to their worship gatherings. They appear to have seen their worship as responding to, reflecting, and attesting heavenly realities (especially the exaltation of Jesus to God's 'right hand'), and also as prefiguring eschatological realities (particularly the universal acclamation of Jesus as 'Lord'). . . . NT texts urge that the worship gathering was not simply a human/earthly transaction but partook in transcendent realities, and was energized and enabled by God's Spirit."

6. Aune, "Worship," 973. See also Campbell, "Worship."

7. Peterson, *Acts*, 159–60: "Some commentators regard the four elements specified here as a primitive liturgical sequence, implying that their meetings regularly involved instruction, (table) fellowship, then the Lord's Supper and prayers. However, vv. 44–47 appear to be an expansion on this initial summary, and some of the things mentioned there clearly took place at different times and in different places."

tic "breaking of the bread," prefigured by the "presentation of the loaves (*prothesis tōn artōn*)" in the tabernacle (9:2; 13:10).[8]

The element of teaching was closely related to the reading of the sacred scriptures that took place in early Christian worship. According to 1 Tim 4:13, Paul instructed Timothy to attend to the "reading," that is, the public reading of the scriptures, to the exhortation inspired by and to the teaching based upon the scriptures. And according to 2 Tim 3:16, "all scripture is inspired by God and advantageous for teaching, for reproof, for correction, for training in righteousness."[9] With his multiple citations and extended explanations of a rich variety of scriptural quotations, the author of Hebrews admirably exemplifies how the sacred scriptures and their interpretation can be adroitly exploited for teaching and exhortation. He presupposes that the members of his audience are thoroughly familiar with these scriptures, which they would have heard regularly as part of their worship services.[10]

The author of Hebrews also presupposes that the members of his audience regularly participated in a sacred eucharistic meal as part of their communal worship.[11] The eucharistic meals celebrated by early Christians commemorated and gave thanks to God for the salvific signifi-

---

8. On the term "breaking of the bread" here as inclusive of a eucharistic meal, see Fitzmyer, *Acts*, 271; Heil, *Meal Scenes*, 237–38.

9. Towner, *Timothy and Titus*, 317: "It is normally assumed, apparently, that the primary function of the public reading of Scripture in the worship setting was to lay the groundwork for the preaching and teaching to follow." Aune, "Worship," 983: "One important feature of Christian worship with close parallels in synagogue Judaism is the practice of reading aloud from sacred texts, usually accompanied by a homiletic explanation of the meaning and significance of the reading. Such reading is not in itself worship, though the context in which it is done is. However, if worship is regarded as communication between God and his people, then the reading of Scripture must be construed as one important mode whereby God's word is mediated to those assembled."

10. On the use and interpretation of the Old Testament in Hebrews, see Docherty, *Use of the Old Testament*.

11. According to Hurtado, *Lord Jesus Christ*, 145, "it is commonly accepted that a sacred meal was a characteristic feature of Christian circles from the earliest years onward... the meal is obviously a 'cultic' occasion that formed a key part of the devotional/liturgical life of early Christian groups. Christians ate these common meals to express their fellowship with one another and also with direct reference to Jesus.... In the tradition that Paul recites in [1 Cor] 11:23–26, he associates the bread and wine of the meal directly with Jesus' redemptive death, which is constitutive of 'the new covenant'; Paul also characterizes the continuing cult-meal practice as a proclamation of the death of 'the Lord' until his eschatological return."

Introduction: Worship in the Letter to the Hebrews 5

cance of Jesus with explicit and/or implicit reference to his redemptive death and resurrection.[12] The author seems to rely upon his audience's general familiarity with key terms employed in the narratives about the institution of the eucharistic Lord's Supper. They may have gained this familiarity from their having heard the traditions behind the gospel passion narratives or other traditions about Jesus's suffering and death, from the ritual they used to celebrate the Eucharist, and/or from eucharistic catecheses.[13] At any rate, the author refers to such eucharistic terms as "body," "blood of the (new) covenant," "on behalf of," "forgiveness of sins" (cf. Matt 26:26–29; Mark 14:22–25; Luke 22:19–20; 1 Cor 11:23–26; Heb 2:9; 5:1; 6:20; 7:25, 27; 9:7, 14–15, 20, 22, 24; 10:5, 10, 12, 18, 29; 12:24; 13:20). Furthermore, all of the various versions of this traditional terminology have their common OT background in such texts as Exod 24:1–11; Jer 38:31–34 (LXX); and Isa 53:10–12, which the author employs throughout his letter (cf. Heb 8:8–12; 9:20, 28; 10:16–17).[14]

---

12. As noted by Hurtado, "Worship," 922, "an explicit reference to Jesus' redemptive death seems not always a feature of Christian sacred meals, as is demonstrated especially in the eucharistic prayers in *Did.* 9–10. This extra-canonical text is widely regarded as preserving liturgical material from a very early time. . . . Although Jesus' redemptive death and resurrection are not directly mentioned in these prayers in *Didache*, he is obviously central, the focus and continuing basis of the thanksgiving given to God. Moreover, there is no reason to read into these prayers some supposed reluctance to see Jesus' death as redemptive or to posit some radically different form of Christianity from which the prayers derive. . . . the explicit references to Jesus' death, and the familiar 'words of institution' setting the bread and cup within the context of Jesus' last supper, when they were used in 1st cent. circles, may have formed part of an introduction to the eucharistic meal and not part of the prayers recited as part of the eucharist." For more on the *Didache*, see Niederwimmer, *Didache*; Milavec, *Didache*. For more on the origins of the Eucharist, see Koenig, *Feast*; Smith, *Symposium*; Bradshaw, *Eucharistic Origins*; Stringer, *Origins of the Eucharist*.

13. For ritualistic traditions about Jesus' suffering and death that developed apart from the gospel passion narratives, see Aitken, *Jesus' Death*. On the words of the institution of the eucharistic meal as interpretive reflections or catecheses, see McGowan, "Liturgical Text."

14. Klauck, "Lord's Supper," 368: "The author of the Epistle to the Hebrews develops his theology in large measure with the help of linguistic models taken from the OT and the Jewish sacrificial cult. Among them one finds also concepts that are known to us from the traditions concerning the Lord's Supper. In 9:20 he quotes the saying about 'the blood of the covenant' from Exod 24:8, and not with the introductory 'behold' (*idou*) as in the LXX, but rather with 'this' (*touto*), a word that one tends to connect with the words of interpretation."

Authorship and Literary Genre of Hebrews

The anonymous author of Hebrews refers to himself with a masculine participle (Heb 11:32). Although unknown to us, he was apparently well known to his audience. At one time he had been with his audience, and now hopes to be restored to them (13:19). Accompanied by "our brother Timothy," who has been "released," he expects to see his audience soon (13:23).[15]

Although Hebrews does not begin with the identification of its sender and recipients, it concludes with customary epistolary characteristics.[16] The author refers to what he has presented in Hebrews as "the word of the encouragement" that "I have written by letter to you" (13:22). The same terminology is used—"a word of encouragement"—to describe the homily or sermon that Paul delivered in the synagogue at Pisidian Antioch (Acts 13:15). Hence, Hebrews may be considered an epistolary homily or sermon, or more precisely in accord with its own self-description, "the word of the encouragement written by letter," and it was intended to be read publicly and heard by its envisioned audience in the communal setting of their worshiping assembly.[17] It not only exemplifies and epitomizes the kind of homily or sermon or "word of encouragement" that was delivered by a leader within a worshiping assembly, but, its main thrust is to deepen the understanding and appreciation of its audience, some of whom are apparently abandoning their liturgical gatherings (Heb 10:25), for the significance of what takes place in and through their communal worship.

---

15. That Apollos, who was known as "an eloquent speaker, powerful in the scriptures" (Acts 18:24), and who was associated with Paul, along with Timothy, in Ephesus when Paul wrote 1 Corinthians (1 Cor 16:8, 10, 12), authored Hebrews in view of its eloquent employment of the Scriptures, is a plausible hypothesis, but only an hypothesis. See Guthrie, "Apollos"; Kistemaker, "Authorship"; Johnson, *Hebrews*, 40–44; Witherington, *Letters and Homilies*, 17–24. For detailed discussions of the possible identity of the author, see Attridge, *Hebrews*, 1–6; Bruce, *Hebrews*, 14–20; Lane, *Hebrews 1–8*, xlix–li; Ellingworth, *Hebrews*, 3–21; DeSilva, *Perseverance*, 23–27; Koester, *Hebrews*, 42–46; Koosed and Seesengood, "Constructions"; Salevao, *Legitimation*, 95–121; Mitchell, *Hebrews*, 2–6; O'Brien, *Hebrews*, 2–9.

16. For an unconvincing attempt to argue that Hebrews 13 was written by a different author than chapters 1–12 and for a different situation, see Wedderburn, "Hebrews." See also Hagner, *Hebrews*, 29–30.

17. Attridge, "Paraenesis"; Wray, *Rest*; Schenck, *Understanding*; Walker, "Hebrews"; Gelardini, "Hebrews"; Lincoln, *Hebrews*, 9–14; Portalatín, *Temporal Oppositions*, 9–26.

Audience and Date of Hebrews

The title of the document, "To Hebrews" (*Pros Hebraious*), was added in the second or third century, and thus cannot be taken as a certain indication of either the geographical destination of the letter or the ethnic composition of its audience.[18] The author's statement that "those from Italy greet you" (13:24) probably indicates that the letter was sent to an audience located somewhere in Italy, with Rome as the most probable destination. It may well have been composed and sent from Ephesus, a city with which Timothy is closely associated (Acts 19:22; 1 Cor 16:8; 1 Tim 1:3; 2 Tim 1:18; 4:12; cf. Heb 13:23). But there is no certainty regarding either the geographical provenance or the destination of the letter.

Regarding the date of the letter, many think it was probably written before the destruction of Jerusalem (70 CE), reasoning that if the sacrificial cult in the temple there had already been terminated, this fact would surely have been employed within the author's argument. But the argument of the letter is based on scriptural references to the sacrificial cult associated with the tabernacle rather than with the temple. And so there are those who argue for a date after the destruction of the temple.[19] Perhaps the most that can be said with relative certainty is that Hebrews was written sometime in the latter half of the first century.[20]

Literary Structure of Hebrews

As I have demonstrated elsewhere, the text of Hebrews divides itself into three distinct but interconnected macrochiastic levels.[21] The first level divides the entire text into three main sections in a basic A-B-A' chiastic pattern. The second level divides each of these three main sections into eleven distinct units arranged in an A-B-C-D-E-F-E'-D'-C'-B'-A' pattern. The third level divides the first five as well as the final five units of each of these main sections into a total of six A-B-C-B'-A' patterns. Furthermore, each of the thirty-three distinct units of the letter exhibits

---

18. On the title, see Koester, *Hebrews*, 171–73.

19. For a possible date after the destruction of the temple in Jerusalem, see Schenck, *Cosmology*, 195–98. See also Aitken, "Portraying the Temple," 133–36.

20. Attridge, *Hebrews*, 9: "The most probable range of dates within which Hebrews was composed is thus 60 to 100 CE. Decisive reasons for a precise dating or narrower range have not been adduced."

21. Heil, *Hebrews*.

its own microchiastic structure, with some of them containing additional smaller chiastic patterns. All of these various levels of chiastic structures are consistently based on very precise linguistic parallels found within the text itself. The goal has been not to insert the text within a predetermined structural mold, but to discover the structure(s) that the text itself projects. In addition, there are various transitional words that connect each unit to the unit that immediately precedes it. These transitional words indicate that the chiastic units are heard by the audience of Hebrews as a closely interconnected and cohesive sequence.

First Macrochiastic Level

A   1:1—5:10: Be Faithful in Heart to Grace from the Son and High Priest

    B   5:11—9:28: We Await the High Priest Who Offered Himself to Intercede

A'   10:1—13:25: By Faith with Grace in Heart Let Us Do the Will of the Living God

In the A section (1:1—5:10) of this first macrochiastic level the audience of Christian believers are exhorted to be faithful in their hearts to the grace of God now generously available to us from Jesus as the Son in whom God, as the "living" God, is still speaking to us, and as the faithful and merciful high priest who has become a source of eternal salvation for all who faithfully obey him.[22] The B section (5:11—9:28) then deepens the audience's appreciation for the death and resurrection/exaltation of Jesus as his heavenly high-priestly act of worship in which his unique self-sacrifice expiated our sins. This enabled him to continually intercede for us, so that we may offer worship pleasing to the living God, as we eagerly await the second coming of the Christ in hope for final salvation from death to eternal life, the life of the living God. In the A' section (10:1—13:25), by way of chiastic development of the A section, the audience is exhorted, by their persevering faith and with their hearts confirmed by God's generous grace, with and through Jesus to offer worship pleasing to God in hope for final salvation from death to eternal life by doing the will of the living God.

---

22. The collective noun "audience" will be used as a plural rather than singular noun, so that it better conforms to the Greek text of Hebrews, which employs plural terms in reference to its audience, envisioned as composed of various individual members.

Second Macrochiastic Level

A   1:1—5:10: Be Faithful in Heart to Grace from the Son and High Priest

  AA   1:1-4: *God Spoke* to Us in a *Son* Who Made a Cleansing for *Sins*

    AB   1:5-14: Angels Are *Spirits* to Assist Those Inheriting Salvation

      AC   2:1-4: How Will We Escape, Neglecting the *Word* of Salvation?

        AD   2:5-9: We *Note* Jesus Who on Behalf of All Might Taste Death

          AE   2:10-18: Those Who Are *Being Tested* He Is Able to Help

            AF   3:1-6: Jesus as Son Faithful beyond Moses

          AE'   3:7-11: Those Who *Tested* Will Never Enter into My Rest

        AD'   3:12-19: We *Note* the Unfaithful Were Not Able to Enter the Rest

      AC'   4:1-11: The *Word* of Rest They Heard Did Not Benefit Them

    AB'   4:12-13: The Living Word of God Penetrates Soul and *Spirit*

  AA'   4:14—5:10: *God Spoke* to the *Son* as a Priest Who Sacrifices for *Sins*

B   5:11—9:28: We Await the High Priest Who Offered Himself to Intercede

BA   5:11—6:12: Imitate Those Inheriting the Promises of *Salvation*

  BB   6:13-20: As *Heirs* Hold Fast to the Hope as a *Firm* Anchor

    BC   7:1-10: See How Great Is Melchizedek Who Goes On *Living*

      BD   7:11-17: According to the Order of Melchizedek not Aaron

        BE   7:18-28: He Is Able to Save the *People* from *Sins*

          BF   8:1-6: High Priest of Things Shown to Moses

>>>> **BE'** 8:7–13: The *People* Whose *Sins* God Does Not Remember

>>> **BD'** 9:1–10: *Aaronic* Sacrifices Do Not Perfect Us in Conscience

>> **BC'** 9:11–14: Blood of Christ Cleanses Our Conscience for *Living* God

> **BB'** 9:15–23: We May Receive the Eternal *Inheritance* of *Firm* Covenant

BA' 9:24–28: Christ Will Bring *Salvation* to Those Eagerly Awaiting Him

A' 10:1—13:25: By Faith with Grace in Heart Let Us Do the Will of the Living God

A'A 10:1–14: You Have *Provided* a Body for Me *to Do* Your *Will* for the *Good*

> **A'B** 10:15–30: *Hearts Made Holy* Not *Abandoning* as the Lord *Will Judge*

>> **A'C** 10:31–39: *Fearful* of *Hands* of the *Living God* for What *Remains*

>>> **A'D** 11:1–7: An Heir of *Righteousness* according to Faith

>>>> **A'E** 11:8–19: With *Promises* He *Acquired* Him from the *Dead*

>>>>> **A'F** 11:20–31: Moses a Model of Faith in Christ

>>>> **A'E'** 11:32–40: Their *Dead* Not the *Promise* Did They *Acquire*

>>> **A'D'** 12:1–11: The Peaceful Fruit of *Righteousness*

>> **A'C'** 12:12–29: *Unfearful Hands* for What *Remains* from the *Living God*

> **A'B'** 13:1–16: God *Will Judge* Not *Abandon* the *Heart Made Holy* by Jesus

A'A' 13:17–25: May God *Provide* You with Every *Good* to *Do* His *Will*

The above schematic overview illustrates how each of the main A-B-A' sections of the first macrochiastic level is divided into eleven units arranged in chiastic patterns that constitute the second macrochiastic level. The sixth unit in each eleven-unit section, that is, 3:1–6, 8:1–6, and 11:20–31, forms the central and pivotal unit for that section. The chiastic parallels are indicated by the words in italics in the titles of each unit.

Third Macrochiastic Level

Aa 1:1—2:18: Let Us Not Neglect So Great a Salvation

Aaa 1:1–4: Having Made a Cleansing for *Sins*

    Aab 1:5–14: God Will Place Your Enemies as a *Footstool for Your Feet*

        Aac 2:1–4: The Confirmed Word of Salvation

    Aab' 2:5–9: We Do Not Yet See All Things Subjected *under His Feet*

Aaa' 2:10–18: Tested to Expiate *Sins* of Those Being Tested

Ab 3:1–6: We Are His House If We Hold to the Hope

Aa' 3:7—5:10: For All Who Obey He Became a Source of Eternal Salvation

Aa'a 3:7–11: Do Not Harden Your Hearts Like Those Who *Tested*

    Aa'b 3:12–19: Take Note That You Do Not Fall Away from the *Living God*

        Aa'c 4:1–11: The Word for Hearing

    Aa'b' 4:12–13: *Living* is the Word of *God* That Penetrates to the Spirit

Aa'a' 4:14—5:10: We Have a High Priest Who Has Been *Tested* in All Things

Ba 5:11—7:28: Let Us Approach God through Jesus Who Is Able to Save Us

Baa 5:11—6:12: The *Word* of Righteousness

    Bab 6:13–20: High Priest Forever *according to the Order of Melchizedek*

        Bac 7:1–10: A High Priest Who Goes On Living

    Bab' 7:11–17: Priest Forever *according to the Order of Melchizedek*

Baa' 7:18–28: The *Word* of the Oath

Bb 8:1–6: Guarantor of a Better Covenant with Better Promises

Ba′ Heb 8:7—9:28: The Christ Who Offered Himself We Await for Salvation

Ba′a 8:7–13: The *Sins* of Them I Will Remember No Longer

    Ba′b 9:1–10: The Tablets of the *Covenant*

        Ba′c 9:11–14: That We May Offer Worship to the Living God

    Ba′b′ 9:15–23: Guarantor of a New *Covenant*

Ba′a′ 9:24–28: Offered for the *Sins* of Many He Will Be Seen Again Without *Sin*

A′a 10:1—11:19: With Faith Let Us Approach the Living God To Live

A′aa 10:1–14: *Waiting* until His Enemies Are Placed as a Footstool for His Feet

    A′ab 10:15–30: The Holy Spirit *Testifies* for Us To *Approach*

        A′ac 10:31–39: Fearful to Fall into the Hands of the Living God

    A′ab′ 11:1–7: Abel and Enoch *Testified* To *Approach* God

A′aa′ 11:8–19: *Waiting* for the City Having Foundations Made by God

A′b 11:20–31: By Faith Moses Endured the Reproach of the Christ

A′a′ 11:32—13:25: To Live Let Us Offer Worship Pleasing to the Living God

A′a′a 11:32–40: Women Received Their *Dead* from Resurrection

    A′a′b 12:1–11: The Peaceful *Fruit* of Righteousness through Discipline

        A′a′c 12:12–29: Not What Is Fearful But the City of the Living God

    A′a′b′ 13:1–16: Offer to God the *Fruit* of Lips Confessing His Name

A′a′a′ 13:17–25: God Led Up from the *Dead* the Great Shepherd of the Sheep

The above schematic overview illustrates how each of the eleven-unit main sections of the second macrochiastic level is further divided into three chiastically arranged subsections. The first subsections consist of the first five units of each main section (1:1—2:18; 5:11—7:28; 10:1—11:19), in which each five-unit subsection exhibits its own chiastic arrangement. The second subsections consist of the single sixth unit of each main section (3:1–6; 8:1–6; 11:20–31). And the third subsections consist of the last five units of each main section (3:7—5:10; 8:7—9:28; 11:32—13:25), in which each five-unit subsection exhibits its own chiastic arrangement. The single-unit second (b) subsections thus function as the pivotal sections in the chiastic alternation between the first five-unit (a) subsections and the last five-unit (a′) subsections in each main section. The chiastic parallels within each five-unit subsection are indicated by the words in italics within the titles of each unit.

It should be noted that the illustrations of all of the above chiastic levels and patterns are merely a visual attempt to indicate to a modern reader what structural patterns the ancient audience were experiencing, but not necessarily consciously detecting, as they listened to the oral performance of the letter. These visual illustrations help us to better see, understand, and appreciate what the original audience experienced as they listened to the oral performance of the letter to the Hebrews. In addition, they provide us with a structural organization as the basis for a close reading or listening to the text for the purpose of a consistent and complete text-centered exegesis.

The Plan of This Book

The above structural delineation of thirty-three distinct chiastic units will guide our investigation into the vibrant theme of worship in the letter to the Hebrews. Chapter 1 will consider worship in the first five chiastic units (1:1–4; 1:5–14; 2:1–4; 2:5–9; 2:10–18) of the first main (A) eleven-unit section, which form a chiastic pattern in themselves in accord with the third macrochiastic level. Chapter 2 will consider worship in the final six chiastic units of the first eleven-unit section. After an examination of the central and pivotal sixth unit (3:1–6), we move to the concluding five chiastic units (3:7–11; 3:12–19; 4:1–11; 4:12–13; 4:14—5:10), which form a chiastic pattern in themselves in accord with the third macrochiastic level.

Chapter 3 will consider worship in the first five chiastic units (5:11—6:12; 6:13–20; 7:1–10; 7:11–17; 7:18–28) of the second main (B) eleven-unit section, which form a chiastic pattern in themselves in accord with the third macrochiastic level. Chapter 4 will consider worship in the final six chiastic units of the second eleven-unit section. After an examination of the central and pivotal sixth unit (8:1–6), we move to the concluding five chiastic units (8:7–13; 9:1–10; 9:11–14; 9:15–23; 9:24–28), which form a chiastic pattern in themselves in accord with the third macrochiastic level.

Chapter 5 will consider worship in the first five chiastic units (10:1–14; 10:15–30; 10:31–39; 11:1–7; 11:8–19) of the third main (A′) eleven-unit section, which form a chiastic pattern in themselves in accord with the third macrochiastic level. Chapter 6 will consider worship in the final six chiastic units of the third eleven-unit section. After an examination of the central and pivotal sixth unit (11:20–31), we move to the concluding five chiastic units (11:32–40; 12:1–11; 12:12–29; 13:1–16; 13:17–25), which form a chiastic pattern in themselves in accord with the third macrochiastic level. Finally, in the conclusion I will sum up and present the results of the investigation. I now invite you to join me in an endeavor to deepen and enrich our Christian worship by deepening and enriching our understanding of and appreciation for the intriguing and inspiring letter to the Hebrews.

1

Hebrews 1:1—2:18

I. 1:1–4

A ¹:¹ Multifacetedly and multifariously much time ago God, having spoken to the fathers in the prophets, ²ᵃ at the end of these days has spoken to us in a Son, whom he *placed* (*ethēken*) as *heir* of all things (Ps 2:8),

   B ²ᵇ through whom also he *made* the ages,

      C ³ᵃ who, being radiance of the glory and representation of the reality of *him*,

      C′ ³ᵇ and bearing up all things by the pronouncement of the power of *him* (Wis 7:25–26),

   B′ ³ᶜ having *made* a cleansing for sins (Job 7:21),

A′ ³ᵈ *sat* (*ekathisen*) at the right of the Majesty in the heights (Ps 109:1), ⁴ having become so far better than the angels to the degree that more excellent beyond them he has *inherited a name*.[1]

WITH AN ALLURINGLY ALLITERATIVE and sonorously appealing introduction, "multifacetedly and multifariously," the audience are

---

1. In this and all subsequent chapters references to OT passages are from the LXX, following that version's numbering system. The translation of this and all subsequent biblical texts is my own, presenting what I call an "exegetical" translation. The aim is to present a strictly literal translation that attempts, as far as possible, to follow the Greek word order and to render the same Greek words with the same English equivalents. Where possible, I have also tried to represent some of the noteworthy alliteration in the Greek text, e.g., "Multifacetedly and multifariously much time ago" for the impressive alliteration in *Polymerōs kai polytropōs palai* that introduces the letter in 1:1. The italicized words indicate the chiastic parallels.

alerted to the rich variety of ways that in past times God spoke to their ancestors in the prophets (1:1). It is in a context of liturgical worship, which included the reading of the OT scriptures, that the audience can be expected to have heard the diverse ways that God spoke much time ago to their ancestors in the prophets.[2] But "at the end of these days," that is, in the time of the final and definitive fulfillment of what God spoke in the prophets, God has spoken to "us"—the author, his audience, and all Christians—in a Son.[3] The audience begin to hear how God spoke to us in a Son with the description of him as a Son whom God "placed as heir of all things" (1:2a). This tells the audience, presumed to be able to recognize the allusion here to Ps 2:8,[4] that God has placed his royal Son as heir not just of the nations and the ends of the earth, as promised in the psalm, but of absolutely all things in the cosmos.[5] As included within "all things" divinely inherited by this Son as his possession, the audience are to begin to appreciate how God's Son has been included, along with God himself, as a worthy focus of their worship in response to God's word.

The way God spoke to us in a Son by what God did *for* his Son in placing him as heir of all things in the cosmos (1:2a) progresses to the way God spoke to us in a Son by what God did *through* his Son—"through whom also he made the ages" (1:2b). The term, "the ages," here refers to the world in both its temporal and spatial dimensions, the world in which

---

2. Lane, *Hebrews 1–8*, 11: "The conviction that God cares for people and relates himself to them through his spoken word is developed as a major motif by the writer. In the opening lines he concentrates his hearers' attention on the authority of the God who speaks. The locus of God's spoken word for him was the Scriptures. He customarily introduces passages from the OT as God's direct speech (e.g., 1:5–13; 5:5–6; 7:17, 21). The persuasion that God's word is living and active in human experience (4:12) undergirds the appeal to the authority of the Scriptures throughout Hebrews and prepares the hearers for the solemn exhortation not to refuse the God who is speaking (12:25) at the conclusion of the sermon." Johnson, *Hebrews*, 65: "As it is used in the prologue, therefore, the term [prophets] is probably meant to suggest all the agents by whom God's word and will were disclosed to the people, including angels, Moses and Joshua, and the priestly cult, in addition to all the heroes of faith recorded in chapter 11. But the term in the plural may also refer to the very texts of Scripture that report all these acts of revelation, and thereby also reveal them." O'Brien, *Hebrews*, 48–49: "But for the author of Hebrews what God said through the prophets is to be found in the Old Testament Scriptures."

3. On the overall continuity here, despite the contrast, see Smillie, "Contrast."

4. Throughout this study "audience" refers to the audience implied in the text, which is an ideal audience presupposed to possess all the knowledge needed to grasp the author's discourse.

5. Guthrie, "Hebrews," 924.

the audience are now living "at the end of these days" (1:2a).[6] That God made the ages that embrace the entire cosmos through his Son tells the audience that both God and his Son are deserving of their worship as the divine co-creators of the universe.

Having heard of what God has done for and through his Son, the audience now hear the way God has spoken to us through the distinctive divine status the Son possesses as one who is continually existing as radiance of the glory and representation of the reality "of him," that is, of God himself (1:3a). This Son continues to exist with a very active divine status, doubly designated for added emphasis. First, he continues in "being," an ongoing action expressed with the present active participle, as a "radiance," an active, luminous radiating or shining forth of the heavenly "glory" of God himself. Second, he continues in being as a "representation," of the very "reality," the "substance" or "essence," of God as the Father who positioned his Son to be heir of all things (1:2a), and as the Creator who made the ages through the agency of this Son (1:2b). That this Son projects divine "glory" serves as a motivation for the audience to give glory to or glorify both God and God's divine Son in their worship.[7]

The Son whom God placed as heir of "all things" (1:2a) that God created, and the Son through whom God made the ages (1:2b), is the one who continually "bears up" (*pherōn*, present active participle), "sustains," and "carries" to their completion "all the things" that constitute and comprise the universe God created.[8] That he does this by the active "pronouncement" of the very power "of him" (1:3b), the pivotal chiastic

---

6. BDAG, 32–33; Johnson, *Hebrews*, 67. See also Schenck, *Cosmology*; Adams, "Cosmology."

7. Newman, "Glory," 576: "Glory-language in the Bible has both subjective and objective senses. Subjectively, glory refers to the act of worship (e.g., 'give glory to God'). Objectively, glory denotes the object of worship (i.e., God's revealed presence, God's glory). In both its subjective and objective senses, glory-language became an important marker in the development of Israel and the church's faith (monotheism) and practice (worship). What was once reserved for Israel's one true God ('giving glory to God,' 'glorifying God'), early Christians ascribed to the resurrected Jesus. Further, Christians claimed that Jesus was the glory of God, God's revealed presence. Glory-language was thus an important way for conveying the Christian understanding of God."

8. Wright, "Seal." O'Brien, *Hebrews*, 56–57: "The verb used here, *pherō*, has the primary sense of 'sustain or uphold'. The immediate context, however, suggests the additional nuance of the Son's 'carrying' all things to their appointed end or goal. The notion of direction or purpose seems to be included . . . the language implies a 'bearing' that includes movement and progress towards an objective."

parallel with the reality "of him" (1:3a), of God himself, tells the audience, as those included among all the things the Son continues to bear up and carry, that they, as creatures of God, are dependent for their continued existence upon a Son in whom God has spoken to us (1:2a).[9] When the audience hear the Son described as "a radiance of the glory" of God, who bears up all things by the pronouncement of "the power" of God (1:3ab), they are reminded of an impressive resemblance of the Son to the personified divine wisdom described in Wis 7:25–26: "For she is an aura of the power of God and a pure effusion of the glory of the Almighty . . . a radiance of eternal light."[10] This scriptural allusion underscores for the audience the truly sublime divine status of the Son. The audience are thus further induced to worship both God and his Son, who sustains and carries all things to completion, including themselves, by the pronouncement of the power of the God who has spoken to us in a Son.

In accord with the chiastic parallels, the audience hear a progression from the agency of the Son in God's creative making—"through whom he *made* the ages" (1:2b)—to the Son as subject of an expiatory making—"having *made* a cleansing for sins" (1:3c). The audience, already attuned to the wisdom tradition by the allusion in 1:3ab, may now recall Job's address to God for insight into the Son's cultic act of "having made a cleansing for sins" as a key for the continuance and fulfillment of their own lives: "And why did you not *make* oblivion for my lawlessness and a *cleansing for my sin*? For I will go away into the ground, and I will no longer be rising early in the morning" (Job 7:21).[11] The audience are to appreciate that the Son not only is continually bearing them up and carrying them to completion within their cosmic, creaturely existence as part

---

9. On "pronouncement" (*rhēmati*) in reference to the word of God's power spoken by the Son here, see Radl, "*rhēma*," 210. Mitchell, *Hebrews*, 38: "Since the instrument of sustenance is the powerful word of God, the sense is that the universe continues to exist because of the powerful word, which caused it to exist in the first place (Genesis 1). The difference, of course, is that here it is the Son's word that does the sustaining, so he has been given the role of the creator God in keeping all things in existence. This verse offers yet another example of how Hebrews identifies the Son and the Father closely in the exordium."

10. For a detailed illustration of the comparison, see Gheorghita, *Septuagint*, 93. Gheorghita, however, neglects the parallel with "the power." That these are the only two occurrences in both the OT and NT of the word "radiance" (*apaugasma*) enhances the significance of this allusion.

11. The allusion is noted by Westcott, *Hebrews*, 15; Lane, *Hebrews 1–8*, 15.

of all things (1:3b), but that he has made a cultic cleansing for their sins within their earthly, human existence, as a basis for them to go on living and worshiping God. Having accomplished the cultic cleansing of sins, an act of ritual worship, the Son has removed a major barrier preventing access to God. Thanks to the Son's own act of worship the audience may now enter into the presence of God to worship God together with God's divine Son.[12]

The audience then hear a chiastic progression from the Son as the object of a verb with God as the subject who "placed" (*ethēken*) the Son as heir of all things (1:2a) to the Son, as subject of the alliterative counterpart of the verb, who "sat" (*ekathisen*) at the right of the Majesty in the heights (1:3d). The Son, having made a cleansing for the sins of human beings on earth, sat "at the right," the authoritative position of power, of "the Majesty," that is, of God himself, "in the heights," that is, in heaven.[13] The audience are to realize, then, that the Son has been privileged to obey the inviting command of God as "the Lord," who "said to my Lord, 'Sit at my right'" (Ps 109:1).[14] The chiastic parallelism thus facilitates the audience's understanding that it is because the Son, through divine entitlement, "sat" at the powerful right of God in heaven that God "placed" him as heir of all things. In other words, because of the Son's act of ritualistic worship in having made a cleansing for sins (1:3c), he was divinely authorized to sit at the right of God and become an object of worship as the divinely placed heir of all things.

The audience hear another chiastic progression from the Son whom God placed as "heir" of all things (1:2a) to the Son who has become vastly superior to the angels, because he has "inherited a name" (1:4).

12. O'Brien, *Hebrews*, 58: "It is significant that the Son's earthly ministry is described from the first in cultic categories. The purification of sins is one of the author's major concerns, but at this stage there is no explicit mention of high-priestly terminology or any direct reference to the cross.... By making purification for sins the Son accomplished something which no one else could achieve. The forgiveness he has won is permanent, and, because the barrier between God and humanity has been removed, it results in entry into the presence of God himself. Such a provision on our behalf, which has perfectly dealt with the defilement of sin, calls forth from us a response of wholehearted gratitude."

13. O'Brien, *Hebrews*, 59–60: "The term *Majesty* is a circumlocution for God and underscores the impression of the Son's surpassing glory. His enthronement at 'the right hand of the divine Majesty' shows that the rank and rule of God the Father is not compromised in any way, while the addition of 'on high' focuses attention on the heavenly sphere of Christ's exaltation."

14. Attridge, "Psalms," 197.

As the final, climactic word, with a reverberating assonance, the "name" (*onoma*) that the Son conclusively "inherited" and continues to possess (*keklēronomēken* in the perfect tense) underscores the divine, heavenly status of the Son as "heir" (*klēronomon*) of all things. This "name" is not limited to a single identifying title, such as "Son" or "Lord." Rather it refers to all of the various dimensions, which the audience have heard and will yet hear, that characterize the divine status of the Son. Indeed, the audience have heard how God "multifacetedly and multifariously" has spoken to us in a Son (1:1–2a) through what God has done for and through a Son and what the Son has been divinely empowered to do for us. All of this is part of what constitutes the "name" the Son inherited from God his Father. Thus, the Son has been divinely "named" as the heir of all things (1:2a), the agent of creation (1:2b), radiance of the glory and representation of the divine reality (1:3a), the one bearing up all things by the pronouncement of divine power (1:3b), and the one who, having made a cleansing for sins (1:3c), sat at the right of the Majesty in the heights (1:3d), vastly superior to the angels (1:4).[15]

That the Son has inherited a "name," a divine status, vastly superior to the angels means not only that God's speaking to us in a Son surpasses the way God has spoken through angels (cf. 2:2), but also that, unlike the angels, the Son, who now sits enthroned with God in heaven (1:3d), is entitled and worthy to be worshiped along with God. At this point the audience not only have heard some of the ways God has spoken to us in a Son, but also have been drawn into a worshipful response by the aesthetically elevated and hymn-like language with its strikingly uncommon vocabulary in this first unit (1:1–4).[16] In other words, the author's

---

15. On "name" as not merely an identifying label, but as a term expressing the essential characteristics or status of a person, see BDAG, 712; Hartman, "*onoma*," 519. On the background and significance of the terms "heir" and "inherit" here, see Friedrich, "*klēronomeō*," 298–99.

16. Although probably not a preexisting early Christian hymn, this elegant introduction of the letter (1:1–4) exhibits noteworthy hymnic characteristics. O'Brien, *Hebrews*, 47: "Balanced clauses that describe the Son are introduced by the relative pronoun 'who' which is typical of hymnic passages (note Phil. 2:6; Col. 1:15; 1 Tim 3:16), and along with unusual vocabulary, such as *radiance, exact representation, purification,* and *sustaining*. . . . Further, the passage describes the movement of the Son from his preexistence to his sharing in humanity and exaltation, a progress similar to that in other so-called hymnic passages." Farris, "Hymns," 923: "Hymns, more narrowly defined, can be discerned by their apparent metric form, by the parallelism so characteristic of Hebrew poetry, or by vocabulary or concepts different from the surrounding prose. These hymns

awe-inspiring and poetically hymnic way of informing the audience of how God has spoken to us in a Son serves at the same time as an act of laudatory worship, leading his audience to join him in grateful praise and reverent awe of God and his divine Son. This initial hymnic act of worship thus establishes an overall context of worship for the discourse to follow. The audience are now poised to hear the author elaborate more ways that God has definitively spoken to us in a Son worthy to be worshiped along with God, since this Son has inherited a divine, heavenly status far better and more excellent than the angels themselves.[17]

II. 1:5–14

A[5] For to *which* of *the angels* did he *ever* say, "Son of mine are you, today I have begotten you (Ps 2:7)?" And again, "I will be to him as Father, and he will be to me as Son (2 Sam 7:14)?" [6] And again, when he leads the firstborn into the heavenly world, he says, "And let all the angels of God worship him (Deut 32:43; Ps 96:7)." [7] And of the angels he says, "He who makes his angels *spirits* and his *ministers* a flame of fire (Ps 103:4)," [8] but of the Son, "Your throne, O God, is forever and ever, and the staff of uprightness is a staff of your kingdom. [9] You loved righteousness and hated lawlessness; therefore God, your God, anointed you with the oil of gladness beyond your partners (Ps 44:7–8)." [10] And, "You at the beginnings, Lord, founded the earth, and the heavens are the works of your hands.

B[11a] They will perish, *but you* are continuing,

    C[11b] and all *like a garment* will become old,

        D[12a] and like a cloak you will roll them up,

    C'[12b] *like a garment* indeed they will be changed.

B'[12c] *But you* are the same and your years will not cease (Ps 101:26–28)."

---

may be examples of early Christian praise or may have been composed by the authors of the books in which they are found. Even where the latter is true, these hymns might have been modeled on praise that was current in the church. . . . Hymns both reflect and form the core identity of a worshiping community."

17. Attridge, *Hebrews*, 48. See also Schenck, "Keeping His Appointment"; Mackie, "Confession"; Bauckham, "Divinity"; Webster, "One Who Is Son."

> A'¹³ But to *which* of *the angels* has he *ever* said, "Sit at my right, until I place your enemies as a footstool for your feet (Ps 109:1)"? ¹⁴ Are they not all *ministering spirits* sent for assistance on account of those who are going to inherit salvation?

With the occurrences of the term "angels" (1:4, 5) as the transitional catchwords connecting the first unit (1:1–4) with the second (1:5–14), the audience's focus remains on the comparison of the angels with the divinely exalted Son. An interrogative prelude, "For to which of the angels did he ever say?" (1:5a), introduces a chain of scriptural quotations linked by words they share. The audience continue to hear how God has definitively spoken to us in a Son (1:1–2), with a direct address never spoken to any of the angels (1:5a), in a quotation of Ps 2:7, "Son of mine are you, I today have begotten you" (1:5bc). The one whom God himself has installed as messianic king (Ps 2:6) God emphatically declares as his very own Son—"Son of mine are you" (1:5b). With an explicit employment of the otherwise superfluous (in Greek) first-person singular pronoun for added emphasis, God himself declares to his Son that "*I* today have begotten you" (1:5c). God has implicitly become the Father of his royal Son "today," that is, when God placed the Son who sat at his right in heaven (1:3d) as heir of all things (1:2a; cf. Ps 2:8). But the "today" of this solemn pronouncement also refers to the liturgical "today" when the audience, gathered together as a worshiping assembly at the eschatological "end of these days" (1:2a), hear it made present for them as a basis for their worship.¹⁸

With the quotation of 2 Sam 7:14 (cf. 1 Chr 17:13), the audience hear a progression in God's emphatic declaration concerning his Fatherhood of his royal Son. Whereas God implicitly declared himself to be the Father of his Son in a direct address to his Son with the second-person singular pronoun, "I today have begotten *you*" (1:5c), God now promises that he himself will be explicitly the Father of his Son in an indirect address to the audience by referring to his Son with the third person singular pronoun, "I will be to *him* as Father" (1:5d). And whereas God declared the Son to be his very own Son in a direct address to the Son with the second-person singular pronoun, "Son of mine are *you*" (1:5b), God now promises a rela-

---

18. Regarding "today" here, Docherty, *Use of the Old Testament*, 151, points out "that the author was operating within an eschatological framework in which God's action through the messiah is envisaged as happening in the present." This liturgical "today" will be further developed in 3:7, 13, 15; 4:7; 5:5.

tionship of mutual allegiance between himself and his Son in an indirect address to the audience by referring to his Son with the third-person singular pronoun, "and *he* will be to me as Son" (1:5e). Induced to listen to how God has spoken to us in a Son (1:2), the audience have heard God's voice speak with scriptural authority both to the Son and to them about the mutual allegiance of the Son with his divine Father, preparing them for an elaboration of this mutual, paternal-filial allegiance that God never promised for any of the angels (1:5a).

The scriptural promise from 2 Sam 7:14 that "I will be to him as Father, and he will be to me as Son" (1:5de) closely resembles the traditional formula expressing the covenantal relationship between God and his people Israel: "I will be to them as God, and they will be to me as people." The audience will hear it quoted later from Jer 38:33 in Heb 8:10, but it occurs frequently in the OT, including in 2 Sam 7:24 (cf. 1 Chr 17:22) in the immediate context of 2 Sam 7:14.[19] Furthermore, the royal Son serves as the representative leader of his people Israel, considered to be the corporate "Son" of God (Exod 4:22; cf. Hos 11:1). As the "Son" of God, however, the people of Israel frequently failed to fulfill their covenantal obligations by being unfaithful to God, which rendered them incapable of true and authentic worship of God as their Father, as evident especially in their worship of false gods. The quotation from 2 Sam 7:14 thus promises that the royal Son will be a truly faithful and obedient covenantal Son who offers proper and authentic worship to the God who is his Father. The audience have now been alerted to listen to what this scriptural promise entails for their own faithfulness and capability to worship as God's people.

In a manner reminiscent of God leading his chosen people Israel as his "firstborn" son/heir into the promised land long ago in the exodus event, when God now leads his firstborn Son into the heavenly world,[20] he

---

19. See also Zech 8:8; Jer 7:23; 11:4; 24:7; 38:1; 39:38; Bar 2:35; Ezek 11:20; 14:11; 36:28; 37:33.

20. There is a noteworthy similarity between Hebrews, which states, "when" God "leads" the "firstborn," the Son whom God placed as "heir" of all things (1:2a), who "inherited" a name (1:4), into the "heavenly world (*oikoumenēn*)" (1:6), and the address to Israel in Deut 11:29. It states, "when the Lord your God leads you into the land into which you are crossing there to inherit it." And see the use of the same form of the verb for the same event in Exod 13:5, 11; 23:20; Deut 6:10, 23; 7:1. In addition, in Exod 4:22 God declares that Israel is "my firstborn son." On *oikoumenēn* in 1:6 as a reference to the heavenly world, see Balz, "*oikoumenē*," 504; Caneday, "Eschatological World"; Allen,

says, "And let the angels of God worship him (Deut 32:43; Ps 96:7)" (1:6).[21] Not only has God placed the Son as the filial "heir" of all things (1:2a), who, more excellent beyond the angels, has "inherited" a name (1:4), but God leads this Son into the heavenly world as his specially chosen and favored "firstborn." Both Israel and the Davidic messianic king are declared to be God's "firstborn" in a context of worship. As God's "firstborn" son, Israel is to be sent away from Egypt by the Pharaoh so that God's "firstborn" may "offer worship" to God (Exod 4:22-23). To the Davidic king, who in an act of worship will call upon God, praying, "You are my Father, my God, and the protector of my salvation" (Ps 88:27; cf. 2 Sam 7:14 in Heb 1:5), God promises, "And I will place him as firstborn, high beyond the kings of the earth" (Ps 88:28). But in Hebrews the royal covenantal Son not only will offer worship to God his Father, but will himself be worshiped by the angels of God.[22]

Thus, as the chain of scriptural quotations linked by words they share continues, God calls for all the angels of God to worship "*him*," the Son concerning whom God pledged that "I will be to *him* as Father" (2 Sam 7:14 in 1:5). God's authoritative invitation to let all the angels of God worship his firstborn Son, as God leads him into the realm of heavenly worship, underscores the divine status of the Son as vastly superior to the angels of God (1:4-5). The audience, gathered together as a worshiping assembly, are thus further persuaded to listen to God's scriptural voice definitively speaking to us in a Son (1:1-2). As God's covenantal and specially favored "firstborn," this Son is worthy of their attention both as the Son who will faithfully and obediently worship God (1:5) as well as be worshiped by the angels of God (1:6).

After the invitation for the "*angels*" of God to worship the firstborn Son whom God leads into the heavenly realm (1:6), the audience hear the scriptural voice of God through Ps 103:4 say of the "*angels*," "He who

---

Deuteronomy, 55. On the significance of the Exodus event in Hebrews, see Thiessen, "End of the Exodus."

21. The scriptural quotation in Heb 1:6 exhibits noteworthy similarities to both Deut 32:43 and Ps 96:7. For the discussion of this and other OT background, see Cockerill, "Hebrews 1:6"; McLay, *Use of the Septuagint*; idem, "Biblical Texts"; Gheorghita, *Septuagint*; Allen, *Deuteronomy*; Docherty, *Use of the Old Testament*, 133-34, 156-60.

22. Docherty, *Use of the Old Testament*, 158: "David is described as the 'firstborn' in Ps 88:28, a verse immediately following one in which he is said to cry, 'You are my father, my God . . .' (Ps 88:27), and part of a section (Ps 88:21-38) in which God promises that his throne will be established forever, a passage very reminiscent of 2 Sam 7."

makes his *angels* spirits and his ministers a flame of fire" (1:7). That God "makes" his angels spirits continues the demonstration of the Son's superiority over them, as they are embraced by the ages God "made" through the Son (1:2). And that the angels are further described as God's "ministers" extends their role in worship. Not only are the angels themselves to worship the firstborn Son whom God leads into the heavenly realm, but, as "ministers" (*leitourgous*) of God they also are to assist others, particularly the audience, in this heavenly worship. The audience are thus to appreciate that through their earthly worship they can also be participants, along with and through the assistance of the angels, in the heavenly worship of God's Son.[23]

The chain of quotations continues with a link contrasting what God's scriptural voice says "of" (*pros*) the angels (1:7a) with what it says "of" (*pros*) the Son (1:8a). But the verbal linkage within the quotations themselves continues not with the immediately preceding scriptural quotation, which speaks only of the angels (1:7), but with the one prior to that, which includes a reference to the Son. The God who said, "And let all of the angels of *God* worship him" (1:6), now says of the Son through Ps 44:7–8, "Your throne, O *God*, is forever and ever, and the staff of uprightness is a staff of your kingdom. You loved righteousness and hated lawlessness; therefore *God*, your *God*, anointed you with the oil of gladness beyond your partners" (1:8–9).[24] Through this verbal linkage the audience experience a remarkable progression from God inviting the angels of "God" to worship his Son, to God addressing and acknowledging his Son to be also "God" (1:8), to God affirming himself as the "God," who, emphatically as the "God" of his Son, anointed him (1:9).

The royal status of the Son, himself "God," is developed. The "throne" on which the royal Son "sat at the right of the Majesty in the heights" of heaven (1:3d) is now described as an eternal throne, remaining "forever and ever," while the "staff" or rule that characterizes his kingdom or reign is that of uprightness (1:8). Because he loved righteousness and hated lawlessness, God, the God who pledged to be to him as a Father (1:5), anointed him as his royal Son with the oil of festive "gladness" or "re-

---

23. On the "ministry" of the angels as pertaining to the service of worship, see Spicq, "*leitourgeō*," 382n16; see also BDAG, 591; Cockerill, *Hebrews*, 42. On the OT background of Heb 1:7, see Swinson, "Hebrews 1:7"; Docherty, *Use of the Old Testament*, 160–63.

24. Bateman, "Psalm 45:6–7"; Gert Jacobus Steyn, "Hebrews 1:8–9"; Docherty, *Use of the Old Testament*, 163–66.

joicing" (*agalliaseōs*) appropriate for him as the object of worship (1:9).[25] That the Son loved the righteousness that accords with God's will and hated the "lawlessness" (*anomian*) equivalent to sinfulness against God resonates with the Son's having made a cleansing for sins (1:3c).[26] Just as the Son, having made a cleansing for sins, sat at the right of God in heaven as an object of worship, so the Son, who loved righteousness and hated lawlessness, was anointed by God as an object of worship. That God himself anointed him "beyond" (*para*) his "partners," that is, the angels as his heavenly companions or associates (1:9), adds to the audience's appreciation of the superiority of God's divine royal Son, who "beyond" (*par'*) the angels themselves has inherited a name (1:4). He is worthy to be worshiped in heaven not only by the angels but by the audience.[27]

The scriptural voice of God continues to address the divine royal Son through Ps 101:26, "You at the beginnings, Lord, founded the earth, and the heavens are the works of your hands" (1:10). At this point in the chain of scriptural quotations the author enables his audience to hear the authoritative voice of God himself reinforcing his direct address of his royal Son as "God" (1:8) by also addressing him as divine "Lord." And that at the beginnings God's royal Son, as the divine Lord, founded the earth and the heavens are the works of his hands develops the royal Son's role in creation as the one through whom God made the ages (1:2). The audience are to appreciate that the royal Son, whom God himself adopted and pledged that he would be a Son to him as the Father (1:5), God addressed not only as divine "Lord" but as also "God." God the Father anointed him as greatly superior to the angels with the oil of a festive gladness appropriate to worshiping him as the divine royal Son of God eternally enthroned in heaven (1:8–9). Both the Father, who is God and Lord, and the Son, who is also God and Lord, are to be the focus of the audience's worship.

The audience continue to hear the scriptural voice of God speaking to us *in* a Son (1:2) through his direct address *to* the Son, as the divine royal Son (1:5–10) superior to the angels (1:4–5), as the same scriptural quotation continues with Ps 101:27a, "They will perish, but you are con-

---

25. BDAG, 4; Weiser, "*agalliaō*," 8: "with the 'oil of gladness,' i.e., with the ointment used at joyous celebrations."

26. Limbeck, "*anomia*," 106: "*Anomia* can also refer to breaking of the law and thereby come to mean offense and sin."

27. That these are the first two occurrences in Hebrews of the preposition "beyond" (*para*) facilitates this connection.

tinuing" (1:11a). At this point the audience have heard a progression from God's direct and emphatic addresses of the Son's adoption, "Son of mine are *you*" (1:5), and of his royal Son's divine lordship, "*You* at the beginnings, Lord" (1:10), to God's direct and emphatic address of his royal Son's eternity, "But *you* are continuing." Since the earth and the heavens that form the framework for the audience's existence will eventually perish, they are to keep the focus of their worship on God and God's royal Son, whose heavenly throne is "forever and ever" (1:8) and who is continuing to exist for all eternity.

After hearing God's direct address to his divine royal Son, promising that he will roll up all of creation like a worn-out cloak (Ps 101:27c in 1:12a), the audience experience a chiastic progression in the description of the earth and heavens as *like a garment* that will become old (Ps 101:27b in 1:11b) to *like a garment* that indeed will be changed (Ps 101:27d in 1:12b).[28] The intensified progression from a pejorative expression, "will become old," to a more optimistic one, "indeed will be changed" (by God, divine passive), raises a hope for the audience that all of creation will one day be divinely transformed into something new and different, implying that it will become a more suitable framework for the worship of the eternal divine Son. This hope contributes to the future focus of the audience's worship.

The audience continue to hear the scriptural voice of God speaking to them through a direct address to the royal Son, as the quotation concludes with Ps 101:28, "But you are the same and your years will not cease" (1:12c). At this point the audience are presented with a chiastic progression from "*but you* are continuing" (1:11a) to "*but you* are the same and your years will not cease" (1:12c). The audience are to appreciate that, in contrast to all of creation, which will become old, be "rolled up," and indeed be radically changed (1:11b–12b), the divine royal Son will be unchangeably the same forever. As one who is ever continuing to exist (1:11a), his years will never cease. God's promise, continuing his pledge to be the Father to his divine Son (1:5), that "your years will not cease" climaxes the threefold scriptural declaration of the eternal nature of the Son, whose "throne will be forever and ever" (1:8) and who is ever "continuing" in existence (1:11). All of this scriptural description of his divine character continues to add to the audience's appreciation of God's

---

28. The addition of the words "like a garment" in 1:12b, which do not appear in the LXX of Ps 101:27d, facilitate the parallelism with 1:11b.

royal Son as a most worthy and appropriate object of worship not only by the angels of God (1:6) but by themselves as well.

At the climactic conclusion of this chain of scriptural quotations (1:5–13), in which God is speaking to us in a Son (1:2) through direct addresses to his Son, the audience are again presented with rhetorically potent questions comparing the angels to the divine royal Son (1:5): "But to which of the angels has he ever said, 'Sit at my right, until I place your enemies as a footstool for your feet (Ps 109:1)'? Are they not all ministering spirits sent for assistance on account of those who are going to inherit salvation?" (1:13–14). At this point the audience are presented with a chiastic progression in questions about the angels. "For *to which of the angels* did he *ever* say?" (1:5), the angels, whom God "makes his *spirits* and his *ministers*" (1:7), progresses to "But *to which* of *the angels* has he *ever* said?" (1:13), the angels, who are "*ministering spirits* sent for assistance on account of those who are going to inherit salvation" (1:14). Furthermore, the only occurrences in this unit of the first-person genitive singular pronoun as emphatic references to God himself in "Son of *mine* are you," introducing the first scriptural quotation of Ps 2:7 in 1:5, and in "Sit at *my* right," concluding the final, climactic quotation of Ps 109:1 in 1:13, serve as a literary inclusion appropriately enclosing the entire chain of quotations.

Although the divine royal Son has already gained the privilege of sitting at the right of God in the heavenly heights (1:3), there remains a future, yet-to-be-fulfilled dimension of the divinely issued invitation for him to do so. The God who "*placed*" the Son as heir of all things (1:2) is the Father who now promises his divine royal Son that he will sit at his right until "I *place* your enemies as a footstool for your feet" (1:13). God himself pledges that he will place the enemies of his royal Son, which are yet to be specifically identified, in utter subjection to the rule of the "throne" and "staff" of his kingdom (1:8). The reverberating redundancy of references to "foot/feet" in the phrase "*foot*stool for your *feet*" intensively reinforces the extreme subjugation of the enemies beneath the triumphant divine royal Son enthroned eternally in heaven.[29]

A provocative rhetorical question elicits the audience's appreciation that all of the angels, whom God makes his "*spirits* and his *ministers*" (1:7), God sends as his "*ministering spirits*" on a mission to assist in their

---

29. On the meaning of making someone a "footstool" for someone else, BDAG, 1040, states: "subject one person to another, so that the other can put a foot on the subject's neck."

worship of the divine royal Son (1:6) those who are going to inherit salvation (1:14). The audience are to see themselves among those who are going to "inherit" salvation from the divine royal Son, who, as "heir" of all things (1:2), has, beyond the angels themselves, "inherited" a name (1:4), and who, as God the Father's favored "firstborn" Son, is entitled to the inheritance (1:6). What this "salvation" more precisely entails has yet to be fully disclosed and described. However, the implication at this point is that the audience are to have the hope of inheriting the "salvation" resulting from the Son's having made purification for sins (1:3) and from God's pledge to place "enemies" in utter subjugation to his divine royal Son (1:13). For their own worship as those who are going to inherit salvation, the audience are to avail themselves of the assistance of the angels of God as spirits ministering at the heavenly worship (1:6–7) of God's divine royal Son triumphantly enthroned at the powerful and authoritative right side of God (1:13).[30]

III. 2:1–4

A [2:1] Therefore it is necessary for *us* all the more to attend to the things that have been *heard*, lest we drift away. [2a] For if the word *spoken through* angels became *firm*

    B [2b] and every transgression and disobedience *received* a just recompense,

        C [3a] how will we escape, neglecting so great a salvation,

    B' [3b] which, having *received* a beginning

A' [3c] of being *spoken through* the Lord, was *confirmed* for *us* by those who *heard*, [4] God additionally testifying with signs together with wonders and various acts of power and distributions of the Holy Spirit according to his willing?

The term "angels," which occurs near the conclusion (1:13) of the previous unit, recurs near the beginning (2:2a) of this unit to function as a thematically key transitional term. The theme regarding the angels moves the focus of the audience from what God did not speak *to* any of the angels to what God spoke *through* the angels. Having heard God speaking to them in a Son (1:1–2) by directly addressing the divine royal Son, rather

---

30. Marshall, "Soteriology in Hebrews."

than any of the angels, through a cohesive chain of scriptural citations (1:5–14), the audience are presented with an exhortation that serves as a warning: "Therefore it is necessary for us all the more to attend to the things that have been heard, lest we drift away" (2:1). It is necessary for "us," that is, the audience and the author as those included among the "us" to whom God has now spoken in a Son (1:2), all the more to attend to "the things that have been heard" (2:1a). These are the things that have been heard in a context of worship. They refer to the things that have been heard by "us" in the things God has spoken to us in addressing his divine royal Son through the preceding chain of scriptural quotations (1:5–14), heard by the audience as a worshiping assembly. They also refer to the things that have been heard by the ancestral fathers to whom God has spoken in the past in the prophets through the scriptures (1:1) heard during public worship services.

In an alliterative wordplay, the audience and author are "all the more to attend" (*perissoterōs prosechen*) to the things that have been heard, lest "we drift away" (*pararyōmen*, 2:1). The audience are thus warned that their inattentiveness to what God has spoken to them as a worshiping assembly, both in the prophets heard in the scriptures (1:1) and in a Son heard through the preceding chain of scriptural quotations (1:5–14), may result in their "drifting away" or "being washed away" in the manner of an unanchored or unsteady ship at sea.[31]

The audience are then presented with the beginning of a conditional clause, reminding them that "the word spoken through angels," a reference to the Mosaic law given by God to his chosen people, Israel, which was regarded in some traditions as spoken to Moses through the mediation of angels (Gal 3:19; Acts 7:30, 38, 53), "became firm" (2:2a). That the word of God, the law spoken at Sinai, became "firm" (*bebaios*) means not only that it offers a firm, steady, or secure foundation or "anchor" as a counter to the danger of the audience "drifting away" (2:1), but also that it is "firm" in the sense of having binding judicial validity for the audience.[32]

---

31. O'Brien, *Hebrews*, 84: "The peril against which the community is to be on guard is that of 'drifting away,' like a boat that is gradually slipping away from its moorings. This suggests a movement that may be subtle and undetected by those on board, and along with the term 'neglect' (v. 3) points to a gradual, unthinking movement away from the faith."

32. BDAG, 172; Fuchs, "*bebaios*," 211.

The judicial dimension of the legally "firm" or "valid" word spoken through angels (2:2a) is developed with the reminder that every transgression and disobedience of this "word," that is, the Mosaic law, received a just recompense (2:2b), thus underlining the need for the audience all the more to be attentive to it, in order to avoid the just penalty of the recompense rendered by God. The alliteration reverberating throughout the vocabulary employed here contributes to the close connection between the audience's possible inattentiveness to "every transgression and disobedience" (*pasa parabasis kai parakoē*) and the danger of them "drifting away" (*pararyōmen*, 2:1). That "every transgression and disobedience," terms synonymous with "lawlessness" and "sins," received a just recompense contributes to the audience's appreciation for the salvific activity of the Son, who hated "lawlessness" (1:9) and made a cleansing for "sins" (1:3).

At the center of this chiastic unit the audience are presented with an ominously potent, thought-provoking, rhetorical question: "How will we escape, neglecting so great a salvation?" (2:3a). The implication is that "we," audience and author, will not be able to escape the just penalty of a recompense from God, if, through inattentiveness to the things that have been heard during worship (2:1), we neglect so great a salvation. The attractiveness of the salvation the audience are to have the hope of inheriting (1:14) is developed with a description enhancing its significance as "so great a salvation." The audience are thus attuned for further delineation of why this salvation, which includes the divine royal Son's cultic act of having made a cleansing for sins (1:3) and anticipates the further salvific action that God will place his enemies as a footstool for his feet as the Son now sits enthroned in heavenly exaltation at the powerful right side of God (1:3, 14), is "so great a salvation."

The audience then experience a chiastic progression from a just recompense that every transgression and disobedience "received" (2:2b) to a beginning which so great a salvation "received" (2:3b). This progression establishes for the audience a noteworthy contrast between the just penalty of the recompense received for every transgression and disobedience under the Mosaic law and the beginning received for so great a salvation, which the audience hope to inherit (1:14). The implication is that this salvation is "so great" because it includes being saved from the just penalty of the recompense received for every transgression and disobedience, every act of lawlessness and sin, against God under the Mosaic law.

Next, the audience are presented with a chiastic progression from "the word *spoken through* angels became *firm*" (2:2a) to "being *spoken through* the Lord, was *confirmed*" (2:3c). And, "it is necessary for *us* all the more to attend to the things that have been *heard*" during worship (2:1) progresses to "it was confirmed for *us* by those who *heard*" (2:3c). In contrast to "the word," the Mosaic law, which was spoken by God through angels (2:2a), "so great a salvation," which the audience are not to neglect (2:3a), received a beginning of being spoken and thus effected by God through the Lord (2:3c).[33] This contrast deepens the audience's appreciation for the superiority of the divine royal Son, whom God addressed as "Lord" of creation (1:10), and in whom God has spoken to us (1:2) by directly addressing him through the scriptural quotations the audience just heard as a worshiping assembly (1:5–14), to the angels, none of whom God addressed as his "Son" (1:5, 13). But the audience are also alerted to a superiority of "so great a salvation," which was spoken through the divine royal Son as Lord, to "the word" of the Mosaic law, which was spoken merely through angels.[34]

Whereas the word of the Mosaic law became "firm" (2:2a), so that it is necessary for "us" all the more to attend to the things that have been "heard" in it, lest we drift away (2:1), "so great a salvation" was "confirmed" for "us" by those who "heard" (2:3c). That this great salvation was "confirmed," and not merely became "firm" like the word of the Mosaic law, indicates that it is an even more secure "anchor," assuring that, by heeding it, we will not "drift away." That there are those who "heard" the beginning (2:3b) of so great a salvation (2:3a) being spoken through the Lord, so that they have confirmed it for "us," audience and author, strengthens the appeal for "us" all the more to attend to the things that have been "heard" (2:1). These things included especially the preceding chain of scriptural quotations (1:5–14), in which God spoke to "us" (1:2) as a worshiping assembly through addressing his Son as "God" (1:8) and "Lord" (1:10).

Along with this confirmation for us by those who heard the beginning of so great a salvation before the audience have heard it (2:3c), is God's additional "testifying with signs together with wonders and various

---

33. O'Brien, *Hebrews*, 87: "The word of God not only announces salvation; it also effects it."

34. The only preceding occurrence of "Lord" at this point in Hebrews refers to the Son (1:10), who has also been addressed as "God" (1:8). God the Father, however, is the one speaking. Hence, God as "Lord" Father has spoken through his "Lord" Son.

acts of power and distributions of the Holy Spirit according to his willing" (2:4). Such testifying by God often occurred in the context of a worshiping assembly.[35] That God's testifying included distributions of the Holy "Spirit," often manifest and evident in the worshiping assembly, resonates with the worship dimension heard earlier by the audience regarding the angels.[36] After God invited the angels to worship his firstborn Son (1:6), they are described as his "spirits" and his "ministers" of worship (1:7). And the audience have been induced to acknowledge that all the angels are "ministering spirits" sent to assist in their worship those who are going to inherit salvation (1:14). The confirmation given us by those who heard previously, as well as God's further testifying, provide the audience with a firm "anchor," lest they "drift away" (2:1) and neglect "so great a salvation" that they can hear spoken about especially and preeminently in their worshiping assembly.

IV. 2:5–9

A ⁵ For not to *angels* did he subject the heavenly world, the one coming, about which we are speaking. ⁶ But someone testified somewhere, saying, "What is man that you remember him, or a son of man that you care for him? ⁷ You *made* him *lower briefly beyond the angels, with glory and honor you crowned* him,

B ⁸ᵃ *all things you subjected* under his feet" (Ps 8:5–7). In *subjecting* to *him all things* he left nothing to *him* unsubjected.

B′ ⁸ᵇ Yet now we do not see *all things subjected* to *him*,

A′ ⁹ but we are taking note of Jesus, the one *briefly beyond the angels made lower*, on account of the suffering of death, *with glory and honor crowned*, so that, by the grace of God, on behalf of all he might taste death.

Verbs to express "testifying"—"God additionally *testifying with*" (2:4) and "someone *testified* somewhere" (2:6)—serve as the transitional words linking this unit (2:5–9) to the previous one (2:1–4). The transition keeps

---

35. Acts 14:1–3: in the Jewish synagogue at Iconium; 1 Cor 12:4–11: in the worshiping assembly at Corinth.

36. On the role of the Holy Spirit in 2:1–4, see Emmrich, *Pneumatological Concepts*, 64–68; Allen, "Holy Spirit."

the audience's attention on listening to the divine testimony, available to them as a worshiping assembly, that they have been given to confirm so great a salvation they are not to neglect as a focus for their worship (2:3–4).

In addition, within the third macrochiastic level of the letter to the Hebrews, this unit in 2:5–9, which occurs after the central and pivotal unit in 2:1–4, exhibits a parallel relationship with the unit in 1:5–14. The parallelism is evident, first of all, in the occurrences of the term "heavenly world"—"when he [God] leads the firstborn into the *heavenly world*" (1:6) and "not to angels did he [God] subject the *heavenly world*" (2:5). Also contributing to the parallelism is the verbal form to express "going" or "coming"—"those who are going [*mellontas*] to inherit salvation" (1:14) and "the heavenly world, the one coming [*mellousan*]" (2:5). Finally, the parallelism is confirmed by expressions involving subjugation under the "feet" of the divine royal Son—God promises to "place your enemies as a *footstool for your feet*" (1:13) and God "subjected all things *under his feet*" (2:8).[37]

Having heard the questions that introduce the comparison of the angels to the superior divine royal Son—"For to which of the angels did he ever say?" (1:5a) and "But to which of the angels has he ever said?" (1:13)—the audience now hear the blunt assertion, "For not to angels did he subject the heavenly world, the one coming, about which we are speaking" (2:5). Although, as the audience have heard, God invited, through a quotation of scripture, all the angels of God to worship his firstborn divine royal Son, when God leads him into the "heavenly world" (1:6), God did not subject under the power and authority of the angels this "heavenly world." That this heavenly world is described as "the one coming" (*mellousan*), that is, the one that is destined to arrive at the future, final time of salvation, links it to the audience as among "those who are going" (*mellontas*) to inherit salvation (1:14). This "so great a salvation" (2:3) that the audience are "going" to inherit is thus implicitly part of the "coming" heavenly world, about which "we"—author and audience—are speaking, in which the angels themselves worship and, as "ministering spirits," assist others to worship the firstborn divine royal Son (1:14). This further contributes to the future focus of the audience's worship.

---

37. For the outline and description of the third macrochiastic level, see the Introduction.

In development of "God additionally *testifying with* signs together with wonders and various acts of power and distributions of the Holy Spirit according to his willing" (2:4), to further confirm "so great a salvation" the audience are not to neglect (2:3), the audience hear, "But someone *testified* somewhere, saying" (2:6a). In contrast to God, whose testifying included his speaking to us by directly addressing his divine royal Son through scriptural quotations (1:1-2, 5-13), "someone"—an anonymous, generic, representative human being—testified "somewhere," that is, somewhere in scripture as the word of God.[38] But this scriptural word of God is spoken to God by a human being, and thus serves as an act of worship in response to what God has done.

This "someone" testified "somewhere" (2:6a) by quoting from Ps 8:5-7.[39] Whereas God spoke to us by directly addressing his divine royal Son through quotations of scripture (1:1-2, 5-13), this "someone" directly addressed God, speaking through a quotation of scripture on behalf of all human beings: "What is man that you remember him" (2:6b). When the audience hear the continuation of the quote, "or a son of man that you care for him?" (2:6c), they experience a progression from a reference to humankind in general, "what is *man that* you remember him," to a reference to God's royal Son as a member of humankind, "or a son of *man that* you care for him?" The audience's identification of a "son" here as God's royal Son has been prepared by the previous references to him with the only other occurrences at this point in Hebrews of "son" in 1:2, 5 (*bis*), and 8. The question of God's care for his divine royal Son as a "son of man" thus has implications for God's providential remembrance of humankind in general.[40]

Although not to "angels" did God subject the coming heavenly world (2:5), the continuation of the scriptural quotation acknowledges that God made his divine royal Son, as a member of humankind (2:6c), lower briefly beyond the "angels" (2:7a). That God made his divine royal Son lower

---

38. Koester, *Hebrews*, 214; Guthrie, "Hebrews," 944; O'Brien, *Hebrews*, 94: "For our author the Old Testament is a divine oracle, the voice of the Holy Spirit. Since it is God who speaks in Scripture, the identity of the person who uttered his word is relatively unimportant."

39. Steyn, "Heb 2:6-8"; Guthrie and Quinn, "Hebrews 2:5-9"; Guthrie, "Hebrews," 944-47.

40. "Son of man" here, however, is not used as the christological title found elsewhere in the NT; see Rascher, *Schriftauslegung*, 55.

briefly "beyond" (*par'*) the angels further elaborates for the audience the "name," that is, the identifiable characteristics and essential qualities, which the divine royal Son inherited as more excellent "beyond" (*par'*) the angels (1:4). In other words, the divine royal Son is more excellent "beyond" the angels because of his seat at the right of the Majesty in the heights of heaven (1:3d), where all the angels of God and the audience are to worship him (1:6). But, before taking that heavenly seat, he was made lower briefly "beyond" the angels on the earth by becoming a human being, a situation that likens him to each member of the audience.

That "with (divine) glory (cf. 1:3) and honor" God "crowned" his divine royal Son (2:7b) develops his significance as a "son of man" (2:6c). The audience are to appreciate that it is precisely from the divine royal Son's status as a son of humankind, a human being like them, made briefly lower beyond the angels, that God exalted and "crowned" him "with glory and honor." With this divine glory and honor, he took his seat at God's right in the heights of heaven (1:3), worthy to be worshiped not only by all the angels of God (1:6), but by the audience as well as by all human beings with the assistance of the angels as God's "ministering spirits" (1:7, 14).

With the conclusion of the scriptural quotation of Ps 8:5–7, "all things you subjected under his feet" (2:8a), the audience hear the completion of a hymnic act of worship spoken to God by a representative human being in which they have been drawn to participate by praising God for what he has done for all human beings (cf. the hymnic dimension of 1:1–4).[41] They then hear a further elaboration of the psalm by the author: "In subjecting to him all things he left nothing to him unsubjected" (2:8a). In contrast to the angels, to whom God did not "subject" the coming heavenly world (2:5), God "subjected" all things under the feet of his divine royal Son. That God subjected "all things" under his feet develops the audience's appreciation of the divine royal Son not only as the one bearing up "all things" by the pronouncement of God's power (1:3), but as a Son whom God placed as heir of "all things" (1:2). And the assertion from a scriptural quote (Ps 8:7) that God subjected all things "under his feet"

---

41. O'Brien, *Hebrews*, 94: "Psalm 8 is a hymn of praise for God's work in creation in which two major themes are set in contrast to each other. First, the psalmist is overcome with wonder as he contemplates the majesty and power of God (vv. 1–2). But when he looks at the starry heavens and contemplates their vastness, his mind turns to the insignificant but remarkable dignity of man."

reinforces God's promise from a scriptural quote (Ps 109:1) of placing the enemies of his Son, seated at God's right in heavenly enthronement, in a position of utter subjugation to the Son, as a "footstool for your feet" (1:13).

Having heard the completion of the scriptural quotation from Ps 8:5–7, the audience are then impressed with a striking intensification of God's subjection of all things under the feet of his divine royal Son. In his own words of authoritative explanation, the author assures his audience that in subjecting to his divine royal Son all things God left absolutely nothing to him unsubjected (2:8a). This further enhances the worthiness of the divine royal Son, who is also a human "son of man," as an object of worship for not only the audience but all human beings.

The author then speaks for himself, his audience, and all human beings, in enunciating the yet-to-be-fulfilled promise of God regarding his heavenly enthroned divine royal Son: "Yet now we do not see all things subjected to him" (2:8b). At this point the audience are presented with a chiastic parallelism. The audience heard the human speaker of the scriptural quotation acknowledge that God "subjected all things" under the feet of his divine royal Son (2:8a). The author intensively reinforced this for his audience by pointedly asserting that in "subjecting to him all things" God left nothing "to him" unsubjected. And now, the author draws his audience as well as all human beings into his declaration that now "we" do not yet see "all things subjected to him." This further contributes to the future focus of the audience's worship, as oriented to the ultimate fulfillment and completion of God's promised salvific activity.

For the first time in Hebrews, the audience hear the divine royal Son identified by name: "but we are taking note of Jesus, the one briefly beyond the angels made lower, on account of the suffering of death, with glory and honor crowned, so that, by the grace of God, on behalf of all he might taste death" (2:9). At this point the audience have heard that God "made lower" his divine royal Son, as a son of humankind (2:6c), "briefly beyond the angels"—the "angels" to whom God did not subject the coming heavenly world (2:5), and that "with glory and honor you crowned" him (2:7). And now, as a chiastic progression, the audience hear that we are taking note of Jesus, the one "briefly beyond the angels made lower," and "with glory and honor crowned." Thus, the heavenly enthroned divine royal Son, briefly beyond the angels made lower as a human being, is now explicitly identified for the audience as "Jesus," the one of whom we are taking note as both the divine and the human focus of our worship.

Although we do not yet physically "see" (*orōmen*) all things subjected to the divine royal Son (2:8b), as authoritatively asserted by the scripture quotation (2:8a), we are presently "taking note" (*blepomen*), that is, directing our attention to, Jesus as the focus of our worship that is directed to this future divine subjecting of all things to him as the human and divine royal Son.[42] As a "son of man" (2:6c), a human being, Jesus was briefly beyond the angels made lower by God "because of" or "on account of" the suffering of death—that is, so that he might suffer his own death as a human being, as well as on account of the suffering of death that all human beings in general must undergo. Furthermore, it is on account of this human suffering of death that Jesus was crowned by God with glory and honor in heavenly enthronement. The ultimate purpose within God's plan of Jesus becoming a human being by being made lower beyond the angels was so that, by the grace of God, on behalf of all human beings, he might "taste" (*geusētai*), that is, "fully experience" the suffering of death (2:9).[43]

Along with the explicit identification of the divine royal Son, who is also a "son of man" (2:6c), a human being, as "Jesus" (2:9), the audience receive further implicit delineation of the great salvation they are not to neglect as a worshiping assembly (2:3). This salvation that the audience hope to inherit (1:14) is "so great" because it includes salvation from the power of death (2:9), implicitly among the "enemies" God will place in total subjection as a "footstool for the feet" of his heavenly enthroned divine royal Son (1:13). This salvation is for all human beings, on behalf of whom Jesus, himself a human being, fully experienced the death all human beings must experience, before he was exalted from this death to a seat at God's right (1:3), crowned with heavenly glory and honor (2:7, 9). The audience are thus further persuaded of the worthiness of Jesus, the human "son of man" who is also the divine royal Son of God in heaven,

---

42. On the meaning of *blepō* in Hebrews as "take note," "pay attention to," or "be concerned about," see Müller, "*blepō*," 222. Thus, *blepomen* in 2:9 is distinct in meaning from the physical seeing expressed by *orōmen* in 2:8; see Westcott, *Hebrews*, 45; *contra* Ellingworth, *Hebrews*, 154.

43. BDAG, 195; van der Minde, "*geuomai*," 246. See also Blomberg, "But We See Jesus."

to be worshiped by them, with the assistance of the angels as God's "ministering spirits" (1:14).

V. 2:10–18

A ¹⁰ For it was fitting for him, for whom are all things and through whom are all things, in leading many sons into glory, to make the *initiator* (*archēgon*) of their salvation, through *sufferings*, perfect.

    B ¹¹ For indeed he who makes holy and those who are being made holy are all from one, for which reason he is not ashamed to call them *brothers*, ¹² saying, "I will proclaim your name to my *brothers*, in the midst of the assembly I will praise you (Ps 21:23),"

        C ¹³ᵃ *and again*, "*I* will be confident in him (Isa 8:17b; cf. 2 Sam 22:3a),"

        C' ¹³ᵇ *and again*, "Behold *I* and the children whom God gave to me (Isa 8:18a)."

    B' ¹⁴ Since then the children have shared in blood and flesh, he also similarly partook with them, so that through death he might destroy the one who has the strength of death, that is the devil, ¹⁵ and free those, as many as by fear of death through all their life were held in slavery. ¹⁶ For surely not angels does he take hold of, but rather the descendants of Abraham he takes hold of, ¹⁷ᵃ whence he was obligated in all things with his *brothers* to be likened,

A' ¹⁷ᵇ so that he might become a merciful and faithful *high priest* (*archiereus*) in things regarding God in order to expiate the sins of the people, ¹⁸ for in what he himself *suffered* in being tested, those who are being tested he is able to help.

The close connection between the previous unit (2:5–9) and this unit (2:10–18) is secured by a chiastic sequence of transitional words. After hearing the center of this chiastic sequence in the declaration, "for it was fitting for" God (2:10a), the audience are presented with a pivotal progression making them realize that "all" human beings on behalf of whom Jesus might fully experience death by the grace of God (2:9d) are among "all" the things that are from God and "all" the things that are through

God (2:10b). The audience are among the many sons God is leading to heavenly "glory" (2:10c), the same heavenly "glory" and honor with which Jesus, the divine royal Son, is crowned (2:9c). And it was fitting for God to make Jesus, as the initiator of their salvation, perfect through "sufferings" (2:10d), which includes the "suffering" of death all human beings must undergo (2:9b).[44]

On the macrochiastic level, the audience are to appreciate the appropriate progression from Jesus as the one who, beyond the angels, has inherited a "name" (1:4), a divine status, to Jesus' scriptural promise to perform an act of worship in proclaiming to his brothers the "name" of God and praising him in the midst of the liturgical assembly (2:12). Furthermore, the audience experience a progression from Jesus as the heavenly enthroned divine royal Son having made purification for the "sins" that prevent proper worship (1:3) to Jesus becoming a merciful and faithful high priest in order to expiate, through his act of cultic worship, the "sins" of the people of God (2:17b), among whom are the members of the audience.

The audience have heard that God has spoken to us in a "Son" (1:2), whom God, through scriptural quotations, addressed as "*Son* of mine" and promised that "he will be to me as a *Son*" (1:5). Indeed, God addressed the "Son" as God himself, whose heavenly throne is forever and ever (1:8). This divine royal Son was also referred to as a "*son* of man" (2:6), a member of humankind, a human being. And now the audience are to consider themselves to be among the many "sons," "sons" both of mankind and of God, whom God is "leading into" the heavenly "glory" that implies their participation in heavenly worship. This is the same heavenly "glory" with which Jesus, the royal Son of God and a son of humankind, is crowned (2:9), when God "leads" him as the firstborn "into" the heavenly world to be worshiped by the angels (1:6), and with the assistance of the angels, by the audience (1:14).

That it was fitting for God to make the initiator of the "salvation" of the many "sons" God is leading into glory perfect (2:10) further elucidates the "salvation" the audience, as among the many human "sons" of God, have the hope of "inheriting" (1:14). The audience are not to neglect, as a motivation for their worship, a "salvation" that is so great (2:3). Indeed, it was through the suffering of death (2:9), which all human beings must

---

44. For a more detailed illustration and explanation of the chiastic sequence connecting 2:5–9 with 2:10–18, see Heil, *Hebrews*, 64–65.

undergo, that God made Jesus, the initiator of this salvation, "perfect" (*teleiōsai*), that is, capable of being seated at the right of God in heavenly glory (1:3, 13), worthy not only to perform an act of cultic worship but ultimately to be worshiped (1:6).[45]

The alliteration between God's "leading" (*agagonta*) and the term "initiator" (*archēgon*) lends a connotation of "leader" to the word here translated as "initiator" (2:10). On the other hand, the wordplay between the term "perfect," with its connotation of "bringing to an end," "finishing," or "completing," highlights the connotation of "initiating" or "beginning" present in the term *archēgon*, which, through the combined effect of the alliteration and wordplay, acquires a sense of "initiating leader." The Jesus "perfected" for worship through the suffering of death on behalf of all human beings (2:9) is thus the "Son" who serves as both the "initiator" and "leader" for the many "sons," including the audience. The salvation he both initiates and leads them to is so great that they ought not to neglect it as the basis for their worship (2:3).

The Jesus whom, through the sufferings of death, God perfected (2:10) both to perform worship and to be an object of heavenly worship (1:6) is the one who "makes holy" (*hagiazōn*), that is, sets apart from the common, profane, or unclean and dedicates or consecrates for the purpose of honoring or worshiping God.[46] The audience are to consider themselves as among those who are "being made holy" by Jesus (2:11). That Jesus, himself perfected, is making them holy means that they are on the way of being perfected for their role in the heavenly worship. As among those who are going to inherit the salvation Jesus initiated, they are being made holy and thus being perfected to approach and worship God, as well as Jesus, the divine royal Son, who is also God (1:8–12), with the assistance of the angels God sent as ministering spirits (1:14).

That he who makes holy and those who are being made holy are "all from one" (2:11) means that both Jesus and those, including the audience, he is making holy have a common human as well as divine origin. Jesus and those he is making holy are "all from one" humankind, "sons" of humankind, as indicated by the scriptural quotation of Ps 8:5 in 2:6. And not only is Jesus the royal "Son" of God (1:2, 5, 8), but the human beings

---

45. On the cultic sense of being made "perfect" in Hebrews, see Hübner, "*teleioō*," 345. See also Peterson, *Hebrews and Perfection*; McCruden, "Christ's Perfection"; Thomas, "Perfection of Christ."

46. Balz, "*hagios*"; BDAG, 9–10.

he is making holy for their role in worship are also the many "sons" God is leading to the glory of heavenly worship, the "one" God "for whom" are all things and "through whom" are all things (2:10).[47]

In a preceding chain of scriptural quotations God spoke directly to and about his divine royal Son to the audience (1:5–13). Now the divine royal Son, Jesus, through a scriptural quotation of Ps 21:23, responds to that concerted address, speaking directly to and about God for the benefit of the audience as among his "brothers" (2:12). With his scriptural voice Jesus promises God an act of worship in which he will proclaim God's "name" to "my brothers." As the audience hear this scriptural promise in the context of their communal worship, it functions as a speech act, that is, an act that begins to accomplish the worship that it promises for the benefit of the audience.

While the "name" of God refers to the totality of the essential qualities and attributes that identify God and thus cannot be limited to any one word, the preeminent attribute by which God has identified himself at this point is that of "Father." At the beginning of the scriptural sequence (1:5–13) God, with his scriptural voice, emphatically promised his royal Son that "I will be to him as a Father, and he will be to me as a Son" (2 Sam 7:14 in 1:5). Now that "Son," who, being more excellent beyond the angels, has inherited a "name" (1:4), a divine status, emphatically promises God that "I will proclaim your *name* to my brothers" (2:12). Thus, the audience are to realize that God is the Father not only of Jesus, his divine royal "Son," but also of them as among the many "sons" God is leading to the glory of heavenly worship (2:10). They are those whom Jesus, without shame, calls his "brothers."

In a continuation of his scriptural voice (Ps 21:23) Jesus promises that he will praise God "in the midst of the assembly," which, in accord with the poetic parallelism of the psalm, further describes "my brothers" as a communal "gathering" or "assembly" of Jesus' human brothers on earth (2:12). That "I will praise" (*hymnēsō*) God in the midst of this brotherly "assembly" underlines its worshiping dimension.[48] The heavenly enthroned divine royal Son worthy of the audience's worship, together with and assisted by God's angels (1:6, 14), is the Jesus who promises to worship God by "praising" him in the midst of an earthly assembly of his

---

47. For a different interpretation of "all from one" as a reference to descent from Abraham, see Swetnam, "Hebrews 2:11."

48. Rutenfranz, "*hymneō*," 393; BDAG, 1027.

brothers. As a speech act, this promise begins to be fulfilled in the very hearing of it by the audience as they listen to the letter as a worshiping assembly. As among the brothers of Jesus, the audience now anticipate hearing how Jesus will continue to fulfill this promise of worship by praising God in their midst and proclaiming God's name to them.

Continuing his act of hymnic worship with a quotation from Isa 8:17b, Jesus' promise that "I will be confident in him" (2:13a)," that is, place his trust or faith in the God who promised to be a Father to him (1:5), begins to delineate one of the ways in which Jesus "will praise" God in the midst of the worshiping assembly of his brothers (2:12). This "confidence" of Jesus, the divine royal Son, in God as his Father thus serves as a model for the members of the audience. They are also to be confident in their divine Father as among the "brothers" of this "Son" of God (2:11–12), the many "sons" God is leading to the glory of heavenly worship (2:10).

At this point the audience are presented with a chiastic progression from "and again, 'I will be confident'" from Isa 8:17b (2:13a) to "and again, 'Behold I and the children whom God gave to me'" from Isa 8:18a (2:13b). As among the many "sons" God is leading to heavenly glory, the "brothers" of Jesus, the audience are now to consider themselves among the "children" God gave to Jesus, his divine royal Son. Jesus, who professed his confident faith and trust in God as his Father, God has entrusted with God's "children," who include the audience, to make them holy as the initiating leader of their salvation, so that they, like him, may be perfected for their role in heavenly worship (2:10–12).

Since the "children," that is, the "children" whom God gave to Jesus (2:13b), "have shared in blood and flesh," that is, possess a common humanity, so Jesus, the divine royal Son, demonstrated his solidarity with them by similarly partaking of their human condition (2:14a). That through "death" Jesus might destroy the one who has the strength of "death" (2:14b) elucidates for the audience why, on account of the suffering of "death," Jesus might fully experience "death" on behalf of all human beings by the grace of God (2:9). The one who has the strength of death is identified as "the devil" (*diabolon*, 2:14c). As the leader of all demonic powers, he is the chief adversary or enemy of God, preeminent among the "enemies" God has promised to place in total subjugation "as a footstool for the feet" of his divine royal Son (1:13), an object of heavenly worship by both the angels (1:6) and the audience (1:14).[49]

After the identification of the devil (2:14c) as the one who has the strength of death, the audience are presented with a progression from Jesus, through his "death," destroying the one who has the strength of "death" (2:14b) to Jesus freeing those who as by fear of "death" through all their life were "held" or "bound" in slavery (2:15). Jesus was to "free" the "children" God gave him, his fellow human "brothers" (2:11–14), from the "slavery" of their life-long fear of death. This further specifies for the audience what is involved in the "salvation" to which Jesus is leading them as among the many sons of God (2:10), the "salvation" they, as "sons," hope to inherit (1:14), the "salvation" that is so great they ought not to neglect it as the basis for their worship (2:3).[50]

That Jesus surely does not take hold of, as the initiating leader of salvation (2:10), "angels" (2:16) continues the various contrasts that have been developed for the audience between angels and the divine royal Son (1:4–7, 13; 2:5, 7, 9). But that Jesus rather takes hold of the "descendants of Abraham" (2:16), the preeminent ancestor of God's chosen people, further solidifies his solidarity with the human condition of the audience. They are among the "children" God gave him (2:13–14), his fellow "brothers" (2:11–12), the many "sons" of God (2:10), who hope to "inherit" salvation and, with the assistance of the angels, to participate in heavenly worship (1:14).

That Jesus was obligated in all things with his "brothers" to be likened (2:17a) further underscores his solidarity with the audience as his human "brothers." And that Jesus was obligated in all things with his brothers "to be likened" reinforces his partaking of the human "blood and flesh" that the audience as among the children God gave him (2:13b) "have shared in" (2:14a). Jesus promises, in an act of worship, to proclaim God's name to them as a worshiping assembly (2:12), to those he is not ashamed to call his "brothers" (2:11).

At this point the audience are presented with another chiastic progression. Jesus is the "initiator" or "initiating leader" (*archēgon*), whom God made perfect through "sufferings" (2:10). This progresses to Jesus as a merciful and faithful "high priest" (*archiereus*) in things regarding God

---

49. Böcher, "*diabolos*," 297–98; BDAG, 226–27.
50. Gray, *Godly Fear*, 111–38.

(2:17b), for in what he himself "suffered" in being tested, those who are being tested he is able to help (2:18). Jesus becomes a merciful and faithful high priest in order to perform a cultic act of worship in expiating the "sins" of the people (2:17b). This makes more explicit for the audience the high priestly character of Jesus as the heavenly enthroned divine royal Son, who, having made purification for the "sins" that prevent worship, sat at the right of God in heaven (1:3) to be worshiped both by angels and human beings (1:6, 14).

Jesus' becoming a merciful and faithful high priest to expiate the sins of the "people" of God (2:17b) continues this unit's various designations that characterize the social groupings of which the audience are a part. The audience are among the many "sons" God is leading to glory (2:10), the "brothers" Jesus is not ashamed to acknowledge as such and to whom he promises to proclaim God's name (2:11–12), and the "children" whom God gave to Jesus and with whom Jesus, the divine royal Son, shared a common humanity (2:13–14). The audience are now to consider themselves as members of this chosen "people" of God whose sins Jesus expiated as a merciful and faithful high priest. Furthermore, the audience are among those who are "being made holy" for worship by the one who "makes holy," the Jesus made perfect for worship through sufferings (2:10–11). They are also to see themselves among those who are "being tested," whom Jesus, in what he himself suffered in "being tested," is able to help (2:18). As a merciful and faithful high priest who performed a cultic act of worship in expiating the sins that prevent worship, Jesus is able to help the audience as a worshiping assembly.[51]

Conclusion

I. As included within all things divinely inherited by God's Son (1:2a), and as living in the ages that embrace the entire cosmos God made through his Son (1:2b), the audience are to appreciate how God's Son has been included, along with God himself, as a worthy focus of their worship in response to God's having spoken to us definitively in a Son (1:1). That this Son projects divine glory (1:3a) serves as a motivation for the audience to give glory to or glorify both God and God's divine Son in their wor-

---

51. Swetnam, "Hebrews 2:17"; DeYoung, "Divine Impassibility." The presentation of Jesus as a high priest in Hebrews has its closest parallels in the Qumran texts, according to Mason, *You Are a Priest Forever*.

ship. The audience are to appreciate that the Son not only is continually bearing them up and carrying them to completion (1:3b), but that he has made a cultic cleansing for their sins as a basis for them to go on living and worshiping God (1:3c). Thanks to the Son's own act of cultic worship, the audience may now enter into the presence of God to worship God together with God's divine Son. Because of the Son's act of ritualistic worship in having made a cleansing for sins, he was divinely authorized to sit at the right of God and thus become an object of worship (1:3d).

That the Son has inherited a "name," a divine status, vastly superior to the angels (1:4) means not only that God's speaking to us in a Son surpasses the way God has spoken through angels, but also that, unlike the angels, the Son is entitled and worthy to be worshiped along with God. The author's awe-inspiring and poetically hymnic way of informing the audience of how God has spoken to us in a Son serves at the same time as an act of laudatory worship, leading his audience to join him in grateful praise and reverent awe of God and his divine Son. This initial hymnic act of worship (1:1–4) thus establishes an overall context of worship for the remainder of this epistolary homily.

II. The "today" of God's solemn pronouncement to his Son from Ps 2:7, "Son of mine are you, I today have begotten you" (1:5a), also refers to the liturgical "today" when the audience, as a worshiping assembly at the eschatological end of these days (1:2a), hear it made present for them as a basis for their worship. The quotation from 2 Sam 7:14, "I will be to him as Father, and he will be to me as Son" (1:5b), promises that the royal Son will be a truly faithful and obedient covenantal Son who offers proper and authentic worship to the God who is his Father. The audience have thus been alerted to listen to what this scriptural promise entails for their own faithfulness and capability to worship as God's people. Not only are the angels themselves to worship the firstborn Son whom God leads into the heavenly realm (1:6), but, as ministers of God, they also are to assist others in this heavenly worship (1:7). The audience are thus to appreciate that through their earthly worship they can also be participants, along with and through the assistance of the angels, in the heavenly worship of God's Son.

God the Father anointed his Son as greatly superior to the angels with the oil of a festive gladness appropriate to worshiping him as the divine royal Son of God eternally enthroned in heaven (1:8–9). Both the

Father, who is God and Lord (1:9), and the Son, who is also God (1:8) and Lord (1:10), are to be the focus of the audience's worship. God's scriptural pronouncement that the earth and the heavens like a garment will not only become old, but indeed be changed (1:11–12), raises a hope for the audience that all of creation will one day be divinely transformed into something new and different, implying that it will become a more suitable framework for the worship of the eternal divine Son. This hope contributes to the future focus of the audience's worship. The audience are to have the hope of inheriting the salvation (1:14) resulting from the Son's having made purification for sins (1:3) and from God's pledge to place enemies in utter subjugation to his divine royal Son (1:13). The audience are thus to avail themselves of the assistance of the angels of God as spirits ministering at the heavenly worship (1:6–7, 14) of God's divine royal Son enthroned at the powerful and authoritative right side of God (1:13).

III. It is necessary for "us," that is, the audience and the author, as those included among the "us" to whom God has now spoken in a Son (1:2), to all the more attend to the things that have been heard (2:1a). These are the things that have been heard in a context of worship. They refer to the things God has spoken to us in addressing his divine royal Son through the chain of scriptural quotations (1:5–14), heard by the audience as a worshiping assembly. They also refer to the things that have been heard by the ancestral fathers to whom God has spoken in the past in the prophets through the scriptures (1:1) heard during public worship services. "We," audience and author, will not be able to escape the just penalty of a recompense from God (2:2), if, through inattentiveness to the things that have been heard during worship (2:1), we neglect so great a salvation (2:3). The confirmation given us by those who heard previously (2:3), as well as God's further testifying (2:4), provide the audience with a firm anchor, lest they drift away (2:1) and neglect so great a salvation proclaimed to them, especially and preeminently in their worshiping assembly.

IV. The "so great a salvation" (2:3) that the audience are going to inherit is implicitly part of the coming heavenly world (2:5) in which the angels themselves worship (1:6), and, as ministering spirits, they assist others to worship the firstborn divine royal Son (1:14). This further contributes to the future focus of the audience's worship. And with the conclusion of the scriptural quotation of Ps 8:5–7 in 2:6–8, "all things you subjected under his feet" (2:8a), the audience hear the completion of a hymnic act of worship spoken to God by a representative human being into which the members of the audience have been drawn to participate by praising God for what he has done for all human beings.

Along with the explicit identification of the divine royal Son, who is also a son of man (2:6c), a human being, as Jesus (2:9), the audience receive further implicit delineation of the great salvation they are not to neglect as a worshiping assembly (2:3). This salvation that the audience hope to inherit (1:14) is so great because it includes salvation from the power of death (2:9), implicitly among the enemies God will place in total subjection as a footstool for the feet of his heavenly enthroned divine royal Son (1:13). This salvation is for all human beings, on behalf of whom Jesus, himself a human being, fully experienced the death all human beings must experience, before he was exalted from this death to a seat at God's right (1:3), crowned with heavenly glory and honor (2:7, 9). The audience are thus further persuaded of the worthiness of Jesus, the human son of man who is also the divine royal Son of God in heaven, to be worshiped by them.

V. That it was fitting for God to make the initiator of the salvation of the many sons God is leading into the glory of heavenly worship perfect (2:10) further elucidates the salvation that the audience, as among the many human sons of God, have the hope of inheriting (1:14). It was through the suffering of death (2:9) that God made Jesus, the initiator of this salvation, perfect, that is, capable of being seated at the right of God in heavenly glory (1:3, 13), worthy not only to perform an act of cultic worship but ultimately to be worshiped (1:6). The audience are being made holy by Jesus (2:11) and thus being perfected to approach and worship God, as well as Jesus, the divine royal Son, who is also God (1:8–12).

With his scriptural voice Jesus promises God an act of worship in which he will proclaim God's name to my brothers (Ps 21:23 in 2:12). And, in a continuation of this scriptural voice Jesus promises that he will praise God in the midst of the assembly, which, in accord with the poetic parallelism of the psalm, further describes "my brothers" as a communal gathering or assembly of Jesus' human brothers (2:12). That "I will praise" God in the midst of this brotherly assembly underlines its worshiping dimension. The heavenly enthroned divine royal Son worthy of worship is the Jesus who promises to worship God by praising him in the midst of an earthly assembly of his brothers. As a speech act, this promise begins to be fulfilled in the very hearing of it by the audience as they listen to the letter as a worshiping assembly.

Jesus, who professed his confident faith and trust in God as his Father, God has entrusted with God's children (2:13), who include the audience, to make them holy as the initiating leader of their salvation, so that they, like him, may be perfected for their role in heavenly worship (2:10-12). After the identification of the devil (2:14c) as the one who has the strength of death, the audience are presented with a progression from Jesus, through his death, destroying the one who has the strength of death (2:14b) to Jesus freeing those, as many as by fear of death through all their life were held or bound in slavery (2:15). Jesus was to free the children God gave him, his fellow human brothers (2:11-14), from the slavery of their life-long fear of death (2:15). This further specifies for the audience what is involved in the salvation to which Jesus is leading them as among the many sons of God (2:10), the salvation they, as sons, hope to inherit (1:14), the salvation that is so great they ought not to neglect it as the basis and motivation for their communal worship (2:3).

Jesus' becoming a merciful and faithful high priest to expiate the sins of the people of God (2:17b) continues the various designations that characterize the social groupings of which the audience are a part. The audience are among the many sons God is leading to glory (2:10), the brothers Jesus is not ashamed to acknowledge as such and to whom he promises to proclaim God's name (2:11-12), and the children whom God gave to Jesus and with whom Jesus, the divine royal Son, shared a common humanity (2:13-14). The audience are also to consider themselves as members of the chosen people of God whose sins Jesus expiated as a merciful and faithful high priest. The audience are also to see themselves among those who are being tested, whom Jesus, in what he himself suffered in being tested, is able to help (2:18). As a merciful and faithful high priest who performed an act of worship in expiating the sins that prevent worship, Jesus is able to help the audience as a worshiping assembly. Thus, the audience are persuaded to seek help and the expiation of their sins from the Jesus who is worthy of their worship as the heavenly enthroned divine royal Son, who is also a merciful and faithful high priest.

2

Hebrews 3:1—5:10

I. 3:1-6

A ^{3:1} Whence, holy brothers, partners of a heavenly calling, turn attention to the apostle and high priest of *our* confession, Jesus,

   B ² being *faithful* to the one who made him, as also *Moses in (all) his house* (Num 12:7). ^{3a} For this one has been considered worthy of greater glory beyond *Moses*,

      C ^{3b} just as greater honor than the house has the *one who furnishes* it.

         D ^{4a} For every house is furnished by someone,

      C' ^{4b} but the *one who furnishes* all things is God.

   B' ⁵ And *Moses* was *faithful in all his house* as an attendant for testimony of the things that would be spoken,

A' ⁶ but Christ as Son over his house, whose house are *we*, if to the boldness and to the boast of the hope we hold.

THE FIRST TWO OCCURRENCES in Hebrews of the term "high priest"—"a merciful and faithful *high priest*" in 2:17b and "the apostle and high priest" in 3:1—serve as the transitional words connecting the previous unit (2:10-18) to this one (3:1-6). These transitional words keep the audience's attention focused for a further development of the character of Jesus as a "high priest," one who has the role of offering cultic worship.

    The author applies his reasoning regarding the necessity for Jesus to suffer death like all of his human brothers (2:14-16), "*whence* he was obligated in all things with his *brothers* to be likened" (2:17a), directly to the audience, "*whence*, holy *brothers*." That the audience are addressed as "holy" brothers resonates with their "being made holy" by the Jesus "who makes holy" (2:11), that is, consecrates or dedicates them to be "perfected," so that they are worthy and fit to participate in heavenly worship (2:10). That they are "*partners* of a heavenly calling" reinforces this worshiping resonance, as it associates them with the angels as the heavenly "partners" of the Jesus (1:9) the angels are called to worship when God leads him into the heavenly world (1:6).

The designation of Jesus as a "merciful and faithful" high priest is now developed, as the audience are directed to turn their attention to Jesus as the "apostle" and high priest of our confession (3:1). That Jesus is the high priest as well as "apostle" (*apostolon*), that is, one sent by God, continues the focus on heavenly worship, as it recalls for the audience the angels being "sent" (*apostellomena*) by God as "ministering spirits" to assist them in their heavenly worship as those who are going to inherit salvation (1:14).[1] The audience are to direct their attention to Jesus as the apostle and high priest of our "confession," that is, as the object of our public confession of faith, allegiance, and homage that takes place preeminently in the worshiping assembly, but extends as well to the domain of daily living in the society outside of the worshiping assembly. The "Jesus" of whom we are taking note (2:9) is the "Jesus" of our public confession, the worthy object of our faith and worship.

The audience learn that for Jesus to be a "faithful" high priest (2:17b) means his being "faithful" to the one who made him, faithful to God not only as the God who created him, but as the God who "made," that is, sent, placed, or appointed him in his position as high priest in the heavenly worship. This is similar to God "making" the angels his spirits and his ministers (1:7), so that they can be ministering spirits sent by God for assistance in the heavenly worship (1:14). Jesus is faithful to the God who made him, as also Moses was faithful to God in all God's "house" (3:2), that is, in accord with the scriptural allusion to Num 12:7, in all God's "household" as a designation for the people of God entrusted to the leadership of Moses.[2] This designation of God's people as a "house," which

---

1. Bühner, "*apostolos*," 146: "Only in Heb 3:1 is Christ called *apostolos*: he is *apostolos* as the high priest in the heavenly sanctuary, entrusted with this task by God." See also Swetnam, "Hebrews 3,1," 252–62.

2. O'Brien, *Hebrews*, 131: "Moses was faithful to God despite opposition from others, including Israel who wanted to return to Egypt because they lacked food and water

often refers to the temple where God dwells and is worshiped, points to God's people as a worshiping assembly.³ The audience are being invited to compare the faithfulness of Jesus as the high priest sent by God for his role in heavenly worship (3:1) to the faithfulness of Moses within God's "house," that is, within God's people as a worshiping assembly.

Jesus, being radiance of the "glory" of God (1:3), has been considered worthy by God (divine passive) of greater "glory" beyond Moses (3:3a). Indeed, God crowned him, as his divine royal Son enthroned at the right of God (1:4, 13), with heavenly "glory" and honor (2:7, 9), the same heavenly "glory" to which God is leading the "many sons" that include the audience (2:10). Not only has Jesus as the divine royal Son inherited a name "beyond" the angels (1:4), and been anointed by God with the oil of gladness "beyond" the angels as his heavenly partners (1:9), but he has been considered worthy of greater glory "beyond" Moses. This underscores his worthiness to be glorified by both the angels and the audience in heavenly worship.

As the divine royal Son crowned by God with glory and "honor" in his heavenly enthronement (2:7, 9), Jesus has greater "honor" than the "house," God's people as a worshiping assembly, because he is the one who "furnishes" (*kataskeuasas*), that is, prepares or equips the "house" for its worship (3:3b).⁴ As the audience must admit, every "house" needs to be "furnished," that is, prepared or equipped by someone in order to fulfill its function and purpose (3:4a). The audience then experience a chiastic progression from the "one who furnishes" the house (3:3b), namely, Jesus (3:1–3a), to the "one who furnishes" all things for a house (3:4a), namely, God (3:4b). This means that both God the Father (1:5) and Jesus as the royal Son who is also God (1:8) furnish everything the "house" as God's people need to fulfill their function as a worshiping assembly.

(Num. 11:4–6), as well as Miriam and Aaron who challenged his leadership (12:1–2). Against this opposition God replies: 'my servant Moses is faithful in all my house' (12:7). The 'house' of Numbers 12:7 in which Moses served so faithfully was not the tent of meeting but the people of Israel, the family of God. This divine word of affirmation for Moses sets the stage for Hebrews 3:7–4:11, where the author will set Jesus and Moses, who were faithful, over against the wilderness generation, who were not (see 11:23–28)."

3. Matthews, "House," 902: "When speaking of God's temple, *house* may refer to any place dedicated to God's worship."

4. On the meanings of "prepare," "furnish," or "equip" for *kataskeuazō*, see BDAG, 526–27.

At this point the audience have been given various indications of what God—both the Father and Son—has provided for the "house" of God to fulfill its function as a worshiping assembly. First, the scriptural voice of God the Father indicates that the Son is an *object* of heavenly worship. When he leads the firstborn into the heavenly world, he says, "Let the angels of God worship him" (1:6). Not only are the angels themselves to worship the divine royal Son, but God has sent them, as "ministering spirits" (1:7), to assist in the heavenly worship of the Son by those who are going to inherit salvation (1:14), the members of God's "house" as a worshiping assembly.

Second, God has testified "with signs together with wonders and various acts of power and distributions of the Holy Spirit" (2:4) to confirm the word of "so great a salvation" (2:3) as the *motivation* "furnished" for the heavenly worship in God's "house." Jesus is the initiator of this salvation as the divine, but also human, Son who, by the grace of God, suffered death on behalf of all human beings to free them from enslavement to the power of the death they fear all their lives (2:9–15). This great salvation thus reinforces the worthiness of the divine Son as an object of the heavenly worship God has "furnished" for the "house" as a worshiping assembly.

Third, the divine Son, Jesus, the "apostle" sent by God as a merciful and faithful high priest in things pertaining to God (2:17; 3:1), serves as a *mediator* "furnished" for the heavenly worship of God's "house." As high priest, the divine Son made an expiatory cleansing for the sins of the people (1:3; 2:17), making them holy, so that they can be "perfected" (2:10–11), and thus made worthy and fit for the heavenly worship of God. And, as the divine Son, Jesus is the one in whom God the Father has spoken the word of "so great a salvation" (1:1–2; 2:3) that "furnishes" the motivation for the heavenly worship in God's "house," thus serving as a mediator between God and God's "house" to enable the worship of God by God's people.

Moses was faithful in all God's "house" as an "attendant" (*therapōn*), that is, an "aide" or "servant" in a cultic setting of worship in the "house" of God, God's people as a worshiping assembly (3:5).[5] That Moses was faith-

---

5. BDAG, 453. Ellingworth, *Hebrews*, 207: "*therapōn* is used of a temple servant; otherwise it implies a cultic office. Moses is referred to, or refers to himself, as God's *therapōn*." Koester, *Hebrews*, 246: "A 'servant' [*therapōn*] was also one who ministered in the Temple or 'house' of God (Tob 1:7)."

ful in God's "house" as a cultic "attendant for testimony" complements, as "furnishings" God provides for his "house" (3:4) to be a worshiping assembly, the angels God sent as "ministering spirits for assistance" (1:14).

God's promise that "mouth to mouth I will speak" to Moses (Num 12:8) as the faithful attendant in all God's house (Num 12:7) serves as the scriptural basis for his testimony of "the things that would be spoken" (*lalēthēsomenōn*, 3:5) by God (divine passive).[6] Moses provides testimony that God, "having spoken to the fathers in the prophets" (1:1), has now "spoken" to us in a Son (1:2). This "word spoken through angels" (2:2) anticipates the word of salvation that received "a beginning of being spoken through the Lord" (2:3), the salvation concerning the heavenly world and worship within it about which "we are speaking" (2:5) in this letter. Moses was thus faithful in all God's house as an attendant for testimony of "the things that would be spoken" as the basis and motivation for the audience's heavenly worship.

The designation of Jesus, the high priest and divine royal Son, as "Christ" (3:6)—"anointed one"—has its basis in the authoritative scriptural address of God the Father to God the Son, as heard previously by the audience: "God, your God, *anointed* you with the oil of gladness beyond your partners" (Ps 44:8 in 1:9). As Son, Jesus is the "Christ" anointed by God beyond the angels, his "partners" in the heavenly world, with the oil of "gladness" or "rejoicing" appropriate for him as an object of joyous worship. Whereas Moses was faithful to God "in" all God's "house," the worshiping assembly or household of God, as an "attendant" to assist in the worship (3:5), Christ was faithful to God as the "Son" who is "over" God's "house" (3:6), the Son, Jesus Christ, who is the object of heavenly worship (1:6).

The emphatic affirmation, "whose house are *we*" (3:6), explicitly and poignantly identifies the author and audience with the "house" of God as a worshiping assembly or household. It keeps the audience's focus on their hope for the salvation initiated by the Son enthroned over them as the "house" of the Son. It does so by recalling the only previous emphatic utterance in Hebrews of the first person plural pronoun in the author's earnest warning, "how will we escape, neglecting so great a salvation?" (2:3)—the salvation that provides the basis and motivation for heavenly worship.

---

6. Swetnam, "Hebrews 3,5."

But there is a condition the audience must meet to remain identified as the familial "house" of the divine royal Son. They are to hold to "the boldness and the boast of the hope" (3:6). The "boldness" (*parrēsian*) to which they are to hold connotes a confident and courageous speaking out freely, publicly, and openly.[7] It resonates with "our confession" of the apostle and high priest, Jesus (3:1), and thus includes speaking out boldly not only within but outside of the "house" as a worshiping assembly. The "boast of the hope" to which they are to hold similarly connotes a proud assurance, joyous exulting, and public proclaiming, both inside and outside of their worshiping assembly. They are to confidently and courageously "boast" of their hope to inherit salvation (1:14), the "so great a salvation" they are not to neglect (2:3) in their worship. The hope is that of inheriting "so great a salvation" from enslavement to the fear of death, the salvation that has been initiated by Jesus (2:10-15), the Christ who is the high priest faithful to God as the divine royal Son enthroned over us as his familial "house" of worship (3:1, 6).[8]

II. 3:7-11

A [7] *Therefore*, as the Holy Spirit *says*, "Today when you hear his voice, [8a] 'do not harden your *hearts*

    B [8b] as in the rebellion during the day of the *testing* in the wilderness,

    B' [9] where your fathers *tested* by trial though they saw my works [10a] for forty years.

A' [10b] *Therefore* I became provoked with that generation and I *said*, "They are always wandering in the *heart*, and they have not known my ways," [11] as I swore in my anger, "They will never enter into my rest!"'" (Ps 94:7-11).

The closely related expressions for divine revelation—"the things that would be *spoken*" (3:5) and "the Holy Spirit *says*" (3:7)—serve as the link connecting the previous unit (3:1-6) to this one (3:7-11).[9] These expres-

---

7. Koester, *Hebrews*, 247: "'Boldness' includes both the internal disposition of confidence or courage and the external expression of clear and public speaking." According to Attridge (*Hebrews*,112), "boldness" here "refers to a public demonstration of Christian commitment." See also Johnson, *Hebrews*, 110-11; Gray, *Godly Fear*, 138-43; Mitchell, "Holding on to Confidence."

8. Whitfield, "Pioneer and Perfecter."

9. The audience have previously heard the verb "to speak" (*laleō*) as an expression

sions keep the focus of the audience on the word that God is speaking to us, the word heard preeminently in the "house," their worshiping assembly, the word of God that calls for a worshipful response.[10]

With regard to the second macrochiastic level, after the central and pivotal unit (3:1-6) the audience experience a chiastic relationship between the units in 3:7-11 and in 2:10-18 provided by expressions for "testing." Passive expressions of "testing"—"for in what he himself suffered in being *tested*, those who are being *tested* he is able to help" (2:18)—progress to active expressions—"as in the rebellion during the day of the *testing* in the wilderness, where your fathers *tested*" (3:8b-9).[11]

Having heard of God's additionally testifying, with distributions of the "Holy Spirit" (2:4), to "so great a salvation" that began to be spoken through the Lord (2:3), the audience are now told what the "Holy Spirit" says. Having heard scriptural quotations spoken by God the Father (1:5, 6, 7, 13), by a representative human being (2:6), and by God the Son (2:12), the audience now hear a quotation from Psalm 94 spoken by the Holy Spirit.[12] The previous scriptural quotations addressed the audience indirectly by directly addressing either God the Son (1:5, 6, 7, 13) or God the Father (2:6, 12). But this one spoken by the Holy Spirit addresses the audience directly and explicitly with an urgent appeal: "Today when you hear his voice" (Ps 94:7b in 3:7). As part of the psalm, "today" referred to the festival day of worship on which the psalm was sung. But now it is applied to the days of the audience. Indeed, "the psalm was composed in such a way that the prophetic warning contained in vv. 7-11 always referred to the *hic et nunc*."[13] It thus now applies to the "here and now," the "today," on which the audience are listening to this homiletic letter as a worshiping assembly.[14]

---

for divine revelation in 1:1, 2; 2:2, 3, and the verb "to say" (*legō*) as an introduction to the divine revelation expressed in explicit quotations of scripture in 1:5, 6, 7, 13; 2:6, 12.

10. On 3:7-11 as the beginning of an exegetical homily on Psalm 94, see Attridge, "Psalms," 205-6; Rascher, *Schriftauslegung*, 196-200.

11. For an outline of the second macrochiastic level of Hebrews, see the Introduction.

12. On the interpretation of Psalm 94 (MT 95) here, see Guthrie, "Hebrews," 952-56.

13. Thiessen, "End of the Exodus," 357.

14. The previous verse of the psalm has summoned the congregation to the worship of God: "Come, let us worship and fall prostrate before him" (Ps 94:6). See also Attridge, "Psalms," 206.

That "today" the audience are to "*hear* his voice" (3:7), that is, the voice of God the Father, who has spoken to us in his divine royal Son and high priest, reinforces the previous exhortation for the audience "to attend to the things that have been *heard*, lest we drift away" (2:1). These "things that have been heard" include preeminently the word of "so great a salvation" that received a beginning of being spoken through the Lord, and was confirmed for us by those who "heard" (2:3). The audience are now likewise urged to "hear" and thus attentively listen to the voice of God that has spoken to them throughout the letter to this point, the voice of God that is still speaking to them "today," and that calls for their obedient response in worship.[15] As part of their worship "today," the audience are to hear the "voice" of God that implores them, "Do not harden your hearts" (Ps 94:8a in 3:8a). The audience are not to metaphorically "harden," that is, close their "hearts" in resistance to God's will.[16] They are rather to open their "hearts" (*kardias*), that is, their inner persons, the very center or core of their beings, which are determinative for their lives and for their worship, to the voice of God.[17]

At this point the audience are presented with this unit's chiastic pivot of parallels from "the *testing* in the wilderness" (3:8b), with its connotation of being tested by and testing of God, to the further specification of "where your fathers *tested* by trial" (3:9). In addition, the audience experience the ironic distortion from a passive to an active "testing" with regard to God—from God the Son and high priest, who, through what he suffered in "being tested," is able to help those who are "being tested" (2:18), to the "fathers" who "tested" God "the Father" (1:5) in the wilderness. The ancestral "fathers" tested God by trial despite the fact that they saw the miraculous works of God that sustained them in the wilderness for forty years, the works that are among the multifaceted and multifarious ways in which God spoke of old to the "fathers" (1:1), the works that should evoke a response of faith and worship.

The audience are then presented with a chiastic progression from what the Holy Spirit says in quoting from Psalm 94—"*therefore*, as the

15. Laansma, "Hidden Stories," 11.

16. Koester, *Hebrews*, 255: "Hardness of heart is a metaphor for those who refuse to do God's will."

17. Sand, "*kardia*," 250–51: "*Kardia* refers thus to the *inner person*, the seat of understanding, knowledge, and will, and takes on as well the meaning *conscience* . . . the center of the person, that which determines one's life and from which one must determine one's life."

Holy Spirit *says*" (3:7)—to what God says within the same psalm—"*therefore* I became provoked with that generation and I *said*" (3:10b). In addition, the audience experience a chiastic progression from God's warning regarding their own hearts—"do not harden your *hearts*" (3:8a)—to the provoked God's declaration regarding their ancestors' hearts—"They are always wandering in the *heart*" (3:10b).

The audience are to avoid not only "hardening" their own hearts (3:8a) but the example of their ancestral fathers who were always "wandering" in the heart (3:10b). This reinforces the author's previous exhortations "to attend to the things that have been heard, lest we *drift away*" (2:1) and that "we," who are the "house" of Jesus Christ as the divine royal Son and high priest, "*hold* to the boldness and to the boast of the hope" (3:6). Not only are the audience to keep their hearts open rather than closed in hardened resistance to God's will, but to keep their hearts attentively focused on what God is speaking to them, particularly as a worshiping assembly, rather than "wandering" in their heart or "drifting away."

Not only has "that generation" of the audience's ancestral fathers always been wandering in the heart, but they have not known "my ways" (3:10b), the ways that God prescribed for them to behave and the ways that God himself acts, despite the fact that "they *saw* my works" (3:9).[18] This alerts the audience, who, although they do not yet "see" all things subjected to God's Son (2:8b), "are taking note" of Jesus (2:9a) to learn to obey the ways of God from him. He knew God's ways as the one who, on account of the suffering of death, was crowned by God with heavenly glory and honor, so that, by the grace of God, on behalf of all he might fully experience death (2:9). And he knew God's ways as the divine royal Son who was obligated by God in all things with his human brothers to be likened, "so that he might become a merciful and faithful high priest in things pertaining to God in order to expiate the sins of the people, for in what he himself suffered in being tested, those who are being tested he is able to help" (2:17–18). As a merciful and faithful high priest, the divine royal Son is able to help the audience to avoid the failures of their ancestral fathers to properly worship God.

---

18. Koester, *Hebrews*, 256: "Not recognizing the ways of God meant that Moses' generation did not grasp either the favor that God had shown them or the consequences of rebelling against him." Johnson, *Hebrews*, 116: "Their 'not knowing' is not really a form of ignorance, but a form of rebellious disobedience."

Although the audience's ancestral fathers saw "my" works for forty years (3:9–10a), they have not known "my" ways (3:10b). Consequently, God swore in "my" anger that they will never enter into "my" rest (3:11). For the wilderness generation, that they will never "enter into my rest (*katapausin*)" meant that they will not enter into the land of Canaan as their promised rest and inheritance. Moses told them that "you have not yet come into the rest [*katapausin*] and into the inheritance which the Lord your God is giving you" (Deut 12:9). But God's "rest" also refers to the place of worshiping God in the sanctuary in Jerusalem/Zion, which has its counterpart in the sanctuary in heaven. Within the Jerusalem temple Solomon declared, "Blessed be the Lord today who has given rest [*katapausin*] to his people Israel" (3 Kgdms 8:56). In reference to chosen Zion God declares, "This is my rest [*katapausis*] forever" (Ps 131:14). And God indicates that "my rest" is ultimately in heaven, when he says, "Heaven is my throne . . . what is the place of my rest [*katapauseōs*]?" (Isa 66:1).[19]

The audience then are not to harden their hearts in resistance to God's will, but open them to attentively listening to and learning God's ways from the divine royal Son, who promises that he will proclaim God's name to his brothers in the midst of the worshiping assembly (2:12). Unlike their ancestral fathers with wandering hearts, the audience will then be able to "enter into my rest" (3:11), the "rest" of God's heavenly sanctuary where they will be able to worship God. The audience will then be among the many sons God is "leading into glory" (2:10), the heavenly glory of God's rest. They will then not have "drifted away" (2:1) and neglected "so great a salvation" (2:3) that they hope to inherit as God's sons (1:14b). Indeed, they, along with the angels of God as ministering spirits (1:14a), will then be able to worship the divine firstborn Son, whom God "leads into the heavenly world" (1:6), into God's heavenly rest where God is worshiped in glory.[20]

---

19. Koester, *Hebrews*, 257–58; Son, *Zion Symbolism*, 138. Hofius, "*katapausis*," 266: "The author understands the *katapausis* mentioned in the Psalm to be the heavenly dwelling of God, which God has appointed as the eschatological *resting place* for his people." See also Hofius, *Katapausis*; Wray, *Rest*.

20. On entering God's rest as indicating the opportunity to worship God joyfully in the heavenly security of God's presence, see Gleason, "Rest in Hebrews 3:7—4:11."

III. 3:12–19

A ¹² *Take note*, brothers, lest there be in anyone of you an evil heart of *unfaithfulness* in falling away from the living God,

   B ¹³ but encourage one another during each day, while it is called "today," so that not anyone of you may become hardened by the deceit of *sin*,

      C ¹⁴ *for* we have become partners of the Christ, if we hold the beginning of the reality firm until the end, ¹⁵ while it is said, "Today when you *hear* his voice, 'do not harden your hearts as in the *rebellion*'" (Ps 94:7–8).

      C' ¹⁶ *For* which of those who *heard* rebelled? Was it not all those who came out of Egypt through Moses?

   B' ¹⁷ With whom was he provoked for forty years? Was it not those who *sinned*, whose corpses fell in the wilderness?

A' ¹⁸ And with whom did he swear that they should not enter into his rest, if not those who disobeyed? ¹⁹ And we *take note* that they were not able to enter because of *unfaithfulness*.

The occurrences of the word "heart"—"they are always wandering in the *heart*" (3:10b) and "lest there be in anyone of you an evil *heart*" (3:12)—serve as the transitional words that connect 3:7–11 to 3:12–19. After the negative example of the ancestral fathers in the wilderness, whom God declared "always wandering in the heart," the focus returns to the "heart" of the audience, who have already been warned, "do not harden your hearts" (3:8a).

With regard to the second macrochiastic level, the audience experience a chiastic relationship between 2:5–9 and 3:12–19 provided by the first three occurrences in Hebrews of the verb "take note." The declaration that "we are *taking note* of Jesus" (2:9) progresses to both the imperative "*take note*, brothers" (3:12), and the declaration that "we *take note* that they were not able to enter" (3:19).

Not only are the audience in a "brotherly" relationship with one another and with the author, but they are "brothers" of Jesus (3:12). Previously addressed as "holy *brothers*," who are "partners of a heavenly calling," they were directed to "turn attention to the apostle and high priest of our professing, Jesus" (3:1). Jesus "was obligated in all things with his *brothers* to be likened, so that he might become a merciful and faithful high priest" (2:17). The audience are numbered among those whom Jesus is not ashamed to call "brothers" (2:11), the "many sons" God is leading into heavenly glory (2:10). Indeed, hearing the letter while gathered together as "brothers" in their liturgical assembly, the audience have been attuned to listen for the fulfillment of the scriptural promise that Jesus will proclaim God's name "to my *brothers*" in the midst of their worshiping assembly (2:12).

Especially as "brothers" of Jesus, the audience are to take note lest there be any individual among them with "an evil *heart* of unfaithfulness" (3:12), which would liken them to their ancestral fathers, who were "wandering in the *heart*" (3:10), forbidden to enter into God's own heavenly rest (3:11). Furthermore, if the audience were to have any member with an evil heart of "unfaithfulness," they would not be like their "brother," Jesus, who likened himself to his "brothers" in all things, so that he might become a merciful and "faithful" high priest (2:17). Indeed, Jesus was "faithful" to the God who made and sent him as high priest (3:1–2), "faithful" as the messianic Son over God's "house"—the people of God as a worshiping "household" or assembly, among whom are the audience (3:5–6). And Jesus faithfully placed his confidence in the God who entrusted him with the "children" (2:13) within God's plan of leading "many sons," including the audience, into the glory (2:10) and divine rest of heavenly worship.

The "unfaithfulness" of having an evil heart is further explained by its dire consequence, namely, "in falling away from the living God" (3:12). To fall away from the living God would mean for the audience not to enter into God's own heavenly "rest" (3:11), the heavenly glory (2:10) and the heavenly world where God and his Son are worshiped (1:6). For the audience to fall away from the "living" God underscores that they would be falling away from the eternally "living" God who grants eternal "life" after death. This "living" God sent Jesus as his faithful Son and high priest (2:17; 3:1–6) to be like his "brothers," the "children" God gave him (2:13), in all things, including the undergoing of death, "so that through death he might destroy the one who has the strength of death, that is the devil, and free those, as many as by fear of death through all their life were held in slavery" (2:14–15). The audience are not, through unfaithfulness, to fall away from the eternally "living" God, who can free them from the fear of an eternal death that enslaves them through all of their mortal "living" (2:15).[21]

In contrast to "during the day" on which (3:8) the ancestral fathers tested God (3:9), the audience of "brothers" are to encourage one another "during each day" (3:13). They are to encourage one another during each day, while it is called "today" (3:13), that is, each day on which it is called by God (divine passive) as the "today" when they are to hear God's voice (3:7), in other words, each day on which they are gathered together to listen to God speaking to them as a worshiping assembly. If the audience are encouraging one another within their worshiping assembly, then they will not be "drifting away" (2:1), "wandering in the heart" like their ancestral fathers (3:10).

That the audience are to encourage one another, so that not anyone of them may become "hardened" by the deceit of sin (3:13), reinforces God's scriptural command that they not "harden" their hearts (3:8) when they hear his voice (3:7). Not anyone of them is to become hardened by "the deceit of *sin*," because sin, as an offense against God, renders one incapable of worshiping God. It was to expiate the "sins" of the people, so that they could be capable of worshiping God, that Jesus became a merciful and faithful high priest in things pertaining to God (2:17). And having made a cleansing for "sins," he sat at the right of God in the height of heaven (1:3), thus becoming a worthy object of worship.

That we have become "partners" of the "Christ" (3:14) reminds the audience of "brothers" (3:1, 12) that they are "partners" of a heavenly calling (3:1). They have been called to be heavenly partners of the "Christ" who is over them as the "house" of the worship of God (3:6), like the angels, who are "partners" beyond whom God "anointed" his Son as the "Christ," the "anointed one" (1:9). As God called the angels, so he is calling the audience, who have become heavenly partners of the Christ, to worship this Christ as his anointed firstborn Son whom he led into the heavenly world (1:6).[22]

---

21. On the designation "living" God, see Koester, *Hebrews*, 258–59; Johnson, *Hebrews*, 117: "The use of the designation is particularly apt here, since to turn away from the living God is to turn toward death." Schnabel, *Paul the Missionary*, 166: "God is the 'living God' because he is the source of life. The predicate *living* also indicates that the one true God is the Creator of life who also saves from death."

22. Being a "partner" connotes being a "partaker" or "participant," according to Nardoni, "Partakers."

For the audience to be partners of the Christ in heavenly worship, they must "hold the beginning of the reality firm until the end" (3:14). The beginning of the "reality," resonating with the Son's being the representation of the "reality" of God (1:3), refers to the beginning of the divine reality of the word of God's great salvation. The audience are to persevere in holding the "beginning" of the reality "firm" until the end. This reinforces the exhortation that they are not to neglect so great a salvation, the divine word of which, having received a "beginning" of being spoken through the Lord, was "confirmed" for us by those who heard (2:3), thus made "firm" like the word spoken through angels (2:2). The audience may hold the beginning of the divine reality of the word of God's great salvation firm until the end by persevering in their response to this reality as a worshiping assembly called to participate in heavenly worship.

The encouragement of the audience is further motivated by a repetition of the scriptural voice of God, as recorded in Ps 94:7–8, which they heard in 3:7–8. They are to hold the beginning of the word of their great salvation, spoken by the divine voice, firm until the end, "while it is said (by the Holy Spirit of God; cf. 3:7), 'Today when you hear his voice, "do not harden your hearts as in the rebellion"'" (3:15). When the audience, during the "today" in which they have gathered as a worshiping assembly to listen to this letter, hear the voice of God speaking of their great salvation, they are to heed that voice by not hardening their hearts, not closing them in resistance, to that divine word of salvation, as in the rebellion of their ancestral fathers.

The audience are led to admit that absolutely "all" of those who came out of Egypt through Moses rebelled against God (3:16). Even though the ancestors heard the very voice of God, they still rebelled. And the fact that it was through Moses, who was faithful in all of God's house (3:2, 5), that they came out of Egypt did not prevent them from rebelling against God. This alerts the audience to the possibility that anyone or all of them, despite hearing the very voice of God, and despite being the very worshiping "house" of Christ himself (3:6), the faithful Son considered worthy of greater glory beyond Moses (3:3), could rebel against God, as did all of their ancestral fathers in the wilderness.

The audience then experience a chiastic progression from the warning that not anyone of them become hardened by the deceit of "sin" (3:13) to the negative example of their ancestors who "sinned" in the wilderness (3:17). That it was those who sinned whose corpses fell "in the wilderness," in fulfillment of the prophetic warning by Moses (Num 14:29, 32), recalls the rebellion during the day of testing "in the wilderness" (3:8), and thus underlines how sin resulted in the death that prevented the ancestors from entering into God's own rest (3:11). That their ancestral fathers fell to their death rather than entering into God's own rest bolsters the exhortation for the audience to take note lest there be anyone of them with an evil heart of unfaithfulness in falling away from the "living God" (3:12). Indeed, it is the living God who grants eternal life after death to those who enter into his heavenly rest to participate in the heavenly worship.

Next the audience experience a chiastic progression from the command to "take note" lest anyone have an evil heart of "unfaithfulness" (3:12) to the declaration that "we take note" that the ancestors were not able to enter God's rest because of "unfaithfulness" (3:19). Reminded of God's scriptural pronouncement that "I swore in my anger, 'They will never enter into my rest!'" (Ps 94:11 in 3:11), the audience are led to admit that those with whom God swore that they should not enter into his rest were those who disobeyed (3:18). That it was those who "disobeyed" indicates to the audience that when they hear the voice of God as a worshiping assembly, they are to respond not with hardness of heart that leads to testing and rebellion against God but with faithful and worshipful obedience to what they hear.

Having been commanded to "take note" regarding themselves, lest there be in anyone of them an evil heart (3:12), the audience are joined with the author in their communal declaration that "we take note" regarding those who were not able to enter into God's rest (3:19). But this ominous observation of which "we are taking note" regarding those whose deaths prevented them from entering into God's rest stands in contrast with the optimistic observation of which "we are taking note" regarding Jesus, who, by the grace of God, tasted death on behalf of all (2:9). And this is in accord with God's salvific plan of leading many sons into glory (2:10), the glory of worshiping God in God's heavenly rest.

That we take note that the ancestors were not able to enter into God's rest because of "unfaithfulness" (3:19) further describes the consequence of those who "disobeyed." But this ominous observation regarding the consequence of their "unfaithfulness" also reinforces the exhortation for the audience to take note lest there be in anyone of them an evil heart of "unfaithfulness" in falling away from the living God (3:12). In contrast to the negative example of their ancestral fathers in the wilderness, who were not able to enter into God's own rest, the audience are to respond with obedience and faithfulness when, as a worshiping assembly, they hear the voice of the "living" God. This is the God who invites them to enter into the heavenly rest of his eternal "living" to participate in heavenly worship.

IV. 4:1–11

A **4:1** Let us be afraid *then*, lest, while the promise *to enter into his rest* is left, *anyone* of you seem to have been lacking. ² For indeed we have *received good news* just as they did, but the word for *hearing* did not benefit them, who were not united in faith with those who *heard*. ³ᵃ For we are entering into the rest, we who believed,

B ³ᵇ just as *he has said*, "As I swore in my anger, '*They will never enter into my rest!*'" (Ps 94:11),

B' ³ᶜ and yet the works have been produced from the founding of the world. ⁴ For *he has said* somewhere about the seventh day thus, "And God rested on the seventh day from all his works" (Gen 2:2), ⁵ and in this again, "*They will never enter into my rest!*" (Ps 94:11).

A' ⁶ Since *then* it remains for some *to enter* into it, and those who previously *received good news* did not enter because of disobedience, ⁷ again he sets a certain day, "Today," in David saying after so long a time, just as it was said before, "Today if you *hear* his voice, do not harden your hearts" (Ps 94:7–8). ⁸ For if Joshua gave them rest, he would not have spoken after these things about another "day." ⁹ So a Sabbath rest remains for the people of God. ¹⁰ For the one who enters *into his rest* also himself rests from his works just as God from his own works. ¹¹ Let us strive *then to enter* into that rest, so that not *anyone* may fall in the same pattern of disobedience.

The occurrences of the infinitive "to enter"—"we take note that they were not able *to enter* because of unfaithfulness" (3:19) and "let us be afraid then, lest, while the promise *to enter* into his rest is left, anyone of you seem to have been lacking" (4:1)—serve as the transitional words that link 3:12–19 to 4:1–11. The transition keeps the focus of the audience on the theme of entering into God's own heavenly rest to participate in heavenly worship.

With regard to the second macrochiastic level, the occurrences of the term "word"—"for if the *word* spoken through angels became firm" (2:2) and "the *word* for hearing did not benefit them" (4:2)—function as the parallels between the 2:1–4 and 4:1–11 units. That these are the first two occurrences of the term "word" in Hebrews enhances the significance of this parallelism. These key occurrences of the term "word" refer to the word of God that calls for a response of obedient worship.

God has sworn that those who disobeyed would not "enter into his rest" (3:18) because of unfaithfulness (3:19). But the audience are reminded that the promise "to enter into his rest" still remains, and that is why they are to be afraid lest anyone of them seem to have been lacking (4:1). We have received the good news promising entrance into God's own rest, "just as they did" (4:2). The ancestral fathers received good news "as a promise that God would deliver them from slavery and bring them to Canaan (Exod 3:16–17; 4:27–31; cf. 6:1–9)."[23] We also received good news as the "word" (2:2) of so great a salvation (2:3), the salvation that frees those held in slavery by the fear of death through all their life (2:15), with its promise of entrance into the glory of heavenly worship (1:14; 2:10), the eternal rest of the living God (3:11–12). That the "word" for "hearing" did not benefit them (4:2) recalls and reinforces for the audience that those ancestors who "heard," nevertheless, rebelled against God in the wilderness (3:16). They thus failed to heed the urgent appeal of Ps 94:7 to "hear" the voice of God's word promising good news (3:7, 15). As a worshiping assembly, the audience are not to fail to heed this voice.

The word for "hearing" did not benefit them, because they were not united in faith with those who "heard" (4:2), that is, those who really "heard" by responding with faith and obedience. They were not "united" or "joined" in faith with the exceptions to those who heard but rebelled in the wilderness (3:16), namely, Joshua and Caleb (Num 14:26–30).[24] But they also did not share the faith of those who "heard" and confirmed for us the word of so great a salvation (2:3), the word included among the things spoken by God and "heard" by us (2:1). We who have received the good news (4:2), with its still remaining promise "to enter into his rest" (4:1), have begun to realize the fulfillment of that promise, as we are already "entering into the rest, we who believed" (4:3a). That we are

---

23. Koester, *Hebrews*, 269.

24. On the allusion to Joshua and Caleb here, see Ellingworth, *Hebrews*, 243; Koester, *Hebrews*, 270.

those who have in fact "believed" means that we are united in "faith" with those who really "heard" in the sense of responding to what they heard by believing (4:2). That we are already "entering" into the rest impresses upon the audience that, although not yet complete, the process of their entering into the heavenly glory of the eternal rest of the living God to participate in heavenly worship has begun and is underway.

The divine voice, "he has said," introduced the quotation from Ps 94:11 that reiterated God's decisive declaration, "They will never enter into my rest!" (4:3; cf. 3:11, 18). Now that same divine voice, "he has said," introduces a quotation from "somewhere," that is, from somewhere in scripture as the word of God (cf. 2:6), in this case from Gen 2:2 about the seventh day, thus, "And God rested on the seventh day from all his works" (4:4). That God "rested" on the seventh day of creation from all his works expands the previous references to God's "rest" (3:11, 18; 4:1, 3) beyond the "rest" of the promised land intended for the ancestors after they saw God's "works" for forty years in the wilderness (3:9) to the more fundamental "rest" of God after creation. All of the "works" from which God rested on the seventh day include the "works" of God's creation (1:10) that have been produced and are still being produced from the founding of the world (4:3).

The words, "and in this again," that is, in "this" quoting of scripture (cf. 1:5, 6; 2:13), introduce yet another reiteration of Ps 94:11, with particular focus on the concept of God's "rest": "They will never enter into my rest!" (4:5; cf. 3:11, 18; 4:3). When the audience hear the words "my rest" this time, they know that they refer to the "rest" of God on the seventh day of creation when God "rested" from all his works (4:4), and thus that the promise to enter into this "rest" to participate in the heavenly worship still remains for them (4:1).

The statement, "since then it *remains* for some *to enter* into it" (4:6a), begins to draw out the consequences for the audience of the fact that the promise to enter into God's rest was not limited to the rest their ancestors failed to enter, despite seeing the works of God for forty years in the wilderness (4:5; cf. 3:7–11, 16–19). The promise to enter was constituted more broadly and fundamentally by God's rest on the seventh day of creation from all of his works (Gen 2:2), the works that have been and still are being produced from the founding of the world (4:3–4). It confirms for the audience that the promise "to enter" is still "left" and "remains" for them (4:1).

Indeed, although "those who previously received good news did not enter because of disobedience" (4:6b), we also "have received good news" (4:2a) of the promised rest of God, and are already entering into that rest (4:3a). Having taken note that the ancestors in the wilderness were not able to enter "because of unfaithfulness" (3:19), the audience are now told that their ancestors did not enter "because of disobedience," thus underlining the need for the audience, as a worshiping assembly, to hear and heed the voice of God with a response not only of faith but of the obedience required for proper worship.

The ancestors in the wilderness were not united in faith with those who "heard," and, consequently, the word for "hearing" did not benefit them (4:2). In contrast, the audience are not to harden their hearts when "you hear" the voice of God "today" (4:7), that is, here and now, the "day" on which the audience are listening to this homiletic letter as a worshiping assembly. This reinforces for the audience the exhortation that "*Today* when you *hear* his voice, 'do not harden your hearts as in the rebellion'" (Ps 94:7–8), when those who "heard," nevertheless rebelled (3:15–16). It reinforces what the Holy Spirit says to the audience, namely, "*Today* when you *hear* his voice, 'do not harden your hearts'" (3:7–8). Finally, it reinforces the exhortation for the audience not to neglect the word of so great a salvation that was confirmed for us by those who "heard" (2:3), but rather to attend to the things that have been "heard," lest we drift away from the basis and motivation of our worship (2:1).

In the next statement—"for if Joshua gave them rest" (4:8a)— "Joshua" (*Iēsous*) refers to the faithful leader who brought those ancestors who did not rebel and die in the wilderness under the leadership of Moses (3:16–17) into the promised land of Canaan (cf. Josh 21:43; 22:4). This faithful leader of the past shares the name of the faithful leader of the present, "Jesus" (*Iēsoun*), of whom the audience are taking note (2:9) and to whom they are to turn their attention as the apostle and high priest of our professing (3:1). "If Joshua *gave rest* to them" refers not to the "rest" of the promised land of Canaan, but to the more fundamental "rest" promised by God who "rested" on the seventh day of creation from all his works (4:4). If Joshua had given those he led this "rest," then God would not have spoken after these things regarding the wilderness generation "*about* another *day*" (4:8b). God spoke not only "about" the seventh "day" of creation on which he rested (4:4), but the "certain *day*," that is, the "today" of Ps 94:7–8, when God spoke through David long after the wilderness generation. God still speaks "today," calling the audience, as a worshiping assembly, not to harden their hearts when they hear the voice of God (4:7) promising them entrance into God's own rest to participate in heavenly worship.

That a "Sabbath rest" remains for the people of God (4:9) confirms that the "other day" about which God has spoken (4:8) refers both to the "seventh day," the day for observance of God's Sabbath rest (4:4), and to the "day," the liturgical "today," for hearing the voice of God during worship (4:7). This resonates with the "Sabbath rest" (*sabbatismos*) as a day not only for rest but for the worship of God.[25] That a Sabbath rest "remains" for the people of God (4:9) also confirms that it "remains" for some to enter into God's own rest (4:6). The audience are to appreciate, then, that a Sabbath rest remains for them as among the chosen "people" of God, the "people" whose sins Jesus expiated as the merciful and faithful high priest of God (2:17; 1:3). He thereby eliminated an obstacle preventing them from entering into God's own Sabbath rest to participate in heavenly worship.[26]

Since "the promise to enter into his rest is left" (4:1), every member of God's people who "enters into his rest" also himself "rests" from his works just as God "rested" (4:4) from his own works of creation on the seventh day (4:10). This is thus God's own eternal and heavenly "rest," the "rest" that Joshua did not give to the wilderness ancestors (4:8). It is available to each and every member of the audience as the rest that is part and parcel of their participation in heavenly worship.

With regard to the concern for each and every individual member among them, the audience were told to take note lest there be in "anyone" of you an evil heart of unfaithfulness (3:12; cf. 3:19). They are to encourage one another, so that not "anyone" of them may become hardened by the deceit of sin (3:13: cf. 3:17). They are to be afraid lest "anyone" of them seem to have been lacking" (4:1). And now, they are to strive to enter into that rest, so that not "anyone" of them may fall in the same pattern of disobedience (4:11; cf. 4:6; 3:18). At this point, then, each and every member of the audience has been urged to avoid not only unfaithfulness,

---

25. Hofius, "*sabbatismos*," 219: "The statement in Heb 4:9f. remains dependent on a Jewish sabbath theology that associates the idea of sabbath rest with ideas of worship and praise of God. Accordingly, the author of Hebrews understands by *sabbatismos* the eternal sabbath celebration of salvation, i.e., the perfected community's worship before God's throne."

26. Weiss, "*Sabbatismos*."

the deceit of sin, and being deficient, but also the disobedience of a heart hardened to the salvific voice of God that prevents final entrance into the eternal and heavenly rest of the living God to participate in heavenly worship.[27]

V. 4:12–13

A [12a] For living is *the word* of God

>   **B** [12b] and effective and sharper than *every* two-edged sword and penetrating as far as a division of soul and spirit, as well as of joints and marrow, and able to scrutinize deliberations and thoughts of the heart. [13a] And no creature is invisible before *him*,
>
>   **B'** [13b] but *all things* are naked and laid bare to the eyes of *him*,
>
> **A'** [13c] regarding whom there is upon us *the word*.

The term "God" occurs in the assertion, "For the one who enters into his rest also himself rests from his works just as *God* from his own works" (4:10), toward the conclusion of 4:1–11. This occurrence serves as the transitional word that connects this unit to 4:12–13, which begins with the assertion, "For living is the word of *God*" (4:12a). Through this linguistic linkage the audience experience a transition in themes from that of entering into God's very own heavenly rest to that of the word of God that is continually "living."

With regard to the second macrochiastic level, the occurrences of the term "spirit"—"he who makes his angels *spirits*" in 1:7 and "are they not all ministering *spirits*" in 1:14, as well as "penetrating as far as a division of soul and *spirit*" in 4:12—function as the parallels between the units of 1:5–14 and 4:12–13. These are the only occurrences of "spirit" to this point in Hebrews that do not refer to the "Holy Spirit" (cf. 2:4; 3:7). And with regard to the third macrochiastic level, the unit in 4:12–13, which occurs after the central and pivotal unit in 4:1–11, exhibits a parallel relationship with the unit in 3:12–19. This parallelism is evident in the occurrences within these two units of the terms "living" and "God"—"in

---

27. See also DeSilva, "Entering God's Rest"; Bénétreau, "Le repos"; Allen, "More than Just Numbers."

falling away from the *living God*" in 3:12 and "*living* is the word of *God*" in 4:12a.

Having been exhorted to join the author in striving to enter into the Sabbath rest that remains for the people of "God" (4:9), the rest that includes resting from one's own works as "God" rests from his works (4:10), the audience are told that the word of "God" regarding this rest is living (4:12a). That the word of God is "living," with "living" accentuated as the emphatic initial word of the sentence, first of all, refers to its vital relevance and vibrancy for the lives of those who hear it. For the audience as a worshiping assembly, the "word" of God is "living" as the vibrant "voice" of God from Ps 94:7–11. This voice is actively available and "alive" for them to hear during the liturgical "today," inviting them not to harden their hearts but rather to enter into God's own rest (3:7, 15; 4:7).

That emphatically "living" is the word of God (4:12a) also means that this word not only offers life but, as a performative speech act heard during worship, produces and makes "living" a reality for the audience as among those who are to respond obediently to the word's invitation to enter into God's own rest. The "living" that the word of God makes possible is that of the "living" God himself (3:12), the God who lives eternally, resting from his works. This "living" rest is available also to everyone who enters into God's own rest (4:10). By making the "living" of God's own eternal life of rest a reality for those who obey, the "living" word of God frees those held in slavery by the fear of death through all their "life" (2:15).[28]

The "word" of God that is living (4:12a) is the "word" for hearing, which did not benefit the ancestors of the wilderness generation who were not united in faith with those who heard (4:2). The audience have already been exhorted not to neglect to hear with a response of obedient faith, in contrast to the wilderness generation, the "word" of so great a salvation (2:2–3). This is the living word that not only promises but can produce for each and every one of them a living beyond this mortal life entangled in slavery to the fear of death (2:15), a living of the eternal life and heavenly rest that includes worship of the living God himself (3:12).[29]

---

28. On Deut 32:47 as the most prominent OT background to Heb 4:12a, see Allen, *Deuteronomy*, 94–97.

29. For a proposal that the "living word of God" is a christological personification, see Swetnam, "Jesus as *logos*"; idem, "*Logos* as Christ," 129–33. But the context does not seem to substantiate this. See also Koester, *Hebrews*, 273.

That the living word is "effective" indicates its ability to make its promise of "life" presently active. The word's effectiveness as a "living" word reaches into the inner depth of one's being. As sharper than every double-edged cutting instrument, the word penetrates into a person's "soul and spirit, as well as joints and marrow," otherwise impenetrable and indivisible dimensions of a person's inner being (4:12b). The living and powerfully effective word of God that penetrates to the human "spirit" is included in what is said by the Holy "Spirit" of God (3:7), and resonates with the acts of power that come from this divine Holy "Spirit" (2:4). That the living word of the living God (3:12) reaches to the human "spirit" reminds the audience that human beings have a spiritual dimension which likens them to the angels, whom God makes "spirits" and ministers (1:7) in accord with their role of worshiping the firstborn Son in the heavenly world (1:6). That the word of God touches the human "spirit" with its promise of the eternal life of the living God thus facilitates the participation of the audience as human beings in the heavenly worship of the divine Son through the assistance of angels as ministering "spirits" sent by God (1:14).

That the living and effective word of God is able to scrutinize deliberations and thoughts of the "heart" (4:12b) reinforces the previous pleas for the audience as a whole not to harden their "hearts" (3:8, 15; 4:7). That this "living" word of God is able to scrutinize the deliberations and thoughts of the "heart" of every individual human being sharpens the warning for the audience to take note that there not be in anyone of them an evil "heart" of unfaithfulness in falling away from the "living" God (3:12). In contrast to the wilderness generation who were wandering in the "heart" (3:10) which God's living word can scrutinize, the audience are to know the ways of God in their "heart," lest they fall short of entering into God's own eternal life of heavenly rest and worship (3:16–19).[30]

But this living, effective, penetrating, and innerly scrutinizing dimension of the word of God, in accord with its comparison to a double-edged sword, cuts both ways. It not only warns but encourages the audience. As the word of so great a salvation (2:2–3), the "living" word (4:12a) of the "living" God (3:12) is the word about the Jesus who shared in our humanity so that through "death" he might destroy the one who has the strength of "death," the devil (2:14). The living word about the

---

30. The warning aspect of the "word of God" here is denied by Smillie, "Hebrews 4:12–13."

eternal life that conquers the power of death through the death of Jesus is innerly effective, working interiorly (*en-ergēs*) and able to scrutinize the inner deliberations (*en-thymēseōn*) and inner thoughts (*en-noiōn*) of the heart. This assures the audience at the very inner core and depth of their persons of their freedom from the fear of death in which they were held or innerly entangled (*en-ochoi*) in slavery all of their life (2:15).[31]

The assertion that "no creature is invisible before him" (4:13a) moves the focus of the audience from the living word of God (4:12a) to the living God himself.[32] That no creature, and thus no individual member of the audience, is invisible before God reinforces the warning that there not be in anyone in the audience an evil heart of unfaithfulness in falling away from the living God (3:12), since hardened and wandering hearts (3:8, 10, 15; 4:7) cannot be hidden from the penetrating scrutiny of God himself. But that no creature is invisible before God also encourages each individual member of the audience, as an earthly creature who will perish (1:11). Each human, mortal creature, enslaved by the fear of a final and definitive death (2:15), is not hidden before God, who offers entrance into a Sabbath rest and worship. Thus, each creature of God may rest from his or her own works, just as the Creator, in the heavenly rest and worship of the eternal life of the living God (4:9–11).

The focus of the audience on the living word of God as effectively sharper than "every" two-edged sword in its penetrating ability (4:12b) broadens to a focus on "all things" in general being naked and laid bare to the eyes of "him," God himself (4:13b), an elaboration upon the assertion that no creature is invisible before "him," God himself (4:13a). This elaborated assertion reinforces the warning that there not be in anyone in the audience an evil, hardened, or wandering heart of unfaithfulness in falling away from the living God (3:12; cf. 3:8, 10, 15; 4:7), since all things are susceptible to the searching, scrutinizing "eyes" of the God able to see whether a person knows the ways of God or not (3:10).

This elaborated assertion (4:13b) also reinforces the encouragement for every individual in the audience that God has the merciful "eyes" to see everyone who is enslaved by the fear of a death that can deprive one

---

31. Gray, *Godly Fear*, 114–15; Johnson, *Hebrews*, 101: "The author suggests that fear of death leads to a slavery that is not acute—arising in moments of crisis—but rather chronic, and therefore more fundamentally shapes human choices."

32. The genitive "God" (*theou*) rather than the nominative "word" (*logos*) in 4:12a serves as the antecedent for the genitive "him" (*autou*) in 4:13a.

of God's eternal life (2:15). That "*all things* are naked and laid bare" to the "eyes" of God, in other words, that "all things" are in a position of being at the mercy of God, assures the audience that God "sees," as do we, that "all things" have not yet been "subjected" to Jesus, the divine Son (2:8). Among all these things yet to be subjected under the feet of the heavenly enthroned Jesus are his enemies (1:13), preeminent among whom is the devil, who wields the power of death (2:14). That all things are naked and laid bare to the eyes of the living God thus bolsters the hope of the audience that God sees their vulnerability to the fear of a death preventing their entrance into the heavenly rest and worship of God's eternal life.

The phrase "regarding whom" (4:13c) keeps the focus of the audience on "him," the God to the eyes of whom all things are naked and laid bare (4:13b), on "him," the God before whom no creature is invisible (4:13a), and on the God whose word is living, effective, penetrating, and scrutinizing (4:12). As the audience recall, it was in things "regarding God" that Jesus became a merciful and faithful high priest (2:17), able to help those being tested (2:18). The audience as a worshiping assembly, then, have been attuned and alerted to look to Jesus for help as they are confronted with the things "regarding God." These are the things involved especially in hearing the living word of the living God with a heart open to knowing the ways of God (3:10) in leading many sons into the glory of heavenly worship (2:10), into the Sabbath rest and worship of God's eternal life (4:9–11). And this confrontation is reinforced as "there is upon *us*," the audience, "the word" (4:13c), recalling that God has spoken to "us" in a Son (1:2).

That regarding God there is upon us "the word" (4:13c) presents the audience with a double meaning. First, "the word" refers to "the word" from God that is living (4:12a) and that is now directed "to" or "upon" us, with its innerly effective, powerfully penetrating, and sharply double-edged message of both warning and encouragement. As the word voiced by God himself that we, the audience as a worshiping assembly, are to hear during the liturgical "today" (3:7, 13, 15; 4:7), it warns against a hardened heart of unfaithfulness closed to knowing the ways of God (3:8, 10, 12, 15; 4:7). But, at the same time, as the "living" word of the "living" God (3:12), it encourages faithful obedience to God with its promise of entrance into the heavenly Sabbath rest and worship of the eternal life of God himself (4:9–11).

Secondly, that regarding God there is upon us "the word" (4:13c) refers to "the word" that we, the audience as a worshiping assembly, are to return to God in response to God's word to us. In other words, we are now confronted with the decision of how we are going to respond to the "living" word of God with its double-edged message of both warning and encouragement. The expectation is for the audience to respond with "the word" of their communal confession of faithful obedience to "the word" of God. This accords with the previous exhortation that the audience, as holy brothers and partners of a heavenly calling, are to turn attention to the apostle and high priest of "our confession," Jesus (3:1), who was faithful to the one who made him (3:2a). Thus, "the word" that is incumbent upon "us" as our response to "the word" (*ho logos*) of God to us resonates with "our confession" (*homologias*) as our communal word of worshipful response to the faithfulness of Jesus with our own faithful obedience.[33]

VI. 4:14—5:10

A ¹⁴ Having then a great high priest who has passed through the heavens, Jesus the Son of God, let us hold fast to the confession. ¹⁵ For we do not have a high priest who is not *able* to *sympathize* (*sympathēsai*) with our weaknesses, but one who has been tested in all things in likeness, yet without sin. ¹⁶ Let us approach then with boldness the throne of grace, so that we may receive mercy and may find grace for timely help. ⁵:¹ For every high priest from men taken, on behalf of men is appointed in things regarding God, so that he may *offer* both gifts and sacrifices on behalf of sins, ² being *able* to *deal patiently* with those who are ignorant and wandering, since he himself is surrounded by weakness ³ and on account of this he is obligated, *just as* concerning the people, so also concerning himself, to *offer* concerning sins.

B ⁴ And *not* by *himself* does anyone take the honor *but* is called by God even as also Aaron.

---

33. Smillie, "'Heb. 4:13," 25: "Not only is *homologia* cognate with *logos* (from *homologeō*, literally 'to say together the same words,' hence 'con-fession'), but it is also the natural sequence to what the author has just been saying . . . *Homologia* and *hēmin ho logos*, then, are both invitations to affirm or profess the word the readers have heard. At the end of v. 13, the author says in effect, 'Now it is our turn to return the word to him.'" See also Becker, "Heb 4,12–13."

B′ ⁵ So also the Christ did *not* glorify *himself* in becoming high priest, *but* the one who spoke to him, "Son of mine are you, I today have begotten you" (Ps 2:7).

A′ ⁶ *Just as* also in another place he says, "You are a priest forever according to the order of Melchizedek" (Ps 109:4), ⁷ who in the days of his flesh *offered* both prayers and supplications with strong outcrying and tears to the one who is *able* to save him from death, and he was heard from his reverence, ⁸ although being a Son, he learned from the things he *suffered* (*epathen*) obedience, ⁹ and having been made perfect, he became for all those who obey him a source of eternal salvation, ¹⁰ having been designated by God high priest according to the order of Melchizedek.

The declaration that "the word" is incumbent upon us (4:13), which brings the unit in 4:12–13 to its climactic conclusion, provides the transitional word that connects this unit with the following unit in 4:14–5:10. The link occurs at the beginning of this unit in the exhortation, "let us hold fast to the confession" (4:14). The term "confession" (*homologias*), literally "a saying together of the same words," shares a similar sound and meaning with the term "the word" (*ho logos*). These transitional words keep the focus on the communal response of the audience as a worshiping assembly to the living word of God.

With regard to the second macrochiastic level, there are a number of parallels indicated between the 1:1–4 and the 4:14—5:10 units. A first parallelism involves the term "Son" in reference to Jesus—"in a *Son*" in 1:2, "*Son* of God" in 4:14, "my *Son* are you" in 5:5, and "although being a *Son*" in 5:8. A second concerns references to "God"—"much time ago *God*" in 1:1, "Son of *God*" in 4:14, "things regarding *God*" in 5:1, "is called by *God*" in 5:4, and "having been designated by *God*" in 5:10. A third features occurrences of the term "sin"—"having made a cleansing for *sins*" in 1:3, "yet without *sin*" in 4:15, "on behalf of *sins*" in 5:1, and "concerning *sins*" in 5:3. A fourth parallelism is exhibited by occurrences of the verb "speak" with God as subject—"God, having *spoken* to the fathers . . . has *spoken* to us" in 1:1–2, and "the one who *spoke* to him" in 5:5. With regard to the third macrochiastic level, this unit in 4:14—5:10 exhibits a parallel relationship with the unit in 3:7-11. This parallelism is evident in the occurrences in these two units of the verb "test"—"where your fathers *tested*" in 3:9, and "one who has been *tested* in all things in likeness" in 4:15.

Regarding God "there is upon us the word" (*ho logos*, 4:13), with its implication that it is incumbent upon us to respond to "the word" (*ho logos*) of God that is living and effective (4:12). The audience are thus exhorted to continue to make that response by holding fast to the "confession" (*homologias*)—their saying together, as a worshiping assembly, of words in response to the word of God (4:14). That they are to hold fast to the "confession" because they have "a great high priest who has passed through the heavens, Jesus the Son of God" (4:14), reinforces the previous exhortation for the audience, as "partners of a heavenly calling," to "turn attention to the apostle and high priest of our *confession*, Jesus" (3:1).

As a worshiping assembly, the audience are to hold fast to the "confession" in response to the living word of God concerning the great salvation accomplished by Jesus as the great high priest and Son of God.[34] Jesus has passed through the "heavens" (4:14) in a celestial, ceremonial procession preliminary not only to his role as the great high priest in the heavenly worship but to his exaltation as the royally enthroned Son of God and object of heavenly worship by the angels (1:6; cf. 1:3, 13; 2:9–10). The audience are invited to this heavenly worship as "partners of a *heavenly* calling" (3:1).[35]

The double negative expression, "we do *not* have a high priest who is *not* able to sympathize with our weaknesses" (4:15), underscores that we have a high priest definitely able to "sympathize" or "suffer with" us in our weaknesses.[36] That we have a high priest "able" to "suffer with" us in our weaknesses, as one who has been "tested" (4:15), stands in stark contrast to the rebellion during the day of the "testing" in the wilderness (3:8), where the fathers "tested" God by trial though they saw God's works (3:9). It reinforces the previous assertion that "in what he himself *suffered* in being *tested*, those who are being *tested* he is *able* to help" (2:18). And that we have as "high priest" one who has been tested "in all things" in

---

34. Attridge, *Hebrews*, 140: "The maintenance of the confession probably involved preservation of a commitment made in a liturgical context, but cannot be limited to that."

35. Koester, *Hebrews*, 282: "Jesus passes through the heavens like a priest moving through the forecourt of a sanctuary and into the holy of holies." See also Johnson, *Hebrews*, 139.

36. Johnson, *Hebrews*, 141: "Christ entered fully into the human experience of suffering."

"likeness" to us (4:15) reaffirms that he was obligated "in all things" with his brothers to be "likened," so that he might become a merciful and faithful "high priest" (2:17).

We have a high priest able to sympathize with our weaknesses as one tested in all things in likeness to us, yet without "sin" (4:15). This encourages the audience not to become hardened by the deceit of "sin" (3:13). As the audience have been informed, Jesus became a merciful and faithful high priest in things regarding God in order to expiate the "sins" of the people (2:17), the sins that prevent the audience as the people of God from the worthy worship of God. Indeed, having made a cleansing for "sins," Jesus, as the exalted Son of God, "sat at the right of the Majesty in the heights" (1:3), and thus became an object of heavenly worship for the audience, assisted by the ministering angels (1:6–7, 13–14; 3:1; 4:14).

As the worshiping "house" or household of Christ, the audience were previously exhorted that they are to hold to the confident and openly expressed "boldness" (3:6) that accompanies their confession of Jesus as the high priest (3:1). And now they are exhorted that, with the "boldness" that accompanies this confession to which they are to hold fast (4:14), they are to approach the "throne" of grace (4:16).[37] The exalted Jesus as the divine Son of God sits upon this "throne" of grace (1:3, 13), the eternal "throne" of God in heaven (1:8). Since Jesus, as the great high priest and Son of God, "has passed through" the heavens in a cultic procession preliminary to his role in the heavenly worship, the audience are now able, with boldness, to cultically and continually "approach" (*proserchōmetha*), within their communal worship, this heavenly throne of divine grace.[38]

That the audience, as a worshiping community, are to approach with boldness the heavenly throne of grace so that they may receive "mercy" (4:16) resonates with Jesus becoming a "merciful" and faithful high priest

---

37. Koester, *Hebrews*, 284: "Boldness (*parrēsia*) includes both an internal disposition of confidence and an external expression that is clear and public."

38. Ellingworth, *Hebrews*, 269: "*Proserchomai* in Hebrews is always used in a cultic sense, of worshippers approaching God, either generally (11:6), in the OT ritual (10:1; 12:18), or through Christ, as here." O'Brien, *Hebrews*, 185: "The challenge for the listeners here at 4:16 is to persistent, confident prayer. Based on Jesus' high-priestly work that leads to an opening of the heavenly sanctuary for men and women in a new way, this direct approach to God is an ongoing and regular expression of the definitive 'drawing near' to him. . . . The imperfective aspect of the verb (*proserchōmetha*) views the action as open-ended: the 'approach' should therefore be ongoing or occur again and again (n. 181)."

in things regarding God in order to expiate the sins of the people (2:17; cf. 1:3). The audience, then, are to approach the throne of grace in order to receive divine mercy with regard to their weaknesses and sins. That the audience are to approach the throne of "grace" in order to find "grace" for timely help (4:16) encourages them to experience, within their communal worship, the "grace" of God that allowed Jesus to taste death on behalf of all people (2:9). This is the salvific death that frees all people from slavery to the fear of a death that deprives one of eternal life with God (2:14–15). That they may find grace for timely "help" follows upon the assertion that Jesus, as the merciful and faithful high priest, tested in all things in likeness to us, yet without sin (4:15), is able to "help" the audience as among those who are being tested with regard to the weaknesses and sinfulness that prevent their full and proper worship of God (2:18).

Having been presented with the question of God's concern for humanity in the quotation of Ps 8:5, "What is *man* that you remember him, or a son of *man* that you care for him?" (2:6), the audience now hear of God's establishment of the high priesthood from and for the sake of human beings. Every high priest is taken by God (divine passive) from "men," and on behalf of "men" is appointed by God in things regarding God (5:1). Every high priest is a human being appointed by God on behalf of human beings "in things regarding God," so that he may offer both gifts and sacrifices on behalf of "sins" (5:1). This further explains the obligation for Jesus to become in all things like his fellow human beings, so that he might become a merciful and faithful high priest "in things regarding God" in order to expiate the "sins" of the people (2:17) and thus enable them to worship God.

Every high priest is "able" to "deal patiently" with those who are ignorant and wandering, since he himself is surrounded by "weakness" (5:2). This reinforces the exhortation for the audience to approach with boldness the throne of grace, in order to receive mercy and find grace for timely help (4:16) from Jesus as the great high priest "able" to "sympathize" with our "weaknesses" (4:15). And that Jesus, like every high priest, is able to deal patiently with those who are "ignorant" and "wandering" (5:2) reassures the audience of his timely help for them (4:16) in their vulnerability to become like their ancestors who were always "wandering" in their heart and did "not know" the ways of God (3:10).

Every high priest is "obligated," just as concerning the "people," so also concerning himself, to offer concerning "sins" (5:3; cf. 5:1). This further explains for the audience why, although Jesus is without "sin" (4:15), he was "obligated" in all things with his brothers to be likened, so that he might become a merciful and faithful high priest in things regarding God in order to expiate the "sins" of the "people" (2:17). And it reinforces the exhortation for no member of the audience to become hardened by the deceit of "sin" (3:13). In dealing with their weaknesses and sinfulness, the audience, as among the "people" of God for whom a heavenly sabbath rest and worship remains (4:9), have been assured that they may approach with boldness the heavenly throne of grace. They may receive mercy and find grace for timely help (4:16) from Jesus, the great high priest and divine Son of God (4:14). Indeed, having made a cleansing for "sins," he sat at the right of God on that heavenly throne and became an object of worship (1:3).

At this point the audience are presented with a pivot of parallels at the center of this chiastic unit. They hear a progression from "*not by himself* does anyone take the honor but is called by God even as also Aaron (5:4) to "the Christ did *not* glorify *himself* in becoming high priest, *but* the one who spoke to him" (5:5). That the Christ did not "glorify" himself in becoming high priest but was glorified by God reminds the audience that Jesus has been considered by God to be worthy of greater "glory" beyond Moses (3:3). With "glory" and honor God crowned him (2:7, 9), as the heavenly enthroned divine Son, who is the radiance of God's heavenly "glory" (1:3). It is through this glorified Son that God intends to lead his many sons to this same "glory" of heavenly worship (2:10), the many "sons" who include the audience.

The audience were made aware of how God's Son is distinguished beyond the angels by the God who "spoke" to us in a Son (1:2) through his scriptural voice that with divine authority pronounced to the Son (Ps 2:7), "Son of mine are *you*, I today have begotten you" (1:5). And now the audience realize that the authoritative call which God "spoke" in glorifying Christ to become a high priest is the same as the call to his divine Sonship through that same scriptural voice, "Son of mine are *you*, I today have begotten you" (5:5). And this is confirmed and reinforced as the audience are informed that "just as in another place" in scripture (Ps 109:4) the voice of God says, "*You* are a priest forever according to the order of Melchizedek" (5:6). Furthermore, just as the heavenly throne of Jesus as the exalted divine Son is "*forever* and ever" (1:8), so the Son is a priest "*forever* according to the order of Melchizedek."³⁹

As the audience were reminded, every high priest is taken from men and appointed on behalf of men in things regarding God, "so that he may *offer* both gifts and sacrifices on behalf of sins" (5:1) and "to *offer* concerning sins" (5:3). And now they are informed that Jesus, as high priest, "*offered* both prayers and supplications" (5:7). And that he did so "in the days of his *flesh*" (5:7) reminds the audience that Jesus, as high priest, was a human being who shared in their "blood and *flesh*" (2:14). The audience are to appreciate that he offered prayers and supplications not just for himself but for them as his fellow human beings.⁴⁰

As a high priest, Jesus is "able" to deal patiently with those who are ignorant and wandering, since he himself is surrounded by weakness (5:2), "able to sympathize with our weaknesses (4:15), and is "able" to help those who are being tested (2:18). He thus offered both prayers and supplications with strong outcrying and tears to the God "able" to save him from death (5:7). That Jesus prayed so ardently to be saved from "death" resonates with his sharing in the human condition of the audience, so that through "death" he might destroy the one who has the strength of "death," the devil, and free those, as many as by fear of "death" through all their life were held in slavery (2:14–15). The audience are to appreciate that Jesus became their fellow human being, so that through his suffering of "death," by the grace of God, he might taste "death" on behalf of all (2:9).

That Jesus "was heard from his reverence" (5:7) means that his prayer was answered in the sense not of his escaping the physical death all human beings undergo, but of being saved from eternal death by the God who raised him from the dead and exalted him to a seat at his right on the heavenly throne.⁴¹ That the prayers and supplications Jesus offered as high priest on behalf of human beings to the God able to "save" him from death were answered deepens the audience's appreciation for the signifi-

---

39. Farrow, "Melchizedek."

40. Clivaz, "Hebrews 5.7"; McCormick, "Humanity of the Son." O'Brien, *Hebrews*, 197–98: "The opening temporal phrase, (lit.) 'during the days of his flesh', recalls Jesus' incarnation (2:14), while the term 'flesh' reinforces the reality of his humanity. Although this expression encompasses Jesus' entire life, Hebrews focuses on his passion. No precise indication of the time when his prayers were offered can be inferred."

41. Koester, *Hebrews*, 288: "God did not deliver Jesus from crucifixion, but he did deliver him from death by raising him to life again."

cance of Jesus suffering death on behalf of all. Through the sufferings that culminated in his death and perfected him, Jesus became the initiator of "salvation" from eternal death (2:10), the great "salvation" from eternal death that the audience are not to neglect as a worshiping assembly (2:3), the "salvation" from eternal death they are going to inherit as participants in heavenly worship (1:14).

Although being a "Son," indeed the "Son" of God (4:14), to whom the scriptural voice of God (Ps 2:7) declared, "*Son* of mine are you" (5:5; cf. 1:2, 5, 8; 3:6), Jesus learned from the things he suffered obedience (5:8). The close connection between what Jesus "learned" (*emathen*) from the things he "suffered" (*epathen*) is underscored by the similar sound of the two verbal forms employed. The audience have heard previously that in what Jesus himself "suffered" in being tested, those who are being tested he is able to help (2:18). That Jesus, as a Son of God, learned from the things he suffered obedience to God thus implies that he is able to help the audience learn obedience to God from the things they suffer. And for the audience to learn "obedience" to God from the things they suffer would help them to avoid falling in the same pattern of "disobedience" of their ancestors (4:11) who, as those "disobedient" to God (3:18), did not enter into the glory of God's own heavenly rest and worship because of their "disobedience" (4:6).[42]

Jesus was made "perfect" as a "Son" who learned from the things he "suffered" obedience (5:8), so that he became for all those who obey him a source of eternal "salvation" (5:9). This recalls and reinforces for the audience how it was fitting for God in leading many "sons" to the glory of heavenly worship to make the initiator of their "salvation," through "sufferings," "perfect" (2:10). As a worshiping assembly, the audience are not to neglect so great a "salvation" (2:3) they are going to inherit as participants in heavenly worship (1:14), because it is an "eternal" salvation that saves them from their life long fear of an eternal death (2:14–15) that would prevent their entering into the eternal life in the heavenly rest and worship of the living God. To gain this eternal salvation the audience are thus to "obey" the Son who learned from the things he suffered "obedience" to God. That Jesus was designated by God high priest according to the order of Melchizedek (5:10) reinforces God's scriptural declaration

---

42. Swetnam, "Crux"; idem, "Context of the Crux"; Richardson, "Passion."

(Ps 109:4) to his Son, "You are a priest *forever* according to the order of Melchizedek" (5:6).

Conclusion

I. The audience are to direct their attention to Jesus as the apostle and high priest of our confession (3:1), that is, as the object of our public confession of faith, allegiance, and homage that takes place preeminently in the worshiping assembly, but extends as well to the domain of daily living in the society outside of the worshiping assembly. The audience are invited to compare the faithfulness of Jesus as the high priest sent by God for his role in heavenly worship (3:1) to the faithfulness of Moses within God's house (3:2), that is, within God's people as a worshiping assembly. Not only has Jesus as the divine royal Son inherited a name beyond the angels (1:4), and been anointed by God with the oil of gladness beyond the angels as his heavenly partners (1:9), but he has been considered worthy of greater glory beyond Moses (3:3a). This underscores his worthiness to be glorified by both the angels and the audience in heavenly worship.

Both God the Father and Jesus as the royal Son who is also God furnish everything the "house" as God's people need to fulfill their function as a worshiping assembly (3:3–4): 1) The divine royal Son is furnished as an *object* of worship; 2) so great a salvation (2:3) is furnished as the *motivation* for the heavenly worship in God's house; 3) the Son is furnished as a *mediator* between God and God's house to enable the worship of God by God's people. Moses was faithful to God in all God's house, the worshiping assembly or household of God, as an attendant to assist in the worship (3:5). But Jesus Christ was faithful to God as the Son who is over God's house (3:6), the Son who is the object of heavenly worship (1:6). The audience are to hold to the boldness and the boast of the hope (3:6), the hope of inheriting (1:14) so great a salvation (2:3), if they are to remain identified as the familial "house" of worship of the divine royal Son.

II. As part of their worship today (3:7), the audience are to hear the voice of God that implores them, "Do not harden your hearts" (Ps 94:8a in 3:8a). They are rather to open their hearts, their inner persons, the very center or core of their beings, which are determinative for their lives and for their worship, to the voice of God. Although the audience's ancestral fathers saw God's works for forty years (3:9–10a), they did not know God's ways (3:10b). Consequently, God swore in his anger that they will never enter into God's own rest (3:11). God's rest refers to the place of worshiping God in the sanctuary in Jerusalem/Zion, which has its counterpart in heaven. The audience then are not to harden their hearts in resistance to God's will, but open them to attentively listening to and learning God's ways from the divine royal Son, who promises that he will proclaim God's name to his brothers in the midst of the worshiping assembly (2:12). Unlike their ancestral fathers with wandering hearts, the audience will then be able to "enter into my rest" (3:11), the rest of God's heavenly sanctuary where they will be able to worship God.

III. The danger of the audience having an evil heart of unfaithfulness carries a dire consequence—falling away from the living God (3:12). To fall away from the living God would mean for the audience not to enter into God's own heavenly rest (3:11), the heavenly glory (2:10) and the heavenly world where God and his Son are worshiped (1:6). That the audience are to encourage one another during each liturgical "today," so that not anyone of them may become hardened by the deceit of sin (3:13), reinforces God's scriptural command that they not harden their hearts (3:8) when they hear his voice (3:7). For the audience to be partners of the Christ in heavenly worship, they must hold the beginning of the divine reality of the word of God's great salvation firm until the end (3:14) by persevering in their response to this reality as a worshiping assembly called to participate in heavenly worship. In contrast to the negative example of their ancestral fathers in the wilderness, who were not able to enter into God's own rest, the audience are to respond with obedience and faithfulness when, as a worshiping assembly, they hear the voice of the living God. This is the God who invites them to enter into the heavenly rest of his eternal living to participate in heavenly worship (3:15–19).

IV. We who have received the good news (4:2), with its still remaining promise to enter into God's rest (4:1), have begun to realize the fulfillment of that promise, as we are already "entering into the rest, we who believed" (4:3a). That we are already entering into the rest impresses upon the audience that, although not yet complete, the process of their entering into the heavenly glory of the eternal rest of the living God to participate in heavenly worship has begun and is underway. The promise to enter was constituted more broadly and fundamentally by God's rest on the seventh day of creation from all of his works (Gen 2:2), the works that have been and still are being produced from the founding of the world (4:3–4). The audience are told that their ancestors did not enter because of disobedience (4:6), thus underlining the need for the audience, as a worshiping assembly, to hear and heed the voice of God with a response not only of faith but of the obedience required for proper worship.

That a Sabbath rest remains for the people of God (4:9) confirms that the "other day" about which God has spoken (4:8) refers both to the seventh day, the day for observance of God's Sabbath rest (4:4), and to the day, the liturgical "today," for hearing the voice of God during worship (4:7). This resonates with the Sabbath rest as a day not only for rest but for the worship of God. The audience are to appreciate that a Sabbath rest remains for them as among the chosen people of God, the people whose sins Jesus expiated as the merciful and faithful high priest (2:17; 1:3). He thereby eliminated an obstacle preventing them from entering into God's own Sabbath rest to participate in heavenly worship. Each and every member of the audience has been urged to avoid not only unfaithfulness, the deceit of sin, and being deficient, but also the disobedience of a heart hardened to the salvific voice of God that prevents final entrance into the eternal and heavenly rest of the living God to participate in heavenly worship (4:10–11).

V. The word of God that is emphatically living (4:12a) is the word for the audience to hear during their liturgical worship. It is the living word that not only promises but can produce for each of them a living beyond this mortal life entangled in slavery to the fear of death (2:15), a living of the eternal life and heavenly rest that includes worship of the living God himself (3:12). The living, effective, penetrating, and innerly scrutinizing dimension of the word of God, in accord with its comparison to a double-edged sword (4:12b), cuts both ways. It not only warns but encourages the audience. That no creature is invisible before God (4:13a) reinforces the warning that there not be in anyone in the audience an evil heart of unfaithfulness in falling away from the living God (3:12). But that no creature is invisible before God also encourages each member of the audience with an offer of entrance into the heavenly rest and worship of the living God (4:9–11).

That all things are naked and laid bare to the eyes of the living God (4:13b) bolsters the hope of the audience that God sees their vulnerability to the fear of a death preventing their entrance into the heavenly rest and worship of God's eternal life. And that regarding God there is upon us the word (4:13c) presents the audience with a double meaning. First, the word refers to the word from God that is living (4:12a) and that is now directed to or upon us, with its innerly effective, powerfully penetrating, and sharply double-edged message of both warning and encouragement. Secondly, the word refers to the word that we, the audience as a worshiping assembly, are to return to God in response to God's word to us. The audience are expected to respond with the word of their communal confession of faithful obedience to the living word of the living God.

VI. The audience are to hold fast to the confession, because they have a great high priest who has passed through the heavens, Jesus the Son of God (4:14). Jesus has passed through the heavens in a celestial, ceremonial procession preliminary not only to his role as the great high priest in the heavenly worship but to his exaltation as the royally enthroned Son of God and object of heavenly worship by the angels (1:6). That every high priest is a human being appointed by God on behalf of human beings in things regarding God, so that he may offer both gifts and sacrifices on behalf of sins (5:1), further explains the obligation for Jesus to become in all things like his fellow human beings. That every high priest is able to deal patiently with those who are ignorant and wandering, since he himself is surrounded by weakness (5:2), reinforces the exhortation to approach with boldness the throne of grace, in order to receive mercy and find grace for timely help (4:16) from the great high priest able to sympathize with our weaknesses (4:15). And that every high priest is obligated, with regard to the people and himself, to offer for sins (5:3) further explains why, although Jesus is without sin (4:15), he was obligated in all things with his brothers to be likened, in order to expiate the sins of the people (2:17).

The audience realize that the authoritative call which God spoke in glorifying Christ to become a high priest is the same as the call to his divine Sonship (1:5) through that same scriptural voice (Ps 2:7), "Son of mine are *you*, I today have begotten you" (5:4–5). And this is confirmed and reinforced as the audience are informed that just as in another place in scripture (Ps 109:4) the voice of God says, "*You* are a priest forever according to the order of Melchizedek" (5:6). That the prayers and supplications Jesus offered as high priest on behalf of human beings to the God able to save him from death were answered (5:7) deepens the audience's appreciation for the significance of Jesus suffering death on behalf of all. Through the sufferings that culminated in his death and perfected him, Jesus became the initiator of salvation from eternal death (2:10), the great salvation from eternal death that the audience are not to neglect as a worshiping assembly (2:3), the salvation from eternal death they are going to inherit as participants in heavenly worship (1:14).

Jesus was made perfect as a Son who learned obedience from the things he suffered (5:8), so that he became for all those who obey him a source of eternal salvation (5:9). As a worshiping assembly, the audience are not to neglect so great a salvation (2:3), because it is an eternal salvation that saves them from their life long fear of an eternal death (2:14–15) that would prevent their entering into the eternal life in the heavenly rest and worship of the living God. To gain this eternal salvation the audience are thus to obey the Son who learned from the things he suffered obedience to God. That Jesus was designated by God high priest according to the order of Melchizedek (5:10) reinforces God's scriptural declaration (Ps 109:4) to his Son, "You are a priest *forever* according to the order of Melchizedek" (5:6).

3

Hebrews 5:11—7:28

I. 5:11—6:12

A ¹¹ Concerning which much for us is the word, and it is difficult to explain in speaking it, since you have *become sluggish* in hearing. ¹² For though you ought to be teachers by this time, you again *have* need for someone to teach you the elements of the beginning of the sayings of God, and you have *become* those *having* a need of milk and not solid food. ¹³ For everyone who partakes of milk is inexperienced of the word of righteousness, for he is an infant. ¹⁴ But solid food is of the *perfected*, of those who because of their maturity *have* faculties trained for distinguishing of the beneficent and of the baneful.[1] ⁶:¹ᵃ Therefore, departing from the word at the beginning about the Christ, let us *bear* forward toward the *perfection*,

> **B** ¹ᵇ not again laying down a foundation of *repentance* from dead works and of faith in God, ² of teaching about baptisms, of laying on of hands, of resurrection of the dead, and of eternal judgment. ³ And this we will do, if God permits.
>
>> **C** ⁴ᵃ For it is impossible for those once enlightened, having *tasted* of the heavenly gift,
>>
>>> **D** ⁴ᵇ and having become partners of the Holy Spirit,
>>
>> **C'** ⁵ and having *tasted* the beneficent pronouncement of God and the powers of the age to come,

---

1. On the translation "because of their maturity" for *dia tēn hexin*, see Lee, "Hebrews 5:14." The translation "of the beneficent and of the baneful" is an attempt to convey a sense of the alliterative artistry in *kalou te kai kakou*, as well as to use terms more specific than the general terms "good and evil."

B′ ⁶ and having fallen away, again to renew to *repentance*, recrucifying for themselves the Son of God and holding him up to contempt.²

A′ ⁷ For earth that drinks the rain coming upon it repeatedly and produces useful vegetation for those on account of whom it is cultivated, shares a blessing from God. ⁸ But *bearing* forth thorns and thistles, it is rejected and near a curse, whose *end* is a burning. ⁹ But we are confident concerning you, beloved, of better things, indeed those *having* to do with salvation, even if we speak thus. ¹⁰ For God is not unjust so as to neglect your work and the love which you demonstrated for his name, having assisted the holy ones, and continuing to assist. ¹¹ But we desire each of you to demonstrate the same eagerness for the assurance of the hope until the *end*, ¹² so that you may not *become sluggish*, but imitators of those who through faith and patience are inheriting the promises.

The occurrence of what the scriptural voice of God "says" in the quotation of Ps 109:4 toward the conclusion (5:6) of the unit in 4:14—5:10 provides the transitional word for the connection to the following unit in 5:11—6:12. This unit begins with a reference to the "word" that is difficult to explain in "speaking" it (5:11). The connection thus creates a transition from what God "speaks" to what the author is "speaking" about and by means of a "word."

"Concerning which much for us is the word" (5:11a) recalls and resonates with "regarding whom there is upon us the word" (4:13b), in which "the word" refers both to the living word of God heard during worship (4:12) and the word of our necessary obedient and worshipful response to it. Most recently the audience heard the word of God spoken in the quotation of Ps 109:4 in which God, in reference to Jesus Christ as his divine Son (5:5), "says," "You are a priest forever according to the order of Melchizedek" (5:6). The "word" concerning which there is much for us refers not only to this scriptural word of God and the necessary word of our response to it, but to the word of the author's explanation of it. This is confirmed as the author tells the audience, "and it is difficult to explain in *speaking* it, since you have become sluggish in hearing" (5:11b).

---

2. On "recrucifying" as the appropriate translation for *anastaurountas* because of the context, see BDAG, 72.

The accusation that the audience have become sluggish in their "hearing" of the word (5:11) alerts them to the danger of becoming like their unfaithful and disobedient ancestors whom the word for "hearing" did not benefit, since they were not united in faith with those who "heard" (4:2). It reinforces the refrain of the warning from Ps 94:7–8, "Today if you *hear* his voice, do not harden your hearts" (3:7, 15; 4:7). The audience are not to become like those in the wilderness who "heard" but rebelled (3:16). Rather, they are to become like those who "heard" and confirmed for us the word of so great a salvation (2:3). Indeed, they are to attend to the things that have been "heard," lest they drift away (2:1) from and neglect the great salvation that should inspire their worship and prevent their sluggishness.

As those who have "become" sluggish in hearing (5:11), the audience have "become" as those having a need of "milk" and not "solid food" (5:12). Although the audience have need for someone to teach them the elements of the beginning of the sayings of God, they are prodded to want to become the teachers they ought to be by this time (5:12).[3] No one in the audience should want to be considered an "infant," one who partakes of "milk" and is thus inexperienced of the "solid food" of the word of righteousness (5:13). The "word" of God that demands the word of our worshipful response and that is difficult for the author to explain (5:11) is now described as the "word" of "righteousness," the word concerned with God's doing of what is right for us as our God and Father and our response of doing God's will as his people and sons. Reminded that the divine Son loved "righteousness" and hated lawlessness (1:9), the audience are attuned to hear more about what is involved in this "word of righteousness."

That "solid food" is of the "perfected" (5:14a) connotes that the "solid food" of the word of righteousness is a matter of those who are "perfected" in the sense of having become adults rather than infants (5:13). But it also reminds the audience that "solid food" is a matter of those who are "perfected" in the sense of having been made fit or worthy for their role in worship. Having learned obedience from what he suffered, Jesus was made "perfect," that is, fit for his role in worship as high priest, so that he

---

3. O'Brien, *Hebrews*, 207n116: "Milk and solid food were often used as metaphors for levels of instruction. Paul told the Corinthians that when he first preached to them, 'I fed you with milk . . . for you were not ready for solid food'. What is more, at the time he wrote to them, 'you are *still* not ready' (1 Cor. 3:1–4)."

became a source of eternal salvation for all who obey him (5:9). As among those who obey him, the audience are among those who are being made holy for worship by the Jesus who makes holy (2:11), since God made him "perfect" through sufferings (2:10). The audience are thus being persuaded to become "perfected"—mature adults fit for proper worship.

Instead of those who "have" need for someone to teach them the elements of the beginning of the sayings of God, and those "having" a need of milk rather than solid food (5:12), the audience should be those who because of their maturity "have" faculties trained for distinguishing of the beneficent and of the baneful (5:14b). To be able to distinguish what is beneficial and what is harmful will aid their worship. But since the audience again have need for someone to teach them the elements of "the beginning" of the sayings of God (5:12a), the author will commence his instruction departing from the word at "the beginning" about the Christ (6:1a). Departing from the "word" at the beginning about the Christ is aimed at making the audience experienced for the "solid food" of the "word" of righteousness (5:13). They are thus invited to bear forward with the help of the author toward the "perfection" (6:1a), toward becoming "perfected" as mature adults made fit for proper liturgical and ethical worship (5:14).

Although the audience again have need for someone to teach them the elements of the beginning of the sayings of God (5:12), the author is not going to give a detailed explanation of them. He presupposes their familiarity with the foundational teaching by reminding them of what they have already experienced in becoming believers. They have repented from "dead works," the sinful works that lead to eternal death, and placed their faith in God (6:1b). They know the difference between the ritual baptism they underwent in becoming Christians and other baptisms, the significance of the ritual laying on of hands,[4] the fundamental teaching about the final resurrection of the dead and the "eternal" judgment (6:2) involved in "eternal" salvation (5:9). Finally, the audience are made aware that bearing forward toward the perfection (6:1a) is a matter of the gracious permission of the God in whom they believe (6:3).

---

4. Tipei, *Laying on of Hands*, 225: "[T]he LH [laying on of hands] had become the established rite for the reception of the Holy Spirit. Its association here in 6.2 with baptism indicates that the rite continued to be administered in close assocation with baptism, perhaps subsequent to water-baptism, but clearly distinct of it."

The audience begin to be alerted to what is impossible for them as among those once "enlightened" (6:4) by God (divine passive) in becoming believers at their baptism. Their having been enlightened includes having "tasted" of the heavenly gift (6:4) given them as a result of the grace of God by which Jesus might "taste" death on behalf of all (2:9), the death through which he destroyed the power of death and freed those enslaved by the life long fear of a death depriving them of eternal life (2:14–15). This "tasting" (*geusamenous*) alludes to but is not limited to their communal eating of the eucharistic meal.[5] As partners of a "heavenly" calling (3:1) to participate in the heavenly worship, the audience have already begun to experience and share in this "heavenly" gift of God's grace.

That the audience have become partners of the "Holy Spirit" (6:4b) reminds them of the distributions of the "Holy Spirit" they shared in (2:4) when they were enlightened after their initial hearing of the word of so great a salvation (2:2–3). They have become partners of the Holy Spirit as those who have together shared in hearing the "Holy Spirit" speak to them, as a worshiping assembly, the exhortation of Ps 94:7–8, "Today when you hear his voice, 'do not harden your hearts'" (3:7–8a). As "partners" of the Christ (3:14), as those who together comprise the "house" of Christ (3:6), the worshiping assembly of "partners" called to partake of and share in the heavenly liturgy (3:1), the audience have also become "partners" of the Holy Spirit (6:4b). Following upon the reference to "partaking" (*metechōn*) in the sense of sharing in the drinking of milk (5:13), and to having "tasted" of the heavenly gift as an allusion to sharing in the eucharistic meal (6:4a), having become "partners" (*metochoi*) in the sense of "partakers" reinforces the allusion to sharing in the eucharistic meal as a heavenly gift of the Holy Spirit.[6]

---

5. Ellingworth, *Hebrews*, 320: "*Geuomai* is used in connection with the Lord's Supper in Acts 20:11.... The language of the present passage is not specific enough either to limit the reference to the eucharist, or to exclude such a reference entirely."

6. Ibid., 321: "The meaning of *metochos* varies between companionship and participation; here the latter predominates." See also Allen, *Deuteronomy*, 128n96. O'Brien, *Hebrews*, 222: "The language of participation calls to mind the earlier references in which the members of the community are addressed as 'sharers in a heavenly calling' (3:1) and are 'partners of Christ' himself, assuming that they hold their original conviction firmly to the end (3:14). The Spirit was powerfully active at the founding of the congregation, with various gifts proceeding from him as a conclusive demonstration and seal of the truth of the gospel."

That the audience have "tasted" or experienced the pronouncement of God (6:5a), with its allusion to their hearing the word of God that is proclaimed to them in the worshiping assembly, complements their having "tasted" of the heavenly gift (6:4a), with its allusion to their partaking of the eucharistic meal in the worshiping assembly. That they have tasted the "beneficent" pronouncement of God implies their status as adults who because of their maturity have faculties trained for distinguishing of the "beneficent" and of the baneful (5:14). Their having tasted the "powers" of the age to come (6:5b) reminds the audience of the various "acts of power" they experienced together with those who heard the word of so great a salvation (2:4). As among those who are "going" to inherit salvation (1:14), the audience have already tasted the powers of the age "to come," that is, of the heavenly world, the "coming" one (2:5) that has been subjected under the feet of Jesus as the heavenly enthroned divine Son (2:8–9). They have already tasted and thus experienced the beneficent "pronouncement" of God (6:5a), that is, the word of so great a salvation (2:2–3), initiated by Jesus (2:10), the Son of God who is bearing up all things by the "pronouncement" of the "power" of God (1:3) and who has become an object of their worship.

The audience have been exhorted to attend to the things that have been heard "lest we drift away" (2:1). They have been warned lest there be in anyone of them an evil heart of unfaithfulness in "falling away" from the living God (3:12). They have been exhorted to strive to enter into God's own rest so that not anyone of them may "fall" in the same pattern of disobedience (4:11) as their rebellious and sinful ancestors who were not able to enter into God's rest because of their disobedience and unfaithfulness (3:16–19; 4:6). And now they are warned that in the event of their having "fallen away," it will be impossible for them, whose faith has already been founded on their repentance (6:1b), to again renew to repentance (6:6). The God who swore in his anger that the rebellious and fallen away ancestors will never enter into his rest (3:7, 18; 4:3, 5) will surely not restore the audience to repentance, if they should fall away as apostates, failing to appreciate what is involved in their worship.

It is impossible for those who would fall away to renew again to repentance, since, by falling away from the foundation of their repentance (6:1b), namely the high-priestly sacrificial death of Jesus (2:14–18), they would in effect be recrucifying for themselves the Son of God and holding him up to contempt (6:6).⁷ That it is as impossible again to renew to repentance as it is unthinkable disgracefully to recrucify for themselves the Son of God is underscored by the alliterative link between "renew" (*anakainizein*) and "recrucifying" (*anastaurountas*). The warning against falling away from the faith they confess as a worshiping community and thus recrucifying for themselves and holding up to contempt "the Son of God" reinforces the exhortation that we are to hold fast to the confession, since we have a great high priest who has passed through the heavens, Jesus "the Son of God" (4:14).⁸

By means of agricultural imagery and in view of the divine gifts they have graciously been granted (6:4–5), the audience are exhorted to compare themselves with earth that drinks the rain that comes upon it repeatedly as a divine gift. It produces useful vegetation for those on account of whom it is cultivated, and thus shares a blessing from God (6:7). With a continuation of the imagery, they are warned not to be like earth bearing forth "thorns and thistles" as a result of their sinfulness (cf. Gen 3:17–18). Such earth is rejected and near a curse, so that its end or destiny is a "burning," an image of divine judgment (6:8).⁹ That the audience are not to become like earth "bearing forth" thorns and thistles, so that its end or destiny is a burning, reinforces the author's exhortation, "let us *bear forward* toward the perfection," the end or destiny divinely intended for them (6:1a), the goal of the "solid food" that is "of the perfected" (5:14).¹⁰

Although the author speaks in a way that warns them of bad things, if they fall away (6:6), namely their eternal destruction (6:8), he is confident concerning them, addressed as "beloved," of better things (6:9). These better things that have to do with "salvation" remind the audience that Jesus became a source of eternal "salvation" for all who obey him (5:9), that God made him the initiator of their "salvation" (2:10), the so great a "salvation" they are not to neglect as the motivation that inspires

---

7. Attridge, *Hebrews*, 169: "Christ's sacrificial death is the only way to a true and effective cleansing of conscience and remission of sin. It is the bedrock on which the 'foundation' (6:1) of repentance is built. Those who reject this necessary presupposition of repentance simply, and virtually by definition, cannot repent."

8. Mathewson, "Heb 6:4–6," 209–25; Snyman, "Hebrews 6:4–6," 354–68; Emmrich, "Hebrews 6:4–6," 83–95; Davis, "Hebrews 6:4–6."

9. Koester, *Hebrews*, 316. On the OT background of the blessing/cursing imagery here, see Allen, *Deuteronomy*, 127–34.

10. Gleason, "Hebrews 6:4–8" 62–91; deSilva, "Hebrews 6:4–8 (Part 1)"; idem, "Hebrews 6:4–8 (Part 2)."

their worship (2:3). This is the "salvation" they are on the way to inheriting as participants in heavenly worship (1:14).

The assertion that God is not unjust boosts the assurance that God will surely remember the work and love the audience demonstrated for his "name" (6:10a), the "name" that the scriptural voice of Jesus promised to proclaim to the audience, as his brothers, within their worshiping assembly (2:12). They not only have assisted the "holy ones" among them as "holy" brothers (3:1) of Jesus (cf. 2:11, 12, 17), but are continuing to assist them as part of their ethical worship (6:10bc). Since God will surely not neglect the audience's work and the love which they "demonstrated" for his name (6:10a), the author desires that each individual in the audience "demonstrate" the same eagerness and thus persevere for the assurance of the "hope," the "hope" the audience as the worshiping household of Christ are to hold (3:6), until the "end" (6:11). This reinforces the exhortation that we hold the beginning of the reality firm until the "end" (3:14). Such perseverance will assure that the "end" for the audience is not the "burning" of divine judgment (6:8), and will facilitate their bearing forward with the author toward the "perfection" (6:1a) needed for their participation in heavenly worship.

The audience, who have "become sluggish" in hearing (5:11), are now not to "become sluggish" (6:12). As among those who are going to "inherit" salvation (1:14) as brothers of the divine Son who "inherited" a name more excellent beyond the angels (1:4), they are rather to become imitators of those who through faith and patience are "inheriting" the promises (6:12). These "promises" include the "promise" of entering into God's own rest to participate in heavenly worship (4:1), as well as the promised "blessing" from God (6:7), which implies a response of the blessing and praise of God in worship.[11]

II. 6:13–20

A ¹³ For when God promised to Abraham, since he *had* by no one greater to swear, swore by himself, ¹⁴ saying, "Indeed, blessing I will bless you, and multiplying I will multiply you" (Gen 22:17). ¹⁵ And so having patience, he obtained the promise.

---

11. Koester, *Hebrews*, 318. McBride, "Bless," 476: "Petitions for and pronouncements of divine blessing and responsive benedictory praises of God are constant features of worship." See also Nongbri, "Hebrews 6:4–12."

> **B** ¹⁶ For men swear by someone greater, and, for confirmation, a limit to all dispute for them is the *oath*.
>
> **B′** ¹⁷ When God even more planned to show to the heirs of the promise the unchangeableness of his plan, he guaranteed it with an *oath*, ^{18a} so that through two unchangeable things, in which it was impossible for God to lie,
>
> **A′** ^{18b} we who have taken refuge may *have* a strong encouragement to hold fast to the hope lying ahead, ¹⁹ which we *have* as an anchor of the soul, both sure and firm, and which enters into the interior of the veil, ²⁰ where as forerunner on behalf of us Jesus entered, according to the order of Melchizedek having become high priest forever.

The last word of the unit in 5:11—6:12, "promises," serves as the thematic catchword connecting this unit to the next unit in 6:13–20, which commences, "For when God *promised* to Abraham." There is thus a transition from being imitators of those who through faith and patience are inheriting the "promises" (6:12) to the example of what was involved when God "promised" to Abraham (6:13).

The audience have been exhorted not to become sluggish, but rather to become imitators of those who through faith and patience are inheriting the "promises" (6:12) that include the "promise" to enter into God's own heavenly rest for participation in heavenly worship (4:1), as well as the promised "blessing" from God (6:7). And now, as those among Abraham's descendants of whom Jesus has taken hold (2:16), their attention is focused on what was involved when God "promised" to Abraham (6:13a).

Regarding their faithless ancestors, the audience have heard the scriptural voice of God decisively pronounce, "As I *swore* in my anger, 'They will never enter into my rest!' (Ps 94:11)" (3:11; 4:3). The audience were also confronted with a question warning them against the disobedience of their ancestors, "And with whom did he *swear* that they should not enter into his rest, if not those who disobeyed?" (3:18). And now, in contrast, regarding their faithful ancestor Abraham, they again hear the scriptural voice of God, who since he had by no one greater to "swear," "swore" by himself (6:13bc), emphatically promise, "Indeed, *blessing I will bless* you, and multiplying I will multiply you (Gen 22:17)" (6:14). Abraham thus exemplifies for them how "earth that drinks the rain coming upon it repeatedly and produces useful vegetation for those on account of whom it is cultivated, shares a *blessing* from God" (6:7). That, "having patience," Abraham obtained the "promise" (6:15) of the blessing reinforces the exhortation for the audience to become imitators of those who through faith and "patience" are inheriting the "promises" (6:12).[12]

At this point the audience are presented with a pivotal progression of parallels involving the term "oath." They hear a progression from "a limit to all dispute for them is the *oath*" (6:16) to "he guaranteed it with an *oath*" (6:17c). Just as an "oath" is required for the confirmation that puts a limit to all dispute when men swear, so God guaranteed the promise made to Abraham with an "oath." God did this in planning to show the unchangeableness of his plan to the "heirs" of the "promise" made to Abraham (6:17ab), among whom are the audience as imitators of those who through faith and patience are "inheriting" the "promises" (6:12). Consequently, in going beyond human swearing, God guaranteed the promise even more with an oath, so that two unchangeable things—both the promise and the oath—were involved (6:18a). In these it was "impossible" for God to lie (6:18b), recalling and reinforcing how it is "impossible" for those once enlightened (6:4), and having fallen away, again to renew to repentance (6:6).

When God promised to Abraham, since he "had" by no one greater to swear, he swore by himself (6:13), and thus guaranteed the promise with an oath (6:17). Consequently, "we," including author and audience, who have taken refuge in the security provided by God may "have" a strong encouragement because of the hope we "have" as an anchor of the soul (6:18c–19). That we may have a "strong" encouragement echoes the "strong" outcrying of the prayers and supplications of Christ that were heard by God (5:7). And that we may have a strong encouragement to "hold fast" to the "hope" lying ahead (6:18c) reinforces the exhortations that, as a worshiping assembly, we "hold fast" to the confession (4:14), that to the boldness and to the boast of the "hope" we hold (3:6), and that we show eagerness for the assurance of the "hope" until the end (6:11).

We have this hope lying ahead as an anchor of the "soul" (6:19), the "soul" that the living word of God profoundly penetrates (4:12). That this hope is an anchor of the soul that is both sure and "firm" (6:19), "firm" like the word of God spoken through angels (2:2), reinforces the exhorta-

12. The "promise" Abraham obtained refers to the birth and preservation of Isaac; Koester, *Hebrews*, 326; see also Ellingworth, *Hebrews*, 338–39; Johnson, *Hebrews*, 168–69.

tion that we hold the beginning of the reality "firm" until the end (3:14). As a secure and firm "anchor" of the soul, this hope encourages us to attend to the things that have been heard during worship, lest we "drift away" like an unanchored ship (2:1).[13] It further encourages us not to be "wandering" in heart or to "fall away" like the unfaithful and disobedient ancestors (3:10, 12, 16–19; 4:6, 11), but rather to persevere as a worshiping assembly.

In contrast to the unfaithful and disobedient ancestors who failed to "enter" into God's heavenly rest to participate in heavenly worship (3:19; cf. 3:11, 18; 4:3, 5, 6), this hope "enters" into the interior of the veil, the most holy place in the heavenly sanctuary (6:19). This is where, as forerunner on behalf of us, Jesus "entered," according to the order of Melchizedek having become high priest forever (6:20).[14] This "entrance" of Jesus as a hope that is a sure and firm anchor of the soul into the heavenly sanctuary bolsters the exhortation that we strive to "enter" into the heavenly sabbath rest of God to participate in heavenly worship (4:11), the rest we are even now "entering" into as those who believed and those who now worship within the liturgical assembly (4:3).

That Jesus entered "on behalf" of us relates his high priestly activity of cultic worship directly to the audience, as it recalls that every high priest taken from men is appointed "on behalf" of men in things regarding God, so that he may offer both gifts and sacrifices "on behalf" of sins (5:1). It was by the grace of God that Jesus might taste death "on behalf" of everyone (2:9). That Jesus became "according to the order of Melchizedek high priest forever" (6:20) reminds the audience that he was designated by God as "high priest according to the order of Melchizedek" (5:10) in accord with God's authoritative scriptural pronouncement from Ps 109:4, addressed to Jesus, "You are a priest forever according to the order of Melchizedek" (5:6). This unit thus concludes on the emphatically

---

13. On "drift away" (*pararyōmen*) here as a nautical metaphor, see BDAG, 770. O'Brien, *Hebrews*, 241: "The Christian hope is secure and unwavering because God does not lie, and he has given a sure promise and an oath to his people (vv. 17–18)."

14. Regarding "enters into the interior of the veil (*katapetasmatos*)" in 6:19, Hofius ("*katapetasma*," 66) states, "In the heavenly sanctuary a *curtain* . . . veils the dwelling of God with the throne of glory. Heb 6:19 and 10:20 refer to this curtain . . . this 'object of hope' can be described as a 'secure and steadfast anchor of the soul which enters into the [heavenly] most holy place' (6:19f.)." See also BDAG, 524; Gane, "Hebrews 6:19," 5–8; Davidson, "Hebrews 6:19–20"; Young, "Where Jesus Has Gone"; idem, "Hebrews 6:19–20"; Cosaert, "Use of *Hagios*."

climactic note of the eternity of Jesus' high priesthood—that it is according to the order of Melchizedek that Jesus became high priest *forever*.[15]

III. 7:1–10

A [7:1a] For this *Melchizedek*, king of Salem, priest of the God Most High, having *met* Abraham returning from the defeat of the kings

> B [1b] and having *blessed* him, ² to whom also a *tenth* of everything Abraham apportioned, first being interpreted king of righteousness and then king of Salem, that is, king of peace, ³ without father, without mother, without genealogy, neither beginning of days nor end of *life* does he have, having been made like the Son of God, remains a priest for all time. ⁴ See how great is this one, to whom also a *tenth* from the choice spoils Abraham the patriarch gave. [5a] And those of the sons of *Levi* who *receive* the priesthood have a commandment to *tithe* the people according to the law,
>
>> C [5b] that is, *their* brothers,
>>
>>> D [5c] although they have come from the loins of Abraham.
>>
>> C' [6a] But he who was not of *their* ancestry
>
> B' [6b] *took a tithe* from Abraham and *blessed* the one having the promises. ⁷ Without any dispute the inferior is *blessed* by the superior. ⁸ And here, on the one hand, men who die *receive tithes*, but, there, on the other hand, one is testified that he goes on *living*. ⁹ And so to speak, through Abraham even *Levi*, who *receives tithes, was tithed*.

A' [10] For he was still in the loins of his father when *Melchizedek met* him.

The name "Melchizedek" in the conclusion of the unit in 6:13–20 serves as the transitional word connecting this unit to the following one in 7:1–10, which commences with a reference to "Melchizedek" (7:1) as king and priest. This sets the stage for an explanation in 7:1–10 of the climactic emphasis upon the eternity of Jesus' high priesthood at the close of 6:13–20—it is according to the order of Melchizedek that Jesus became "high priest forever" (6:20).

---

15. Worley, "Fleeing to Two Immutable Things."

By way of an allusion to Gen 14:17–20, the audience are reminded that Melchizedek was both a king and a priest (7:1a). This king met Abraham on his return from the defeat of other kings, the Abraham to whom God swore the promise of a blessing (6:13), the preeminent patriarch of whom the audience are to consider themselves descendants (2:16). The Abraham whom God promised to bless (6:13), saying, "Indeed, *blessing I will bless* you" (Gen 22:17)" (6:14), Melchizedek actually "blessed" (7:1b). In addition, Abraham apportioned a tenth of everything he had to Melchizedek. Based on a translation of his name from the Hebrew (*melchi*="my king" and *zedek*="righteousness"), Melchizedek can be interpreted as a "king of righteousness" (7:2).[16] This interpretation hints at his relevance for the audience, who are to be experienced in the word of "righteousness" (5:13), in order to be among the mature and those perfected for worship (5:14—6:1). It also assimilates him to Jesus as the heavenly enthroned divine royal Son, the scepter of whose "kingdom" is uprightness (1:8) and who loved "righteousness" but hated lawlessness (1:9). As king of "Salem," a place many identified with Jerusalem and a name that can be understood as a transliteration of the Hebrew term for "peace," Melchizedek is interpreted as both a king of righteousness and a king of peace (7:2).[17]

Since the scriptural tradition does not mention his father, mother, or genealogy, Melchizedek is understood to have neither the beginning of days nor end of life (7:3). Having been thus made eternal like the divine Son of God, whose heavenly royal throne is "forever and ever" (1:8), Melchizedek remains a priest for "all time" (7:3).[18] This explains for the audience why it is "according to the order of Melchizedek" that Jesus became a high priest "forever" (6:20; cf. 5:6). Both Melchizedek and Jesus have an eternal priesthood.[19]

The audience are to consider how great is "this one," that is, "this" Melchizedek (7:1), as the one to whom Abraham the patriarch gave a tenth

---

16. Schröger, "*Melchisedek*," 405. See also Kruijf, "Priest-King Melchizedek"; Fitzmyer, "Melchizedek"; Steyn, "Heb 7.1–4"; Cockerill, "Melchizedek."

17. Koester, *Hebrews*, 341–42; Johnson, *Hebrews*, 177: "The qualities of righteousness and peace classically represent the prophetic hopes of Israel."

18. Koester, *Hebrews*, 343: "The direction of thought is important: the Son of God is not like Melchizedek; rather, Melchizedek is like the Son of God, who is the principal reality."

19. Neyrey, "'Without Beginning of Days'"; Mason, "Hebrews 7:3."

from the choice spoils (7:4). At this point the audience are presented with a progression concerning Melchizedek as the one to whom Abraham apportioned a tenth of everything (7:2). That Abraham "apportioned," with its connotation of paying what is due from obligation, has progressed to "he gave," with its connotation of freely and spontaneously giving a gift. "Of everything" is now specified as "from the choice spoils." And Abraham is now emphatically described as "the patriarch," with its connotation of "the preeminent patriarch." In other words, the audience are to consider how great this Melchizedek truly must be, if even Abraham, *the* patriarch, freely gave him a tenth from the choice spoils of his victory over the kings.[20]

Abraham, the patriarch, freely gave as a gracious gift a "tenth" or "tithe" from the choice spoils of victory to Melchizedek, the king and priest (7:4). In contrast, those of the sons of Levi who receive the priesthood have a commandment to "tithe" the people according to the law (7:5a).[21] The "people" whom the sons of Levi, as priests, tithe are the "people" for whose sins they are to offer sacrifice in their cultic worship (5:3), the "people" of God for whom a sabbath rest for heavenly worship remains (4:9), and the "people" for whom Jesus became a merciful and faithful high priest in order to expiate the sins that prevent proper worship of God (2:17).

Although the people were equal to them as their fellow "brothers" (7:5b), nevertheless, the Levitical priests took tithes from them. In contrast, Jesus, the merciful and faithful high priest, became like his "brothers" in all things (2:17). He was not ashamed to call his fellow human beings "brothers," saying, in quoting Ps 21:23, "I will proclaim your name to my *brothers*, in the midst of the assembly I will praise you" (2:11-12). Addressed as "brothers" (3:1, 12), the audience are numbered, not among

---

20. Lane, *Hebrews 1-8*, 168: "The term *akrothiniōn*, denoting the best or choicest of the spoils, appears to have been chosen to sharpen the impression of Melchizedek's exalted stature. . . . The term *ho patriarchēs*, "the patriarch," which is placed at the end of the sentence for emphasis, serves to underscore the stature of Abraham as the progenitor of Israel. But Abraham is exalted in v 4 only to emphasize the exalted status of Melchizedek even more." See also Ellingworth, *Hebrews*, 361. Koester, *Hebrews*, 343: "Abraham's relationship to Melchizedek sets a precedent for the relationship of Abraham's descendants (2:16) to Christ."

21. Attridge, *Hebrews*, 196: "The formulation gives an initial hint of the inferior status of the Levites. They have a 'command' to receive tithes based on the law. The collocation of the two terms is common in Hebrews and the negative appraisal of both becomes clear as the argument of the chapter proceeds."

the tithed "brothers" of the Levitical priests, but among the "brothers" to whom Jesus promises to proclaim God's name and in the midst of whose worshiping assembly he promises to praise God. Not only are the people from whom the Levitical priests took tithes their own fellow brothers, but they share a common origin as descendants of Abraham, as those who "have come from the loins of Abraham" (7:5c). This emphatically reinforces for the audience how the Levitical priests take tithes from those who are equal to them in status.[22] In contrast to the Levitical priests who tithed the people who were "their" brothers (7:5b), even though they shared with them descent from Abraham (7:5c), the priest Melchizedek was not of "their" Abrahamic ancestry (7:6a).

Whereas those of the sons of Levi who receive the priesthood have a commandment "to tithe" the people according to the law, even though they share with them descent from Abraham (7:5), the priest Melchizedek "took a tithe" from Abraham himself (7:6b). Having "blessed" Abraham upon his return from the defeat of the kings (7:1), Melchizedek "blessed" the one having the "promises" (7:6c), the "promises" the audience are inheriting (6:12). These include the "promise" Abraham obtained by having patience (6:15, 17), and the "promise" of entering into God's own rest for heavenly worship (4:1).[23] This indicates the superiority of Melchizedek to Abraham, since in this case it is without any dispute that the inferior, Abraham as the one tithed, is "blessed" by the superior, Melchizedek as the one who took the tithe (7:7).[24]

In contrast to Melchizedek, to whom a "tenth" or "tithe" from the choice spoils Abraham the patriarch gave (7:2, 4), the sons of Levi receive "tithes" (7:8) from the people who are their fellow brothers and fellow

---

22. Johnson, *Hebrews*, 179: "The tax, or tithe, in other words, was not paid from outsiders, but from fellow Israelites." Mitchell, *Hebrews*, 140: "The parity of the Levites and their kindred suggests that their reception of tithes is something less than Melchizedek's receiving from Abraham, thus implying the superiority of Melchizedek over Abraham."

23. Ellingworth, *Hebrews*, 366: "The use of the absolute expression 'the promise(s)' is normal in Hebrews, and even where the article is not used, the promise is, or the promises are, assumed to be too well known to need specifying ... Here the point is not the content of the promises, but the status conferred on Abraham by his having received them."

24. Mitchell, *Hebrews*, 141: "The author is not laying down a general rule, as there are biblical examples of greater individuals being blessed by lesser ones. He is merely referring to the case at hand, namely that Abraham in this instance is the lesser and Melchizedek the greater, since the former paid a tithe to the latter."

descendants of Abraham (7:5). Whereas men who "die" "receive" tithes (7:8), namely, the sons of Levi who "receive" the priesthood and have a commandment to tithe the people (7:5a), Melchizedek is testified as one who goes on "living" (7:8), since he does not have an end of "life" (7:3c).[25] The audience are to realize, then, that through Abraham, who gave a tithe to the priest Melchizedek, even Levi, who "receives" "tithes" (7:9), since the sons of Levi who "receive" the priesthood have a commandment to "tithe" the people according to the law (7:5a), was himself "tithed" (7:9).

The audience are thus to appreciate that Levi, who was still in the loins of his father Abraham when he was met by the priest Melchizedek (7:1a, 10), was himself tithed when Abraham gave a tithe to Melchizedek. This means that the Levitical priesthood is inferior to the eternal priesthood of Jesus, which is according to the order of the Melchizedek (5:6, 10; 6:20) who goes on living (7:8). In being made eternal like the Son of God, Melchizedek remains a priest for all time (7:3d). Whereas the sons of Levi who receive the priesthood tithe those who come from the "loins" of Abraham (7:5c), Levi himself was still in the "loins" of his father Abraham when he was tithed by Melchizedek, the eternal priest of the God Most High.[26] It is according to the order of this eternal priest Melchizedek that Jesus became high priest forever (6:20) for the benefit of the audience as a worshiping assembly.

IV. 7:11–17

A **¹¹** If then there was perfection through the Levitical priesthood, for the people on the basis of it were *given law*, what further need *according to the order of Melchizedek* for a different priest to *arise* and not said to be according to the order of Aaron? **¹²** For the priesthood being changed, of necessity a change of *law* also *comes about*.

   B **¹³** For he of whom these things are said, partook in a different *tribe*, from which *no one* attended to the altar.

      C **¹⁴ᵃ** For it is clear that our Lord sprang up from Judah,

---

25. Granerød, "Melchizedek."

26. Ellingworth, *Hebrews*, 369: "[T]he first readers of the epistle needed to be reminded that Levi had not yet begun his independent existence, and was thus involved in all that Abraham did. A logical basis is thus given for the permanent effect of Abraham's submission to Melchizedek, which so far has only been implied. The apparent jump from Abraham to the levitical priests in vv. 5 and 8 is finally justified."

B′ ¹⁴ᵇ about which *tribe* Moses spoke *nothing* concerning priests.

A′ ¹⁵ And it is even more yet quite clear, if according to the likeness of Melchizedek a different priest *arises*, ¹⁶ who not according to a *law* of a fleshly commandment has *come about* but according to the power of an indestructible life. ¹⁷ For it is testified that "you are a priest forever *according to the order of Melchizedek*" (Ps 109:4).

The preceding unit in 7:1–10 concludes with a reference to Melchizedek, noting that Levi was still in the loins of his father Abraham when Melchizedek met him (7:10). This reference to Melchizedek serves as the transitional word for the connection to the next unit in 7:11–17, whose opening verse contains a reference to the order of Melchizedek in relation to that of Aaron (7:11). These transitional words keep the focus of the audience on the comparison between the different priesthoods of Levi and of Melchizedek. In addition, within the third macrochiastic level of the letter to the Hebrews, this unit in 7:11–17, which occurs after the central and pivotal unit in 7:1–10, exhibits a parallel relationship with the unit in 6:13–20. The parallelism is indicated by the only occurrences in this macrochiastic section (5:11—7:28) of the phrase "according to the order of Melchizedek" (6:20; 7:11, 17).

The implication that "perfection" of priestly worship was unattainable through the Levitical priesthood (7:11) alerts the audience to the impossibility for them, by means of this Levitical priesthood, to bear forward toward the mature "perfection" the author envisions for them (6:1). Namely, they are to be numbered among the "perfected," those mature and completely fit for heavenly worship (5:14). The audience are reminded that God made the initiator of their salvation, Jesus, "perfect" through sufferings (2:10), so that having been made "perfect," he became for all those who obey him a source of eternal salvation, having been designated by God as high priest according to the order of Melchizedek (5:9).

Not only do the sons of Levi who receive the priesthood have a commandment to tithe the "people" according to the "law" (7:5), but, as the audience are reminded, the "people were given law" on the basis of the Levitical priesthood (7:11a).[27] Every high priest is obligated by law to offer

---

27. Ibid., 372: "[I]n the author's view, the Mosaic law is essentially a set of cultic regulations in which the role of priests is fundamental. Priesthood and law are indissolubly bound together; and within this relation, priesthood is logically prior. The present clause therefore means 'the levitical priesthood ... was the basis of the Law given to the people.'"

sacrifice concerning the sins of the "people" (5:3). Jesus became a merciful and faithful high priest in order to expiate the sins of the "people" (2:17). And the audience are included in this "people" of God for whom the heavenly sabbath rest of God remains, so that they may participate in heavenly worship (4:9).

There is a question of what further "need" according to the order of Melchizedek for a different priest to "arise," that is, not only to appear but to be raised from the dead to heavenly exaltation, and not said to be according to the order of Aaron, since there was no perfection through the Levitical priesthood (7:11). This recalls and resonates with the "need" for the audience, who have a "need" for "milk" and not "solid food," to be taught the basics (5:12), in order to attain the perfection needed for their heavenly worship (6:1). Although, like "Aaron," Jesus was called to be a priest by God (5:4), he represents a "different" priest to arise and not be "said" or "called" according to the order of "Aaron," the order of the Levitical priesthood, but, as called by God in "another" or "different" place in scripture, "You are a priest forever according to the order of Melchizedek (Ps 109:4)" (5:6).[28]

The rhetorical question has established the "need" for a different priest to arise not according to the order of Aaron but according to the order of Melchizedek, since there was no perfection through the Levitical "priesthood," the basis for the people to be "given law" (7:11). This "need" progresses to the "necessity," with the "priesthood" being changed, of a corresponding change of "law" (7:12). The audience are now prepared to hear more about what is involved in this change of law.[29]

He of whom these things are "said" (7:13) by God (divine passive) refers to the different priest to arise and not "said" by God to be according to the order of Aaron (7:11). He is a "different" priest because not only is his priesthood according to the order of Melchizedek rather than the order of Aaron (7:11), but he partook in a tribe "different" from that of Levi. That he "partook" in a different tribe (7:13) further specifies for the audience the significance of the fact that, since the children whom God gave him (2:13) shared in blood and flesh, he similarly "partook" with

---

28. Koester, *Hebrews*, 353: "The new priest is not 'another' in the same line, but one of a 'different' sort. The verb 'raise up' can be used for someone who assumes a position, such as a king or prophet. The verb was also used for Jesus' resurrection to indestructible life. Both senses fit this context."

29. Joslin, "Hebrews 7–10"; Schmitt, "Hebrews 7:12."

them. This is so that through his death he might destroy the one who has the strength of death, that is the devil (2:14), and free those, as many as by fear of death through all their life were held in slavery (2:15). That from this tribe no one attended to the altar (7:13) indicates the non-priestly nature of his human lineage, underlined by the artful assonance between "partook" (*meteschēken*) and "attended" (*proseschēken*).

The different priest to "arise" according to the order of Melchizedek (7:11) originally "sprang up" from the tribe of Judah (7:14a) rather than from the priestly tribe of Levi.[30] That the different priest is referred to as our "Lord" reminds the audience of his divine lordship over them as a worshiping assembly, even while elaborating on his human origin. The great salvation the audience are not to neglect in their worship received a beginning of being spoken through this divine "Lord" (2:3), with God additionally testifying to it (2:4). And the scriptural voice of God himself addressed his divine royal Son, the object of heavenly worship (1:6), as the Lord of creation: "You at the beginnings, *Lord*, founded the earth, and the heavens are the works of your hands (Ps 101:26)" (1:10).

That Moses spoke nothing concerning priests about the tribe of Judah from which our Lord sprang up (7:14) reinforces for the audience the non-priestly nature of the different tribe in which a different priest to arise according to the order of Melchizedek (7:11) partook, even though no one from that tribe previously attended to the altar (7:13), and thus to sacrificial worship. The Moses who was faithful in all God's house as a cultic attendant for testimony of the things that would be "spoken" (3:5), which included especially the things involving worship, "spoke" nothing concerning priests with regard to the ancestral tribe from which our Lord sprang up (7:14).[31]

Whereas it is "clear" that our Lord sprang up from the tribe of Judah (7:14a), it is "even more" yet "quite clear" in God's plan, if our Lord arises as a different priest according to the likeness of Melchizedek (7:15). This

---

30. Johnson, *Hebrews*, 187: The verb "sprang up" is "used literally for the 'rising' of the stars or the sun 'in the east,' but influenced by the prophecy of Num 24:17, 'a star shall arise from Jacob,' it can also suggest the coming of the Messiah (see Jer 23:5; Zech 3:8; 6:12; Matt 4:16; Luke 1:78; see also Isa 11:1). As with the verb *anistēmi* [in 7:11], the author may deliberately intend this allusion, which gains even further depth if 'arising' also includes the resurrection and exaltation of the Messiah." See also Koester, *Hebrews*, 354–55; Lane, *Hebrews 1–8*, 182.

31. Koester, *Hebrews*, 355: "Moses' blessing to Judah (Deut 33:7) said nothing about priests, whereas Moses asked God to give Levi priestly lots (Deut 33:8–11)."

recalls that when God "even more" planned to show to the heirs of the promise the unchangeableness of his plan, he guaranteed it with an oath (6:17). The high priest who is able to sympathize with our weaknesses, as one who has been tested in all things in "likeness" to us, yet without sin (4:15), is the "different priest who arises" according to the "likeness" of Melchizedek (7:15). He is "the different priest to arise" and not said to be according to the order of Aaron (7:11). As a worshiping assembly, the audience are thus to appreciate not only his difference from Levitical priests but also his likeness to both Melchizedek and to themselves.

According to the likeness of Melchizedek a different priest arises, one who "has come about" not according to a "law" of a fleshly commandment, but according to the power of an indestructible life (7:16). This represents the change of "law," the "law given" on the basis of the Levitical priesthood (7:11a), that "comes about" of necessity when there is a change of priesthood (7:12). This different priest has come about "not according to" a law of a fleshly "commandment," like the "commandment" to tithe the people according to the "law" that those sons of Levi who receive the priesthood have (7:5), "but according to" the power of an indestructible life (7:16).

That this different priest has come about according to the power of an indestructible "life" (7:16) further specifies his likeness to Melchizedek (7:15), who does not have end of "life," but remains a priest for all time (7:3), as he "goes on living" forever (7:8). This life has its source in the "living" God from whom the audience are to make sure that none of them falls away (3:12; cf. 4:12). It reminds the audience that Jesus partook of their humanity, so that through death he might destroy the one who has the strength of death, that is the devil, and free those, as many as by fear of death through all their "life" were held in slavery (2:14–15).

As Melchizedek, who remains a "priest" for all time (7:3), is "testified" that he goes on living (7:8), so regarding the different "priest" who arises (7:15c), it is "testified" by the scriptural voice of God in Ps 109:4 that "you are a *priest* forever" (7:17a). That it is testified that "you are a priest forever *according to the order of Melchizedek*" (7:17b) explains what it means for a different priest to arise "according to the likeness of Melchizedek" (7:15b). It means he arises "according" to the power of an indestructible life (7:16c) that empowers him to remain a priest forever. Since there was no perfection through the Levitical priesthood, so that there was need for a different priest to arise "according to the order of

Melchizedek" (7:11), the audience are now poised to hear how this different, eternal priest brings about the perfection needed for heavenly worship.[32]

V. 7:18–28

A [18] For on the one hand a removal of a former commandment comes about because of its *weakness* and uselessness, [19] for *the law* made nothing *perfect*. On the other hand there is the introduction of a better hope through which we are drawing near to God. [20] And as much as this was not without an *oath-taking*, for they without an *oath-taking* have become priests, [21] but with an *oath-taking* through the one saying to him, "The Lord has sworn and will not change, 'You are a priest forever'" (Ps 109:4), [22] by so much has Jesus become the surety of a better covenant.

> **B** [23] And they, on the one hand, who have become priests were many because they were prevented by death from *remaining on*,
>
> **B′** [24] but he, on the other hand, because he *remains* forever, has the priesthood that is permanent, [25] whence also he is able to save completely those who approach God through him, always living to intercede on behalf of them.

A′ [26] For such a high priest is indeed fitting for us—devout, innocent, undefiled, separated from sinners, having become higher than the heavens, [27] who does not have each day a necessity, just as the high priests, first on behalf of his own sins to offer up sacrifices then of the people, for this he did once for all having offered up himself. [28] For *the law* appoints men having *weakness* as high priests, but the word of the *oath-taking* that is after *the law* a Son who forever has been made *perfect*.

Toward the conclusion of the preceding unit in 7:11–17 is the statement that a different priest arises, who not according to a law of a fleshly "commandment" "has come about" (7:16). This provides the transitional words connecting this unit to the following unit in 7:18–28, which begins by stating that a removal of a former "commandment" "comes about" be-

---

32. Moffitt, "If Another Priest Arises."

cause of its weakness and uselessness (7:18). The transition thus keeps a focus on what comes about when a commandment of the law in regard to priesthood is changed. And within the third macrochiastic level of the letter to the Hebrews, this unit in 7:18-28 exhibits a parallel relationship with the unit in 5:11—6:12. The parallelism is indicated by the only occurrences in this macrochiastic section (5:11—7:28) of terms for "word" (5:11, 13; 6:1; 7:28).

The audience have heard that there was no "perfection" through the Levitical priesthood, on the basis of which the people were "given law," so that there was need for a different priest to arise, meaning that of necessity a change of "law," including especially the cultic law regarding worship, also "comes about" (7:11-12). This change happens when a different priest arises, who not according to the "law" of a fleshly "commandment" "has come about," but according to the power of an indestructible life (7:15-16). And now they hear that a removal of a former "commandment" "comes about" because of its weakness and uselessness, for "the law made nothing perfect" (7:18-19a).[33] The audience are prepared to hear how the arrival of a different priest that brings a removal of a commandment of the law regulating cultic worship results in the perfection needed for heavenly worship.

In contrast to the removal of a weak and useless commandment of the law that made nothing "perfect" for the heavenly worship of God (7:18-19a), there is the "introduction" by God of a better hope through which we are drawing near to God in a complete way, especially for participation in heavenly worship (7:19b).[34] This recalls God "leading in" or "introducing" the firstborn Son into the heavenly world (1:6). This "better" hope takes its place in the line of those things the audience are to appreciate as "better"—Melchizedek as the "superior" or "better one" who blesses Abraham as his inferior (7:7), the "better" things having to do with salvation (6:9), and the divine Son who has become so far "better" than the angels (1:4).

---

33. The alliteration and assonance among the terms "removal" (*athetēsis*), "weakness" (*asthenes*), and "uselessness" (*anōpheles*) underscore their close connection.

34. Mitchell, *Hebrews*, 148-49: "The noun 'introduction,' *epeisagōgē*, means something that is present in a way it was not before. It occurs only here in the NT." Koester, *Hebrews*, 356: "People could draw near to God in prayer and faith under the Mosaic Law, but Hebrews maintains that the priestly work of Christ enables people from all times and places to come before God in this complete way."

The introduction of a better "hope" through which we are drawing near to God (7:19b) refers to the "hope" lying ahead, to which we may have a strong encouragement to hold fast as a worshiping assembly (6:18). This better hope has been described as a sure and firm anchor of the soul that enters into the interior of the heavenly veil, where Jesus entered as forerunner on behalf of us (6:19–20a). The implication is that Jesus himself, as the eternal high priest according to the order of Melchizedek (6:20b), is this "better hope" through which we are drawing near to God in our liturgical worship. This is the "hope" of which each of us—each member of the audience—is to demonstrate the same eagerness for the assurance until the end (6:11). It is the "hope" to whose boldness and boast we are to hold as the worshiping household of Christ (3:6).[35]

"As much as" (*kath' hoson*) this introduction of a better hope was not without an oath-taking (7:20a) resonates with the greater glory of Jesus beyond Moses "just as" (*kath' hoson*) greater honor than the household of worship has the one who furnishes it (3:3). The audience are to appreciate that this introduction of a better hope constituted by the establishment of Jesus Christ as an eternal high priest (7:19b) took place with an oath-taking, the significance of which is emphatically reinforced by means of a double negative—"*not without* an oath-taking" (7:20a). This is in contrast to the sons of Levi who have become priests (7:5) without an oath-taking (7:20b). But Jesus has become an eternal priest with an oath-taking through the God who pronounced the oath to him in Ps 109:4, "The Lord has sworn and will not change, 'You are a priest forever'" (7:21). That the Lord God has "sworn" and will not change stands in contrast to what he "swore" to the unfaithful ancestors who disobeyed during the wandering in the wilderness (3:18). This excluded them from entering into God's rest for heavenly worship, in accord with the oath God pronounced in Ps 94:11, "As I *swore* in my anger, 'They will never enter into my rest!'" (3:11; 4:3).

That the Lord has "sworn" and "will not change" (7:21) stands in continuity with the oath he promised to Abraham when he "swore" by himself, since he had by no one greater to "swear" (6:13). And it confirms that whereas men "swear" by someone greater, and, for confirmation,

---

35. Johnson, *Hebrews*, 189: "Here, as in 6:15–19, the term "hope" is a way of designating Jesus himself. Because he has entered into God's presence (6:20), the author and readers can declare with confidence that 'through it' (the hope that is Jesus) they are 'approaching God.'"

a limit to all dispute for them is the oath (6:16), when God even more planned to show the "unchangeableness" of his plan, he guaranteed it with an oath (6:17). This is so that it was through two "unchangeable" things, in which is impossible for God to lie (6:18). The audience are to appreciate the superior authoritativeness of the unchangeable oath by which God emphatically swore to Jesus, "You are a priest forever" (7:21). The introduction of Jesus as a "better" hope through which we are drawing near to God in worship (7:19b), the "Jesus" who entered into the interior of the heavenly veil as forerunner on our behalf (6:20), has thus progressed to the eternal priest "Jesus" as the surety (*eggyos*) of a "better" covenant (7:22).[36]

Not only did the sons of Levi "become priests" without an oath-taking (7:20), but they who have "become priests" were many (7:23). That they were many because they were prevented by death from "remaining on" (7:23) highlights for the audience their difference from Melchizedek, who "remains" a priest for all time (7:3). That they were prevented by "death" indicates to the audience their contrast with Jesus whom God saved from "death" (5:7), so that through his "death" he might destroy the one who has the strength of "death," that is the devil, and free those who by the fear of "death" were held in slavery through all their life (2:14–15). Jesus underwent the suffering of "death" and was crowned with glory and honor, so that, by the grace of God, he might taste "death" on behalf of all (2:9). This salvation from death is the great salvation (2:3) that motivates and inspires worship.

In contrast to the Levitical priests who were many because they were prevented by death from "remaining on" (7:23), Jesus, because he "remains" a priest "forever," possesses the priesthood that is permanent (7:24). This recalls and reinforces for the audience that Jesus is a priest "forever" according to the order of Melchizedek (5:6; 6:20; 7:17, 21), and that he possesses a heavenly royal throne that is "forever" and ever (1:8).

---

36. The proper name "Jesus" stands in an emphatic final position in 7:22, recalling the previous occurrence of this name in 6:20. Johnson, *Hebrews*, 192–93: "Jesus is called the *eggyos* of a better covenant. This term has the sense of a pledge, surety, or guarantee, for a contract. One party puts up such a pledge to ensure the other party that the contractual obligations will be met, at loss to himself if he fails to meet the obligations." Mitchell, *Hebrews*, 153: "In the Hebrew Bible the word 'covenant' is commonly used to describe a relationship with God, either of an individual or of Israel as a people.... In secular Greek the word *diathēkē* signifies a 'testament' or a 'will.'" See also Gräbe, "New Covenant"; Joslin, *Hebrews*.

The permanent "priesthood" Jesus possesses represents the change of "priesthood" that took place (7:12), since through the Levitical "priesthood" there was no perfection for heavenly worship (7:11).

Although there was no "perfection" through the Levitical priesthood (7:11), since the law involved with it made nothing "perfect" (7:18), Jesus, possessing the priesthood that is permanent (7:24), is able to save "completely" (*panteles*) or "perfectly" for all time (7:25).[37] Having been made "perfect," he became for all those who obey him a source of eternal salvation (5:9). Indeed, it was fitting for God to make Jesus, as the initiator of salvation, "perfect" through sufferings (2:10). Since his prayers and supplications to the God who is "able" to "save" him from death were heard from his reverence (5:7), Jesus is "able" to "save" completely and forever those who approach God for worship through him (7:25). The audience were previously exhorted, "Let us *approach* then with boldness the throne of grace, so that we may receive mercy and may find grace for timely help" (4:16). Now they are to realize that Jesus is able to save them completely and forever as those who, as a worshiping assembly drawing near to "God" (7:19), "approach" "God" through him.[38]

Jesus is always "living" to intercede (7:25), because, according to the power of an indestructible "life" (7:16), he became a priest forever according to the order of Melchizedek, who goes on "living" (7:8), not having an end of "life" (7:3). That Jesus is always "living" connotes his heavenly divine life, resonating with the word of the "living" God (3:12) that is itself always "living" (4:12). He is thus able to free those, as many as by fear of death through all their "life" or "living" were held in slavery (2:15). That Jesus is always living to intercede (*entygchanein*) "on behalf of" them, the

---

37. Regarding *panteles*, Mitchell, *Hebrews*, 154, notes that it "carries both a temporal sense (forever) and a modal sense (completely). Whereas in the past commentators may have been split over which to choose, more recent interpreters prefer to retain the ambiguity of the term by including both meanings. Thus Jesus saves both 'completely' and 'for all time.'" Attridge, *Hebrews*, 210: "[T]he very ambiguity of the phrase probably appealed to our author. Christ, because of his 'inviolable' priesthood, is able to offer participation in the same transcendent sphere of which he is a part. At the same time, the hallmark of Christ's priestly status, and of the salvation it provides, is their eternal quality."

38. Lane, *Hebrews 1–8*, 189: "The designation of those for whom Christ cares continually as *tous proserchomenous*, 'those who approach [God],' which makes use of an equivalent expression for the description of the community in v 19, is appropriate to the cultic imagery in the context. In the LXX the Greek expressions *proserchesthai*, 'to approach,' and *eggizein*, 'to draw near,' are used interchangeably for the approach to God in worship."

audience who are to approach God for heavenly worship through him (7:25), is a consequence of his entrance into the interior of the heavenly veil (6:19) as forerunner "on behalf of" us (6:20).[39]

Just as it was "fitting" for God, in leading many sons into glory, to make the initiator of their salvation, through sufferings perfect (2:10), so such a high priest—devout, innocent, undefiled, separated from sinners, having become higher than the heavens, is indeed "fitting" for us (7:26). "Having become" so far better than the angels as more excellent beyond them he has inherited a name (1:4), Jesus sat at the right of the divine Majesty in the "heights" (1:3). And according to the order of Melchizedek "having become" high priest forever (6:20), Jesus is a high priest "having become" "higher" than the "heavens." These are the "heavens" that are the works of his hands (1:10), the "heavens" through which he has passed as our great high priest to make possible our heavenly worship (4:14).[40]

As one who "has" the priesthood that is permanent (7:24), Jesus does not "have" each day a "necessity"—in accord with the "necessity" of a change in law when there is a change in priesthood (7:12), just as the Levitical high priests, first on behalf of his own sins to offer up sacrifices, then of the people (7:27). Every high priest is appointed by God to offer both gifts and "sacrifices" on behalf of "sins" (5:1). And he is obligated, just as concerning the "people," so also concerning himself, to offer concerning "sins" (5:3). But Jesus, being without "sin" (4:15) and separated from "sinners" (7:26), has no necessity on behalf of his own "sins" to offer up "sacrifices," before offering them up for the sins of the "people" (7:27).

39. Balz, "*entygchanō*," 461-62: "*Entygchanō* . . . belongs primarily to the conceptual world of the ruler's court, where accusations against another and where requests on behalf of another are made with the hope of receiving a hearing. The narrower theological usage of the verbs in Romans 8 and Hebrews 7 take on their meaning from this background. . . . In Heb 7:25 Christ is the one who is high priest for eternity. Early Christian tradition thus brings together the motif of Christ's exaltation with that of the intercessory or priestly approach of the exalted one to God's right hand for the believer. Here Christ does not—as in Jewish texts—declare the merits of the faithful, but as the one who has always stood on their side interceding, he gives assistance." Lane, *Hebrews 1-8*, 190: "With his exaltation to heaven, Jesus became the permanent intercessor for his people. . . . The direct result of his intercessory activity is the sustaining of the people and the securing of all that is necessary to the eschatological salvation mentioned in the previous clause." See also Miller, "Paul and Hebrews," 260-61; O'Brien, *Hebrews*, 275-78.

40. The only two occurrences of the adjective "high" in Hebrews are in 1:3 and 7:26, enhancing this echo. Attridge, *Hebrews*, 213: "That Christ has become 'higher than the heavens' is another retrospective phrase reminiscent of earlier references to the exaltation, as well as of the 'heavenly' dimension of Christ's priesthood as sketched in this chapter."

He became a merciful and faithful high priest to expiate not his own sins but the "sins" of the "people" (2:17). Indeed, having made a cleansing for "sins," he sat at the right of the divine Majesty in the heavenly heights (1:3), empowered to intercede on behalf of the people—among whom are the audience—who approach God for heavenly worship through him (7:25).

The Levitical high priests have a necessity "each day" to "offer up" sacrifices for their own sins before offering for the sins of the people.[41] In contrast, Jesus did this "once for all" (*ephapax*), that is, a completely effective "once" at his sacrificial death and a singularly definitive "for all time," having "offered up" himself (7:27).[42] The Christ who did not glorify "himself" in becoming high priest (5:5) once for all offered up "himself" as his high priestly sacrifice.[43] In contrast to Jesus, a "high priest" separated from sinners (7:26), other "high priests" have a necessity to offer up sacrifices not only for the sins of the people but for their own sins (7:27), because the law appoints men having weakness as "high priests" (7:28). That "the law" appoints men having "weakness" as high priests recalls that every high priest, who is taken from men and appointed by God on behalf of men (5:1) is surrounded by "weakness" (5:2). It also recalls that a removal of a former commandment comes about because of its "weakness" and uselessness (7:18), for "the law" made nothing perfect for heavenly worship (7:19a). In Jesus, however, we have a high priest able to sympathize with our "weaknesses" (4:15).

The word of the "oath-taking" that is after "the law" (7:28) recalls that Jesus became a priest not without an "oath-taking," whereas the sons of Levi without an "oath-taking" have become priests (7:20). But Jesus became a priest emphatically with an "oath-taking" through the God who declared to him, "The Lord has sworn and will not change, 'You are a priest forever' (Ps 109:4)" (7:21). The audience are thus to appreciate that by the authoritative and definitive word of the oath-taking God ap-

---

41. Attridge, *Hebrews*, 213: "But the double offering involved is clearly that of the Day of Atonement, which, as the author knows (9:7), was a once-yearly observance. . . . our author has somehow conflated the daily sacrifices with that of the Day of Atonement, which is for him the paradigm sacrifice."

42. Koester, *Hebrews*, 368: "The terms *ephapax* (7:27; 9:12; 10:10) and *hapax* (6:4; 9:7, 26–28; 10:2; 12:26–27) have the quantitative sense of singularity and the qualitative sense of completeness. Christ's sacrifice was singular because it achieved complete cleansing for sin, whereas the multiple Levitical sacrifices did not achieve complete cleansing, and therefore had to be repeated." See also Thompson, "EPHAPAX," 566–81.

43. Eberhart, "Sacrificial Metaphors"; Joslin, "Christ Bore the Sins."

pointed Jesus not only a priest forever but also a Son. In contrast to "the law" that made nothing "perfect" for heavenly worship (7:19a), as there was no "perfection" through the Levitical priesthood (7:11), Jesus forever has been made permanently, absolutely, and enduringly "perfect" (7:28). He is thus completely and fully fit for his role in the heavenly worship. This is the Jesus whom, through suffering, God made "perfect" (2:10), the Son who learned from the things he suffered obedience (5:8), and having been made "perfect" by God, became a source of eternal salvation for all who obey him as part of their worship (5:9).[44]

Conclusion

I. As those who have become sluggish in hearing (5:11), the audience have become as those having a need of milk and not solid food (5:12). That solid food is of the perfected (5:14a) connotes that the solid food of the word of righteousness is a matter of those who are perfected in the sense of having become adults rather than infants (5:13). But it also reminds the audience that solid food is a matter of those who are perfected in the sense of having been made fit or worthy for their role in worship. They are thus invited to bear forward with the help of the author toward the perfection (6:1a), toward becoming perfected as mature adults made fit for proper liturgical and ethical worship (5:14).

That the audience have tasted or experienced the pronouncement of God (6:5), with its allusion to their hearing the word of God that is proclaimed to them in the worshiping assembly, complements their having tasted of the heavenly gift (6:4), with its allusion to their partaking of the eucharistic meal in the worshiping assembly. The audience are warned that in the event of their having fallen away, it will be impossible for them, whose faith has already been founded on their repentance (6:1), to again renew to repentance (6:6). The God who swore in his anger that the rebellious and fallen away ancestors will never enter into his rest (3:7, 18; 4:3, 5) will surely not restore the audience to repentance, if they should fall away as apostates, failing to appreciate what is involved in their worship.

---

44. Lane, *Hebrews 1–8*, 196: "The verb *teleioun*, 'to perfect,' is accordingly best understood in a dynamic sense as referring to the whole process by which Jesus was personally prepared and vocationally qualified for his continuing ministry in the presence of God. In v 28 that ministry is contemplated as an accomplished fact of singular importance to the stability of the community addressed." See also MacLeod, "Hebrews 7:26–28."

Although the author speaks in a way that warns the audience of bad things, if they fall away (6:6), namely their eternal destruction (6:8), he is confident concerning them of better things that have to do with salvation (6:9), the salvation they are on the way to inheriting as participants in heavenly worship (1:14). They not only have assisted the holy ones among them as holy brothers (3:1) of Jesus (cf. 2:11, 12, 17), but are continuing to assist them as part of their ethical worship (6:10). Since God will surely not neglect the audience's work and the love which they demonstrated for his name (6:10a), the author desires that each individual in the audience demonstrate the same eagerness and thus persevere for the assurance of the hope until the end (6:11). Such perseverance will assure that the end for the audience is not the burning of divine judgment (6:8), and will facilitate their bearing forward with the author toward the perfection (6:1a) needed for their participation in heavenly worship. Rather than becoming sluggish (5:11; 6:12), they are to become imitators of those who through faith and patience are inheriting the promises (6:12). These promises include the promised blessing from God (6:7), which implies their response of the blessing and praise of God in worship.

II. That, having patience, Abraham obtained the promise (6:15) of the blessing reinforces the exhortation for the audience to become imitators of those who through faith and patience are inheriting the promises (6:12). In going beyond human swearing, God guaranteed the promise even more with an oath, so that two unchangeable things—both the promise and the oath—were involved (6:18a). In these it was impossible for God to lie (6:18b), recalling and reinforcing how it is impossible for those once enlightened (6:4), and having fallen away from their faith and worship, again to renew to repentance (6:6). The entrance of Jesus as a hope that is a sure and firm anchor of the soul into the heavenly sanctuary (6:19-20) bolsters the exhortation that we strive to enter into the heavenly Sabbath rest of God to participate in heavenly worship (4:11), the rest we are even now entering into as those who believed and those who now worship within the liturgical assembly (4:3). The Jesus who entered into the heavenly sanctuary is an eternal high priest, since he became according to the order of Melchizedek high priest *forever* (6:20).

III. The audience are to consider how great this Melchizedek truly must be, if even Abraham, *the* patriarch, freely gave him a tenth from the choice spoils of his victory over the kings (7:1-2). In contrast, those of the sons of Levi who receive the priesthood have a commandment to tithe the people according to the law (7:5a). The people whom the sons of Levi, as priests, tithe are the people for whose sins they are to offer sacrifice in their cultic worship (5:3), the people of God for whom a Sabbath rest for heavenly worship remains (4:9), and the people for whom Jesus became a merciful and faithful high priest in order to expiate the sins that prevent proper worship of God (2:17). In contrast to the Levitical priests who tithed the people who were their brothers (7:5b), even though they shared with them descent from Abraham (7:5c), the priest Melchizedek was not of their Abrahamic ancestry (7:6a). Abraham as the one tithed, is blessed by the superior, Melchizedek, as the one who took the tithe (7:7). Through Abraham, who gave a tithe to the priest Melchizedek, even Levi, who receives tithes (7:9), since the sons of Levi who receive the priesthood have a commandment to tithe the people according to the law (7:5a), was himself tithed (7:9).

Levi, who was still in the loins of his father Abraham when he was met by the priest Melchizedek (7:1a, 10), was himself tithed when Abraham gave a tithe to Melchizedek. This means that the Levitical priesthood is inferior to the eternal priesthood of Jesus, which is according to the order of the Melchizedek (5:6, 10; 6:20) who goes on living (7:8). In being made eternal like the Son of God, Melchizedek remains a priest for all time (7:3d). Whereas the sons of Levi who receive the priesthood tithe those who come from the loins of Abraham (7:5c), Levi himself was still in the loins of his father Abraham when he was tithed by Melchizedek, the eternal priest of the God Most High. It is according to the order of this eternal priest Melchizedek that Jesus became high priest forever (6:20) for the benefit of the audience as a worshiping assembly.

IV. There was a need for a different priest to arise according to the order of Melchizedek, that is, not only to appear but to be raised from the dead to heavenly exaltation, and not said to be according to the order of Aaron, since there was no perfection for heavenly worship through the Levitical priesthood (7:11). Jesus is a different priest because he partook in a tribe different from that of Levi. That from this different tribe no one attended to the altar (7:13) indicates the non-priestly nature of his human lineage. That Jesus, as this different priest, is referred to as our Lord (7:14) reminds the audience of his divine lordship over them as a worshiping assembly, even while elaborating on his human origin. The audience are thus to appreciate not only his difference from Levitical priests but also his likeness to both Melchizedek and to themselves. That Jesus has come about as a priest according to the power of an indestructible life (7:16) further specifies his likeness to Melchizedek (7:15), who does not have end of life, but remains a priest for all time (7:3), as he goes on living forever (7:8). This empowers Jesus to remain a priest forever (7:17) on behalf of the audience as a worshiping assembly.

V. In contrast to the removal of a weak and useless commandment of the law that made nothing perfect for the heavenly worship of God (7:18-19a), there is the introduction by God of a better hope through which we are drawing near to God in a complete way, especially for participation in heavenly worship (7:19b). The audience are to appreciate the superior authoritativeness of the unchangeable oath by which God emphatically swore to Jesus, "You are a priest forever" (7:21). The introduction of Jesus as a better hope through which we are drawing near to God in worship (7:19b), the Jesus who entered into the interior of the heavenly veil as forerunner on our behalf (6:20), has progressed to the eternal priest Jesus as the surety of a better covenant (7:22). In contrast to the Levitical priests who were many because they were prevented by death from remaining on (7:23), Jesus, because he remains a priest forever, possesses the priesthood that is permanent (7:24). The audience are to realize that Jesus is able to save them completely and forever (7:25) as those who, as a worshiping assembly drawing near to God (7:19), approach God through him.

That Jesus is always living to intercede on behalf of the audience, who are to approach God for heavenly worship through him (7:25), is a consequence of his entrance into the interior of the heavenly veil (6:19) as forerunner on behalf of us (6:20). Jesus is a high priest who became higher than the heavens (7:26), the heavens through which he has passed as our great high priest to make possible our heavenly worship (4:14). The Levitical high priests have a necessity each day to offer up sacrifices for their own sins before offering for the sins of the people. In contrast, Jesus did this once for all, that is, a completely effective "once" at his sacrificial death and a singularly definitive "for all time," having offered up himself (7:27). Jesus forever has been made permanently, absolutely, and enduringly perfect (7:28). He is thus completely and fully fit for his role in the heavenly worship on our behalf.

4
Hebrews 8:1—9:28

I. 8:1-6

A ^{8:1} The main point of the things being said—we have such a high priest, who sat at the right of the throne of the Majesty in the heavens, ^{2a} a *minister* of the holy things

    B ^{2b} and of the *tabernacle*, the true one, which the Lord, not man, set up.

        C ³ For every high priest is appointed to *offer* both *gifts* and sacrifices; whence it is necessary for this one also to have something which he may *offer*.

            D ^{4a} If then he would *be* on earth,

            D' ^{4b} he would not *be* a priest,

        C' ^{4c} there being those who *offer* the *gifts* according to a law,

    B' ⁵ who offer worship in a pattern and shadow of the heavenly things, just as Moses, who was about to complete the *tabernacle* was warned. For he says, "See that you make everything according to the model shown to you on the mountain" (Exod 25:40).

A' ⁶ But now he has obtained a more excellent *ministry*, to the degree that he is guarantor of a better covenant, which on the basis of better promises was given law.

At the conclusion of the preceding unit in 7:18–28 is the statement that the law appoints men having weakness as "high priests," but the word of the oath-taking that is after the law appoints the Jesus who is a priest forever (7:21) as also a Son who forever has been made perfect (7:28). At the beginning of the next unit in 8:1–6 is the statement that we have such a "high priest" (8:1). These occurrences of terms for "high priest" thus serve as the transitional words connecting these units as they keep a focus on the theme of high priesthood.

The main point of the things the audience as a worshiping assembly have heard "being said," not only by the author but by God (cf. 7:11, 13, 21), is that we have "such" a "high priest" (8:1). We have "such" a "high priest" who is fitting for us—devout, innocent, undefiled, separated from sinners, having become higher than the heavens (7:26), who once for all offered up himself for the sins of the people (7:27). He is such a high priest who is both a priest forever (7:21) and a divine Son who forever has been made perfect for his high priestly role in heavenly worship (7:28). That such a "high priest we have" (8:1) resonates with the hope that "we have" as an anchor of the soul, both sure and firm, and which enters into the interior of the heavenly veil (6:19). This hope is Jesus himself who, as forerunner on behalf of us entered, according to the order of Melchizedek having become "high priest" forever (6:20). It includes the situation of the audience "having" a great "high priest" who has passed through the heavens (4:14). For we do not "have a high priest" who is not able to sympathize with our weaknesses (4:15).

With an allusion to Ps 109:1, the audience have heard that, as the divine Son, Jesus "sat at the right of the Majesty in the heights" (1:3). And now they hear that, as such a high priest, Jesus "sat at the right of the throne of the Majesty in the heavens" (8:1). That as such a high priest Jesus sat at the right of the heavenly "throne" reinforces the exhortation that we, as worshipers, approach with boldness the "throne" of grace, so that we may receive mercy and may find grace for timely help (4:16) from Jesus our sympathetic high priest (4:15), whose "throne" as divine Son is eternal (1:8). That as such a high priest Jesus sat at the right of the throne of the divine Majesty in the "heavens" resonates with his having become higher than the "heavens" as such a high priest (7:26). These are the "heavens" through which he passed as our great high priest (4:14), the "heavens" that are the works of the hands of Jesus as the eternal divine Son (1:10) and object of heavenly worship (1:6, 14).

As the audience have heard, the angels are God's "ministers" (1:7) and "ministering" spirits who assist in the heavenly worship (1:14). But Jesus' divinely authoritative seat as "such" a high priest at the right of the Majesty in the heavens (8:1) positions and empowers him for his high priestly role as "minister" of "the holy things," the things involved in the heavenly worship (8:2a) in which the audience are being invited to participate.[1] Jesus is a minister of the "tent" or "tabernacle," *the* true one, that is the place of heavenly worship, which the Lord, not a human being, erected (8:2b).[2] The "Lord" God, the "Lord" who has sworn that Jesus is a priest forever (7:21), erected it not on earth but in heaven.

"For every high priest is appointed to offer both gifts and sacrifices" (8:3) reminds the audience of what they heard previously: "*For every high priest from men taken, on behalf of men is appointed in things regarding God, so that he may offer both gifts and sacrifices on behalf of sins*" (5:1). Thus it is necessary that "this one," that is, "such" a high priest that we have (8:1), to have something which he may offer (8:3). Whereas in the days of his flesh while on earth he "offered" both prayers and supplications with strong outcrying and tears to the one who is able to save him from death, and he was heard from his reverence (5:7), as a high priestly minister in the heavenly worship it is necessary that he have something which he may "offer." The audience are now awaiting an elaboration on what that "something" entails.

As a heavenly high priest, Jesus is distinct from the priests on earth: "If then he would be on earth, he would not be a priest, there being those who offer the gifts according to a law" (8:4). This reminds the audience that Jesus arose as a different priest who has come about not "according to a law" of a fleshly commandment but according to the power of an

---

1. Lane, *Hebrews 1–8*, 205: "The term *leitourgos* [minister] is here virtually equivalent to *archiereus*, 'high priest,' but emphasizes the cultic rather than the official aspect of the office. It implies activity (cf. 7:25), and not merely status." Although often understood to refer to "the holy place" or "the sanctuary," *tōn hagiōn* literally means "the holy things," the things consecrated to God that render their location "the holy place" or "the sanctuary." See Balz, "*hagios*," 17.

2. Ellingworth, *Hebrews*, 401: "Apart from 11:9, where it has the literal meaning 'tent,' *skēnē* is used in Hebrews of a place of worship, either heavenly, as here and in 9:11, or earthly, under the Mosaic dispensation (8:5; 9:8, 21; 13:10). . . . In the present verse, the article before *skēnēs* indicates assumed information: 'the well-known scriptural tabernacle'; the word order, and the repeated article, of *tēs skēnēs tēs alēthinēs*, are emphatic." Koester, *Hebrews*, 376: "The 'true' is heavenly and abiding in contrast to what is earthly and transient."

indestructible life (7:16). Previously the audience were exhorted to strive to enter into the heavenly rest of God himself, so that not anyone of them may fall in the same "pattern" of disobedience as the wilderness ancestors (4:11), against whom God swore that they will never enter into his heavenly rest (3:11, 18; 4:3, 5). The negativity of this earthly "pattern" is implicitly present now as the audience hear about those who offer worship in a mere earthly "pattern" and shadow of the heavenly things (8:5a). That they offer worship only in a pattern and shadow of the "heavenly" things deepens the audience's appreciation that they are those who have already tasted of the "heavenly" gift (6:4), and who are partners of a "heavenly" calling (3:1), those who are called to participate in heavenly worship.

The audience have heard that in Jesus we have a heavenly enthroned high priest (8:1) who is a minister of the true, heavenly "tabernacle," which the Lord God, not man, set up (8:2). In contrast, they now hear of the earthly "tabernacle" to be completed by Moses, whom the scriptural voice of God warned in Exod 25:40 to see to it that he make everything according to the model shown to him by God (divine passive) on the mountain, an earthly correspondence to heaven (8:5b). This continues the separation from and superiority of the heavenly high priest Jesus with regard to Moses. As the audience were told, Moses spoke nothing concerning priests about the tribe of Judah from which our Lord Jesus sprang up (7:14). Whereas those who came out of Egypt through Moses rebelled against God in the wilderness (3:16), Jesus enters into the interior of the heavenly veil as forerunner on behalf of us (6:19–20), the initiator of our salvation (2:10). And whereas Moses was faithful in all God's house (3:2, 5), Jesus was considered worthy of even greater glory beyond Moses as the heavenly enthroned divine Son over God's house of worship (3:6), as an object of heavenly worship (1:6, 14).

As the heavenly enthroned divine Son (1:3), Jesus has become so far "better" than the angels "to the degree" that "more excellent" beyond them he has inherited a name (1:4). And as the heavenly enthroned high priest who is a minister of the true, heavenly tabernacle (8:1–2), Jesus has obtained a "more excellent" ministry, "to the degree" that he is guarantor of a "better" covenant (8:6). The author has encouraged the audience to obtain the "better" things having to do with salvation (6:9). Abraham was blessed by Melchizedek as the superior or "better" one (7:7). There is the introduction of a "better" hope, Jesus himself, through which we, as worshipers, are drawing near to God (7:19). And Jesus has become the surety of a "better" covenant (7:22). But now the audience are to appreciate that Jesus is guarantor of a "better" covenant, which on the basis of "better" promises was given law (8:6).[3]

The "promise" to enter into God's own heavenly rest and worship still remains for the audience (4:1). The audience are to become imitators of those who through faith and patience are inheriting the "promises" (6:12). Having patience, which serves as an example for the audience to emulate, Abraham obtained the "promise" (6:15). When God planned to show to the heirs, which include the audience, of the "promise" the unchangeableness of his plan, he guaranteed it with an oath (6:17). And Melchizedek blessed Abraham as the one having the "promises" the audience are to inherit (7:6). But now the audience are to appreciate that Jesus is guarantor of a better covenant, which was given law on the basis of better "promises" (8:6).

Those of the sons of Levi who receive the priesthood have a commandment to tithe the people according to the "law" (7:5). But when the priesthood is changed, of necessity a change of "law" also comes about (7:12). Indeed, Jesus, arising as a different priest according to the order of Melchizedek (7:15), has come about not according to the "law" of a fleshly commandment but according to the power of an indestructible life (7:16). For the "law" made nothing perfect for heavenly worship (7:19). Indeed, the "law" appoints men having weakness as high priests, but the word of the oath-taking that is after the "law" a Son who forever has been made perfect" for heavenly worship (7:28). And so the audience are to appreciate that whereas the people were "given law" "on the basis of" the imperfect Levitical priesthood (7:11), Jesus, as heavenly high priest, is guarantor of a better covenant, which "on the basis of" better promises was "given law" (8:6). This sets up a new cultic system for the heavenly worship in which the audience are being called to participate.

---

3. Ellingworth, *Hebrews*, 410: "In Hebrews, as elsewhere in the Bible, the covenant, whether old or new, is not a mutual agreement, contract, or negotiation, for which an arbitrator may be needed; it is a unilateral gift from God.... Christ's mediation is thought of in Hebrews as similarly unilateral. He is an intermediary from God to humanity; his action on behalf of humanity in relation to God, though part of his priestly ministry, is described in other terms." Thus, "guarantor" (*mesitēs*) in 8:6 also means "mediator" or "intermediary"; see Koester, *Hebrews*, 378–79. Sänger, "*mesitēs*," 411: "Jesus as the *mesitēs* is the *guarantor* and pledge of the final divine promise."

II. 8:7–13

A [7] For if that *first* one were faultless, for a second one would not have been sought a place. [8] For finding fault with them, he says, "Behold days are coming, says the *Lord*, when I will complete with the house of Israel and with the house of Judah a *new* covenant, [9] not according to the covenant, which I made with their fathers on the day of my taking hold of their hand to lead them out of the land of Egypt, for they did not stay in my covenant, and I neglected them, says the *Lord*, [10a] for this is the covenant, which I will covenant with the house of Israel after those days, says the *Lord*, giving my laws into their mind and upon their hearts I will inscribe them,

B [10b] and I will be to them *as God*,

B' [10c] and they will be to me *as people*.

A' [11] And they will certainly not teach each his fellow citizen and each his brother, saying, 'Know the *Lord*,' for all of them will know me from small to great, [12] for I will be merciful to the wrongdoings of them and the sins of them I will certainly remember no longer" (Jer 38:31–34). [13] In saying "*new*," he makes old the *first*, and what is becoming old and aging is near to disappearing.

At the conclusion of the preceding unit in 8:1–6 is the assertion that Jesus has obtained a more excellent ministry, to the degree that he is guarantor of a better "covenant" (8:6). Toward the beginning of this next unit in 8:7–13 is the quotation from Jer 38:31: "Behold days are coming, says the Lord, when I will complete with the house of Israel and with the house of Judah a new *covenant*" (8:8). These occurrences of the term "covenant" thus serve as the transitional words connecting these units as they move the focus from the covenant as "better" to the covenant as "new." And with regard to the second macrochiastic level, after the central and pivotal unit in 8:1–6 the audience experience a chiastic relationship between the unit in 8:7–13 and the one in 7:18–28 provided by the terms "people" and "sins." Jesus "does not have every day a necessity, just as the high priests, first on behalf of his own *sins* to offer up sacrifices then of the *people*, for this he did once for all having offered up himself" (7:27). And God's scriptural word promises that "they will be to me as *people*" (8:10c) and "the *sins* of them I will certainly remember no longer" (8:12).

That the first covenant was not "faultless," so that God sought a place for a second (8:7) is reinforced for the audience with the reference to God "finding fault" with "them," that is, with those with whom he made the first covenant (8:8a). Consequently, as God "says" in pronouncing the promise from the quotation of Jer 38:31–34, "Behold days are coming," emphatically underscored as the authoritative word of God by "*says* the Lord," "when I will complete with the house of Israel and with the house of Judah a new covenant" (8:8). Recalling that at the end of these "days" God has spoken to us in a Son (1:2), the audience realize that they are now living in the quotation's coming "days" promised by God.[4] The promise of God that "I will complete" (*syntelesō*) a new covenant connotes its perfection as a covenant that will not be broken.[5] God will complete a new covenant not only with the house of Israel but with the house of "Judah," recalling that, as a heavenly high priest, our Lord sprang up from "Judah" (7:14).

This promised new covenant to be completed in the "days" that are coming will not be in accord with the covenant (8:9a) God made with their "fathers" (cf. 1:1) on that past "day" (8:9b) of his taking hold of their hand to lead "them," the same "them" with whom he found fault (8:8a), out of the land of Egypt (8:9c). God's "taking hold" of their hand to lead them out of the land of Egypt, that is out of slavery, was the precedent for Jesus not "taking hold" of angels but "taking hold" rather of the descendants of Abraham, his fellow human beings (2:16), in freeing them from slavery to the fear of death (2:15). That God led them out of the land of "Egypt" reminds the audience that those who came out of "Egypt" through Moses rebelled against God (3:16), disqualifying them to participate in the heavenly rest and worship of God.

The audience hear the scriptural voice of God declare that as a consequence of their not staying in God's covenant (8:9d), God has "neglected" (*ēmelēsa*) them, emphatically underlined by "says the *Lord*" God (8:9e). This reinforces the previous cohortative question of how we will escape,

---

4. Attridge, *Hebrews*, 227; Koester, *Hebrews*, 385: "In Hebrews the coming days have arrived (Heb 1:2), although final redemption remains future."

5. On the verb "I will complete," Attridge, *Hebrews*, 227 notes: "While the verb used here is not synonymous with *teleioun*, it recalls the prominent motif of Christ's perfection and one of the effects of the new covenant and its sacrifice will be the perfection of believers." According to Ellingworth, *Hebrews*, 416, Hebrews may be following the usage of Jer 41:8, 15, "in reserving *syntelesō* for a covenant which is not broken." See also Joslin, *Hebrews*, 186n49.

"neglecting" (*amelēsantes*) so great a salvation, which received a beginning of being spoken through the "Lord" Jesus Christ (2:3).[6] Since they did not stay in God's first covenant, the scriptural voice of God promises that "this is the covenant" (8:10a) that he will covenant with the house of Israel after "those days," that is, after the promised coming "days" (8:8b) following "that" first covenant (8:7), again, for the third time, emphatically underscored with "says the Lord" (8:10a; cf. 8:8, 9). According to this new covenant, God will give his laws into their mind and upon their hearts he will inscribe "them" (8:10a). God's laws will thus be within "them" with whom he found fault (8:8a), despite leading "them" out of the land of Egypt (8:9c).

The audience have been alerted to anticipate that a change of priesthood brings a necessary change to the external "law" that made nothing perfect for heavenly worship (7:19). This external "law" appoints men having weakness as high priests, but the word of the oath-taking that is after this external "law" appoints a Son who forever has been made perfect (7:28). Jesus has obtained a more excellent ministry, to the degree that he is guarantor of a better covenant, which on the basis of better promises "was given law" (8:6). And now the scriptural voice of God promises the arrival of that necessary change to laws that are internal, "giving my *laws* into their mind and upon their hearts I will inscribe them" (8:10a).[7] The progression from the singular "law" to the plural "laws" indicates that the many individual laws broken in the past can now be kept because they are no longer external but internal.[8]

Previously the audience have heard the scriptural voice of God in the exhortation from Ps 94:7–11, "today when you hear his voice, do not harden your *hearts*" (3:8), and "they are always wandering in the *heart*,

6. Koester, *Hebrews*, 386; Ellingworth, *Hebrews*, 416: "Elsewhere in the Greek Bible, *ameleō* is always used pejoratively with a human subject."

7. Joslin, *Hebrews*, 222–23: The law "is no longer seen as an intimidating external set of regulations, but has been internalized as a blessing of God that renews and changes the heart. . . . The writer of Hebrews can speak of the law's inabilities to bring about perfection and the limits of its cultic requirements (external), and at the same time affirm with Jeremiah that in the New Covenant there is a positive value ascribed to the law (fulfilled and internalized). . . . That which is internalized has significant correspondence to the Mosaic commandments (continuity), yet not complete correspondence due to fulfillment (discontinuity)."

8. Joslin, *Hebrews*, 199–200. Koester, *Hebrews*, 387: "Hebrews warns about hard and evil hearts that lead people astray, and the new covenant is instituted in order that hearts might be true rather than evil, and faithful rather than faithless. Completeness of obedience, rather than internalization, is the concern."

and they have not known my ways" (3:10). They were warned "lest there be in anyone of you an evil *heart* of unfaithfulness in falling away from the living God" (3:12). They were again repeatedly exhorted, "today when you hear his voice, 'do not harden your *hearts* as in the rebellion'" (3:15), and "today if you hear his voice, do not harden your *hearts*" (4:7). They have heard that the living word of God "is able to scrutinize deliberations and thoughts of the *heart*" (4:12). And now, they hear the scriptural word of God promise to give his laws into their mind and "upon their *hearts* I will inscribe them" (8:10a). The audience are thus attracted to what this new covenant can do in their own hearts, so that not anyone of them will have an evil heart of unfaithfulness causing them to fall away from the heavenly worship of the living God who offers eternal life.

God promises that although "they" did not stay in God's first covenant (8:9d), now, in this new covenant, "they" will be to God as a people (8:10c). Just as God's scriptural promise that "I will be to him as a Father" concluded with the reciprocal promise that "and he will be to me as Son" (1:5), so now God's scriptural promise that "I will be to them as God" (8:10b) concludes with the reciprocal promise that "and they will be to me as people." The two parts of this reciprocal promise thus complete the familiar OT covenantal formula uniquely relating God to the people of God.[9]

The audience are thus to appreciate this close relationship between Jesus as the divine Son and high priest with the people of God. They have heard how Jesus became a merciful and faithful high priest in things regarding God in order to expiate the sins of the "people" (2:17), and that a Sabbath rest for heavenly worship remains for the "people" of God (4:9). Every Levitical high priest is obligated, just as concerning the "people," so also concerning himself, to offer concerning sins (5:3). The Levitical priests tithe the "people" according to the law (7:5), and it was on the basis of the Levitical priesthood that the "people" were given law (7:11). Jesus does not have every day the necessity, as the Levitical high priests, first on behalf of his own sins to offer up sacrifices then of the "people," for this he did once for all having offered up himself (7:27). This is the "people,"

---

9. According to Johnson, *Hebrews*, 208, the formula can be translated literally as "I will be God with respect to them and they will be a people with respect to me." Koester, *Hebrews*, 387: "This summarizes the covenantal relationship (Exod 6:7; 29:45; Lev 26:12; Deut 26:17–18; Jer 7:23; 24:7; 30:22; Ezek 11:20; 37:27; Hos 2:23; Zech 8:8; 2 Cor 6:16; Rev 21:3). The formula highlights the uniqueness of God's relationship to his people."

among whom are the audience, and regarding whom God now promises in this new covenant that "they will be to me as *people*" (8:10c). They will be God's own people as a consequence of God's promise to Jesus that "he will be to me as Son" (1:5), since, as the heavenly enthroned divine Son, Jesus is also the eternal high priest of the people of God (7:28—8:6), who makes possible their participation in heavenly worship.

Although the audience have need for someone to "teach" them the elements of the beginning of the sayings of God (5:12), in the new covenant the people of God will certainly not "teach" each his fellow citizen and each his brother to know the Lord (8:11a). The concern for each individual—that "each" will not need to teach his fellow citizen and "each" will not need to teach his brother—reinforces the exhortation that "each" individual in the audience demonstrate the same eagerness for the assurance of the hope until the end (6:11). Although the scriptural voice of God from Ps 94:10 declared of the wilderness generation that "they have not *known* my ways" (3:10), in this new covenant the scriptural voice of God from Jer 38:34 declares that individuals will not need to tell one another, "*Know* the Lord" (8:11b). And that they will not need to teach one another to know the "Lord" follows from the previous threefold emphatic reverberation of "says the *Lord*" (8:8, 9, 10), which undergirds the pronouncement of the new covenant with the definitive authority of the word of God.

In this new covenant all of "them," all of the people of God, from small to great will know the Lord (8:11c) as a God who will be merciful to the wrongdoings of "them" and the sins of "them" he will certainly remember no longer (8:12). That they will "certainly not" need to teach one another to know the Lord (8:11a) is reinforced by the Lord's emphatically authoritative covenantal promise that he will "certainly not" remember their sins "any more." The covenantal promise that "the sins of them *I will* certainly remember no longer" specifies for the audience the significance of the promise that "*I will* be to them as God" (8:10b). The God who "remembers" the people he created (2:6) will certainly "remember" their sins no longer, the sins that prevent them from playing their role in the heavenly worship.

At the beginning of the letter the audience were told that the divine Son, having made a cleansing for "sins," sat at the right of the Majesty in the heights of heaven (1:3). Jesus became a merciful and faithful high priest in things regarding God in order to expiate the "sins" of the people

(2:17). The audience were exhorted to encourage one another that not anyone of them may become hardened by the deceit of "sin" (3:13). In Jesus we have a high priest who is without "sin" (4:15). Every Levitical high priest is to offer gifts and sacrifices on behalf of "sins" (5:1), and is obligated, just as concerning the people, so also concerning himself, to offer concerning "sins" (5:3). But Jesus does not have every day a necessity, like the Levitical high priests, first on behalf of his own "sins" to offer up sacrifices then of the people, for this he did once for all having offered up himself (7:27). The audience are thus to appreciate how the covenantal promise of God that "the sins of them I will certainly remember no longer" (8:12) is based on this definitive self-sacrifice of Jesus, his act of heavenly worship as the divinely enthroned Son and eternal high priest.[10]

God's "saying" "new" (8:13), thus underlining the newness of the "new" covenant (8:8), reinforces his covenantal promise that the people of God will not need to teach one another, "saying," "Know the Lord" (8:11). In saying "new," God "makes old" the "first"—that "first" covenant that was not faultless (8:7), and what is "becoming old" and aging is near to disappearing (8:13), reminding the audience that all of creation "will become old" and perish in contrast to Jesus as the exalted divine Son, who continues eternally (1:11). Just as earth that bears forth thorns and thistles is rejected and "near" a curse, whose end is a burning (6:8), so the first covenant that is becoming old and aging is "near" to disappearing. The audience are thus to deepen their appreciation for what this "new" covenant, which supplants the old and aging one that is near to disappearing, promises for them as a worshiping assembly.

III. 9:1–10

A [9:1] Even the first then had *regulations* for offering of worship and an earthly holy place.

   B [2] For a *tabernacle* was *furnished*, the first, in which were the lampstand and the table and the presentation of the loaves, which is *said* to be "holy things." [3] And behind the *second* veil a *tabernacle* which is *said* to be "holy things of *holy things*,"

      C [4a] *having a golden* altar of incense and the ark of *the covenant*

         D [4b] covered on all sides with gold,

---

10. Fuhrmann, "Failures Forgotten."

C' [4c] in which were a *golden* jar *having* the manna and the staff of Aaron that sprouted and the tablets of *the covenant,*

B' [5] and above it the cherubim of glory overshadowing the place of expiation. Concerning which things it is not now time to *speak* in detail. [6] These things thus *furnished,* into the first *tabernacle* continually go the priests completing the offerings of worship, [7] but into the *second* once a year only the high priest, not without blood which he offers on behalf of himself and of the inadvertent sins of the people, [8] this the Holy Spirit indicating, that the way to "the *holy things*" had not appeared while the first *tabernacle* had standing,

A' [9] which is a parable for the time that has arrived, according to which both gifts and sacrifices are being offered not able according to conscience to make perfect the one offering worship, [10] only on the basis of foods and drinks and various baptisms, *regulations* of the flesh imposed until the time of correction.

At the conclusion of the preceding unit in 8:7–13 is the assertion that God makes old the "first," that is, the first covenant, and that what is becoming old and aging is near to disappearing (8:13). At the beginning of this next unit in 9:1–10 is the assertion that even this "first" covenant had regulations for offering of worship and an earthly holy place (9:1). These occurrences of the term "first" thus serve as the transitional words connecting these units as they retain a focus upon the "first" covenant to be replaced by the "new" covenant. And with regard to the second macrochiastic level, the audience experience a chiastic relationship between the unit in 7:11–17 and this unit in 9:1–10 provided by occurrences of the name of "Aaron" (7:11; 9:4).[11]

Although in announcing a new covenant, God makes old the "first" covenant, so that it is near to disappearing (8:13), even the "first" covenant had regulations for "offering of worship," that is, the sacrificial worship of God, and an earthly holy place where that worship took place (9:1). But, as the audience recall, the earthly priests who offer the gifts according to a law (8:4), "offer worship" in only a pattern and shadow of the heavenly things (8:5). The earthly holy place for sacrificial worship that the cov-

---

11. There are no occurrences in Hebrews of the name of Aaron between these; the only other occurrence is in 5:4.

enant, "the first," had (9:1), that is, "the first" which was not faultless (8:7), is further described as a tabernacle, "the first" (9:2).[12] This pointed designation closely associates this first tabernacle with the faulty first covenant that is becoming old, aging, and near to disappearing (8:13).[13]

That this first tabernacle was "furnished" (9:2) implies that it was ultimately furnished by God (divine passive). About to complete the tabernacle, Moses was warned by the scriptural voice of God in Exod 25:40 to make everything according to the model shown to him by God on the mountain (8:5). And the audience have heard that Jesus has been considered worthy of greater glory beyond Moses, just as greater honor than the worshiping household has the one who "furnishes" it (3:3). For every house is "furnished" by someone, but the one who "furnishes" all things is God (3:4). This first tabernacle that was furnished by God also is "said" by God (cf. 7:13) to be "holy things," since it contains the lampstand (Exod 25:31–39) and the table (Exod 25:23–30) and the presentation of the loaves (Exod 25:30; 2 Chr 13:11) as the "holy things" furnished by God for sacrificial worship (9:2).[14] And behind the "second" veil, analogous to the "second" covenant coming after the faulty first covenant (8:7), is a tabernacle which is "said" by God to be "holy things of holy things" (*hagia hagiōn*, 9:3; cf. Lev 6:10, 18, 22; 7:1, 6; 10:12, 17; 14:13; 1 Chr 23:13; Ezek 43:12).[15]

That this tabernacle is behind the second "veil" (9:3) reminds the audience of the interior of the "veil" (6:19), where as forerunner on behalf of us Jesus entered, according to the order of Melchizedek having become high priest forever (6:20). This "tabernacle," as well as the first "tabernacle" (9:2), also recall for the audience the "tabernacle" completed by Moses in which earthly priests offer worship in only a pattern and shadow

---

12. Mitchell, *Hebrews*, 173: "Although the use of *prōtē*, 'first,' suggests that the author has more than one tent in mind, it will become clear in the next verse that he understands the sanctuary to be divided into two spaces."

13. Stanley, "Hebrews 9:6–10," 386–87: "[T]here is also an aspect of the first tent that makes it inferior to the second tent or holy of holies, just as the first covenant is inferior to the new covenant."

14. Swetnam, "Hebrews 9,2."

15. For detailed discussions of the OT background here, see Lane, *Hebrews 9–13*, 219–20; Ellingworth, *Hebrews*, 421–24; Koester, *Hebrews*, 394; Johnson, *Hebrews*, 217–19; Mitchell, *Hebrews*, 173–74. On the expression *hagia hagiōn*, Lane, *Hebrews 9–13*, 220 notes: "The force of this expression is that of an emphatic superlative ('the Most Holy Place')."

of the heavenly things (8:5). It stands in contrast, then, to the "tabernacle," the true one, which the Lord, not man set up, and of which the high priest Jesus is a cultic minister of the heavenly "holy things" involved in heavenly worship (8:2).

The tabernacle behind the second veil is further described as "having a golden altar of incense and the ark of the covenant" (9:4a).[16] The first tabernacle was appropriately called "holy things," since it was furnished with such holy things for offering of worship as the lampstand, the table, and the presentation of the loaves (9:2). But the second tabernacle was called "holy things of holy things," or "most holy of things," since it had an altar of incense, whose golden adornment is pointedly emphasized. "Golden" is heard by the audience as the first word in the clause, set off from "altar of incense" by the intervening participle "having." In addition, this second tabernacle had "the ark of the covenant," that is, of the first covenant, the one that is old, aging, and near to disappearing (8:13), the one associated with the old earthly worship rather than with the new heavenly worship.[17]

With the reference to a golden jar (9:4c), the audience have heard a triplet of expressions of the golden adornment of items within the second tabernacle. The triplet began with a focus on the second tabernacle as "having a golden altar of incense" (9:4a), in which the adjective "golden" enhances the description of an indefinite "altar of incense." It progressed to a focus on a definite "*the* ark of *the* covenant," whose complete golden adornment is highlighted with the use of the noun "gold" in the description of it as "covered on all sides with gold" (9:4b). And it concludes here with the mention of the first item within the ark of the covenant, "a golden jar having the manna" (9:4c), in which the adjective "golden" enhances the description of an initially indefinite "jar."[18] That these items

---

16. Westcott, *Hebrews*, 247 notes: "It is further to be observed that the word *thymiaterion* is left indefinite. . . . the writer . . . says simply *chrysoun thymiaterion*, 'a golden incense (altar).' The word is descriptive and not the technical name of a special object."

17. Lane, *Hebrews 9–13*, 221: "The ark of the covenant was the most important object located within the Most Holy Place. It was a chest made of acacia wood and was covered on all sides with gold, with rings of gold in each corner through which the staves for lifting and transporting the ark from one place to another were to be permanently inserted (Exod 25:10–15; 37:1–5). The lid of the chest was the focal point for atonement."

18. Koester, *Hebrews*, 395: "Manna was the food that appeared on the ground each day during Israel's sojourn in the wilderness (Exod 16:31). About two quarts of it were

are adorned with the precious metal of gold underscores for the audience their character as among the "holy things of holy things" God has furnished for sacrificial worship in the most holy place of God's presence (9:1-3).[19]

Within the golden ark of the covenant was also "the staff of Aaron that sprouted" (9:4c). The miraculous sprouting of a flower from Aaron's staff divinely confirmed the Levitical priesthood.[20] Hence its appropriateness as one of the "holy things of holy things" that God furnished for sacrificial worship in the tabernacle (9:1-3). The mention of the "staff" of Aaron recalls for the audience the scriptural voice of God from Ps 44:7 addressed to Jesus as the heavenly enthroned eternal divine Son: "Your throne, O God, is forever and ever, and the *staff* of uprightness is a *staff* of your kingdom" (1:8). As the "staff" of Aaron indicated that the tribe of Levi were divinely qualified to be earthly priests, so the audience are to appreciate that the "staff" of Jesus' eternal enthronement indicates that he is divinely qualified to be the heavenly high priest. But that it is the staff of "Aaron" also reminds the audience that Jesus arose as a different priest, not according to the order of "Aaron" (7:11), although he was called by God to be a priest, just as was "Aaron" (5:4).

Also within the golden ark of "the covenant" (9:4a) were the tablets of "the covenant" (9:4c), on which were written the Law God gave to Moses.[21] Hence their appropriateness as among the "holy things of holy things" that God furnished for sacrificial worship in the tabernacle (9:1-3). But the ark and these tablets within it are of the first covenant that is old, aging, and near to disappearing (8:13). This repeated mention of the old

---

preserved in a jar (Exod 16:32-34). The jar was made of gold according to Exod 16:33 LXX (but not MT)."

19. Westcott, *Hebrews*, 248: "The solemn repetition of the word ['gold'] emphasises the splendour of this typical sanctuary. Gold was the characteristic metal of the Holy of Holies."

20. Mitchell, *Hebrews*, 175: "The budding rod of Aaron, according to Num 17:16-24 (LXX), was placed by Moses in the Holy of Holies. Twelve staffs with the names of the heads of the tribes were to be placed in the sanctuary, before the Lord. Aaron's name was to be inscribed on the staff of Levi. When Moses returned the next day he saw that Aaron's rod had sprouted a flower. This indicated that he was chosen by God for the priesthood."

21. Koester, *Hebrews*, 396: "Moses was understood to have received two stone 'tablets of the covenant' (Deut 9:9) on which the Law had been written by the finger of God (Deut 9:10; cf. Exod 34:27-28; 1 Kgs 8:9; 2 Chron 5:10). The tablets were put into the ark (Deut 10:1-5)."

"covenant" reminds the audience of the new "covenant" God promised (8:8), which is not according to the old "covenant," for the people did not stay in that "covenant" (8:9). This is the new "covenant" that, as God promises, "I will covenant" with them, "giving my laws into their mind and upon their hearts I will inscribe them, and I will be to them as God, and they will be to me as people" (8:10). As the heavenly high priest, Jesus is guarantor of this better "covenant" (8:6), having become the surety of this better "covenant" (7:22), the one associated with heavenly, rather than merely earthly, worship.

Climaxing the descriptive enumeration of the "holy things of holy things" God furnished for sacrificial worship in the second tabernacle (9:1–3) is the focus on the "cherubim," that is, the two winged figures, of God's glory above the golden ark of the covenant.[22] They were overshadowing the "place of expiation" or "mercy seat" (*hilastērion*), the special cultic place at which atonement of sins was made during the sacrificial worship in the tabernacle.[23] That they were "overshadowing" (*kataskiazonta*) it resonates alliteratively with the notice that the tabernacle was "furnished" (*kateskeuasthē*) by God for sacrificial worship.[24] The description of them as the cherubim of God's "glory" (9:5) reminds the audience that Jesus has been considered worthy of greater "glory" beyond Moses (3:3). It is through him, who was crowned with divine "glory" and honor (2:7, 9), that God will lead many sons, among whom are the audience, to the "glory" of heavenly worship (2:10). Indeed, Jesus, as God's Son, is the radiance of the "glory" of God (1:3), who thus has become an object of heavenly worship. Indicating that there is more that could be said regarding these things (9:5b), the author abruptly concludes his description, with a poignant implication that at this time there is a more important point for the audience to consider.

---

22. Mitchell, *Hebrews*, 175: "Exodus 25:18–22 describes two cherubim of hammered gold that faced each other with their wings spread. They were placed on each side of the mercy seat that was on the ark itself." Koester, *Hebrews*, 396: "The genitive 'of glory' could describe the cherubim themselves, but the context makes it likely that the glory is 'God's glory.'"

23. Roloff, "*hilastērion*," 186: "*Hilastērion* . . . was the most important cult object in the most holy place in the tabernacle and the temple. It was a gold plate placed on the ark of the covenant. . . . As such it was the place at which atonement was made for the entire community of Israel."

24. Ellingworth, *Hebrews*, 430: "The author's choice of the word [*kataskiazonta*] may be influenced by the wish to make an oral inclusion with *kateskeuasthē* in v. 2."

"These things thus furnished" (9:6a) refers to the things just described as furnished by God for sacrificial worship in the earthly holy place (9:1), a description that began with "the first tabernacle" that was "furnished" by God (9:2). Into "the first tabernacle" continually go the priests "completing" the "offerings of worship" (9:6b).[25] As the audience recall, this is in the earthly tabernacle Moses was to "complete" as only a pattern and shadow of the heavenly things (8:5), the earthly holy place for which there were regulations for "offering of worship" under the first covenant (9:1). Whereas into the first tabernacle continually go the priests completing the offerings of worship (9:6), into the "second," that is, the one behind the "second" veil, the tabernacle which is said to be "holy things of holy things" (9:3), once a year only goes the high priest (9:7a). This, as the audience recall, is the tabernacle analogously associated with the new, "second" covenant God sought to replace the old and aging first one (8:7).

As "high priest" he goes not without blood, which he "offers" on behalf of himself and of the inadvertent sins of the "people" (9:7b).[26] This reminds the audience that every "high priest" is appointed so that he may "offer" both gifts and sacrifices on behalf of sins (5:1). He is obligated concerning both the "people" and himself to "offer" concerning sins (5:3). But, as the audience are to appreciate, Jesus is a heavenly "high priest" (7:26) who does not have every day a necessity, just as the earthly "high priests," first on behalf of his own sins to "offer up" sacrifices then of the "people," for this he did once for all having "offered up" himself (7:27). As every "high priest" is appointed to "offer" gifts and sacrifices, Jesus, the heavenly and eternally perfected "high priest" that we have (8:1), also has something he may "offer" in his act of heavenly worship (8:3).

The audience are aware of the distributions of the "Holy Spirit" according to the will of God (2:4). The "Holy Spirit" drew the audience's attention to the scriptural voice of God (3:7). The audience have become partners of the "Holy Spirit" (6:4). And now the "Holy Spirit" indicates that the way to "the holy things" had not appeared while the first taber-

---

25. Hamm, "Praying."

26. Johnson, *Hebrews*, 223: "This last term, *tou laou agnoēmatōn*, (lit. 'the ignorances of the people') is strange and not well attested in the LXX, but it apparently reflects a distinction made by Num 15:22–30 and Lev 4:2–17 between 'unwitting' sins and others. The distinction does not, however, occur among the regulations for the Day of Atonement. Leviticus 16:16 and 30 declare that 'all sins' are expiated by the ritual."

nacle had standing (9:8). The way to the heavenly "holy things" had not appeared while the first "tabernacle" had standing, because with that tabernacle appeared the way to the second "tabernacle" and the earthly "holy things of holy things" (9:3). But, as the audience are to appreciate, in Jesus we have a heavenly high priest (8:1), who is a minister of the heavenly "holy things" and of the heavenly "tabernacle," the true one, which the Lord, not man, set up (8:2).

That the way to the heavenly holy things had not appeared while the "first" tabernacle had "standing" (9:8) resonates with the fact that the analogous "first" covenant was not faultless, so that for a second one God sought a "place" (8:7). The "standing" the first tabernacle had includes its position as the "first" tabernacle into which the earthly priests go continually (9:6), while into the second once a year only the high priest goes (9:7a). This "first" tabernacle (9:2) refers to the earthly holy place under the "first" covenant (9:1). But in speaking of a new covenant, God makes old the "first," and what is becoming old and aging is near to disappearing (8:13). The implication is that the first earthly tabernacle has likewise become old, as the standing it had prevented the appearance for the way to the heavenly holy things in the heavenly tabernacle for heavenly worship (8:1–2).

The first tabernacle is a "parable," that is, a comparison or analogy, for the present time of the audience, the "end of these days" (1:2), that has now "arrived" (*enestēkota*), with the perfect tense underlining the definitiveness and ongoing nature of the arrival (9:9a). This is the time in which the first covenant is becoming old, aging, and near to disappearing, because God has promised a new covenant (8:13); it is the time in which the audience, as a worshiping assembly, have already "tasted the beneficent pronouncement of God and the powers of the age to come" (6:5). According to this "parable" or "analogy" between the first covenant and the first tabernacle, "both gifts and sacrifices are being offered" (9:9b). This reminds the audience that under the first covenant every high priest is appointed "to offer both gifts and sacrifices" (8:3), and that every high priest is appointed so that he "may offer both gifts and sacrifices" on behalf of the sins (5:1) that prevent proper worship of God.

These gifts and sacrifices are not "able," that is, do not have the power (9:9c), according to conscience to make perfect the one offering worship (9:9d).[27] Their powerlessness aligns them with the wilderness ancestors

---

27. On the significance of "not being able," see Ellingworth, *Hebrews*, 441–42.

who were not "able" to enter into God's promised heavenly rest because of unfaithfulness (3:19). This is in contrast, as the audience are to appreciate, with Jesus, who is "able" to save completely those who approach God through him (7:25). This power comes from the God who was "able" to save him from death (5:7). As a high priest, Jesus is thus "able" to deal patiently with those who are ignorant and wandering (5:2). In Jesus we do not have a high priest who is not "able" to sympathize with our weaknesses (4:15). Indeed, in what Jesus himself suffered in being tested, those who are being tested he is "able" to help (2:18).

The inability (9:9c) of the gifts and sacrifices being offered "according to" the parable (9:9b) pivots the focus of the audience to what is "according to conscience," that is, the consciousness or awareness of the sins on behalf of which the gifts and sacrifices are being offered (9:9d; 5:1; 9:7).[28] They are not able according to conscience to "make perfect" for heavenly worship the one offering worship (9:9d), because under the first covenant the law "made perfect" nothing (7:19) and there was no "perfection" through the Levitical priesthood (7:11). But, in a contrast the audience are to appreciate, Jesus is the initiator of their salvation whom God, through sufferings, "made perfect" (2:10). And having been "made perfect," Jesus became for all those who obey him a source of eternal salvation (5:9). Indeed, as the divine Son appointed by God as a heavenly high priest, Jesus forever has been "made perfect" (7:28). The gifts and sacrifices offered under the first covenant are not able to make perfect the one "offering worship," because the high priests who offer them (8:4) "offer worship" in only a pattern and shadow of the heavenly things (8:5).

These gifts and sacrifices being offered under the first covenant are not able according to conscience to "make perfect" the one offering worship (9:9), since they are offered "only on the basis of foods and drinks and various baptisms" (9:10a).[29] But, as the audience have been exhorted, they are to bear forward toward the "perfection" (6:1) that goes beyond the teaching about "baptisms" (6:2). The implication is that to reach perfection for heavenly worship they are to go beyond the gifts and sacrifices offered under the first covenant.

---

28. For more on "conscience" here, see Attridge, *Hebrews*, 242; Lane, *Hebrews 9–13*, 225; Ellingworth, *Hebrews*, 442; Koester, *Hebrews*, 399; Johnson, *Hebrews*, 226.

29. For more regarding "foods and drinks and various baptisms" here, see Koester, *Hebrews*, 399; Johnson, *Hebrews*, 225–26.

These gifts and sacrifices being offered according to the "regulations" for offering of worship under the first covenant (9:1) are "regulations" of the flesh imposed until the time of correction or setting things right (9:10b).[30] Recalling when Jesus was on earth in the days of his "flesh" (5:7), when he shared in blood and "flesh" (2:14), that these regulations are of the "flesh" underscores their earthly, external dimension and thus their powerlessness to make the one offering worship perfect according to an internal conscience (9:9). But, as the audience are to appreciate, Jesus arises as a different priest who has come about not according to the law of a "fleshly" commandment but according to the power of an indestructible life (7:16). These regulations of the flesh are imposed by God (divine passive) until the "time" of correction, of setting things right. It is the "time" that has now arrived (9:9) for the audience, as the time when the "first" covenant and its analogous "first" tabernacle are becoming old, aging, and near to disappearing, because of the arrival of the new covenant promised by God (8:13), the new covenant with its regulations not for earthly but for heavenly worship.[31]

IV. 9:11–14

A [11] *Christ*, having come as high priest of the good things that have come to be, through the greater and more perfect tabernacle not made by hands, that is, not of this creation,

> B [12a] not through the blood of *goats* and calves but through his own blood,
>
>> C [12b] he entered once for all into "the holy things," finding eternal redemption.
>
> B′ [13] For if the blood of *goats* and bulls and the sprinkling of a heifer's ashes makes holy those defiled for the cleansing of the flesh,

A′ [14] how much more will the blood of the *Christ*, who through the eternal Spirit offered himself unblemished to God, cleanse our conscience from dead works to offer worship to the living God.

---

30. On "correction" or "setting things right" (*diorthōseōs*), Mitchell, *Hebrews*, 178 notes: "'Time to set things right' may also be translated as 'time of correction,' a term that can refer to the correction of a law. The expression occurs only here in the NT."

31. Cortez, "From the Holy."

Toward the conclusion of the preceding unit in 9:1–10 is a reference to the standing of the first "tabernacle" (9:8) under the first covenant. At the beginning of this next unit in 9:11–14 is a reference to the more perfect "tabernacle" not made by hands (9:11). These occurrences of the term "tabernacle" serve as the transitional words connecting these units as they move the focus of the place for sacrificial worship from the earthly to the heavenly tabernacle. And with regard to the second macrochiastic level, the audience experience a chiastic relationship between the unit in 7:1–10 and this unit in 9:11–14 provided by terms referring to living eternally. "One [Melchizedek] is testified that he goes on *living*" (7:8) and the blood of Christ will "cleanse our conscience from dead works to offer worship to the *living* God" (9:14).

The Christ Jesus who, as the divine Son, did not glorify himself in "becoming high priest" (5:5), "has come" as "high priest" of the good things that "have come to be" (9:11). The adroit alliteration underscores for the audience the close connection between the good things that have come to be (*genomenōn*) and the coming (*paragenomenos*) of Christ as heavenly high priest. Although the way to "the holy things" had not appeared while the first tabernacle had standing (9:8), Christ has come as high priest of "the good things that have come to be." These "good things" include the "better promises" and "better covenant" of which Jesus is the guarantor (8:6) and surety (7:22), indeed the "better things" having to do with salvation (6:9), the great salvation (2:3) that is to motivate and inspire the audience's worship.[32]

The audience's attention is drawn to the tabernacle with the heavenly attribute of being "greater" (9:11b), resonating with the God of whom no one is "greater" (6:13, 16). As the "more perfect" tabernacle, it stands in contrast to the first tabernacle's gifts and sacrifices not able to "make perfect" for heavenly worship the one offering worship (9:9), as the law "made perfect" nothing (7:19), for there was no "perfection" through the Levitical, earthly priesthood (7:11). This "more perfect" tabernacle is appropriately associated with Jesus as the heavenly high priest who has been "made perfect" forever (7:28). Having been "made perfect," he became for all those who obey him a source of eternal salvation (5:9), as one whom God "made perfect" through sufferings (2:10). This "more perfect" tabernacle recalls the exhortation for the audience to bear forward toward the

---

32. Fuhrmann, "Christ Grown into Perfection."

"perfection" (6:1), in order to be among those "perfected" for their role in heavenly worship (5:14).

That the greater and more perfect tabernacle is "not made by hands" means that it is heavenly rather than earthly, and thus not of this "creation" (9:11b), in which no "creature" is invisible before God (4:13). It thus resonates with the "tabernacle," the true one, which the Lord, not man, set up, the tabernacle of which Jesus as heavenly high priest is minister of the holy things (8:2). As the greater, more perfect, and heavenly "tabernacle," it stands in sharp contrast to the earthly first "tabernacle," whose standing blocked the appearance of the way to the heavenly "holy things" (9:8), the place for heavenly worship.

Not through the "blood" of goats and calves (9:12a) recalls that once a year only the earthly high priest, not without "blood" offers on behalf of himself and of the inadvertent sins of the people (9:7). Through "his own *blood* (9:12a)" refers to the "blood" that Jesus, as a human being, shares with the children God gave him (2:14). "His own" blood stands in contrast to "his own" sins on behalf of which an earthly high priest offers sacrifice (7:27). And "through his own blood" associates Jesus with the one who enters into God's heavenly rest and rests from his works just as God from "his own" works (4:10), the Sabbath rest that includes heavenly worship.

That Jesus "entered" once for all into the heavenly "holy things" (9:12b) resonates with the description of Jesus as our hope, as an anchor of the soul, which "enters" into the interior of the heavenly veil (6:19), where as forerunner on behalf of us Jesus "entered," according to the order of Melchizedek having become high priest forever (6:20). Although the unfaithful and disobedient ancestors failed "to enter" into God's own heavenly rest (3:11, 18, 19; 4:3, 5, 6), the promise "to enter" into that rest still remains for the audience (4:1). Indeed, we who believed are already "entering" into it (4:3). But the question for the audience is how Jesus' entrance into the heavenly "holy things" relates to the exhortation for them to strive "to enter" into God's own heavenly rest to participate in heavenly worship (4:11).

That, as heavenly high priest, Jesus entered "once for all" into the heavenly "holy things" (9:12b) resonates with the assertion that he does not have a necessity, like earthly high priests, to offer up sacrifices first on behalf of his own sins and then of the people, for this he did "once for all" when he offered up himself (7:27). Jesus' entrance into the heavenly "holy things" indicates that the way to the heavenly "holy things," which was blocked while the earthly first tabernacle had standing, has now appeared (9:8). Upon entering once for all into the heavenly "holy things," Jesus found "eternal" redemption (9:12b). This resonates with Jesus becoming for all those who obey him a source of "eternal" salvation (5:9), a salvation that is vital in view of "eternal" judgment (6:2). Jesus' finding of an eternal "redemption" or "ransoming" (*lytrōsin*) coincides with his "freeing" of human beings held in "slavery" by fear of death all their life (2:15).[33] His "finding" of an eternal redemption provides further basis and impetus to the exhortation for the audience, as a worshiping assembly, to approach with boldness the throne of grace, so that we may receive mercy and may "find" grace for timely help (4:16). We may "find" that grace because Jesus, as heavenly high priest, "found" eternal redemption.

Whereas the "blood" of animals, of goats and bulls, makes holy those "defiled" or "made common" (9:13), Jesus joined his brothers and the children God gave him (2:12–13), who "share in" or "have in common" human "blood" and flesh (2:14).[34] That the blood of goats and bulls and the sprinkling of a heifer's ashes "makes holy" those defiled stands in contrast to Jesus as the one who "makes holy" his brothers, his fellow human beings including the audience, who are being "made holy" (2:11). That animal sacrifices make holy those defiled for the cleansing of the "flesh" (9:13) underscores for the audience that, as regulations of the "flesh" imposed until the time of correction (9:10), they do not have the power according to conscience to make perfect for heavenly worship the one offering worship (9:9).

In contrast to the "blood" of goats and bulls (9:13) offered by earthly high priests is the "blood" of the Christ, who through the eternal Spirit offered himself unblemished to God (9:14a). It is through the assistance of the "eternal" Spirit, the Holy Spirit of God, that Jesus found "eternal" redemption (9:12b), and so became a source of "eternal" salvation for all who obey him (5:9), and who will undergo "eternal" judgment (6:2). Although the divine Holy "Spirit" indicated that the way to the heavenly

33. Johnson, *Hebrews*, 236: "The noun *lytron* is literally the price paid for the release of something held by another, thus a 'ransom' or 'redemption'; *lytrōsis*, in turn, is the act of paying such a ransom, thereby accomplishing the liberation of that which is being held."

34. The verbal root in 2:14 is *koinoō* and in 9:13 *koinōneō*, but their meanings overlap; see BDAG, 552.

"holy things" had not appeared while the earthly first tabernacle had standing (9:8), through the divine eternal "Spirit," Jesus, through the heavenly tabernacle (9:11), entered once for all into the heavenly "holy things" for an act of heavenly sacrificial worship on our behalf (9:12a).[35]

That Jesus "offered himself" unblemished to God (9:14a) reinforces the fulfillment of the necessity for him as a high priest to have something which me may "offer" (8:3). It resonates with the assertion that he does not have the necessity, like earthly high priests, first on behalf of his own sins to offer up sacrifices then of the people, for this he did once for all having "offered up himself " (7:27). And that Jesus offered himself "unblemished" (*amōmon*) to God resonates with the assertions that in Jesus we have a high priest who is "undefiled" (7:26) and able to sympathize with our weaknesses as one tested in all things, but "without sin" (4:15), the sin that prevents the heavenly worship of God.[36]

Gifts and sacrifices are "offered" in the earthly tabernacle that are not able according to "conscience" to make perfect for heavenly worship the one "offering worship" (9:9). But the blood of the Christ, who through the eternal Spirit "offered" himself unblemished to God, will cleanse our "conscience" from dead works to "offer worship" to the living God (9:14). In contrast to the blood of goats and bulls and the sprinkling of a heifer's ashes that makes holy those defiled for the "cleansing" of the flesh (9:13), the blood of the Christ "will cleanse" our conscience.

That the blood of the Christ will cleanse our conscience "from dead works," the sinful "dead" works that are incompatible with and make impossible the worship of the "living" God (9:14), recalls that repentance "from dead works" provides a foundation for the audience to bear forward toward the perfection required for heavenly worship and rest (6:1).

---

35. Emmrich, "Amtscharisma"; idem, *Pneumatological Concepts*, 13: "The Spirit is called '*eternal* Spirit' to bring out the (extraordinary) eschatological significance of the Spirit's assistance in Christ's once-for-all priestly action 'at the conclusion of the ages' (9:26). In fact, the agency of the Spirit in Christ's atoning approach becomes part of the 'time of reconstruction' (9:10) mentioned earlier in the discourse." Ellingworth, *Hebrews*, 457: "Hebrews' explicit references to the Holy Spirit (in contrast to those of Paul) are otherwise related to scripture, which may be why the author chooses a different expression here; more probably, the author wishes to relate the Spirit to the redemption of v. 12 and the inheritance of v. 15, both of which are described as 'eternal.'"

36. Lane, *Hebrews 9–13*, 240: "The word *amōmon* has the ring of sacrificial terminology. In the LXX and elsewhere in Jewish hellenistic sources this term denotes the absence of defects in a sacrificial animal. It was chosen to emphasize the perfection of Christ's sacrifice. The sinless high priest (4:15; 7:26) was also the spotless victim."

The cleansing of our conscience from dead works to worship the "living God" recalls the warning lest there be in anyone within the audience an evil heart of unfaithfulness in falling away from the "living God" (3:12).[37] In contrast to the "dead works" that originated with human sinfulness, the "works" of the living God have been produced from the foundation of the world (4:3). That the living God rested from all his "works" on the seventh day of creation (4:4) is the basis for one who enters into God's own heavenly Sabbath rest to rest from his "works" just as did the living God (4:10). A conscience cleansed from dead works enables the audience to offer worship to the living God, reinforcing the exhortation that we strive to enter into God's own heavenly rest (4:11) to participate in heavenly worship.

V. 9:15–23

A [15] And on account of this he is guarantor of a new covenant, so that, a death having occurred for deliverance from transgressions under the first covenant, those who have been called might receive the promise of the eternal inheritance. [16] For where there is a covenant, there is a *necessity* that a death be borne of the one who covenanted. [17] For a covenant on the basis of the dead becomes firm, since it never has strength while the one who covenanted is living. [18] Whence not even the first was inaugurated without blood.

    B [19a] For every commandment having been spoken *according to the law* to all the people by Moses,

        C [19b] taking the blood of the calves and the goats with water and scarlet wool and hyssop, he *sprinkled* both the book itself and all the people,

            D [20] saying, "This is the blood of the covenant which God has commanded to you" (Exod 24:8).

        C' [21] And the tabernacle and all the vessels of the ministry he likewise *sprinkled* with blood.

    B' [22] And almost everything is cleansed by blood *according to the law*, and without the shedding of blood no forgiveness occurs.

---

37. Johnson, *Hebrews*, 238: "In 3:12 readers were warned not to fall 'away from the living God' (*apo theou zōntos*), which neatly matches *apo nekrōn ergōn* [from dead works] in the present passage."

A′ ²³ There was a *necessity* then that the patterns of the things in the heavens be cleansed with these, but the heavenly things themselves with better sacrifices beyond these.

At the conclusion of the preceding unit in 9:11–14 is a reference to the "eternal" Spirit through which Christ offered himself unblemished to God (9:14). At the beginning of this next unit in 9:15–23 is a reference to the promise of the "eternal" inheritance those who have been called might receive (9:15). These occurrences of the term "eternal" thus serve as the transitional words connecting these units as they move the focus from the eternal Spirit to the eternal inheritance.

With regard to the second macrochiastic level, the audience experience a chiastic relationship between the units in 6:13–20 and 9:15–23 provided by the terms "heirs/inheritance" and "firm." In 6:13–20 are references to "the *heirs* of the promise" of God (6:17) and to an anchor of the soul which is "both sure and *firm*" (6:19). In 9:15–23 are references to "the eternal *inheritance*" of God (9:15) and to a covenant becoming "firm" (9:17). And with regard to the third macrochiastic level, this unit in 9:15–23 exhibits a parallel relationship with the unit in 9:1–10. The parallels are indicated by multiple occurrences of the term "covenant." After the central and pivotal unit in 9:11–14, which contains no references to "covenant," the two occurrences of "covenant" in 9:1–10—"the ark of the *covenant*" and "the tablets of the *covenant*" (9:4)—are paralleled by the five occurrences of "covenant" in 9:15–23. They are climaxed by the scriptural reference to "the blood of the *covenant*" (9:20; cf. 9:15, 16, 17).

Because the blood of the Christ, who entered into the heavenly "holy things" (9:12) and offered himself unblemished to God, will cleanse our conscience from dead works to offer worship to the living God (9:14), he is "guarantor" of a "new covenant" (9:15a; cf. 7:22). This reminds the audience that Jesus, as a heavenly high priest, has obtained a more excellent ministry of worship, to the degree that he is "guarantor" of a better "covenant" (8:6). This better covenant is the "new covenant" promised in Jer 38:31–34 by the scriptural voice of God (8:8). In speaking of this "new" covenant, God makes old the first covenant, and what is becoming old and aging is near to disappearing (8:13).[38]

---

38. Lane, *Hebrews 9–13*, 241. According to Johnson, *Hebrews*, 239, Jesus, as "guarantor" or "mediator" (*mesitēs*) of a new covenant, "does not serve simply as one who negotiates externally between two parties. He bears both parties within himself. His

The Levitical priests were many because they were prevented by "death" from remaining on (7:23). But the "death" of Jesus as heavenly high priest, who in the days of his flesh offered both prayers and supplications with strong outcrying and tears to the God able to save him from "death" (5:7), occurred for deliverance from transgressions under the first covenant (9:15b). This reminds the audience that Jesus shared in the blood and flesh of human beings so that through "death" he might destroy the one who has the strength of "death," that is the devil, and free those, as many as by fear of "death" through all their life were held in slavery (2:14–15). After his suffering of "death," so that, by the grace of God, on behalf of all he might taste "death," Jesus was crowned by God with heavenly honor and glory (2:9), thus becoming an object of heavenly worship (1:6, 14).

That the death of Jesus occurred for "deliverance" (9:15b) resonates with his finding "redemption," when he entered once for all into the heavenly "holy things" (9:12) and offered himself unblemished to God (9:14). That his death occurred for deliverance from transgressions under the "first" covenant (9:15b) recalls the "first" covenant with its regulations for offering of worship and an earthly holy place (9:1). This is the "first" covenant that God makes old in speaking of a new covenant (8:13), for which God sought a place because the "first" covenant was not faultless (8:7). And that his death occurred for deliverance from "transgressions" under the first covenant resonates for the audience with the stipulation that under the first covenant every "transgression" and disobedience received a just recompense (2:2) from God and thus rendered one unworthy for the heavenly worship of God.

Jesus, whose death occurred for deliverance from transgressions under the first covenant, is guarantor of a new covenant, so that those who have been called might receive the promise of the eternal inheritance (9:15). Those who have been "called" refers to those, including the audience, whom Jesus, as the one "called" by God to become a heavenly high priest (5:4), is not ashamed to "call" brothers (2:11). As holy brothers, they are thus partners of a heavenly "calling" (3:1), inviting them to participate in heavenly worship. That those who have been called "might receive" the

---

offering of his own blood makes him at once priest and sacrifice. . . . Christ's 'blameless' offering of himself shows, as Jeremiah prophesied, that this covenant is not only 'new' chronologically but ontologically, for it essentially engages the internal dispositions of humans, enabling them to 'know God' (8:11)."

promise of the eternal inheritance resonates with the exhortation for us, as worshipers, to approach with boldness the heavenly throne of grace, so that we "may receive" mercy and may find grace for timely help (4:16).

That those who have been called might receive the promise of the "eternal inheritance" (9:15) resonates with the "eternal redemption" that Jesus as the heavenly high priest found when he entered once for all into the heavenly "holy things" (9:12), and through the "eternal Spirit" offered himself unblemished to God (9:14) in an act of sacrificial worship. The eternal redemption that Jesus found makes it possible for those who have been called to receive the promise of the eternal "inheritance," as those who are going to "inherit salvation" (1:14). This is the "eternal salvation" of which Jesus became a source for all who obey him (5:9), the "salvation" of which he is the initiator (2:10), the very great "salvation" the audience are to be careful not to neglect as a worshiping assembly (2:3).[39]

The "promise" of this eternal "inheritance" that those who have been called might receive (9:15), the inheritance which is eternal salvation (2:10; 5:9), recalls the "promise" that still is left for the audience to enter into the heavenly rest for worship of the eternally living God (4:1).[40] It resonates with the exhortation for the audience to become imitators of those who through faith and patience are "inheriting the promises" (6:12). Having patience, Abraham obtained the "promise" as a model for the audience (6:15). The audience are thus to consider themselves as among the "heirs of the promise" to whom God determined to show the unchangeableness of his plan, as he "guaranteed" it with an oath (6:17). And Jesus, as "heir" of all things (1:2), who through his heavenly enthronement has "inherited" a name beyond the angels (1:4), is "guarantor" of a new covenant, so that those who have been called, among whom are the audience, might receive "the promise of the eternal inheritance" (9:15) and thus take their place in the heavenly worship of God.

By way of further explanation for the audience, where there is a "covenant" (9:16a), whether the first "covenant" or the new "covenant" of which Jesus is the guarantor (9:15), there is a necessity that a death be borne of the one who covenanted (9:16b). The dimension of a "will" or "testament" for inheritance that is connoted by the concept of a "cove-

---

39. Lane, *Hebrews 9–13*, 241: "The promise concerns the enjoyment of eternal salvation."

40. An artful alliteration underlines the close association between "those who have been called" (*keklēmenoi*) and the eternal "inheritance" (*klēronomias*).

nant" now comes into play for the audience.[41] The necessary "death" to be borne is the "death" of Jesus himself, his act of sacrificial worship, which occurred for deliverance from transgressions under the first covenant (9:15). As heavenly high priest, Jesus does not have a "necessity," like the earthly Levitical high priests, first on behalf of his own sins, to offer up sacrifices then of the people, for this he did once for all having offered up himself (7:27). But there is the "necessity" that a death, his own death, be borne by him as the one who covenanted (9:16b) a new covenant of which he is guarantor (9:15). This accords with the "necessity" of a change in law, when there is a change from an earthly to a heavenly priesthood (7:12).

His own death is "borne" by Jesus (9:16b), the divine Son who "bears" up all things by the pronouncement of God's power (1:3). This "bearing" of his own death by Jesus reinforces the exhortation that we "bear" forward toward the perfection this death makes available to us for our role in heavenly worship (6:1). That Jesus, the heavenly divine Son and high priest, bore his own death as the one who "covenanted" (9:16b) explicates how he is guarantor of a new covenant as a "will" or "testament," so that those called might receive the eternal inheritance (9:15). Jesus as the one who "covenanted" a new covenant of which he is guarantor thus coincides with God as the one who promised a new covenant that "I will covenant" with the people of God (8:10), among whom are the audience.[42]

That a "covenant" on the basis of the "dead" becomes firm (9:17a) further explains the necessity for Jesus to bear his own "death," and thus become one of the "dead," as the one who "covenanted" (9:16), so that he is guarantor of a new covenant (9:15). But the generalizing plural in the phrase "on the basis of the *dead*" also resonates with the result of this self-

---

41. Allen, *Deuteronomy*, 180–81: "Hebrews is engaging in some form of word play in 9:15-17; there is some development from 'covenant' (v15) to 'covenant-testament' (vv16-17) and back to 'covenant' (v18) that permits Hebrews to illustrate its argument. The wordplay, however, remains thematically consistent with the overall Sinai covenant discourse and similarly does not require a move to another semantic domain; *diathēkē*-as-covenant-testament is merely one element of the Sinai covenant narrative in which Hebrews is interested, namely the precedent for a transfer of Mosaic authority. No tangential argument is being made.... Hebrews' wordplay in 9:16-17 invites the scenario of a *diathēkē* that is both covenantal *and* testamentary, both cultic *and* hereditary." See also Murray, "Concept of *diathēkē*"; Johnson, *Hebrews*, 240–41.

42. Koester, *Hebrews*, 418: "Although God promised the new covenant (8:10), Jesus is the testator who dies."

sacrificial death of Jesus in cleansing our conscience from "dead" works, the "dead" works from which we are to repent (6:1), so that we may offer worship to the living God (9:14). As a reference to the new covenant, that a covenant on the basis of the "dead" becomes firm reminds the audience of the "dead" who are to be raised (6:2).

That the new covenant on the basis of the self-sacrificial death Jesus offered upon entering into the heavenly tabernacle (9:11–14) becomes "firm" (9:17a) reinforces the hope we have in Jesus as an anchor of the soul, both sure and "firm." It enters into the interior of the heavenly veil (6:19), where as forerunner on behalf of us Jesus entered as the eternal high priest (6:20). It bolsters the exhortation for the audience's perseverance. To become partners of the Christ, we must hold the beginning of the reality "firm" until the end (3:14), inspired by the authoritative "firmness" of this new covenant that resonates with the word spoken by God through angels that became "firm" (2:2), and with the great salvation spoken through the Lord and divinely "confirmed" for us by those who heard (2:3).

It was necessary for Jesus to bear his own death as the one who "covenanted" (9:16b), and thus became guarantor of a new covenant (9:15), since no covenant, but specifically this new covenant, has strength while the one who "covenanted" is living (9:17b). The new covenant "has strength," then, because of the self-sacrificial death of Jesus. Such "strength" bolsters the exhortation for the audience to have a "strong" encouragement to hold fast to the hope lying ahead (6:18), the hope that Jesus himself represents as a sure and "firm" anchor of the soul, because of offering himself when he entered into the interior of the heavenly veil as heavenly high priest (6:19–20). And such "strength" is the result of the self-sacrificial death of Jesus as the eternal high priest, who in the days of his flesh offered both prayers and supplications with "strong" outcrying and tears to the God able to save him from death, and he was heard from his reverence (5:7). In other words, the new covenant "has strength" because of the "strong" offering of Jesus as heavenly high priest.

The new covenant did not have strength while Jesus, as the one who covenanted, was "living" (9:17b), that is, living with human beings who through all their "life," their earthly "living," were held in slavery by fear of death (2:15). But as the eternal, heavenly high priest according to the order of Melchizedek who goes on "living" (7:8), Jesus is able to save completely those who approach God through him, always "living" to intercede on behalf of them (7:25). Through his self-sacrificial death Jesus enables the audience, who are to heed the "living" word of God (4:12), to offer worship to the "living" God (9:14), rather than falling away and failing to enter into the heavenly, Sabbath rest and worship of the eternally "living" God (3:12).

After the assertion that Jesus is guarantor of a "new" covenant, whose death occurred for deliverance from transgressions under the "first" covenant (9:15), the attention of the audience is drawn to that first covenant with the statement that not even the "first" was "inaugurated" without blood (9:18). The focus thus moves from the deaths (9:15–17) to the sacrificial blood involved in covenant making. That not even the first covenant was inaugurated "without blood" recalls that into the second tabernacle once a year only the earthly Levitical high priest enters, not "without blood" which he offers on behalf of himself and of the inadvertent sins of the people (9:7). But as the heavenly high priest, Christ entered the heavenly "holy things" not through the "blood" of goats and calves but through his own "blood" (9:12). If the "blood" of goats and bulls and the sprinkling of a heifer's ashes makes holy those defiled for the cleansing of the flesh (9:13), even more will the sacrificial "blood" of the Christ cleanse our conscience from dead works to offer worship to the living God (9:14).

The audience have heard that it was not through the blood of "goats" and "calves" but through his own blood that Jesus entered once for all into the heavenly "holy things," finding eternal redemption (9:12). For the blood of "goats" and bulls and the "sprinkling" of a heifer's ashes makes holy those defiled for the cleansing of the flesh only (9:13). And now they hear that when Moses inaugurated the first covenant, he took the blood of the "calves" and the "goats" along with water and scarlet and hyssop and "sprinkled" both the book that contained every commandment of the law and all the people to whom every commandment was spoken by Moses (9:19).[43] The audience are then reminded of the words from Exod 24:8

---

43. Koester, *Hebrews*, 419: "The author seems to conflate details from various rituals. Hyssop was a plant that was used to daub blood on the doorposts at Passover (Exod 12:22) and as a flail for purification (Ps 51:7). Hyssop, scarlet material, and water were used in the cleansing of lepers (Lev 14:4–6, 49–52) and in the rite of the red heifer that purified those defiled by contact with a corpse (Num 19:1–10, 17–18; cf. Heb 9:13). . . . Exodus and Hebrews agree that blood was spattered upon the people but where Exod 24:6 says that blood was poured on the *altar*, Hebrews says that Moses spattered blood upon the *book*. For Hebrews, the Law and sacrifices are inseparable. 'The book' presumably included the Ten Commandments (Exod 20:1–17) and the covenant code

that Moses pronounced when he sprinkled the blood on both the book of the law and all the people: "This is the blood of the covenant which God has commanded to you" (9:20). That "this," that is, the "blood" of the calves and of the goats (9:19b), is the "blood" of the covenant provides the audience with scriptural confirmation that not even the first covenant was inaugurated without "blood" (9:18). And that this is the blood of the covenant that God has "commanded" to you reminds the audience that every "commandment" that Moses spoke according to the law to all the people (9:19a) was commanded by God himself.[44]

"The tabernacle" that Moses sprinkled with blood (9:21) refers to "the tabernacle" on earth about which Moses, in completing it, was warned in Exod 25:40 to make everything according to the model shown to him by God on the heavenly mountain (8:5). That Moses likewise sprinkled all the vessels of the "ministry" for earthly worship reminds the audience that Jesus, as the heavenly high priest, has obtained a more excellent "ministry" for heavenly worship (8:6). The "blood" with which Moses sprinkled the earthly tabernacle and the vessels for the ministry of worship is the "blood" of the covenant (9:20), the sacrificial "blood" of the calves and the goats (9:19). It presents the audience with a sharp contrast to Jesus' own "blood" through which he entered once for all into the heavenly tabernacle (9:12) to perform his act of self-sacrificial worship as the heavenly high priest.

Not only "all" the people (9:19) and "all" the vessels of the ministry that Moses sprinkled with blood (9:21), but almost "everything" is cleansed by blood according to the law (9:22). That no forgiveness of sins "without the shedding of blood" (*haimatekchysias*) occurs (9:22) presents the audience with an emphatic intensification of the assertion that not even the first covenant was inaugurated "without blood" (9:18). Indeed, once a year only the high priest enters into the earthly tabernacle, not "without blood" which he offers on behalf of himself and of the inadvertent sins of the people (9:7).[45] This shifts the focus of the audience

---

(Exod 21:1–23:33)." See also Attridge, *Hebrews*, 257; Johnson, *Hebrews*, 241.

44. On how the quotation of Exod 24:8 in Heb 9:20 differs from the LXX, see Attridge, *Hebrews*, 257–58. He adds: "The use of *toutou* may indicate the influence of the eucharistic words of institution" (cf. Matt 26:28; Mark 14:24; Luke 22:20: 1 Cor 11:24–25). See also Ellingworth, *Hebrews*, 469.

45. Lane, *Hebrews 9–13*, 246. On *haimatekchysia*, Ellingworth, *Hebrews*, 474, notes that "this is the first extant occurrence of this term. Scholars disagree about whether it

from the cleansing with sprinkled blood to the basis for it in the sacrificial shedding of blood. Forgiveness of sins occurs with the shedding of blood and everything is "cleansed" by blood, a "cleansing" of the flesh only (9:13). This reminds the audience that the blood of the Christ, who through the eternal Spirit offered himself unblemished to God, having made a "cleansing" for sins (1:3), "will cleanse" our conscience from sinful dead works to offer worship to the living God (9:14).[46]

There was a necessity that the "patterns" of the things "in the heavens," that is, "in the heavens" where the high priest Jesus sat at the right of the throne of the divine Majesty (8:1), be "cleansed" with these (9:23a), with the items, especially the blood of the animals (9:19–21), by which everything is "cleansed" (9:22).[47] This resonates with what the audience have heard about the worship offered by earthly priests, namely, that they offer worship in merely a "pattern" and shadow of the "heavenly things" (8:5), the "heavenly things" which are to be cleansed with better sacrifices beyond these animal sacrifices (9:23b).

That there is a necessity for the heavenly things themselves to be cleansed with "better" sacrifices (9:23), which points to the self-sacrifice of Jesus as a "better" sacrifice, adds to what the audience have heard regarding the "better" things associated with Jesus. He has become so far "better" than the angels to the degree that more excellent beyond them he has inherited a name (1:4). He represents a "better" hope through which we, as worshipers, are drawing near to God (7:19). He has become the surety of a "better" covenant (7:22). And he is guarantor of a "better" covenant, which on the basis of "better" promises was given law (8:6).

The audience were informed that every high priest is appointed to offer both gifts and "sacrifices" on behalf of sins (5:1; 8:3). But the gifts and "sacrifices" offered in the earthly tabernacle are not able according to conscience to make perfect the one offering worship (9:9). The heav-

---

is coined by the author. . . . There are many OT references to the pouring out of blood in sacrifice on or around the altar. It is the cultic act of applying the blood to the altar, rather than directly the killing of the victim, which is crucial, but in OT ritual the two are closely associated, and in the death of Christ they coincide. Here there is possible a distant allusion to the eucharistic tradition." Note the references to "shedding" or "pouring out" (*ekchynnomenon*) of blood in Matt 26:28; Mark 14:24; Luke 22:20.

46. Wiid, "Testamental Significance"; Lincoln, "Hebrews 9:15–22"; Hahn, "Broken Covenant"; idem, "Covenant."

47. According to Attridge, *Hebrews*, 261, "these" (*toutois*) is "a disparaging reference to the animals' blood and purifying implements listed in vs 19."

enly high priest Jesus, however, does not have a necessity, like the earthly high priests, first on behalf of his own sins to offer up "sacrifices" then of the people, for this he did once for all having offered up himself (7:27). And so, that there is a necessity for the heavenly things themselves to be cleansed with better "sacrifices" than these animal sacrifices (9:23) prepares the audience to hear more about the better sacrifice Jesus offered as heavenly high priest.

VI. 9:24-28

A ^{24a} For *Christ* did not enter into "holy things" made by hands, a copy of the true ones, but into heaven itself,

    B ^{24b} *now* to be *manifested* (*emphanisthēnai*) in the presence of God on behalf of us.

        C ^{25a} Not that *repeatedly* he might offer himself,

            D ^{25b} just as the high priest enters into "the holy things" each year with blood not his own,

        C′ ^{26a} since then it would be necessary for him *repeatedly* to suffer from the founding of the world.

    B′ ^{26b} But *now* once at the completion of the ages for the removal of sin through his sacrifice he has *appeared* (*pephanerōtai*).

A′ ^{27} And just as it is appointed for men to die once, and after this judgment, ^{28} so also the *Christ* offered once "to offer up the sins of many" (Isa 53:12), a second time without sin will be seen, by those eagerly awaiting him, for salvation.

At the conclusion of the preceding unit in 9:15-23 are references to "the things in the *heavens*" and "the *heavenly things* themselves" (9:23). At the beginning of this next unit in 9:24-28 is a reference to "*heaven* itself" (9:24). These occurrences of terms for "heaven" thus serve as the transitional words connecting these units as they move the focus from the earthly to the heavenly location of sacrificial worship.

With regard to the second macrochiastic level, the audience experience a chiastic relationship between the unit in 5:11—6:12 and this one in 9:24-28 provided by the term "salvation." In 5:11—6:12 is a reference to the better things having to do with "salvation" (6:9). And in 9:24-28 is the assertion that Christ will be seen a second time for "salvation" (9:28). And with regard to the third macrochiastic level, this unit in 9:24–28 exhibits a parallel relationship with the unit in 8:7–13. The parallels are indicated by occurrences of the term for "sins." In 8:7–13 is the promise of God in Jer 38:34 that "the *sins* of them I will certainly remember no longer" (8:12). And in 9:24–28 are the assertions that Christ "now once at the completion of the ages for the removal of *sin* through his sacrifice has appeared" (9:26) and that "the Christ offered once 'to offer up the *sins* of many' (Isa 53:12), a second time without *sin* will be seen" (9:28).

The audience have heard that when Christ came as high priest of the good things that have come to be, through the greater and more perfect tabernacle not "made by hands," that is, not of this creation (9:11), he "entered" once for all into the heavenly "holy things" (9:12). And now they hear that Christ did not "enter" into "holy things" "made by hands," a copy of the true ones, but into heaven itself (9:24a). That the earthly holy things made by hands are a mere copy of the "true" heavenly holy things reminds the audience that Christ is a minister of the holy things and of the tabernacle, the "true" one, which the Lord, not man, set up (8:2). The earthly holy things are a mere "copy" or "antitype" of the heavenly holy things, because God told Moses to make everything in the earthly tabernacle according to the "model" or "type" shown to him on the heavenly mountain (8:5).[48] That Christ entered into "heaven" itself (9:24a) resonates with the necessity that the "heavenly" things themselves be cleansed with better sacrifices than those employed to cleanse the earthly patterns of the things in the "heavens" (9:23). It recalls that in Christ we have a high priest who sat at the right of the throne of the divine Majesty in the "heavens" (8:1), who is higher than the "heavens" (7:26), who has passed through the "heavens" (4:14), and the works of whose hands are the "heavens" (1:10).

That Christ "entered" into heaven itself to be manifested in the very presence of, literally before the "face" of, God himself "on behalf of us" (9:24b) reminds the audience that it was into the heavenly interior of the veil (6:19) that Jesus "entered" as forerunner "on behalf of us," according

---

48. Koester, *Hebrews*, 421: "The Tabernacle was the earthly 'antitype' of the heavenly 'type'. . . . God commanded Moses to make the earthly tent (Heb 8:5), but the contrasts between heaven and earth, and the pejorative 'made with hands' imply that it was inferior to its heavenly type."

to the order of Melchizedek having become high priest forever (6:20).[49] Because Jesus remains forever and has the priesthood that is permanent (7:24), he is able to save completely those, among whom are the audience, who approach God in worship through him, always living to intercede "on behalf of them" (7:25).[50]

As high priest Christ entered into the heavenly "holy things" not that he might "repeatedly" "offer" "himself" (9:25a), like the rains that come upon the earth "repeatedly" (6:7). This reminds the audience that Christ, who did not glorify "himself" in becoming high priest (5:5), does not have every day a necessity, like the earthly high priests, first on behalf of his own sins to "offer up" sacrifices then of the people, for this he did once for all having "offered up" "himself" (7:27). Indeed, the blood of the Christ, who through the eternal Spirit "offered" "himself" unblemished to God, in contrast to the earthly high priest who "offers" merely on behalf of "himself" (9:7), will cleanse our conscience from dead works to offer worship to the living God (9:14).

In contrast to Christ, who did not "enter" into the "holy things" made by hands but into heaven itself (9:24), not that repeatedly he might offer himself (9:25a), the Levitical high priest "enters" into the "holy things" on earth each year. That he enters "each year" with "blood" not his own (9:25b) reminds the audience that into the earthly tabernacle enters "once a year" the high priest, not without "blood" which he offers on behalf of himself and of the inadvertent sins of the people (9:7). And that the earthly high priest enters each year with blood "not his own" stands in keen contrast to Christ's entrance into heaven to offer "himself" in an act of self-sacrificial worship as the heavenly high priest.

The notion of Christ repeatedly offering himself (9:25a) presents the audience with a glaring absurdity. It would be necessary for him repeatedly to "suffer" from the founding of the world (9:26a), as the divine Son who learned from the things he "suffered" obedience (5:8), and as the merciful and faithful high priest who "suffered" in being tested like his

---

49. On the verb "to be manifested" (*emphanisthēnai*) in 9:24b, Westcott, *Hebrews*, 272, notes that it "conveys the thought of that being made a clear object of sight, which under ordinary circumstances is not so."

50. Mitchell, *Hebrews*, 194: "In the LXX people come 'before the face of God' in a worship setting." Koester, *Hebrews*, 422: "The Hebrew expression 'appear before the face of God' referred to people coming to the sanctuary. In the LXX seeking God's face meant seeking help in prayer and seeing God's face meant receiving favor from God. This sense is appropriate here."

fellow human beings (2:18). For Christ repeatedly to suffer "from the founding of the world" would be a ridiculous necessity, as it would mean his suffering, as the one through whom God made the ages (1:2), from the time the works of creation were produced, that is, "from the founding of the world" when time began (4:3).[51]

Christ entered into heaven itself "now" to be manifested in the presence of God on behalf of us (9:24b) for the removal of sin through his sacrifice "now" that he has appeared at the completion of the ages (9:26b). Instead of repeatedly offering himself (9:25a) and repeatedly suffering from the founding of the world (9:26a), Christ "once" at the completion of the "ages," the "ages" made through him, the divine Son in whom God has spoken to us at the end of these days (1:2), for the removal of sin has appeared. This is in contrast to the earthly high priest, who "once" a year offers on behalf of himself and of the inadvertent sins of the people (9:7). That Christ has appeared for the "removal" of sin resonates with the need for the "removal" of a former commandment because of its weakness and uselessness (7:18).

Christ's "sacrifice" of himself in heaven through which was the removal of sin (9:26b) serves as the preeminent example of the better "sacrifices" necessary to cleanse the heavenly things themselves (9:23). It provides the alternative for the earthly "sacrifices" that are not able according to conscience to make perfect for heavenly worship the one offering worship (9:9). It satisfies the necessity for Christ as a high priest to have something to offer, since every high priest is appointed to offer both gifts and "sacrifices" (8:3), that is, "sacrifices" for sins (5:1). And it reinforces for the audience that Christ does not have every day a necessity, like the earthly high priests, first on behalf of his own sins to offer up "sacrifices" then of the people, for this he did once for all having offered up himself (7:27) in an act of high priestly worship in heaven.

The Christ who entered into heaven itself now to be "manifested" in the presence of God on behalf of us (9:24), now at the completion of the ages for the removal of sin through his sacrifice has "appeared" on earth (9:26b). This "appearance" of Christ indicates that the way to the heavenly

---

51. Ellingworth, *Hebrews*, 484: "[T]he author does not distinguish between the creation of the universe and that of the human race." Koester, *Hebrews*, 422: "The author assumes that the Son of God existed from the foundation of the world (1:2) when God's works were completed (4:3). He also assumes that sin has been in the world virtually since its founding, so that human beings have needed atonement since primeval times."

"holy things," which the Holy Spirit indicated had not "appeared" while the earthly tabernacle had standing (9:9), has now appeared on earth for the benefit of the audience as a worshiping assembly.[52]

That it is appointed for men to die "once" (9:27a), and after this judgment (9:27b) for eternity (cf. 6:2), so that the Christ was offered "once" (9:28a), corresponds to his appearance "once" at the completion of the ages for the removal of sin through his self-sacrifice (9:26b). That it is appointed for "men" to "die" once recalls for the audience that, in contrast to "men" who "die," the priest Melchizedek goes on living forever (7:8). And it is according to the order of Melchizedek that Christ is a high priest forever (5:6; 6:20; 7:17).

That the "Christ," the "Christ" who entered into heaven itself, now to be manifested in the presence of God on behalf of us (9:24), was "offered" once (9:28a) corresponds to the necessity that he not repeatedly "offer" himself (9:25a). With an alliterative allusion to Isa 53:12, it is explained that he was "offered" (*prosenechtheis*) once to take upon himself and "offer up" (*anenegkein*) the sins of many (9:28b). This recalls that he does not have a necessity, like earthly high priests, first on behalf of his own sins to "offer up" sacrifices then of the people, for this he did once for all having "offered up" himself (7:27).

This elaborates for the audience Christ's appearance for the removal of "sin" through his sacrifice (9:26b). It is the removal of the "sins" of "many," which recalls God's plan to lead "many" sons into heavenly glory (2:10), but includes the sins of all people, as "many" can be considered virtually equivalent to "all" (cf. 2:9: "on behalf of *all* he might taste death").[53] This removal of "sin" reminds the audience of the last time they heard about "sin," as it serves to fulfill God's promise from Jer 38:34 that "the *sins* of them I will certainly remember no longer" (8:12). The Christ, who as high priest was "separated from sinners" (7:26) and was "without

---

52. Attridge, *Hebrews*, 265: "The 'manifestation' of Christ in his sacrificial death is the point at which another manifestation or revelation occurs, the opening of the 'way' of access to the 'sanctuary' where God is truly present." Ellingworth, *Hebrews*, 485: "Christ's appearance makes possible believers' access to God. The context requires a reference to Christ's appearance on earth for the sake of humanity, not his appearance in heaven (already mentioned in v. 24)."

53. Ellingworth, *Hebrews*, 487: "Reference to the 'many' is not to be understood as limiting the effects of Christ's sacrifice to those who accept it in faith. The implied contrast . . . is rather between the one sacrifice and the great number of those who benefit from it."

sin" (4:15), has appeared on earth for the removal of "sin" through his sacrifice (9:26b). He will be seen a second time on earth "without sin," that is, not only without his own sin but without the sins of all sinners, by those eagerly awaiting him, including the audience, for salvation (9:28b).[54]

That Christ will be seen by those eagerly awaiting him a second time for "salvation" (9:28b) resonates with the last time the audience heard about "salvation"—the author's disclosure that "we are confident concerning you, beloved, of better things, indeed those having to do with *salvation*" (6:9). It recalls that Christ, the initiator of their "salvation" (2:10), became for all of those who obey him, among whom the audience are to include themselves, a source of eternal "salvation" (5:9). And it reinforces the exhortation for the audience, as those who have the hope of inheriting "salvation" (1:14), not to neglect so great a "salvation" (2:3), the salvation that motivates and inspires their worship, as they await the final fulfillment of this great salvation when Christ comes a second time.

Conclusion

I. Jesus' divinely authoritative seat as high priest at the right of the Majesty in the heavens (8:1) positions and empowers him for his high priestly role as cultic minister of the holy things, the things involved in the heavenly worship (8:2a) in which the audience are being invited to participate. Jesus is a minister of the tent or tabernacle, *the* true one, that is the place of heavenly worship, which the Lord, not a human being, erected (8:2b). Since every high priest is appointed to offer both gifts and sacrifices, it is necessary that Jesus as a high priest have something that he may offer (8:3). But if he would be on earth, he would not be a priest, there being those who offer the gifts according to a law (8:4). That those on earth offer worship only in a pattern and shadow of the heavenly things (8:5a) deepens the audience's appreciation that they are those who have already tasted of the heavenly gift (6:4), and who are partners of a heavenly calling (3:1), those who are called to participate in heavenly worship.

The tabernacle for worship to be completed by Moses, whom the scriptural voice of God warned in Exod 25:40 to see to it that he make everything according to the model shown to him by God on the moun-

---

54. Ibid.: "Despite the author's insistence up to now on the once-for-all nature of Christ's sacrifice, he believes that Christ will appear a second time; but his return, unlike his first coming, will have nothing to do with atonement for sin."

tain, is merely an earthly correspondence to what is in heaven (8:5b). This continues the separation from and superiority of the heavenly high priest Jesus with regard to Moses. Whereas Moses was faithful in all God's house (3:2, 5), Jesus was considered worthy of even greater glory beyond Moses as the heavenly enthroned divine Son over God's house of worship, as an object of heavenly worship by the audience as the worshiping household of Christ (3:6). The audience are to appreciate that whereas the people were given law on the basis of the imperfect Levitical priesthood (7:11), Jesus, as heavenly high priest, is guarantor of a better covenant, which on the basis of better promises was given law (8:6). This sets up a new cultic system for the heavenly worship in which the audience are being called to participate.

II. That the first covenant was not faultless, so that God sought a place for a second (8:7) is reinforced for the audience with the reference to God finding fault with "them," that is, with those with whom he made the first covenant (8:8a). Consequently, as God says in pronouncing the promise from the quotation of Jer 38:31–34, "Behold days are coming, says the Lord, when I will complete with the house of Israel and with the house of Judah a new covenant" (8:8). This promised new covenant will not be in accord with the covenant God made with their fathers on that past day of his taking hold of their hand to lead them out of the land of Egypt (8:9). That God led them out of Egypt reminds the audience that those who came out of Egypt through Moses rebelled against God (3:16), disqualifying them to participate in the heavenly rest and worship of God. According to this new covenant, God will give his laws into their mind and "upon their hearts I will inscribe them" (8:10a). The audience are thus attracted to what this new covenant can do in their own hearts, so that not anyone of them will have an evil heart of unfaithfulness causing them to fall away from the heavenly worship of the living God who offers them eternal life (3:12).

The audience are among the people regarding whom God now promises in this new covenant that "I will be to them as God, and they will be to me as people" (8:10). They will be God's own people as a consequence of God's promise to Jesus that "he will be to me as Son" (1:5), since, as the heavenly enthroned divine Son, Jesus is also the eternal high priest of the people of God (7:28—8:6), who makes possible their participation in heavenly worship. In this new covenant all of the people of God from small to great will know the Lord (8:11) as a God who will be merciful to the wrongdoings of them and the sins of them he will certainly remember no longer (8:12), the sins that prevent them from playing their role in the heavenly worship. The audience are to appreciate how the covenantal promise of God that "the sins of them I will certainly remember no longer" (8:12) is based on the definitive self-sacrifice of Jesus, his act of heavenly worship as the divinely enthroned Son and eternal high priest. And the audience are to deepen their appreciation for what this new covenant, which supplants the old and aging one that is near to disappearing (8:13), promises for them as a worshiping assembly.

III. The earthly holy place for sacrificial worship that the covenant, the first, had (9:1) is further described as a tabernacle, the first (9:2). This pointed designation closely associates this first tabernacle with the faulty first covenant that is becoming old, aging, and near to disappearing (8:13). This first tabernacle is said by God to be "holy things," since it contains the lampstand and the table and the presentation of the loaves as the "holy things" furnished by God for sacrificial worship (9:2). And behind the second veil, analogous to the second covenant coming after the faulty first covenant (8:7), is a tabernacle which is said by God to be "holy things of holy things" (9:3). It contained a golden altar of incense and the ark of the covenant covered on all sides with gold, in which were a golden jar having the manna and the staff of Aaron that sprouted and the tablets of the covenant, and above it the cherubim of glory overshadowing the place of expiation for the sins which prevent proper worship (9:4–5). The staff of Aaron recalls that Jesus arose as a different priest, not according to the order of Aaron (7:11), although he was called by God to be a priest, just as was Aaron (5:4).

Whereas into the first tabernacle continually go the priests completing the offerings of worship (9:6), into the second once a year only goes the high priest (9:7a). This is the tabernacle analogously associated with the new, second covenant God sought to replace the old and aging first one (8:7). As high priest he goes not without blood, which he offers on behalf of himself and of the inadvertent sins of the people (9:7b). That the way to the heavenly holy things had not appeared while the first tabernacle had standing (9:8) resonates with the fact that the analogous first covenant was not faultless, so that for a second one God sought a place (8:7). The gifts and sacrifices being offered under the first covenant are not able according to conscience to make perfect for heavenly worship the one offering worship (9:9), since they are offered only on the basis of foods and drinks and various baptisms (9:10a). These are regulations of the flesh imposed until the time of correction or setting things right (9:10b). That time has arrived when the first covenant and its analogous first tabernacle are becoming old, aging, and near to disappearing, because of the arrival of the new covenant promised by God (8:13), the new covenant with its regulations not for earthly but for heavenly worship.

IV. That the greater and more perfect tabernacle through which Jesus as high priest has come is not made by hands means that it is heavenly and thus not of this earthly creation (9:11). It stands in sharp contrast to the earthly first tabernacle, whose standing blocked the appearance of the way to the heavenly "holy things" (9:8), the place for heavenly worship. Not through the blood of goats and calves but through his own blood Jesus entered once for all into the heavenly holy things, finding eternal redemption (9:12). His finding of an eternal redemption further motivates the exhortation for the audience, as a worshiping assembly, to approach with boldness the throne of grace, so that we may receive mercy and may find grace for timely help (4:16). We may find that grace because Jesus, in his act of worship as heavenly high priest, found eternal redemption. That animal sacrifices make holy those defiled for the cleansing of the flesh (9:13) underscores for the audience that, as regulations of the flesh imposed until the time of correction (9:10), they do not have the power according to conscience to make perfect for heavenly worship the one offering worship (9:9). But the blood of the Christ, who through the eternal Spirit offered himself unblemished to God, will cleanse our conscience from the dead works of sin to offer worship to the living God (9:14).

V. Jesus is guarantor of a new covenant, so that those who have been called, among whom are the audience, might receive the promise of the eternal inheritance (9:15) and thus take their place in the heavenly worship of God. Where there is a covenant (9:16a), whether the first covenant or the new covenant of which Jesus is the guarantor (9:15), there is a necessity that a death be borne of the one who covenanted (9:16b). The necessary death to be borne is the death of Jesus himself, his act of sacrificial worship, which occurred for deliverance from transgressions under the first covenant (9:15). That Jesus, the heavenly divine Son and high priest, bore his own death as the one who covenanted (9:16b) explicates how he is guarantor of a new covenant as a will or testament, so that those called might receive the eternal inheritance (9:15). And that a covenant on the basis of the dead becomes firm (9:17a) further explains the necessity for Jesus to bear his own death, since no covenant, but specifically this new covenant, has strength while the one who covenanted is living (9:17b).

When Moses inaugurated the first covenant, he took the blood of the calves and the goats along with water and scarlet and hyssop and sprinkled both the book that contained every commandment of the law and all the people to whom every commandment was spoken by Moses (9:19). Moses then pronounced the words from Exod 24:8 when he sprinkled the blood: "This is the blood of the covenant which God has commanded to you" (9:20). That "this," that is, the blood of the calves and of the goats (9:19b), is the blood of the covenant provides the scriptural confirmation that not even the first covenant was inaugurated without blood (9:18). The blood of the covenant with which Moses sprinkled the earthly tabernacle and the vessels for the ministry of worship (9:21) is the sacrificial blood of the calves and the goats (9:19). It sharply contrasts Jesus' own blood through which he entered once for all into the heavenly tabernacle (9:12) to perform his act of self-sacrificial worship as the heavenly high priest.

Forgiveness of the sins that prevent worship occurs with the shedding of blood and everything is cleansed by blood (9:22), a cleansing of the flesh only (9:13). This recalls that the blood of the Christ, having made a cleansing for sins (1:3), will cleanse our conscience from sinful dead works to offer heavenly worship to the living God (9:14). That there is a necessity for the heavenly things themselves to be cleansed with better sacrifices than these animal sacrifices (9:23) prepares the audience to hear more about the better sacrifice Jesus offered as heavenly high priest.

VI. Christ did not enter into holy things made by hands, a copy of the true ones, but into heaven itself (9:24a), resonating with the necessity that the heavenly things themselves be cleansed with better sacrifices than those employed to cleanse the earthly patterns of the things in the heavens (9:23). That Christ entered into heaven itself to be manifested in the very presence of God on behalf of us (9:24b) recalls that it was into the heavenly interior of the veil (6:19) that Jesus entered as forerunner on behalf of us (6:20). As high priest Christ entered into the heavenly holy things not that he might repeatedly offer himself (9:25a), in contrast to the Levitical high priest who enters into the holy things on earth each year with blood not his own (9:25b).

Instead of repeatedly offering himself (9:25a) and repeatedly suffering from the founding of the world (9:26a), Christ once at the completion of the ages for the removal of sin has appeared (9:26b). His self-sacrifice for the removal of sin (9:26b) serves as the preeminent example of the better sacrifices necessary to cleanse the heavenly things themselves (9:23). This appearance of Christ indicates that the way to the heavenly "holy things" has now appeared on earth for the benefit of the audience as a worshiping assembly. That it is appointed for men to die once, and after this judgment (9:27) for eternity, so Christ was offered once (9:28a) in accord with his appearance once at the completion of the ages for the removal of sin through his self-sacrifice (9:26b). With an allusion to Isa 53:12, it is explained that Christ was offered once to take upon himself and offer up the sins of many (9:28b). Christ will be seen a second time on earth without sin, that is, not only without his own sin but without the sins of all sinners, by those eagerly awaiting him for salvation (9:28b). This reinforces the exhortation for the audience not to neglect the great salvation (2:3) that motivates and inspires their worship.

5

Hebrews 10:1—11:19

I. 10:1-14

A ¹⁰:¹ *For* the law, having a shadow of the good things to come, not the image itself of the things, each year with the same sacrifices, which they offer for all time, *never is able* those who approach to *make perfect*. ² Otherwise, would they not have ceased to be offered, because *those* offering worship, once having been cleansed, would have had no further consciousness of sins? ³ But in those same (sacrifices) there is remembrance of sins each year. ⁴ *For* it is impossible for the blood of bulls and goats to take away sins.

> **B** ⁵ Therefore entering into the world, he *says*, "Sacrifice and offering *you did not want*, but a *body* you provided for me. ⁶ *Holocausts and sin offerings you took no pleasure in*. ⁷ *Then I said*, '*Behold I have come*, as in the scroll of the book it is written concerning me, *to do*, O God, *your will*'" (Ps 39:7–9).

> **B′** ⁸ *Saying* above, "*Sacrifices and offerings and holocausts and sin offerings you did not want nor take pleasure in*," which according to a law are offered, ⁹ *then he said*, "*Behold I have come to do your will*." He does away with the first, that he might establish the second, ¹⁰ in which will we have been made holy through the offering of the *body* of Jesus Christ once for all.

A′ ¹¹ And every priest stands each day ministering and offering repeatedly the same sacrifices, which *are never able* to cast off sins. ¹² But this one, on behalf of sins one sacrifice having offered *for all time*, sat at the right of God, ¹³ henceforth waiting until his enemies are placed as a footstool for his feet (Ps 109:1). *14 For by one offering he has made perfect for all time those* who are being made holy.

Toward the conclusion of the preceding unit in 9:24–28 is a reference to the singular "sacrifice" of Christ through which is the removal of sin (9:26). At the beginning of this next unit in 10:1–14 is a reference to the yearly "sacrifices" offered by the high priests on earth (10:1). These occurrences of terms for "sacrifice" thus serve as the transitional words connecting these units as they move the focus from the one sacrifice of Christ as the heavenly high priest to the many sacrifices offered by the Levitical priests on earth.

That the law has only a "shadow" of the good things to come (10:1) reminds the audience that the priests on earth offer worship in only a pattern and "shadow" of the heavenly things (8:5). Whereas the law has only a shadow of the "good things" "to come," resonating with "the powers of the age *to come*" (6:5) and with "the heavenly world, the one *coming*" (2:5), Christ has come as high priest of the "good things" that have come to be (9:11). That the law has only a shadow of the good things to come, not the image itself of the "things" (10:1), recalls the unchangeable "things" of God that give the audience, as a worshiping assembly, a strong encouragement to hold fast to the hope lying ahead (6:18).

Although earthly priests "each year" "offer" the same animal sacrifices (10:1), recalling that the high priest enters into "the holy things" "each year" with blood not his own, the heavenly high priest Jesus does not need repeatedly to "offer" himself (9:25). The law, according to which the Levitical high priests "offer" the same "sacrifices," "never is able" those who "approach" to "make perfect" for heavenly worship (10:1). This reminds the audience that in the earthly tabernacle "sacrifices" are being "offered" "not able" according to conscience to "make perfect" the one offering worship (9:9). The "law" is never able to make perfect those who approach, because the "law" appoints men having weakness as high priests, but the word of the oath-taking that is after the "law" appoints a Son, the heavenly high priest Jesus, who forever has been "made perfect" (7:28) for his role in heavenly worship.

In contrast to the eternal Melchizedek, who, having been made like the Son of God, remains a priest "for all time" (7:3), the mortal Levitical priests offer the same sacrifices year after year "for all time" (10:1). And in contrast to the law that is "never able" to make perfect for heavenly worship those who "approach" for worship (10:1), the heavenly high priest Jesus is "able" to save completely those who "approach" God through him, always living to intercede on behalf of them (7:25). This reinforces the exhortation that, since we do not have a high priest who is "not able" to sympathize with our weaknesses (4:15), let us, as a worshiping assembly, "approach" then with boldness the throne of grace, so that we may receive mercy and may find grace for timely help (4:16).

The audience are then presented with a question that leads them to an affirmative answer in agreement with the author. Would the same sacrifices the Levitical priests "offer" for all time but are never able to make perfect those who approach for worship (10:1) not have ceased to be "offered," if those "offering worship," once having been "cleansed," would have had no further "consciousness" of sins? (10:2). This again reminds the audience that sacrifices are being "offered" not able according to "conscience" to make perfect for heavenly worship the one "offering worship" (9:9). But the blood of the Christ, who through the eternal Spirit "offered" himself unblemished to God, will "cleanse" our "conscience" from sinful dead works to "offer worship" to the living God (9:14).

The audience are to appreciate the irony that in those "same" sacrifices, that is, the "same" sacrifices the Levitical high priests offer "each year" for all time (10:1), there is "each year" only the continual remembrance of "sins" (10:3), rather than a cleansing of the consciousness of "sins" (10:2). It is "impossible" for those once enlightened (6:4), and having fallen away, again to renew to repentance (6:6). It is "impossible" for God to lie (6:18). Similarly, it is "impossible" for the "blood of bulls and goats," that is, the "blood of bulls and goats" which cannot make holy those defiled for the cleansing of the flesh (9:13), to "take away" "sins" (10:4). This is in contrast to Christ, who now once at the completion of the ages for the "removal" of "sin" through his sacrifice has appeared (9:26). Indeed, Christ, offered once "*to offer up* the *sins* of many" (Isa 53:12), a second time without "sin" will be seen, by those eagerly awaiting him, among whom are the audience, for final, eternal salvation (9:28).

The scriptural quotation from Ps 39:7–9 attributed to Jesus upon "entering" into the earthly world (10:5) complements what the audience have heard regarding his self-offering upon entering into the heavenly world. In contrast to the Levitical high priest, who "enters" into the earthly "holy things" each year with blood not his own (9:25), Christ did not "enter" into "holy things" made by hands, a copy of the true ones, but into heaven itself, now to be manifested in the presence of God on behalf of us (9:24). Not through the blood of goats and calves but through his own blood he "entered" once for all into the heavenly "holy things," finding eternal redemption (9:12). Jesus represents the hope which we have as an anchor of the soul, both sure and firm, and which "enters" into the interior of the heavenly veil, where as forerunner on behalf of us Jesus "entered," according to the order of Melchizedek having become high priest forever (6:19–20). And when God "leads" the firstborn into the heavenly world, he says, "And let all the angels of God worship him (Deut 32:43; Ps 96:7)" (1:6).

What Jesus "says" (10:5a) in quoting Ps 39:7–9 complements what God "says" (8:8, 9, 10) in quoting Jer 38:31–34, the promise of a new covenant.[1] In contrast to the same animal "sacrifices" which the Levitical priests "offer" repeatedly (10:1), the scriptural voice of Jesus acknowledges that "sacrifice" and "offering" God did not want (10:5b). What the scriptural voice of Jesus then declares to God, "but a body you provided for *me*" (10:5c), resonates with what he said in quoting Isa 8:18a, "behold I and the children whom God gave to *me*" (2:13). This indicates a connection between the "body" God provided Jesus for his self-sacrifice and the "children," including the audience, God entrusted to Jesus as a merciful and faithful high priest (2:14–18). In accord with the assertion that it is impossible for the blood of goats and bulls to take away "sins" (10:4), the scriptural voice of Jesus declares to God, "holocausts and sin offerings [*peri hamartias*] you took no pleasure in" (10:6), even though every high priest is obligated to offer sacrifices "concerning sins" (*peri hamartiōn*, 5:3).[2]

When God became provoked with the faithless and disobedient wilderness generation, his scriptural voice from the quotation of Ps 94:7–11 declared, "*I said*, 'They are always wandering in the heart, and they have not known my ways'" (3:10). The audience are to appreciate the contrast, as the scriptural voice of Jesus now declares, "*I said*, 'Behold I have come,

---

1. The occurrences of the verbal form "he says" (*legei*) in 8:8, 9, 10 are the last times the audience have heard it before hearing it used for Jesus in 10:5. On the two quotations, Guthrie, "Hebrews," 977, notes: "Both emphasize the internalization of the law, rivet attention with *idou* ('behold'), have something 'written,' contain references to 'sin,' and refer to God."

2. Ellingworth, *Hebrews*, 502: "*Peri hamartias* is frequently used in the LXX virtually as a compound noun."

as in the scroll of the book it is written concerning me, to do, O God, your will'" (10:7). In continuity with the scriptural declaration of Jesus, "*Behold* I and the children God gave to me" (2:13), and in correspondence to the scriptural promise of God, "*Behold* days are coming" (8:8), Jesus now declares, "*Behold* I have come." Moses sprinkled the "book" of the covenant containing the written will of God (9:19), and now the scriptural voice of Jesus pledges that he has come, as in the scroll of the "book" it is written concerning him, to do the will of God.[3] Although, as Jesus acknowledged to God, sacrifice and offering "you did not want or *will*," he pronounces that he has come precisely "to do, O God, your *will*."[4]

It is brought to the attention of the audience that the sacrifices and offerings and holocausts and sin offerings, which God did not want nor take pleasure in (10:5-6, 8a), are "offered" "according to a law" (10:8b). This reminds the audience that the "law," according to which each year the Levitical high priests "offer" the same sacrifices, never is able to make perfect for heavenly worship those who approach for worship (10:1). Otherwise, these sacrifices would have ceased to be "offered" (10:2). It underscores how Jesus is a heavenly high priest, as it recalls that if he would be on earth, he would not be a priest, there being those who "offer" the gifts "according to a law" (8:4). And it reminds the audience that Jesus has arisen as a different priest, who not "according to a law" of a fleshly commandment has come about, but according to the power of an indestructible life (7:16).

The scriptural voice of Jesus in the first person, "Then I said, 'Behold I have come, as in the scroll of the book it is written concerning me, to do, O God, your will'" (10:7) is reinforced and refocused for the audience, as it is abbreviated and reported in the third person, "Then he said, 'Behold I have come to do your will'" (10:9a). That Jesus does away with the "first," the will of God as understood under the first covenant, that he might establish the "second," the will of God as now understood under the new, second covenant (10:9b), resonates with the assertion that if that "first" covenant were faultless, for a "second" God would not have sought

---

3. On the phrase "in the scroll (*kephalidi*) of the book," Ellingworth, *Hebrews*, 502, notes: "The *kephalis* is the knob on the end of a book roll, hence by extension the roll itself." Koester, *Hebrews*, 433: "[I]n this context the 'book' is probably the Mosaic Law, as in Heb 9:19."

4. Jobes, "Rhetorical Achievement"; idem, "Hebrews 10:5-7"; van der Bergh, "Hebrews 10:5b-7."

a place (8:7). That Jesus "does away" with the first, in ironic contrast to the impossibility for the blood of bulls and goats to "take away" sins (10:4), indicates his role in the "disappearing" of the "first" covenant that is becoming old and aging, now that a new, second covenant has been announced (8:13), introducing a new system for the worship of God.[5]

The audience are made aware that in this "will," that is, the "will" of God that Jesus has come to do (10:7, 9), we have been "made holy" through the offering of the body of Jesus Christ once for all (10:10). This reminds the audience of their close fraternal relationship to Jesus, as it recalls that the Jesus who "makes holy" and those who are being "made holy" are all from one, for which reason he is not ashamed to call them brothers (2:11). And it implies the cleansing of their conscience for the heavenly worship of God. For if the blood of goats and bulls and the sprinkling of a heifer's ashes "makes holy" those defiled for the cleansing of the flesh (9:13), how much more will the blood of the Christ, who through the eternal Spirit offered himself unblemished to God, cleanse our conscience from sinful dead works to offer worship to the living God (9:14).

In contrast to the "offering" and "offerings" God did not want (10:5, 8), it is through the "offering" of the "body" of Jesus Christ once for all, the "body" God provided for him (10:5), that we have been made holy (10:10). The audience have heard references to "Jesus" (2:9; 3:1; 4:14; 6:20; 7:22) and to "Christ" (3:6, 14; 5:5; 6:1; 9:11, 14, 24, 28), but this is the first occurrence of the two words together, thus emphasizing the identity of the body offered in self-sacrifice. That the body of Jesus Christ was offered definitively "once for all" recalls that he entered "once for all" into the heavenly "holy things," finding eternal redemption (9:12), and that he does not have a necessity, like the Levitical high priests, first for his own sins to offer up sacrifices then of the people, for this he did "once for all" having offered up himself (7:27).

As the audience were informed, "every high priest" is appointed to "offer" both gifts and "sacrifices" (8:3). More precisely, "every high priest" is appointed in things regarding God, so that he may "offer" both gifts

---

5. Ellingworth, *Hebrews*, 504–5; Koester, *Hebrews*, 439: "The principal contrast is between the lack of accomplishment of God's will under the Law and the completion of God's will by Christ. Christ came to do God's will through a blood sacrifice that had an internal dimension of obedience and an external dimension in the offering of his body through crucifixion."

and "sacrifices" on behalf of "sins" (5:1). But now they hear that "every" Levitical "priest" stands each day ministering and "offering" repeatedly the same "sacrifices," which are never able to cast off "sins" (10:11), the sins that prevent one from worshiping God.

That every Levitical priest stands "each day" offering the same sacrifices (10:11) presents a contrast to Jesus, who does not have "each day" a necessity, like the Levitical high priests, first on behalf of his own sins to offer up sacrifices then of the people, for this he did once for all having offered up himself (7:27). In contrast to Jesus, who does not "repeatedly" offer himself (9:25), since then it would be necessary for him "repeatedly" to suffer from the foundation of the world (9:26), every Levitical priest stands each day ministering and offering "repeatedly" the same sacrifices (10:11). Since the same sacrifices offered by all of the Levitical priests are "never able" to cast off sins (10:11), the law is "never able" to make perfect for heavenly worship those who approach for worship (10:1; cf. 7:19, 28; 9:22).

That Jesus Christ is pointedly referred to here as "this one" (10:12) resonates with how great is "this one" (7:4), that is, "this" unique high priest Melchizedek (7:1), who was made like the Son of God (7:3). It reminds the audience that Jesus Christ is "this one," who has been considered worthy of greater glory beyond Moses (3:3). In contrast to every Levitical priest "offering" repeatedly the same "sacrifices," which are never able to cast off "sins" (10:11), Jesus Christ "offered" one "sacrifice" on "behalf of sins," in accord with the duty of every high priest to offer sacrifices "on behalf of sins" (5:1), for all time (10:12). In contrast to the Levitical priests, who each year offer the same sacrifices "for all time" (10:1), Jesus Christ offered one sacrifice, the body God provided him (10:5, 10), "for all time" (10:12), while thus, like Melchizedek, remaining an eternal priest "for all time" (7:3).

That Jesus Christ, having offered one sacrifice for all time on behalf of "sins," "sat at the right" of God (10:12) in accord with Ps 109:1 reinforces for the audience the assertion that in Jesus Christ we have a high priest who "sat at the right" of the throne of the divine Majesty in the heavens (8:1). It recalls that Jesus Christ, as the Son of God, having made a cleansing for "sins," "sat at the right" of the divine Majesty in the heights of heaven (1:3). That henceforth he is waiting "until his enemies are placed as a footstool for his feet" (10:13) echoes the explicit citation of Ps 109:1, addressed directly, not to any of the angels, but to the Son of

God: "Sit at my right, until I place your enemies as a footstool for your feet" (1:13). That the heavenly enthroned Jesus Christ is still "waiting" (10:13) reminds the audience that the great salvation they are not to neglect (2:3) is still to be consummated. Indeed, the Christ, offered once "to offer up the sins of many" (Isa 53:12), a second time without sin will be seen, by those "eagerly awaiting" him, among whom are the audience, for final, eternal salvation (9:28).[6]

By "one offering," the "one sacrifice" offered for all time (10:12), through the "offering" of his body once for all (10:10), Jesus Christ has made perfect for all time those who are being made holy (10:14). In contrast to the law, which never is able to "make perfect" for heavenly worship those who approach for worship (10:1; cf. 9:9; 7:19), Jesus Christ, the divinely appointed Son, who forever "has been made perfect" (7:28; cf. 5:9; 2:10), "has made perfect" for all time those who are being made holy. Through his one sacrifice offered "for all time" on behalf of sins (10:12), Jesus Christ has made perfect "for all time" those who are being made holy (10:14). Although the law never is able to make perfect "those" who approach for worship (10:1), because "those" offering worship still have consciousness of sins (10:2), by one offering of himself, Jesus Christ has made perfect for all time "those" who are being made holy.

This emphatically underscores that we, who "have been made holy" through the offering of the body of Jesus Christ once for all (10:10), are still involved in the ongoing process of "being made holy" and thus fit for worship (10:14).[7] It again reminds the audience that the Jesus who "makes holy" and those who are being "made holy" are all from one, for which reason he is not ashamed to call them brothers (2:11). And it again indicates to the audience the cleansing of their conscience for the heavenly worship of God. For if the blood of goats and bulls and the sprinkling of a heifer's ashes "makes holy" those defiled for the cleansing of the flesh (9:13), how much more will the blood of the Christ, who through the eternal Spirit offered himself unblemished to God, cleanse our conscience from sinful dead works to offer worship to the living God (9:14).

---

6. Koester, *Hebrews*, 435: "'Waiting' suggests rest, but not inactivity, for the seated Christ intercedes for others (4:14–16; 7:25; 9:24). The 'enemies' are not identified. Christ's exaltation was a victory over the devil (2:14–15), and the author may have thought of the enemies as other superhuman powers, but the idea is not developed."

7. Attridge, *Hebrews*, 281: "[T]he appropriation of the enduring effects of Christ's act is an ongoing present reality."

II. 10:15–30

A ¹⁵ The Holy *Spirit* also *testifies* (*martyrei*) to us, for after having said, ¹⁶ "This is the *covenant* which I will covenant with them after those days, says the *Lord*, giving my *laws* upon their hearts and upon their mind I will inscribe them" (Jer 38:33),

> **B** ¹⁷ (he said) also, "Their *sins* and their lawless deeds I certainly will remember *no longer*" (Jer 38:34b). ¹⁸ Where there is forgiveness of these, there is *no longer* offering *for sin*.
>
>> **C** ¹⁹ Having then, brothers, boldness for the entrance to "the holy things" in the blood of Jesus, ²⁰ which fresh and living way he inaugurated for us through the veil, that is, his flesh, ²¹ and a great priest over the house of God, ²²ᵃ let us approach with a true *heart* in assurance of *faith*,
>>
>> **C'** ²²ᵇ sprinkled with regard to the *hearts* from an evil conscience and washed with regard to the body by clean water. ²³ Let us hold to the confession of the hope unwaveringly, for *faithful* is the one who promised, ²⁴ and let us turn attention to one another for stirring up love and beneficent works, ²⁵ not abandoning our own gathering, as is the custom of some, but encouraging, and even more so to the degree that you take note of the day drawing near.
>
> **B'** ²⁶ For if we deliberately go on *sinning* after receiving the knowledge of the truth, a sacrifice *for sins no longer* remains,

A' ²⁷ but a certain fearful expectation of judgment and zeal of fire about to devour the adversaries (Zeph 1:18; Isa 26:11). ²⁸ Anyone rejecting the *law* of Moses dies without pity on the basis of two or three *witnesses* (*martysin*) (Deut 17:6). ²⁹ How much worse a punishment do you think is worthy one who tramples under foot the Son of God and considers unclean the blood of the *covenant*, in which he was made holy, and insults the *Spirit* of grace? ³⁰ For we know the one who said, "Mine is vengeance, I will repay" (Deut 32:35), and again, "The *Lord* will judge his people" (Deut 32:36).

Toward the conclusion of the preceding unit in 10:1–14 is a reference to "sins" on behalf of which Jesus Christ offered one sacrifice for all time (10:12). Near the beginning of this next unit in 10:15–30 is a reference to the "sins" God promises to remember no longer (10:17). These occurrences of the term for "sins" thus serve as the transitional words connecting these units as they move the focus from the sins for which Jesus Christ offered himself to the sins God certainly will remember no longer according to Jer 38:34b.

It is divinely "testified" according to scripture that Melchizedek goes on living (7:8; cf. 7:3). And it is divinely "testified" concerning Jesus Christ according to Ps 109:4 that "you are a priest forever according to the order of Melchizedek" (7:17). The audience now hear that the divine Holy Spirit also "testifies" to us in scripture (10:15)—with "testifies" in an emphatic position—in addition to the testimony given by Ps 109:1 (10:12–13).[8] That "the Holy Spirit" testifies to us as the divine speaker of Jer 38:33 reminds the audience of the scriptural testimony "the Holy Spirit" gave in speaking Ps 94:7–11, with its warning to the audience as a worshiping assembly, "Today when you hear his voice, 'do not harden your hearts'" (3:7–8a).[9]

Previously the audience heard Jer 38:33 quoted as follows: "This is the covenant which I will covenant with the house of Israel after those days, says the Lord, giving my laws into their mind and upon their hearts I will inscribe them" (8:10). But now they hear it quoted a bit differently: "This is the covenant which I will covenant with them after those days, says the Lord, giving my laws upon their hearts and upon their mind I will inscribe them" (10:16). Instead of "with the house of Israel," the covenant is now "with them," a generalization that facilitates the application of the new covenant to the contemporary audience.[10] The inversion of the promise into "giving my laws upon their hearts and upon their mind I will inscribe them" (10:16) not only complements the original "giving my laws into their mind and upon their hearts I will inscribe them" (8:10),

---

8. On the emphatic position of the verb "testifies" (*martyrei*) in 10:15, see Westcott, *Hebrews*, 316.

9. Johnson, *Hebrews*, 254: "This is the third time that Scripture is said to 'bear witness' (see also 7:8, 17), and also the third time that the Holy Spirit is said to speak or reveal through Scripture (see 3:7, and, by implication 9:8). Characteristically, the Scripture is understood as spoken, and as addressed 'to us' rather than simply to the past." Lane, *Hebrews 9–13*, 268: "The Spirit brings the detail of the text from the past into the present and makes it contemporary with the experience of the readers."

10. Koester, *Hebrews*, 435: "By referring generally to 'them' rather than to 'the house of Israel,' the author allows for a connection between the new covenant and all for whom Christ's blood was shed." See also Ellingworth, *Hebrews*, 513; Mitchell, *Hebrews*, 204.

but reinforces that the covenant is with "them." The laws of God will be both given and inscribed both "upon the hearts of them" and "upon the mind of them."[11]

The scriptural testimony of the Holy Spirit in the reprise of the quotation of Jer 38:33 (10:15–16) continues with a reiteration of the quotation of Jer 38:34b, differently accentuated. Previously the audience heard the quotation of Jer 38:34b as follows: "I will be merciful to their wrongdoings and their sins I will certainly remember no longer" (8:12). But now they hear: "Their sins and their lawless deeds I certainly will remember no longer" (10:17). God's promise that "I will be merciful to their wrongdoings" has been eliminated in favor of foregrounding "their sins," accentuated by the addition of "their lawless deeds." This also creates a closer correspondence to the divine promise of "giving my *laws* upon their hearts" (10:16), as it resonates with the scriptural voice of God in the quotation of Ps 44:8, affirming that the Son of God "loved righteousness and hated *lawlessness*" (1:9).[12]

The explanation that where there is "forgiveness" of these sins and lawless deeds, there is no longer offering for sin (10:18) underlines the singularity of the self-offering of the blood that was shed by Christ, as it reminds the audience that without the shedding of blood no "forgiveness" occurs (9:22). In correspondence to the decisive scriptural promise of God in Jer 38:34b that their "sins" and their lawless deeds "I certainly will remember *no longer*" (10:17), there is "no longer" offering "for sin" (10:18). That there is no longer "offering" for sin reinforces for the audience that by one "offering" Christ has made perfect for all time those who are being made holy (10:14), and that we have been made holy through the "offering" of the body of Jesus Christ once for all (10:10). It confirms the scriptural voice of Christ addressed to God in the quotation of Ps 39:7 that sacrifice and "offering" and holocausts and "sin offerings" you did not want nor take pleasure in (10:5, 8).

The audience were exhorted to hold fast to the confession, "having" then a great high priest who has passed through the heavens, Jesus the Son of God (4:14). They were then addressed as having become those

---

11. Guthrie, "Hebrews," 979: "Further, in place of the preposition *eis* before *tēn dianoian*, as at 8:10, the author has written *epi tēn dianoian* at 10:16, perhaps because the phrase is now positioned with the verb *epigrapsō* ('I will write')."

12. Koester, *Hebrews*, 436: "Since the Son of God hates 'lawlessness' (1:9), he purges it from the people of God."

"having" a need of "milk and not solid food," including that "you *have* a need for someone to teach you the elements of the beginning of the sayings of God" (5:12). But now they are addressed as those "having" boldness, as a worshiping assembly, for the entrance to the heavenly "holy things" in the blood of Jesus (10:19).

Addressed as "brothers" (10:19), the audience are reminded that, as holy "brothers" who are partners of a heavenly calling (3:1), they have been warned, as "brothers," to take note lest there be in anyone of them an evil heart of unfaithfulness in falling away from the living God (3:12). That they have "boldness" for the entrance to the heavenly "holy things" (10:19) reverberates with the exhortations for them to approach with "boldness" the throne of grace (4:16), and to hold to the "boldness" and to the boast of the hope (3:6). Although the "way" to the heavenly "holy things" had not appeared while the first earthly tabernacle had standing (9:8), the audience are now assured that we have boldness for the "entrance" to the heavenly "holy things" in the blood of Jesus (10:19), which fresh and living "way" he inaugurated for us through the veil, that is, his flesh (10:20).

We have boldness for the entrance to the heavenly "holy things" in the "blood" of Jesus (10:19), since Christ did not enter into "holy things" made by hands, but into heaven itself (9:24a), as a high priest with "blood" that is his own (9:25b). This adds to the assurance for the audience that the "blood" of the Christ, who through the eternal Spirit offered himself unblemished to God, will cleanse our conscience from sinful dead works to offer worship to the living God (9:14).

Corresponding to the fact that not even the first covenant was "inaugurated" without "blood" (9:18), the bold entrance that we have to the heavenly "holy things" in the "blood" of Jesus, is the fresh and living way he "inaugurated" for us through the veil, that is, his flesh (10:20). That it is a "living" way further reinforces the assurance that the blood of the Christ will cleanse our conscience from dead works to offer worship to the "living" God (9:14), the God who possesses and promises to bestow eternal life in his heavenly sabbatical rest (4:6–11). This "living" way, as the way to the eternal life offered by the ever "living" God, resonates with the fact that Jesus is an eternal high priest, who is able to save completely those who approach God through him, always "living" to intercede on behalf of them (7:25). This is the intercession available to the audience as they strive to make sure that there not be in anyone of them an evil heart of unfaithfulness in falling away from the "living" God (3:12).

In contrast to the "veil" that closed the way to the earthly "holy things" (9:3), and resonating with the entrance into the interior of the heavenly "veil" by Jesus as the firm anchor of our soul (6:19), this fresh and living entrance that Jesus inaugurated for us to the heavenly "holy things" is through the "veil" that is his flesh (10:20). The veil that is "his flesh" reminds the audience that it was in the days of "his flesh" that Jesus offered both prayers and supplications with strong outcrying and tears to the God who was able to save him from death, and he was heard from his reverence (5:7). That our entrance to the heavenly "holy things" is in the "blood" and through the "flesh" of Jesus (10:19–20) leads the audience to appreciate that the self-offering of Jesus as the eternal high priest was accomplished in and through the "blood" and "flesh" he shared with us as our fellow and fraternal human being (2:14).

That the audience are those having in Jesus not only boldness for entrance to the heavenly "holy things" (10:19), but also a "great priest" over the house of God (10:21), reinforces the exhortation for them as those having a "great high priest" who has passed through the heavens, Jesus the Son of God, to hold fast to the confession as a worshiping assembly (4:14). And that Jesus is a great priest "over the house" of God reminds the audience that Christ is such a great priest as the Son "over the house" of God, whose house are we, if to the boldness and to the boast of the hope we hold as a worshiping assembly (3:6).

Since we have boldness for entrance to the heavenly "holy things" and a great priest over the house of God (10:19–21), we are to "approach" for the worship of God with a true heart in assurance of faith (10:22a). This is in contrast to those who "approach" with the same sacrifices never able to make them perfect for heavenly worship (10:1). It resonates with the fact the Jesus is able to save completely those who "approach" God through him (7:25), and with the exhortation for us in our worship to "approach" with boldness the throne of grace (4:16).

We are to approach for the worship of God with a "true" heart (10:22a), that is, a heart appropriate for the "true" "holy things" of heaven itself (9:24), and for the "true," heavenly tabernacle (8:2). That we are to approach with a true "heart" is a consequence of the scriptural promise of God to give and inscribe his laws upon our "hearts" (10:16; 8:10). And that we are to approach with a true heart in "assurance" of "faith" (10:22a) resonates with the author's desire that each member of the audience demonstrate the same eagerness for the "assurance" of the hope until the end (6:11). This is so that the audience may not become sluggish in worship, but imitators of those who through "faith" and patience are inheriting the promises (6:12).

Under the old covenant there was a "cleansing" of the flesh by the "sprinkling" of a heifer's ashes (9:13). And the old covenant was inaugurated through the sprinkling with blood and "water" by Moses, who "sprinkled" both the book of the covenant and all the people (9:19), and the tabernacle and all the vessels of the ministry he likewise "sprinkled" with blood (9:21). In contrast, we have been "sprinkled" with regard to the hearts from an evil conscience and washed with regard to the body by "clean" "water," a reminder of our initiatory, sacramental ritual of baptism (10:22b).[13]

We may approach for the heavenly worship of the living God with a true "heart" in assurance of "faith" (10:22a). The reason is that we have been sprinkled with regard to the "hearts"—the "hearts" upon which God has promised in the new covenant to give and inscribe his laws (10:16; 8:10)—from an "evil" "conscience" and washed with regard to the body by "clean" water (10:22b). This reinforces the exhortations for the audience to take note lest there be in anyone of them an "evil" "heart" of "unfaithfulness" in falling away from the living God (3:12), and to heed the voice of God urging them not to harden their "hearts" (3:8, 10, 15; 4:7). It means they may offer worship as those having no "consciousness" of sins, since they have been "cleansed" (10:2). And in contrast to the offering of gifts and sacrifices not able according to "conscience" to make perfect for heavenly worship the one offering worship (9:9), it boosts the assurance that the blood of Christ will "cleanse" our "conscience" from sinful dead works to offer worship to the living God (9:14).

According to the law of the old covenant almost everything is "cleansed" by blood (9:22). But in the new covenant the heavenly things are to be "cleansed" with better sacrifices (9:23). A better sacrifice was the offering of the "body" of Jesus Christ once for all (10:10), the "body" God provided for him (10:5). The audience are to appreciate that it is as a consequence of this better sacrificial self-offering that we have been washed

---

13. Leithart, "Womb."

with regard to the "body" by "clean" water (10:22b) and thus enabled to participate fully in the worship of God.[14]

The exhortation for us to approach for worship with a true heart in assurance of "faith" is strengthened by the further exhortation that, because the one who promised is "faithful," we "hold" to the "confession" of the "hope" unwaveringly (10:23). This resonates with and reinforces previous exhortations with similar terminology: We may have a strong encouragement to "hold fast" to the "hope" lying ahead (6:18). Each should demonstrate the same eagerness for the assurance of the "hope" until the end (6:11). Let us "hold fast" to the "confession" (4:14). We are to "hold" the beginning of the reality firm until the end (3:14). We are to "hold" to the boldness and to the boast of the "hope" (3:6). And, as a worshiping assembly, we are to turn attention to the apostle and high priest of our "confession," Jesus (3:1).

Just as Moses was "faithful" in all God's house (3:5), and Jesus, as a "faithful" high priest (2:17), was "faithful" to the one who made him (3:2), "faithful" is the God who promised (10:23). That the God who "promised" is faithful reminds the audience that when God "promised" to Abraham (6:13), he guaranteed it with an oath, so that through two unchangeable things, in which it was impossible for God to lie, we may have a strong encouragement to hold fast to the hope lying ahead. This is the hope represented by Jesus himself as the eternal high priest in heaven (6:17–20).

Having been directed to "turn attention" to the apostle and high priest of our confession, Jesus (3:1), the audience are now exhorted, "Let us turn attention" to one another for stirring up love and beneficent works (10:24). Having been assured that God is not unjust so as to neglect their "work" and the "love" which they demonstrated for his name (6:10), the audience are now exhorted to turn attention to one another for stirring up "love" and beneficent "works." They are enabled to stir up "beneficent works," because the foundation of repentance from "dead works" and of faith in God has already been laid down for them (6:1). And they have

---

14. Johnson, *Hebrews*, 258: "Christ has brought about the purification of moral consciousness that the law could never accomplish (9:9, 14; 10:2, 11–14). . . . it is also possible that 'washing' simply carries forward the image of purification, extending it to the body as the outward symbol and instrument of faithful obedience (see 10:5, 10), so that as Christ's faith was enacted by the disposition of his body, so is the faith of his followers expressed fully when the purified internal attitude is expressed in the pure disposition of their bodies."

received the promise that the blood of the Christ will cleanse their conscience from sinful "dead works" to offer worship to the living God (9:14).

The exhortation for the audience to turn attention to one another for stirring up love and beneficent works (10:24) continues, as they are urged not to abandon, as is the custom of some, "their own" gathering for communal worship (10:25a).[15] Rather, they are to be "encouraging" one another, all the more as they "take note" of the "day" drawing near (10:25b). This reinforces, as it resonates with, the exhortation that the audience "take note" lest there be in anyone of them an evil heart of unfaithfulness in falling away from the living God (3:12). They are rather to "encourage one another" during each "day," while it is called "today," so that not anyone of them may become hardened by the deceit of the sin that prevents the worship of God (3:13).

The "day" that is drawing near (10:25) refers to the final, decisive day to come at the end of these "days" in which God has spoken to us in a Son (1:2).[16] The audience may prepare for this decisive day of final salvation at each "day" set as the "today" for listening during their communal worship to the voice of God urging that they not harden their hearts against the ways of God (4:7), as in the rebellion during the "day" of the testing of God in the wilderness (3:8). Each "today" of their communal gathering for worship serves as the other "day" about which God spoke (4:8), the "today" for hearing the voice of God inviting the audience to enter into God's own eternal Sabbath rest and worship in heaven (4:9-11). That the decisive day of final salvation is "drawing near" reminds the audience of the introduction of a better hope, represented by the heavenly high priest Jesus (6:18-20), through which we are "drawing near" to God (7:19).

For the audience deliberately to go on "sinning" after receiving the knowledge of the truth (10:26a) would liken them to the disobedient and unfaithful ancestors with whom God was provoked. They "sinned" and their corpses fell in the wilderness (3:17). A sacrifice "for sins no longer"

---

15. On the term "gathering" or "assembly" (*episynagōgē*), Attridge, *Hebrews*, 290, points out: "It is likely that the author has particularly in mind the assembly of his addressees as a worshipping community." Mitchell, *Hebrews*, 212: "The noun *episynagōgē* is more vivid than the simpler *synagōgē*, and with the *epi* prefix it has a more specific local sense." See also Cahill, "Implications."

16. Attridge, *Hebrews*, 291: "Expectation of 'the day' based upon the Old Testament's prophecies of God's judgment was a common element of the eschatology of early Christians who could, as here, simply refer to the day, or define it as the day of God, or of the Lord. This was a day of judgment and of redemption."

remains (10:26b), since in the new covenant God promises that their "sins" and their lawless deeds he certainly will remember "no longer" (10:17). And where there is forgiveness of these, there is "no longer" offering "for sin" (10:18). A "sacrifice" for sin no longer remains, since now once at the completion of the ages for the removal of "sin" through his "sacrifice" Christ has appeared (9:26). And Christ did not have a necessity first on behalf of his own "sins" (cf. 5:1) to offer up "sacrifices" then for the people, for this he did once for all having offered up himself as an act of high priestly worship (7:27). As the audience have heard, a Sabbath rest "remains" for the people of God (4:9), since it "remains" for some to enter into God's own heavenly rest (4:6). In contrast, a sacrifice for sins no longer "remains" for the audience (10:26b). Consequently, they are not to become apostates who go on deliberately sinning (10:26a). Rather, they are to focus upon entering into God's own eternal Sabbath rest and worship that still remains for them in heaven.

For those who deliberately go on sinning (10:26) there is a fearful expectation of "judgment" (10:27a), the "judgment" that follows upon death (9:27). With allusions to Zeph 1:18 and Isa 26:11, this judgment is further described as a zeal of divine "fire," which can be associated with the angels God made to be a flame of "fire" (1:7), about to devour the adversaries of God (10:27b). As adversaries of God, apostates who deliberately go on sinning thus join the enemies God will place under the feet of his heavenly enthroned Son (1:13; 10:13). In ironic contrast to Jesus "waiting" until his enemies are placed as a footstool for his feet (Ps 109:1 in 10:13), for those who deliberately go on sinning there is a fearful "expectation" of judgment. This warning of a "fearful" expectation of judgment thus reinforces the exhortation for the audience to be "afraid," lest, while the promise to enter into God's heavenly rest is left, anyone of them seem to have been lacking" (4:1). This is the kind of worshipful, reverent fear of God that can dissipate one's human "fear" of death (2:15).

According to Deut 17:6, one of the commandments spoken according to the "law" to all the people by Moses in inaugurating the old covenant (9:19), anyone rejecting the "law" of Moses dies without pity on the basis of two or three witnesses (10:28). The punishment of death on the basis of human "witnesses" for rejecting an external law reminds the audience of a fundamental difference between the old and the new covenant, according to which it is the Holy Spirit who "testifies" (10:15) that God will place his "laws" upon their hearts and minds (10:16). That such a person "dies" recalls that it is appointed for men to "die" before being judged by God (9:27). It is another reminder to the audience that the human condition according to which men "die" is transformed by the human and divine Jesus, an eternal, heavenly high priest according to the order of Melchizedek (7:8).

The seriousness of abandoning the gathering for communal worship (10:25) and deliberately continuing to sin as apostates (10:26) is underscored with a rhetorically provocative question posed to the audience: "How much worse a punishment do you think is worthy one who tramples under foot the Son of God and considers unclean the blood of the covenant, in which he was made holy, and insults the Spirit of grace?" (10:29). If "rejecting" the "law" of Moses leads to the death penalty (10:28), the punishment must be even worse for one who metaphorically "tramples under foot," leaving the community and continuing in apostasy, the very "Son" of God. A punishment that will be "worthy" for one who tramples under foot the Son of God presents the audience with an ironically appropriate but sharp contrast to the assertion that Jesus, as the Son God placed over his house (3:6), is considered "worthy" of greater glory beyond Moses (3:3).

To abandon the gathering for worship (10:25) and deliberately to go on sinning (10:26) is to consider unclean "the blood of the covenant" (10:29). This is the blood that transforms "the blood of the covenant," the blood of animals by which Moses inaugurated the old covenant (9:20). This is the blood of the new "covenant" promised by God (Jer 38:33 in 10:16), which is the "blood" of Jesus by which we, as a worshiping assembly, have boldness for entrance into the heavenly "holy things" (10:19), "the blood of the Christ" that will cleanse our conscience to offer heavenly worship to the living God (9:14).

To abandon the gathering for worship (10:25) and deliberately to go on sinning (10:26) is also to insult the "Spirit" of grace (10:29), that is, the Holy "Spirit" who testifies (10:15) to God's scriptural promise of a new covenant (10:16). The designation of the Holy Spirit as the Spirit of "grace" reinforces the exhortation for the audience to approach with boldness the throne of "grace," so that we may receive mercy and may find "grace" for timely help (4:16). It reminds the audience that they may find this grace as a worshiping assembly, because it was by the "grace" of God that Jesus tasted death on behalf of all (2:9).

How much worse will be the divine punishment under the new covenant is reinforced for the audience by a couplet of sequential scriptural quotations: "For we know the one who said, 'Mine is vengeance, I will repay' (Deut 32:35), and again, 'The Lord will judge his people (Deut 32:36)'" (10:30). The concluding pronouncement in the third person that the Lord will judge his people climactically complements and caps off the emphatic first person pronouncement that "mine" is vengeance, "I" will repay. The "Lord," that is, the "Lord" God who promises the new covenant (10:16), will "judge" his people, in accord with a certain fearful expectation of "judgment" (10:27) for those who deliberately go on sinning (10:26).[17] The Lord will judge his "people," that is, all the "people" with whom he made the covenant (9:19), by which he promised that "I will be to them as God, and they will be to me as *people*" (8:10). The audience are to count themselves as belonging to this "people" of God for whom a heavenly and eternal Sabbath rest and worship remains (4:9), the people who are to be judged by God.[18]

III. 10:31–39

A [31] Fearful it is to fall *into* the hands of the *living* God.

> B [32] Remember the previous days, in which, having been enlightened, you *endured* much conflict of sufferings, [33] on the one hand publicly exposed to reproaches and afflictions, on the other hand becoming partners of those so treated. [34a] *For* you even suffered with the prisoners
>
>> C [34b] and accepted the confiscation of your *possessions* with joy,
>>
>> C' [34c] knowing that you yourselves have a better *possession* that remains.
>
> B' [35] Do not throw away then your boldness, which has great recompense. [36] *For* you have need of *endurance* so that, doing the will of God, you may acquire the promise. [37] "*For* just a little longer (Isa 26:20), the one who is to come will come and he will not delay.

---

17. Proctor, "Judgement."
18. Gleason, "Eschatology"; Tanner, "Hebrews 10:26–31."

A′ ³⁸ My just one from faith *will live*, and if he draws back my soul does not take pleasure in him" (Hab 2:3–4). ³⁹ But we are not of drawing back *into* destruction, but of faith *into* preservation of the soul.

Toward the conclusion of the preceding unit in 10:15–30 is a reference to a certain "fearful" expectation of God's judgment (10:27). At the beginning of this next unit in 10:31–39 is an acknowledgment that it is "fearful" to fall into the hands of the living God (10:31). These occurrences of the adjective "fearful" thus serve as the transitional words connecting these units as they move the focus from a fearful expectation of judgment to the fearful judgment itself.

That it is "fearful," emphatic by virtue of its initial position in the sentence, to "fall" into the hands of the living God (10:31) develops the negative, ominous dimension of the audience's fear of a worse punishment (10:29) from the God who will judge his people. It recalls the punishment of the sinful ancestors with whom God was provoked for forty years. They experienced the fearful punishment of falling into the hands of the living God, as their corpses "fell" in the wilderness (3:17). Thus, through their disobedience and unfaithfulness, they were not able to enter into God's own rest (3:18). Such fearfulness reinforces the exhortation that we strive then to enter into God's rest for heavenly worship, so that not any member of the audience may "fall" in the same pattern of disobedience as the unfaithful ancestors (4:11).

But that it is fearful to fall into the "hands" of the living God (10:31) also develops the positive, hopeful dimension of being fearful with its connotation of respect, reverence, and awe in the presence of the divine.[19] It reminds the audience of God's taking hold of the "hand" of his people (by implication with his own hand[s]) to save them from slavery by leading them out of the land of Egypt (8:9). It was through the laying on of human "hands" (6:2) that the audience have been recipients of the transmission of the divine power of God's Spirit (6:4). And to fall into the hands of the living God means to fall into the divine "hands" that fashioned the heavens (Ps 101:26 in 1:10), the place of God's own heavenly Sabbath rest and worship prepared for the audience (4:6, 9–11). The reverent fear of falling into the hands of the "living God" reinforces the exhortation for the audience to take note lest there be in anyone of them an evil heart of

---

19. Attridge, *Hebrews*, 296: "[T]he connotations of falling into God's hands are usually positive."

unfaithfulness in falling away from the "living God" (3:12), thus failing to enter into the eternal life possessed and provided by the ever living God. It also resonates with the assuring promise that it is the blood of the Christ which will cleanse our conscience from dead works to offer worship to the "living God" (9:14).[20]

The directive for the audience to "remember" the previous "days" of their sufferings (10:32) makes all the more relevant for them God's promise of a new covenant in Jer 38:33–34 that "after those days" (10:16; 8:10) he will "remember" no longer their sins and their lawless deeds (10:17; 8:12). Having been "enlightened," recalling that the audience were once "enlightened" through their initiation as believers (6:4), they endured much conflict of "sufferings" (10:32). Such sufferings assimilate them to the singular self-sacrifice of Jesus, whom God made perfect through "sufferings" (2:10), and whom, on account of the "suffering" of death, God crowned with heavenly glory and honor, so that by the grace of God, on behalf of all he might taste death (2:9). Their sufferings took the form, on the one hand, of being publicly exposed to reproaches and afflictions, and, on the other hand, of becoming partners of those so treated (10:33). That "you even suffered with" the prisoners (10:34a) further assimilates the audience to Jesus as a high priest who is able to "sympathize" with our weaknesses (4:15).

The public persecution of the audience for their faith is thus recognized, and the ready "accepting" or "welcoming" of the confiscation of their property paradoxically "with joy" is affirmed (10:34b).[21] In contrast to the unfaithful wilderness generation who did not "know" the ways of God (3:10), and in resonance with God's new covenant promise that his people will not need to teach each other, saying, "know" the Lord (8:11), the audience "know" that they have a better possession that remains (10:34c). That they have a "better" possession resonates with the divine Son becoming so far "better" than the angels (1:4). It recalls the "better" things having to do with salvation (6:9), the "better" or "superior" one blessing the inferior (7:7), a "better" hope (7:19), a "better" covenant

---

20. Ellingworth, *Hebrews*, 544: "[W]hat is to be feared is to fall away from God as the source of life." See also Swetnam, "Hebrews 10,30–31."

21. Johnson, *Hebrews*, 271: "The verb *prosdechomai* here has the nuance of not only 'accepting,' but even of 'welcoming,' and that nuance is made explicit by the phrase 'with joy' . . . joy is a moral disposition of contentment/receptivity even in the midst of suffering."

(7:22; 8:6) enacted on "better" promises (8:6), and the "better" sacrifices (9:23). And that they have a better possession that "remains" for eternity resonates with Melchizedek "remaining" a priest forever (7:3), as well as with the high priest Jesus who "remains" forever (7:24).

The exhortation for the audience not to throw away their "boldness" (10:35a) reminds them of the "boldness" they have for the entrance to the heavenly "holy things" in the blood of Jesus (10:19). It reinforces the exhortations that we approach with "boldness" the throne of grace, so that we may receive mercy and may find grace for timely help (4:16), and that we, as the worshiping "house" of God, hold to the "boldness" and to the boast of the hope (3:6). In contrast to the just "recompense" that every transgression and disobedience receives (2:2), the boldness the audience are not to throw away has great "recompense" from God (10:35b).[22]

In line with the exhortation that "*you have need* for someone to teach you the elements of the beginning of the sayings of God, and you have become those *having a need* of milk and not solid food" (5:12), the audience are now told that "you have need" of endurance (10:36a). They have need of endurance so that, "doing" the "will" of God, they may acquire the promise (10:36b). This recalls the example provided for the audience by the scriptural voice of Jesus from Ps 39:9, which proclaimed, "Behold I have come, as in the scroll of the book it is written concerning me, *to do*, O God, your *will*" (10:7, 9). Indeed, it is in this "will" of God that we have been made holy through the offering of the body of Jesus Christ once for all (10:10). That the audience may acquire "the promise" refers to "the promise" of an eternal inheritance for those who have been called by God for the entrance into heaven and its worship (9:15; 3:1).

Upon "entering" or "coming into" the world the first time, Christ, in the quotation attributed to him from Ps 39:9, declared that "I have come" to do the will of God (10:7, 9). And now, the exhortation for the audience to acquire the promise of the eternal heavenly inheritance by doing the will of God (10:36) is bolstered by a combined scriptural quotation from Isa 26:20 and Hab 2:3 urging them to wait "just a little longer, the one who is to *come* will *come* and he will not delay" (10:37). This assurance regarding the second coming of Christ thus resonates with the previous prediction that the Christ offered once "to offer up the sins of many" (Isa

---

22. According to Ellingworth, *Hebrews*, 551, the recompense or reward "is, however, not material and earthly, but heavenly and lasting (Heb 10:34), promised (v. 36), given by God (11:6), and consisting of life with him."

53:12), a second time without sin will be seen, by those eagerly awaiting him, for final salvation (9:28).[23]

The scriptural declaration by God from Hab 2:4, "my just one from *faith* will live" (10:38a), continues the quotation from Hab 2:3 (10:37). It reinforces the exhortations for the audience to approach for worship with a true heart in assurance of "faith" (10:22a), and not to become sluggish but rather imitators of those who through "faith"—the fundamental "faith" in God (6:1)—and patience are inheriting the promises (6:12). It reminds the audience not to imitate the wilderness ancestors who were not united in "faith" with those who heard the good news (4:2), even as it reaffirms the faith of the audience, recalling that we who "believed" (4:3) are even now entering into the heavenly rest and worship promised by God.

God's scriptural declaration that my just one from faith "will live" (10:38a) strengthens the hope of the audience of believers that they will live the future, heavenly life of the "living" God (10:31). It resonates with the fresh and "living" way, as the way to eternal life, that Jesus inaugurated for us through the veil, that is, his flesh (10:20). It recalls the promise that the blood of Christ will cleanse our conscience from dead works to offer worship to the "living" God (9:14). God's just one from faith will live eternally, since Jesus is always "living" to intercede on behalf of believers (7:25), the Jesus who is a high priest according to the order of Melchizedek, as one who goes on "living" eternally (7:8). And that God's just one from "faith" will live bolsters the warning that there not be in anyone of the audience an evil heart of "unfaithfulness" in falling away from the eternally "living" God (3:12).

But God's scriptural declaration that my just one from faith "will live" (10:38a) also exhorts the audience to live presently from their fundamental faith in God. They are to live presently as the one who covenanted, Jesus, was "living" before his death that made the covenant firm (9:17). They are to live presently from faith because "living" is the word of God and effective and sharper than every two-edged sword and penetrating as far as a division of soul and spirit, as well as of joints and marrow, and able to scrutinize deliberations and thoughts of the human heart (4:12). And they are to live presently from faith, with the hope of eternal life, as those who by fear of death are held in slavery through all their "life" (2:15).

---

23. For a discussion of the scriptural quotations here, see Guthrie, "Hebrews."

God's scriptural promise and exhortation from Hab 2:4, "my just one from faith will live," concludes with the warning that "if he draws back my soul does not *take pleasure in* him" (10:38). It was the scriptural voice of Jesus from the quotation of Ps 39:7–9 that provided a model for how the audience can ensure that God will take pleasure in them. Upon entering into the world, Jesus proclaimed to God, "Holocausts and sin offerings you *took* no *pleasure in*" (10:6, 8). And then he said, "Behold I have come to do your will" (10:7, 9). This scriptural pronouncement by Jesus thus reinforces the exhortation for the audience to have the endurance to do the will of God, so that they, as a worshiping assembly, may secure the pleasure of the ever-living God and acquire the promise of eternal life (10:36) as participants in heavenly worship.

The audience are then exhorted with the resolution that we are not of drawing back "into" destruction, but of faith "into" preservation of the soul (10:39). This further explicates why it is so fearful to fall "into" the hands of the living God (10:31). The judgment of falling "into" the hands of the living God can lead either "into" eternal destruction or "into" eternal life. That we are not of "drawing back" (*hypostolēs*) into destruction stands in contrast, enhanced by the playful alliteration, to the "endurance" (*hypomonēs*) the audience need to do the will of God (10:36).[24] But that we are of "faith" encourages each member of the audience to continue to be God's just one who, from "faith," will live both presently and eternally in the heavenly rest and worship of the ever living God (10:38).

And that this faith results in the preservation of the "soul" (10:39)—the better possession that remains (10:34)—ensures the pleasure of God's "soul" for each believer (10:38). It reminds the audience that in Jesus, as representative of the hope lying ahead (6:18), we have an anchor of the "soul," both sure and firm, which enters into the interior of the heavenly veil (6:19). This scriptural word of God (10:37–38) thus resonates with how the living word of God is penetrating as far as a division of "soul" and spirit (4:12), calling for a response in and through worship.[25]

---

24. Mitchell, *Hebrews*, 224–25: "The noun *hypostolēs*, 'shrinking back,' plays off the conditional clause, 'if he shrinks back' in the previous verse, in keeping with the sermon's exhortations to advance, approach, and move toward the goal. It has the sense of being in a state of timidity."

25. Rhee, "Christology."

IV. 11:1–7

A [11:1] Faith is the reality of things being hoped for, demonstration of things not being *noticed*. [2] For in this the elders were testified. [3] By faith we understand the ages to have been provided by the pronouncement of God, so that from things not apparent what is being *noticed* came to be.

    B [4a] By faith Abel offered to *God* a greater sacrifice beyond Cain, through which he was testified to be just, God testifying on the basis of his gifts,

        C [4b] And through this, having died, he is still speaking.

    B' [5] By faith Enoch was changed so that he did not see death, and he was not found because God changed him, for before the change he was testified to have pleased *God*. [6] Without faith it is impossible to please, for it is necessary that the one approaching *God* believe that he exists and that for those seeking him he becomes a rewarder.

A' [7] By faith Noah, warned about things not yet being *noticed*, becoming reverent, furnished an ark for the salvation of his house; through which he condemned the world, and of righteousness according to faith he became an heir.

At the conclusion of the preceding unit in 10:31–39 is a proclamation regarding "faith"—"we are not of drawing back into destruction, but of *faith* into preservation of the soul" (10:39). At the beginning of this next unit in 11:1–7 is a description of "faith"—"*faith* is the reality of things being hoped for" (11:1). These occurrences of the term "faith" thus serve as the transitional words connecting these units as they move the focus from the faith the audience possess to a more general consideration of that faith. And within the third macrochiastic level of the letter to the Hebrews, this unit in 11:1–7, which occurs after the central and pivotal unit in 10:31–39, exhibits a parallel relationship with the unit in 10:15–30. The parallels are formed by occurrences of the verbs "testify" and "approach." "The Holy Spirit also *testifies*" occurs in 10:15, "the elders were *testified*" in 11:2, "through which he was *testified* to be just, God *testifying*" in 11:4, and "he was *testified* to have pleased God" in 11:5. "Let us *approach* with a true heart" occurs in 10:22 and "it is necessary that the one *approaching* God" in 11:6.

That faith is the "reality" (*hypostasis*) of things being hoped for (11:1a) indicates that it is a divine "reality" that is made "real" or "realized" in and through one's faith in God. This resonates with the assertion that the divine Son is the representation of the "reality" (*hypostaseōs*) of God himself (1:3), and with the exhortation for the audience to hold the beginning of the "reality" (*hypostaseōs*), the making "real" or "realization" of final salvation as partners of the Christ, firm until the end, the actual completion of that hoped for salvation (3:14).[26]

That "faith" is the reality of "things being hoped for" (11:1a) reinforces the exhortation for the audience to hold to the confession of the "hope" unwaveringly, including the better "hope" of drawing near to God (7:19), for faithful is the God who promised (10:23). It reinforces the exhortations for the audience to have a strong encouragement to hold fast to the "hope" lying ahead (6:18), which we have as an anchor of the soul, both sure and firm, and which enters into the interior of the heavenly veil, where as forerunner on behalf of us Jesus entered (6:19–20). The audience are to demonstrate the same eagerness for the assurance of the "hope" until the end (6:11). And, as God's "house," his worshiping community, the audience are to hold to the boldness and to the boast of the "hope" (3:6).[27]

In contrast to the Mosaic law having only a shadow of the good things to come, not the image itself of those divine "things" (10:1), faith is the demonstration, the giving of proof or evidence (*elegchos*), of divine

---

26. The translation "in faith things hoped for become realized (or, reality)" is suggested by Hoerber, "Translation." Lane, *Hebrews 9–13*, 328–29: "[F]aith celebrates *now* the reality of the *future* blessings that constitute the objective content of hope. The word *hypostasis* thus has reference to the point of departure and the ground for a now unalterable course of events that will culminate in the realization of the promises of God. From this perspective, *pistis*, 'faith,' is something objective that bestows upon the objects of hope even now a substantial reality, which will unfold in God's appointed time. It gives them the force of present realities and enables the person of faith to enjoy the full certainty of future realization." Johnson, *Hebrews*, 278: "Faith, in this understanding, makes actual, or makes 'real,' for the believers the things that are hoped for, as though they were present." Mitchell, *Hebrews*, 228: "The substance of faith, then, is not something the believer can produce at will, because it rests on a reality that transcends the individual. Still, the experience of trust in that transcendent reality cannot be completely excluded from the believer's experience of faith."

27. Mitchell, *Hebrews*, 228: "In Hebrews these objects of hope are things yet to be realized, i.e., the final destination of the believers: salvation (1:14; 2:3; 6:9, 11; 7:19, 25; 9:28; 10:23), rest (4:1, 6, 9), perfection (6:1; 11:40), promises (4:1; 6:12, 17; 8:6; 9:15; 10:36), purification of conscience (9:14), eternal inheritance (1:14; 6:12, 17; 9:15), redemption (9:15), and an unshakeable kingdom (12:28)."

"things" not presently being noticed (11:1b).[28] As divine realities, these "things" not yet being noticed resonate with the two unchangeable divine "things"—God's promise and oath—by which it is impossible for God to lie (6:18).

That faith is a present demonstration of divine things not yet "being noticed" (11:1b) complements the exhortations regarding what the audience are presently to notice. They are not to abandon their own gathering for worship, but rather encourage one another, and even more so to the degree that "you are taking note" of the day of future, final salvation that is drawing near (10:25). With their "faith" as a demonstration of divine things not yet being noticed, the audience are to "take note" lest there be in anyone of them an evil heart of "unfaithfulness" in falling away from the living God (3:12), as "we take note" that the wilderness ancestors were not able to enter into God's own rest because of "unfaithfulness" (3:19). Although presently "we are taking note" of Jesus, who, on account of the suffering of death, was crowned by God with heavenly glory and honor (2:9), we do not yet see all things subjected to him (2:8), which accords with our faith as a demonstration or evidence of divine things not yet being noticed.[29]

Melchizedek "is testified" by God, as evident in the scriptures, that he goes on living forever (7:8). It "is testified" by God, as indicated by the scriptures in Ps 109:4, that Jesus is a priest forever according to the order of Melchizedek (7:17). And the Holy Spirit divinely "testifies," as indicated by the scriptures in Jer 38:33–34, to God's promise of a new covenant (10:15). Similarly, in this faith that the audience possess (10:38–39; 11:1), the elders, their ancestors in the faith, "were testified" by God, with the implication that this is evident in the scriptures (11:2).

That by faith we understand "the ages" to have been "provided" by the powerful "pronouncement" of God (11:3a) coheres with the divine providence acknowledged by the scriptural voice of Jesus from Ps 39:7,

---

28. Lane, *Hebrews 9–13*, 329: "[F]aith demonstrates the existence of reality that cannot be perceived through objective sense perception. As the complement to *hypostasis*, 'reality,' *elegchos* must be understood in the objective sense of 'proof' or 'demonstration,' the evidential character that deprives uncertainty of any basis. Thus faith confers upon what we do not see the full certainty of a *proof* or *demonstration*; it furnishes *evidence* concerning that which has not been seen." Johnson, *Hebrews*, 279: "[F]aith acts on unseen things as though they were capable of being seen, because they are understood to be as real, or even more real, than things that can be 'seen,' that is, verified by the senses."

29. Brawley, "Discoursive Structure."

"a body you *provided* for me" (10:5), the body Jesus offered in his self-sacrificial doing of the will of God (10:6–10). It was through Jesus as the divine Son that God made "the ages" (1:2), and this Son is bearing up all things by the "pronouncement" of the power of God (1:3). This deepens the audience's appreciation that, as those enlightened by faith (6:4), they have already, as a worshiping assembly, "tasted" the beneficent "pronouncement" of God and the powers of the "age" to come (6:5).

By faith, the faith that is a demonstration of divine things not yet "being noticed" (11:1), we understand the ages to have been provided by the pronouncement of God, so that from divine things not now readily apparent, the divine reality that is now "being noticed" by faith, came to be through the powerful activity of God (11:3). The powerful pronouncement of God is thus the foundation of faith. The divine realities that the audience are now noticing by faith include that "you are taking note" that the day of the consummation of God's salvation is drawing near (10:25), and that "we are taking note" of Jesus as the divine Son crowned by God with heavenly glory and honor (2:9) to be the object of heavenly worship.[30]

That by faith Abel offered to God a "greater" sacrifice "beyond" his brother Cain (11:4a) likens him to Jesus as the one who has been considered worthy of "greater" glory "beyond" Moses, just as "greater" honor than "the house," the worshiping community, has the one who furnishes it for worship (3:3). The greater "sacrifice" Abel "offered" "to God" recalls the one "sacrifice" Jesus "offered" for all time (10:12), his own body, which he "offered" unblemished "to God" (9:14), in contrast to the "sacrifice" and offering God did not want (10:5).

As one of the elders "testified" by God in their faith (11:2), Abel was "testified" to be just through his faith, God "testifying" on the basis of Abel's sacrificial gifts (11:4a). That Abel was testified by his "faith" to be "just" reminds the audience of God's hortatory promise from Hab 2:4, "My *just one* from *faith* will live" (10:38). That Abel was testified by God to be just on the basis of his "gifts," the "sacrifice" he offered to please God, further likens him to Jesus. As a high priest, Jesus is to offer both "gifts" and "sacrifices" for sins (5:1; 8:3). In contrast to the "gifts" and "sacrifices" offered according to a law (8:4), but not able according to conscience to make perfect for heavenly worship the one offering worship (9:9), Jesus, through the eternal Spirit, offered himself unblemished to God. It is the

---

30. Lane, *Hebrews 9–13*, 330: "[T]hrough the visible we perceive the invisible divine reality as the actual ground of all things because of the intervention of faith."

sacrificial blood of the Christ that will cleanse our conscience from sinful dead works to offer worship to the living God (9:14). Thus, the sacrifice of Abel prefigures that of Jesus and provides the audience with a model of a just one who will live from faith.

Abel's having "died" (11:4b) is in accord with the human condition in which anyone may "die" without pity on the basis of two or three witnesses (10:28), in which it is appointed for men to "die" once (9:27), and in which men who "die" stand in contrast to one testified to go on living forever (7:8). God, who in the past has "spoken" to the fathers in the prophets (1:1), has now "spoken" to us in a Son (1:2). In Ps 94:7–8 the scriptural voice of God has "spoken" to the audience of another "day" to heed his word in order to enter into his heavenly, eternal Sabbath rest and worship (4:8). That Abel, although having died, is still "speaking" (11:4b) thus means that he is still speaking to the audience, as a worshiping assembly, in a divinely revelatory way through this scriptural account about him (11:4b).

Abel, although already having died, still reveals how the audience can conduct themselves in accord with the hortatory promise of God from Hab 2:4, namely, "My just one from faith will live" (10:38). Through "this," that is, through the faith by which Abel offered to God sacrificial gifts, he was testified to be just (11:4a)—to be God's just one who lives his life from faith. Abel's offering of sacrificial gifts, which prefigures Jesus' offering of himself as a sacrifice, thus indicates how each member of the audience can likewise be God's just one who presently lives from faith by similarly offering sacrificial gifts to God. That Abel is still speaking, although having died (11:4b), with its implication that there is a sense in which he is still living, bolsters for the audience the promise that, as God's just ones who presently live from faith, they will also live eternally as heavenly worshipers of the living God.[31]

---

31. According to Lane, ibid., 335, the statement in 11:4b "is distinguished from the Jewish traditions about Abel because it reflects no interest in the act of fratricide nor in Abel as the proto-martyr. All of the emphasis falls on the fact that it is *by his faith* (and not by his blood) that Abel continues to speak. The allusion is thus not to Gen 4:10, which speaks of the cry of Abel's blood from the ground for retribution or reconciliation, but to the record of God's approval of his integrity and his sacrifice in Gen 4:4. . . . The writer affirms that Abel's faith continues to speak *to us* through the written record of his action in Scripture, which transmits to us the exemplary character of his offering." Johnson, *Hebrews*, 281: "Abel anticipates resurrection and demonstrates that 'the righteous one will live from faith.'" See also Lohr, "Righteous Abel, 494; Moberly, "Exemplars," 353–63.

The audience have already heard how a "change" from an earthly to a heavenly reality is accomplished by God. Since the Levitical, earthly priesthood is being "changed" by God (divine passive) to the heavenly priesthood of Jesus, of necessity a "change" of law also comes about by God (7:12). Jesus is thus a different, heavenly priest forever according to the order of Melchizedek (7:17), since Jesus has come about as a heavenly priest not according to a law of a fleshly commandment but according to the divine power of an indestructible, eternal life (7:16). And now the audience hear of a divinely accomplished change from the earthly to the heavenly involving the exemplary faith of Enoch. By faith Enoch was "changed" so that he did not see death, and he was not found on earth because God "changed" him into a heavenly being, for before the "change" he was testified to have pleased God (11:5; cf. Gen 5:24).

Enoch complements Abel as a model of faith for the audience. Whereas Abel, although having "died," is still speaking to the audience (11:4b), Enoch was changed by God into a heavenly being so that he did not see "death" while on earth (11:5a). Before the change Enoch was "testified" to have pleased "God" (11:5b), thus making explicit the implication that Abel likewise pleased God when he offered to "God" a greater sacrifice beyond Cain, through which he was "testified" to be just, God "testifying" on the basis of his gifts (11:4a). The faith of Enoch together with the faith of Abel provide the audience with a model for pleasing God by offering sacrificial gifts as worship in order to experience a heavenly existence beyond death.

That Enoch was changed by God into a heavenly being without seeing "death" (11:5a) deepens the appreciation of the audience for the significance of the death of Jesus while on earth for his status in heaven. The "death" of Jesus that occurred for deliverance from transgressions under the first covenant (9:15b) represents the necessary "death" to be borne of the one who covenanted (9:16), making him the guarantor of a new covenant (9:15a), so that those who have been called, including the audience, might receive the promise of the eternal inheritance in heaven (9:15c). In contrast to the many earthly priests prevented by "death" from remaining on (7:23), Jesus, who was heard from his reverence after praying to the God able to save him from "death" (5:7), became a heavenly priest who remains forever (7:24). It was through his "death" that Jesus might destroy the one who has the strength of "death," that is the devil (2:14), and free those, as many as by fear of "death" through all their life were held in slavery (2:15). On account of his suffering of "death" on earth, so that on behalf of all he might taste "death," Jesus was crowned with heavenly glory and honor (2:9), becoming an object of heavenly worship.

Whereas Enoch was changed by God into a heavenly being so that he did not "see" death (11:5a), Jesus was to "taste" death so that all who must see and taste death on earth may attain to a heavenly existence (2:9).[32] That Enoch was no longer "found" on earth but in heaven (11:5b) reminds the audience of what Jesus "found" in heaven that has significance for them on earth. As high priest, Jesus entered once for all into the heavenly holy things, "finding" eternal redemption from death (9:12). This means that the audience, as a worshiping community, are to approach with boldness the heavenly throne of grace, in order to receive mercy and "find" divine grace for timely help on earth (4:16).

The focus then moves from the model of Enoch's pleasing God (11:5) to pleasing God in general (11:6). Without faith it is impossible for anyone in the audience to "please" God (11:6a). For it is necessary that the one approaching "God" in worship, following upon the example of Enoch, who "pleased God" (11:5c), and of Abel, who offered to "God" a greater sacrifice (11:4a), believe that God exists and is faithful and that for those seeking him he becomes a "rewarder" (11:6b).[33] That God becomes a "rewarder" for those seeking him resonates with the warning that every transgression and disobedience received a just "recompense" from God (2:2), but also with the promise of a great "recompense" or "reward" from God for the boldness of the audience as a worshiping assembly (10:35).[34]

This continues the complementarity of Enoch and Abel as models of faith for the audience. From his faith Abel was testified by God to be just (11:4a), exemplifying the first part of the quotation of Hab 2:4—"My just one from faith will live" (10:38a). From his faith Enoch, who did not see death on earth but lives in heaven (11:5a), was testified to have "pleased" God (11:5c), exemplifying both the first ("from faith will live") and second part of the same quotation—"and if he draws back my soul does not *take pleasure* in him" (10:38bc). Just as Abel's offering a greater sacrifice to God prefigured Jesus' offering of himself to God, so Enoch's having

---

32. Lane, *Hebrews 9–13*, 336: "The phrase 'to see death,' like the related expression 'to taste death' (2:9), is a Semitism for the experience of death."

33. Hartley, "Heb 11:6."

34. Mitchell, *Hebrews*, 231: "God is presented in Hebrews as a God who rewards justly."

pleased God prefigures Jesus' pleasing of God when, rather than offerings God took no "pleasure" in (10:6, 8), Jesus offered his own body in doing the will of God (10:5–10).

The exemplary faith of both Enoch and Abel demonstrates how without "faith" it is impossible for anyone in the audience to please God through worship, for it is necessary that the one "approaching" God in worship "believe" that God exists and that for those seeking him becomes a "rewarder" (11:6). The faith of Enoch and Abel thus bolsters the exhortation that we "approach" God in worship with a true heart in assurance of "faith" (10:22). That God rewarded both Abel and Enoch with a significant status beyond death inspires the audience, by approaching God in worship and with faith in his eternal existence, to seek him as the God who can reward them with a heavenly existence beyond death.[35]

Similar to Moses having been "warned" by God about the heavenly things that provide the model for worship on earth (8:5), by faith Noah was "warned" by God about heavenly things not yet being "noticed" on earth (11:7a). This recalls that the heavenly reality being "noticed" came to be from things not apparent (11:3), so that faith is a demonstration of heavenly things not being "noticed" on earth (11:1). Noah, then, was warned by God about the heavenly realities that are the object of faith. That by his faith Noah became "reverent" toward God places him in a disposition proper for worship as a model for the audience (11:7b). This is confirmed by the description of the worship of Jesus, who in the days of his flesh offered both prayers and supplications with strong outcrying and tears to the God able to save him from death, and he was heard from his "reverence" toward God (5:7).

The association of Noah's faith with worship continues. That the reverent Noah "furnished" an "ark" for the salvation of his "house" (11:7c) associates him with the things "furnished" for worship in the earthly tabernacles (9:6). The first tabernacle was "furnished" with various things for worship (9:2), and the second even included an ark—the "ark" of the covenant—as a furnishing for worship (9:4).[36] As a model of faith, Noah further illustrates for the audience how greater honor than "the house"

---

35. Ellingworth, *Hebrews*, 577: "In Enoch's case, the reward was doubtless that of removal by God from earth to heaven."

36. Ibid., 578: "[I]t appears natural to distinguish sharply between Noah's ark and the ark of the covenant referred to in 9:4; but in fact Noah's ark was also associated with the making of a covenant (Gn. 6:19; Sir. 44:18), and this fact may have been significant for the author and his readers."

has the one who "furnishes" it for worship (3:3). That Noah furnished an ark "for the salvation" of his "house" enhances him as a model of faith for the audience, who, as the "house" of Christ (3:6), are among those who are going to inherit "salvation" (1:14), those eagerly awaiting the final coming of Christ "for salvation" (9:28).

It was through his faith by which the reverent Noah furnished an ark for the salvation of "his house" that he condemned the world (11:7) of his day to destruction rather than salvation from the great deluge (Gen 6:13; 7:22–23). The implication is that he condemned "the world" on account of unfaithfulness in failing to do the will of God, and thus worship God properly with reverence. The world failed to imitate his reverent faith as the proper disposition for the worship of God.[37] This is confirmed by the recall of Jesus, who, upon entering into "the world" (10:5) demonstrated for the world his reverence in the proper worship of God (5:7) as well as his faithfulness as the divine Son over "his house," the house of God that includes the audience (3:6), by his proclamation that he has come to do the will of God (10:7, 9).

Of "righteousness" according to faith, the righteousness desirable to God, Noah became an heir (11:7). This associates him with Melchizedek as king of God's "righteousness" (7:2), with the word of God's "righteousness" in which the audience are to be experienced (5:13), and with God's "righteousness" rather than lawlessness that the divine Son of God loved (1:9). As a reverent heir of "righteousness" according to faith, Noah joins Enoch, who "pleased" God (11:5), and Abel, who was "just" (11:4), as models for the audience of the hortatory scriptural promise of God from Hab 2:4, "My *just one* from faith will live, and if he draws back my soul takes no pleasure in him" (10:38). That of God's righteousness according to faith Noah became an "heir" associates him with the audience as "heirs" of God's promise (6:17), and with Jesus as the Son God placed as "heir" of all things (1:2). This further motivates the audience to imitate Noah's faith in their worship of God.[38]

---

37. Mitchell, *Hebrews*, 231: "So Noah's faith itself is the instrument of condemnation."

38. Lane, *Hebrews 9–13*, 341: "The concept of 'an heir of the righteousness according to faith' implies that others who respond to God with the faith that Noah demonstrated will share with him in the righteousness God bestows upon persons of faith."

V. 11:8–19

A ⁱⁱ:⁸ By faith *Abraham*, being *called*, obeyed to go out to a place which he was about to receive as an inheritance, and he went out not knowing where he was going. ⁹ By faith he sojourned in the land of the promise as (land) of another, having dwelt in tents with *Isaac* and Jacob, the fellow heirs of the same promise.

    B ¹⁰ For he was waiting for the *city* having foundations, whose architect and builder is God. ¹¹ By faith, even though Sarah herself was barren, he received power for the founding of descendants, though beyond the *time* of maturity, since he considered faithful the one who promised. ¹² And *therefore* from one man there were begotten, and these of one who had become dead, "just as the stars of *heaven* in multitude and as the innumerable sand beyond the shore of the sea" (Gen 22:17). ¹³ᵃ In accord with faith these all died, not receiving the promises but from afar seeing them and greeting and confessing

        C ¹³ᵇ *that* they are strangers and sojourners on the earth.

            D ¹⁴ᵃ For those saying such things manifest

        C' ¹⁴ᵇ *that* they are seeking a fatherland.

    B' ¹⁵ And if they were remembering that from which they came out, they would have had *time* to return. ¹⁶ But now they long for a better one, that is a *heavenly one*. *Therefore*, God is not ashamed to be called their God, for he has made ready for them a *city*.

A' ¹⁷ By faith *Abraham*, being tested, offered *Isaac*, and the one who accepted the promises was ready to offer his only begotten, ¹⁸ to whom it was spoken, "In *Isaac* descendants will be *called* for you" (Gen 21:12), ¹⁹ reasoning that God is able to raise even from the dead, whence him, indeed in a parable, he acquired.

At the conclusion of the preceding unit in 11:1–7 is the statement that of righteousness according to faith Noah became an "heir" (11:7). The term "heir" provides the transitional word connecting this unit to the next one in 11:8–19, which begins by stating that Abraham obeyed to go out to a place which he was about to receive as an "inheritance" (11:8). The transition thus keeps a focus on the theme of "inheriting" in the progression from the exemplary faith of Noah to that of Abraham. And within the third macrochiastic level of the letter to the Hebrews, this unit in 11:8-19 exhibits a parallel relationship with the unit in 10:1-14. The parallelism is indicated by the only occurrences in Hebrews of the verb "waiting"—"henceforth *waiting* until his enemies are placed as a footstool for his feet" in 10:13 and "he was *waiting* for the city having foundations" in 11:10.

That by faith Abraham, being "called" by God, as Aaron was "called" by God to be a high priest (5:4), "obeyed" to go out to a place which he was about to "receive" as an "inheritance," not knowing where he was going (11:8), facilitates the audience's identification with him as a model for their faith. As those who have been "called" by God that they might "receive" the promise of the eternal "inheritance" (9:15), the audience are to "obey" Jesus as a source of eternal salvation (5:9), who himself learned from the things he suffered "obedience" (5:8).

That the earthly high priest enters into "the holy things" each year with sacrificial blood "not his own" but of "another," namely of animals, underscores the divine significance of the very own blood of the heavenly high priest Jesus which he offers as a sacrificial gift to God (9:25). Similarly, that by faith Abraham sojourned in the land of the promise as land "not his own" but of "another" (11:9a) underscores the divine significance of this land, which is to become Abraham's very own, as an inheritance promised by God. The uncertainty of Abraham's not knowing where he was "going" contrasts with the certainty promised to the audience that Jesus, the one who is to "come," will come and he will not delay (10:37).[39]

By faith Abraham sojourned in the land of the "promise," having dwelt in tents with Isaac and Jacob,[40] the "fellow heirs" of the same "promise" (11:9). This associates these three patriarchs with Noah, an "heir" of God's righteousness according to faith (11:7), as well as with Jesus, the divine Son whom God placed as "heir" of all things (1:2). This enhances the significance of these figures as models for the communal faith of the audience, who are "heirs" of the "promise" (6:17), the "promise"

---

39. Ibid., 349-50: "In setting out, 'not knowing where he was going,' Abraham exemplified the faith that invests events not seen with the substantial reality of a demonstration or proof (v 1b)."

40. Koester, *Hebrews*, 485: "The word 'tents' suggests the temporary nature of their situation." Mitchell, *Hebrews*, 236: "The mention of Abraham, Isaac, and Jacob together is common in the biblical tradition."

of an eternal "inheritance" (9:15), and who are to be imitators of those who through faith and patience are "inheriting" the "promises" (6:12). Especially the example of Abraham, who through patience obtained the "promise" (6:15), reinforces the exhortation for the audience to have endurance so that, doing the will of God, they may acquire the "promise" (10:36), since the "promise" to enter into the heavenly rest and worship of God still remains for them (4:1).

Just as the heavenly enthroned high priest Jesus is "waiting" for God to place his enemies as a footstool for his feet (10:13), as part of God's final salvific activity, so Abraham was "waiting" for God's final salvation that includes a divinely constructed heavenly city, whose architect and builder is God himself (11:10).[41] That Abraham was waiting for the city having divine "foundations" reminds the audience of the initial divine "foundation" of their faith—a "foundation" of repentance from dead works and of faith in God (6:1).

According to the divine "power" of an indestructible life Jesus became an eternal high priest (7:16). By the pronouncement of the "power" of God the divine Son is bearing up all things (1:3). Resonating with this, even though his wife Sarah herself was barren,[42] Abraham, by faith, received divine "power" for the divinely initiated "founding" of descendants (11:11a), reminiscent of the divinely initiated "founding" of the world (4:3; 9:26). That Abraham received power from God for the founding of "descendants," literally "seed," enhances his significance as a patriarchal model of faith for the audience, who are among the "descendants" or "seed" of Abraham (2:16), as children of God and brothers of Jesus (2:11–17).

That God acted beyond the humanly opportune "time" of maturity (11:11b) in giving Abraham the power for the founding of descendants resonates with God's bringing about the "time" of correction (9:10), the "time" that has now arrived to make perfect, according to conscience, the one offering worship (9:9). As a model for the audience, warned against "considering" unclean the blood of the new covenant, the blood of the

---

41. Mitchell, *Hebrews*, 236: "Confirmation of this city's location comes in the identification of its architect, *technitēs*, and builder, *dēmiourgos*, as God. The LXX uses *technitēs* in relation to God only at Wis 13:1. Philo uses both terms synonymously in the same order of God."

42. Greenlee, "Sarah's Faith" 37–42; idem, "By Faith Sarah"; van der Horst, "Sarah's Seminal Emission"; idem, "Did Sarah."

Son of God (10:29), Abraham "considered" faithful the one who promised (11:11c). That Abraham considered "faithful" the God who "promised" bolsters the exhortation for the audience to hold to the confession of the hope unwaveringly, for "faithful" is the God who "promised" (10:23), indeed, the God who "promised" to Abraham (6:13).

Therefore, by faith, from this one man, Abraham, as he considered faithful the God who promised (11:11), there were "begotten" descendants by the power of God (11:12a), reminiscent of the power pronounced by God in begetting his divine Son in accord with the scriptural quotation of Ps 2:7: "Son of mine are you, I today have *begotten* you" (1:5; 5:5). Since Abraham was beyond the time of maturity (11:11), beyond the time for begetting new human life, these descendants were begotten of one who had become as good as dead (11:12b). In accord with the scriptural promise of God in Gen 22:17b these descendants were so numerous that they were "just as the stars of heaven in multitude and as the innumerable sand beyond the shore of the sea" (11:12c). The descendants were as numerous as the stars of "heaven," the very "heaven" itself into which Christ entered as high priest on our behalf (9:24). This quotation of Gen 22:17b thus complements the quotation of Gen 22:17a, when God promised to Abraham a multitude of descendants among whom are the audience (2:16): "Indeed, blessing I will bless you, and multiplying I will multiply you" (6:14).

Through faith Abel, although having "died," still speaks to the audience (11:4). Similarly, in accord with faith, these patriarchs (11:8–9) all "died," not receiving the fulfillment of the promises but from afar seeing them and greeting and confessing (11:13a), which contains a message of encouragement for the audience. Although these patriarchs did not receive the fulfillment of the "promises," including the land of the "promise" Abraham was to receive as an inheritance, along with Isaac and Jacob as fellow heirs of the same "promise" (11:9), they were seeing the fulfillment of these promises from afar and greeting them and confessing as models for the audience. That these models of faith and hope were "confessing" assists the audience, as a worshiping assembly, to hold to their own "confession" of the hope unwaveringly (10:23), to hold fast the "confession" of Jesus as our heavenly high priest (4:14), and to turn attention to the apostle and high priest of our "confession," Jesus (3:1).

That these patriarchs were confessing that they are strangers "on the earth" (11:13b) accords with the statement that by faith Abraham sojourned in the "land" of the promise as (land) of another, having dwelt in tents with Isaac and Jacob (11:9). It implies that the true and lasting home of them as well as of the audience is heaven, as it resonates with the notice that if Jesus would be "on earth," he would not be a priest (8:4), indeed, the high priest, who sat at the right of the throne of the Majesty in the heavens (8:1).

What the patriarchs "manifest" (11:14a) on earth by confessing that they are merely strangers and sojourners on the earth associates them with the heavenly "manifestation" of Jesus, as it reminds the audience that Christ did not enter into earthly "holy things" made by hands, a copy of the true ones, but into heaven itself, now to be "manifested" in the presence of God on behalf of us (9:24). In contrast to a temporary homeland on earth (11:13b), the patriarchs were seeking a lasting "fatherland" (11:14b), the heavenly home of God the Father, the God whose scriptural voice in 2 Sam 7:14 declared about Jesus, "I will be to him as a *Father*, and he will be to me as a *Son*" (1:5). That the patriarchs manifest that they are "seeking for" a heavenly fatherland models for the audience the kind of faith needed to please God as they approach him in worship. To truly worship God, they must believe that God exists and that for those "seeking him out" he becomes a "rewarder" (11:6).

Abraham received divine power for the founding of descendants, even though he was beyond the opportune "time" of maturity (11:11). In contrast, by their human capability, if the patriarchs were remembering that earthly land from which they came out in seeking a fatherland (11:14), they would have had the opportune "time" to return (11:15). Instead, the patriarchs were longing for a "better" fatherland, indeed, a "heavenly" one (11:16a). This assimilates them with the audience, who accepted the confiscation of their earthly possessions with joy, knowing that they have a "better" heavenly possession that remains (10:34). It recalls the association of "better" with "heavenly" in that "heavenly things," the "heavenly things" serving as the pattern for worship (8:5), need to be cleansed with "better" sacrifices (9:23). This "better" fatherland adds to the series of "better" things presented for the benefit of the audience (1:4; 6:9; 7:7, 19, 22; 8:6). The patriarchs' longing for a fatherland that is "heavenly" thus further associates them with the audience, who, as a worshiping assembly, have already tasted of the "heavenly" gift (6:4) and are partners of a "heavenly" calling (3:1) to participate in heavenly worship.

Just as "therefore," by the power of God, from the one man Abraham there were begotten numerous descendants (11:12), so "therefore," God is "not ashamed" to be "called" the God of the patriarchs (11:16b). This further links the patriarchs to the audience, as among those whom Jesus, the divine Son, is "not ashamed" to "call" brothers (2:11). With regard to the faith of Abraham, who was waiting for the "city" having foundations, whose architect and builder is God (11:10), God has made ready for the patriarchs and for the audience as a worshiping assembly a "city," indeed, a heavenly one (11:16c) with a heavenly worship.

Recalling that by faith Abel "offered" to God a greater sacrifice beyond Cain (11:4), by faith Abraham, being tested, "offered" Isaac, and the one who accepted the promises was ready to "offer" his only begotten (11:17). That Abraham was "tested" likens him to Jesus as a model of faith for the audience. In Jesus we have a high priest who has been "tested" in all things in likeness to us, yet without sin (4:15). And in what Jesus himself suffered in being "tested," those who are being "tested," particularly the audience, he is able to help (2:18).

As the one who accepted "the promises" from God, "the promises" of which the patriarchs, having died, did not receive the fulfillment (11:13), Abraham was ready to offer his only begotten son, Isaac (11:17), a fellow heir with Abraham of the same "promise" of an inheritance (11:9). This further associates the audience, exhorted to be imitators of those who through faith and patience are inheriting "the promises" (6:12), with Abraham, the one having "the promises" (7:6).

Abraham was ready to offer his only begotten son, Isaac, even though to Abraham it was spoken by the scriptural voice of God in Gen 21:12 that "in Isaac descendants will be called for you" (11:18). God's promise to Abraham that in Isaac descendants will be "called" for him adds to God's promise of a place Abraham was being "called" to receive as an inheritance (11:8). God's promise to Abraham that in Isaac "descendants" will be called for him accords with the notice that by faith Abraham received divine power for the founding of "descendants" (11:11). This further enhances the significance of Abraham as a paternal model of faith for the audience, who are numbered among Abraham's "descendants" as those taken hold of by Jesus (2:16).

Abraham's reasoning that God is able to raise even from the "dead" (11:19a) further associates him with the audience, who have already been taught about God's resurrection of the "dead" (6:2). That God is "able" or has the "power" to raise from the dead accords with the divine "power" the believing but aged Abraham, as one who had become as good as "dead" (11:12), received for the founding of descendants (11:11). The first, earthly tabernacle, in which the way to the heavenly "holy things" had not appeared (9:8), is a "parable," that is, a comparison or analogy, for the present time of the audience that has now arrived (9:9), the time when the way to the heavenly "holy things" has appeared with the heavenly exaltation of the high priest Jesus. Similarly, Abraham, by faith reasoning that God is able to raise even from the dead, acquired Isaac, without his dying and being raised, in a "parable" (11:19)—a comparison or analogy for God's resurrection of the dead.[43] That by faith Abraham "acquired" Isaac, the beginning of God's promise of descendants, reinforces the exhortation for the audience to have endurance so that, doing the will of God, "you may acquire" the promise of final salvation (10:36).[44]

Conclusion

I. Ironically, in the same sacrifices the Levitical high priests offer each year for all time (10:1), there is each year only the continual remembrance of sins (10:3), rather than a cleansing of the consciousness of sins (10:2). It is impossible for the blood of bulls and goats to take away sins (10:4). In contrast to the same animal sacrifices which the Levitical priests offer repeatedly (10:1), the scriptural voice of Jesus (Ps 39:7-9) acknowledges that sacrifice and offering God did not want, "but a body you provided for me" (10:5). Although, as Jesus acknowledged to God, sacrifice and offering "you did not want or *will*," he pronounces that he has come precisely "to do, O God, your *will*" (10:6-9). This gives Jesus his role in the disappearing of the first covenant that is becoming old and aging, now that a new, second covenant has been announced (8:13), introducing a new system for the worship of God (10:9).

---

43. Johnson, *Hebrews*, 295: "Abraham received Isaac 'back' literally, when God stopped the sacrifice and Isaac was able to accompany his father home. . . . But this return is 'figuratively' a resurrection from the dead, since, like Sarah and Abraham at the time of the child's birth, Isaac himself was 'as good as dead' with the knife to his throat. As in the use of the same phrase in 9:9, however, the author may also imply another symbolic dimension, namely the resurrection from the dead that occurred in Christ and is anticipated by believers. The rescue of Isaac, at the very least, points forward to a full realization of God's power to bring life from death."

44. Bockmuehl, "Abraham's Faith."

In contrast to the offerings God did not want (10:5, 8), it is through the offering of the body of Jesus Christ once for all, the body God provided for him (10:5), that we have been made holy (10:10). In contrast to every Levitical priest offering repeatedly the same sacrifices, which are never able to cast off the sins that prevent worship (10:11), Jesus Christ offered one sacrifice on behalf of sins for all time (10:12). That the heavenly enthroned Jesus Christ is still waiting until his enemies are placed as a footstool for his feet (10:13) reminds the audience that the great salvation they are not to neglect (2:3) as a worshiping assembly is still to be consummated. They are those eagerly awaiting him for final, eternal salvation (9:28). Although the law never is able to make perfect those who approach for worship (10:1), because those offering worship still have consciousness of sins (10:2), by one offering of himself, Jesus Christ has made perfect for all time those who are being made holy (10:14) for their role in heavenly worship.

II. That the Holy Spirit testifies to us as the divine speaker of Jer 38:33 (10:15–16) reminds the audience of the scriptural testimony the Holy Spirit gave in speaking Ps 94:7–11, with its warning to the audience as a worshiping assembly, "Today when you hear his voice, 'do not harden your hearts'" (3:7–8a). In correspondence to the decisive scriptural promise of God in Jer 38:34b that their sins and their lawless deeds "I certainly will remember no longer" (10:17), there is no longer offering for sin (10:18). That our entrance to the heavenly "holy things" is in the blood and through the flesh of Jesus (10:19–20) leads the audience to appreciate that the self-offering of Jesus as the eternal high priest was accomplished in and through the blood and flesh he shared with us as our fellow and fraternal human being (2:14). Since we have boldness for entrance to the heavenly "holy things" and a great priest over the house of God (10:19–21), we are to approach for the worship of God with a true heart in assurance of faith (10:22a). It is as a consequence of the better sacrificial self-offering of the body of Jesus (10:5, 10) that we have been washed with regard to the body by the clean water (10:22b) of baptism and thus enabled to participate fully in the worship of God.

The exhortation for us to approach for worship with a true heart in assurance of faith is strengthened by the further exhortation that, because the one who promised is faithful, we hold to the confession of the hope unwaveringly (10:23). Exhorted to turn attention to one another for stirring up love and beneficent works (10:24), the audience are urged not to abandon, as is the custom of some, their own gathering for communal worship (10:25a). Rather, they are to be encouraging one another, all the more as they take note of the day drawing near (10:25b). The audience are not to become apostates who go on deliberately sinning (10:26a), since a sacrifice for sins no longer remains for them (10:26b). They may prepare for the decisive day of final salvation at each day set as the "today" for listening during their communal worship to the voice of God inviting them to enter into God's own eternal Sabbath rest and worship that remains for them in heaven (4:7–11).

To abandon the gathering for worship (10:25) and deliberately to go on sinning (10:26) is to consider unclean the blood of the covenant (10:29). This is the blood of the new covenant promised by God (Jer 38:33 in 10:16), which is the blood of Jesus by which we, as a worshiping assembly, have boldness for entrance into the heavenly "holy things" (10:19), the blood of the Christ that will cleanse our conscience to offer heavenly worship to the living God (9:14). The Lord God will judge his people, in accord with a certain fearful expectation of judgment (10:27) for those who deliberately go on sinning (10:26). The audience are to count themselves as belonging to this people of God for whom a heavenly and eternal Sabbath rest and worship remains (4:9), the people who are to be judged by God (10:27–30).

III. That it is fearful to fall into the hands of the living God (10:31) develops the negative, ominous dimension of the audience's fear of a worse punishment (10:29) from the God who will judge his people. But it also develops the positive, hopeful dimension of being fearful with its connotation of respect, reverence, and awe in the presence of the divine. The audience endured much conflict of sufferings (10:32), of being publicly exposed to reproaches and afflictions and of becoming partners of those so treated (10:33). They even suffered with the prisoners and accepted the confiscation of their property with joy, knowing that they have a better possession that remains forever (10:34). The boldness the audience as a worshiping assembly have for the entrance to the heavenly "holy things" in the blood of Jesus (10:19) they are not to throw away as it has great recompense from God (10:35). They have need of endurance so that, doing the will of God, they may acquire the promise (10:36) of an eternal inheritance for those who have been called by God for the entrance into heaven and its worship (9:15; 3:1).

That we are of faith encourages each member of the audience to continue to be God's just one who, from faith, will live both presently and eternally in the heavenly rest and worship of the ever living God (10:38). And that this faith results in the preservation of the soul (10:39)—the better possession that remains (10:34)—resonates with how the living word of God is penetrating as far as a division of soul and spirit (4:12), calling for a response in and through worship.

IV. That faith is the reality of things being hoped for (11:1a) indicates that it is a divine reality that is made real or realized in and through one's faith in God. Faith is the demonstration, the giving of proof or evidence, of divine things not presently being noticed (11:1b). The divine realities that the audience are now noticing by faith (11:3) include the taking note of Jesus as the divine Son crowned by God with heavenly glory and honor (2:9) to be the object of heavenly worship. The exemplary faith of both Enoch (11:5) and Abel (11:4) demonstrates how without faith it is impossible for anyone to please God through worship, for it is necessary that the one approaching God in worship believe that God exists and that for those seeking him he becomes a "rewarder" (11:6). That God rewarded both Abel and Enoch with a significant status beyond death inspires the audience, by approaching God in worship and with faith in his eternal existence, to seek him as the God who can reward them with a heavenly existence beyond death. That of God's righteousness according to faith the reverent Noah became an heir (11:7) associates him with the audience as heirs of God's promise (6:17), motivating them to imitate Noah's faith in their worship of God.

V. That by faith Abraham, being called by God, obeyed to go out to a place which he was about to receive as an inheritance, not knowing where he was going (11:8), facilitates the audience's identification with him. As those who have been called by God that they might receive the promise of the eternal inheritance (9:15), the audience are to obey Jesus as a source of eternal salvation (5:9), who himself learned from the things he suffered obedience (5:8). By faith Abraham sojourned in the land of the promise, having dwelt in tents with Isaac and Jacob, the fellow heirs of the same promise (11:9). The example of Abraham, who through patience obtained the promise (6:15), reinforces the exhortation for the audience to have endurance so that, doing the will of God, they may acquire the promise (10:36), since the promise to enter into the heavenly rest and worship of God still remains for them (4:1).

That Abraham received power from God for the founding of descendants (11:11) enhances his significance for the audience, who are among the descendants of Abraham (2:16), as children of God and brothers of Jesus (2:11–17). By faith, from this one man, Abraham, as he considered faithful the God who promised (11:11), there were begotten numerous descendants by the power of God, begotten of one who had become as good as dead (11:12). Abraham and his fellow patriarchs, who were seeing the fulfillment of the promises from afar and greeting them and confessing (11:13), serve as models for the audience. As a worshiping assembly, the audience are to hold to their own confession of the hope unwaveringly (10:23), to hold fast the confession of Jesus as our heavenly high priest (4:14), and to turn attention to the apostle and high priest of our confession, Jesus (3:1). That the patriarchs manifest that they are seeking for a heavenly fatherland (11:14) exemplifies the kind of faith the audience need to please God as they approach him in worship.

The patriarchs' longing for a fatherland that is heavenly (11:15–16) associates them with the audience, who have already tasted of the heavenly gift (6:4) and are partners of a heavenly calling (3:1) to participate in heavenly worship. With regard to the faith of Abraham, who was waiting for the city having foundations, whose architect and builder is God (11:10), God has made ready for the patriarchs and for the audience a city, indeed, a heavenly one (11:16) with a heavenly worship. Abraham was ready to offer his only begotten son, Isaac (11:17–18), a fellow heir with Abraham of the same promise of an inheritance (11:9). This further associates the audience, exhorted to be imitators of those who through faith and patience are inheriting the promises (6:12), with Abraham, the one having the promises (7:6). Abraham, by faith reasoning that God is able to raise even from the dead, acquired Isaac, without his dying and being raised, in a "parable" (11:19)—a comparison or analogy for God's resurrection of the dead. That by faith Abraham "acquired" Isaac, the beginning of God's promise of descendants, reinforces the exhortation for the audience to have endurance so that, doing the will of God, "you may acquire" the promise of final salvation that includes heavenly rest and worship (10:36).

6

Hebrews 11:20—13:25

I. 11:20-31

A ²⁰ By faith even concerning things to come Isaac blessed Jacob and Esau. ²¹ By faith Jacob, as he was dying, blessed each of the sons of Joseph and worshiped *on* the top of his *staff* ([*rhabdou*], Gen 47:31). ²² By faith Joseph, coming to an end, reminded the sons of Israel concerning the exodus and concerning his bones commanded (Gen 50:24–25).

    B ²³ By faith Moses, when he was born, was hidden for three months by his parents, because they saw the child was beautiful and were not *afraid* of the edict of *the king*.

        C ²⁴ By faith Moses, having become great, refused to be said to be a son of the daughter of Pharaoh, ²⁵ choosing rather to be mistreated with the people of God than to have a temporary enjoyment of sin, ²⁶ᵃ having considered greater wealth than the treasures of *Egypt*

            D ²⁶ᵇ the reproach of the Christ, for he was looking away to the recompense.

        C' ²⁷ᵃ By faith he left *Egypt*,

    B' ²⁷ᵇ not *afraid* of the fury of *the king*, for as if seeing the one who is invisible he persevered. ²⁸ By faith he kept the Passover and the applying of the blood, so that the one who was to destroy the firstborn might not touch them (Exod 12:7, 13).

A' ²⁹ By faith they went through the Red Sea as through dry land, in which, taking an attempt, the Egyptians were drowned. ³⁰ By faith the walls of Jericho fell, having been encircled *on* seven days. ³¹ By faith *Rahab* (*Rhaab*) the harlot did not perish together with those who disobeyed, having welcomed the spies with peace (Josh 6:1–17).

Toward the conclusion of the preceding unit in 11:8–19 is a reference to "Isaac" in the quotation from Gen 21:12—"In *Isaac* descendants will be called for you" (11:18). The reference to "Isaac" provides the transitional word connecting this unit to the next one in 11:20–31, which begins with the statement that by faith even concerning things to come "Isaac" blessed Jacob and Esau (11:20). The transition thus moves the focus from the faith of Abraham in the promise of Isaac to the faith of Isaac himself. And with regard to the second macrochiastic level, this unit in 11:20–31 is the third and final central and unparalleled unit, each of which refers to Moses in relation to the Christ. The unit in 3:1–6 presents Jesus Christ as the Son of God who is faithful beyond Moses in the house of God. The unit in 8:1–6 presents Jesus as a high priest in the heavenly tabernacle shown to Moses. And this unit in 11:20–31 presents Moses as a model of faith who endured the reproach of the Christ.

By faith even concerning "things to come" (*mellontōn*), that is, concerning the promised good "things to come" (*mellontōn*) regarding the heavenly worship of which the law concerning earthly worship has only a shadow (10:1), Isaac blessed both of his sons, Jacob and Esau (11:20).[1] That Isaac "blessed" Jacob and Esau continues the actualization of God's promise to Abraham, the father of Isaac, from Gen 22:17a: "Indeed, *blessing I will bless* you" (6:14). Melchizedek, priest of the God Most High, began to actualize this divine promise, having "blessed" Abraham (7:1). Exemplifying how an inferior is "blessed" by a superior (7:7), Melchizedek "blessed" Abraham as the one having the promises (7:6). Although Isaac blessed both Jacob and Esau, only Jacob was a fellow heir with Isaac of the promise Abraham received (11:9).

By faith Jacob, as he was "dying" (11:21), recalling that he was among the patriarchs all of whom in accord with faith "died" without receiving the fulfillment of the promises, but from afar was seeing them and greeting and confessing that they are strangers and sojourners on the earth

---

1. Lane, *Hebrews 9–13*, 364: "The formulation of v 20 accentuates Isaac's unqualified adherence to whatever God had planned *kai peri mellontōn*, 'even with respect to the future.' The force of *kai*, 'even,' is intensive; it functions to place the phrase *peri mellontōn* in high relief." On the inclusion of a blessing for Esau here, see Koester, *Hebrews*, 492.

(11:13). And recalling that Abel, although having "died" is still speaking to the audience (11:4), Jacob, as he was "dying," blessed each of the sons of Joseph (11:21). That he "blessed" each of the sons of his son Joseph continues the actualization of the divine promise he received when Isaac "blessed" Jacob and Esau (11:20). The blessing of "each" of the sons of Joseph as inheritors of the divine promise reinforces the exhortation for "each" member of the audience to demonstrate the same eagerness for the assurance of the hope until the end (6:11). This is so that they may not become sluggish, but rather imitators of those who through faith and patience are inheriting the promises (6:12), including these patriarchal models of faith.

By faith, while he was dying and thus leaving this earth where he was merely a stranger and sojourner (11:9, 13), Jacob "worshiped" on the top of his staff (11:21), a direct allusion to Gen 47:31 (LXX).[2] This last act of earthly worship by the dying Jacob anticipates his participation in the heavenly worship of the exalted Son of God, as it resonates with the scriptural proclamation that when God leads the firstborn into the heavenly world, he says, "And let all the angels of God *worship* him (Deut 32:43; Ps 96:7)" (1:6). As an anticipation of heavenly worship, Jacob worshiped on the top of his "staff," recalling the "staff" of the priest Aaron that is associated with worship in the earthly tabernacle (9:4), as well as the "staff" of uprightness that is a "staff" of the heavenly kingdom of the enthroned divine Son of God (1:8). The dying Jacob thus provides the audience with a model of faith that includes the hope of participating in the heavenly worship of the heavenly fatherland.

The faith of Joseph as he was "coming to an end" (11:22a) likewise serves as a model for the audience, who have been exhorted to demonstrate the same eagerness for the assurance of the hope until the "end" (6:11), and, as partners of the Christ, to hold the beginning of the reality firm until the "end" (3:14). The patriarchs did not "remember" the land from which they "came out" (11:15). In contrast, Joseph "reminded" the sons of Israel, resonating with the house of Israel as the recipients of God's promise of a new covenant (8:8, 10), concerning the "exodus" (11:22b) to a land anticipating the heavenly fatherland the patriarchs were seeking (11:15).[3]

---

2. Lane, *Hebrews 9–13*, 365: "Jacob's final act of worship, leaning upon the top of his staff, was characteristic for one who lived his life as a stranger and a sojourner."

3. Johnson, *Hebrews*, 296: "[A]lthough the actual exodus will be in the future, Joseph's

This "exodus" or "way out" of an earthly land (11:22b) thus anticipates the fresh and living "way" into the heavenly holy things that Jesus inaugurated for us (9:8; 10:20). That Joseph "commanded" the sons of Israel concerning his bones (11:22c), which they were to bring with them out of their exodus and into a new land (Gen 50:24–25), anticipates the divine commandment of a new covenant in accord with the proclamation of Moses in Exod 24:8: "This is the blood of the covenant which God has *commanded* to you" (9:20). According to this new covenant commanded by God, the blood of the Christ, who through the eternal Spirit offered himself unblemished to God, will cleanse our conscience from dead works to offer worship to the living God (9:14), so that we may participate in the worship of the heavenly fatherland that was anticipated by the faith of these patriarchs.

When Moses, one of the multitude "begotten" from the one man Abraham in accord with God's promise (11:12), was "born" (11:23), by faith his parents hid him for three months (Exod 2:2), in view of the edict of the king of Egypt that every Hebrew male child be killed (Exod 1:15–22).[4] Their seeing that the "child" was beautiful as a child from God associates Moses with the audience, as the "children" with whom Jesus shared in blood and flesh (2:14), the "children" whom God gave to him (2:13).[5] That they were not "afraid" of the edict of the "king" (11:23), who stands in contrast to Melchizedek as God's "king" of righteousness and of peace (7:1–2), provides the audience with a model for heeding the exhortation for us to be "afraid," lest, while the promise to enter into God's heavenly rest and worship is left, anyone of us seem to have been lacking (4:1).[6]

---

faith is demonstrated by his remembering and trusting—and acting in light of—the *promise* of God's visitation to the people that was stated to Abraham in Gen 15:13–15. His act of memory is therefore also an act of faith that God could accomplish what he had promised."

4. There are references to Moses in 3:2, 3, 5, 16; 7:14; 8:5; 9:19; 10:28. See D'Angelo, *Moses*.

5. On Moses as a "beautiful" (*asteion*) child, Lane (*Hebrews 9–13*, 370) refers to "a well-established tradition of interpretation that found in the word *asteios* an indication that the infant possessed a visible sign of God's elective favor. According to v 23, Moses' parents found in the extraordinary appearance of their son a basis for faith in the as yet unseen purposes of God; his unusual attractiveness was to them a visible sign that he enjoyed God's favor and protection."

6. This "edict" (*diatagma*) of the king for the slaying of infants appears in Wis 11:7, as noted by Ellingworth, *Hebrews*, 610. Koester, *Hebrews*, 501: "Fearing God is appropriate, whereas fearing a king who opposes God is not."

The reference to Moses as *"having become great"* (11:24a) by God (divine passive), associates him with Jesus as a "great" high priest (4:14; 10:21). Jesus "became" higher than the heavens (7:26), "having become" a priest forever according to the order of Melchizedek (6:20), and "having become" so far better than the angels to the degree that more excellent beyond them he has inherited a name (1:4). As one of the "sons" of Israel (11:22), Moses refused to be said to be a "son" of the daughter of Pharaoh (11:24b). That by faith Moses chose rather to be mistreated with "the people of God" than to have a temporary enjoyment of sin (11:25) further commends him as a model of faith for the audience, as among "the people of God" for whom the heavenly Sabbath rest and worship of God still remains (4:9). His refusal of a temporary enjoyment of "sin" aligns him with Jesus as one who is without "sin " (4:15; 9:28). In contrast to one who "considers" unclean the blood of the covenant (10:29), and in line with Abraham, who "considered" faithful the God who promised (11:11), Moses "considered" what was of greater wealth than the treasures of "Egypt" (11:26a). This recalls that God led his people out of the land of "Egypt" through Moses (3:16; 8:9).

That Moses considered the "reproach" of the Christ to be of greater wealth than the treasures of Egypt (11:26) further associates him with the audience, who not only have been publicly exposed to "reproaches" and afflictions, but became partners of those so treated (10:33).[7] Moses' endurance of the reproach of "the Christ," for he was looking away to the recompense (11:26), strengthens the assurance that the blood of "the Christ" will cleanse our conscience from dead works to offer worship to the living God (9:14). It also bolsters the exhortations for the audience to depart from the word at the beginning about "the Christ" in order to bear forward toward the perfection (6:1), and to become partners of "the Christ" by holding the beginning of the reality firm until the end (3:14). That by faith Moses endured the reproach of the Christ, for he was looking away to the "recompense" from God, reinforces the exhortation for

---

7. Attridge, *Hebrews*, 341: "Moses could have been understood to be aware of the ultimate perfecter of the faith, the one who would bring God's promises to reality. Sustained by that awareness, he accepted the reproach that accompanied his association with Christ and Christ's people. . . . Although our author probably assumes some sort of prophetic consciousness on the part of Moses, he is not concerned to make clear precisely how the lawgiver accepts the reproach 'of Christ.'" The phrase "the reproach of the Christ" (*ton oneidismon tou Christou*) may be inspired by Ps 88:51–52. On this, see Lane, *Hebrews 9–13*, 373; Johnson, *Hebrews*, 301.

the audience as a worshiping assembly not to throw away their boldness, which has great "recompense" from God (10:35). Indeed, God becomes a "rewarder" for those seeking him in worship (11:6), and is the giver of a just "recompense" (2:2).

That by faith Moses "left" Egypt (11:27a) in view of a recompense from God serves as a model of the faith associated with the promise God has "left" for the audience. They have been exhorted to be afraid lest, while the promise to enter into God's heavenly rest and worship is still "left" for them, anyone of them seem to have been lacking in faith (4:1). The intensification from both parents together not fearing the "edict" of the king (11:23) to Moses as an individual not fearing the actual "fury" of the king (11:27b) further reinforces, with particular poignancy, the exhortation for the Godly fear of the audience concerning every individual among them: "Let us *be afraid* then, lest, while the promise to enter into his rest is left, anyone of you seem to have been lacking" (4:1).

That Moses did not fear the fury of the king because of the insight of his faith—"for" as if "seeing" the God who is invisible he persevered (11:27)—complements how he endured the reproach of the Christ because of the foresight of his faith—"for" he was "looking away" to the recompense from God (11:26).[8] The faith of Moses thus exemplifies for the audience how faith is the reality of things being hoped for and the demonstration of things not yet being "noticed" (11:1). It serves as a model for the insight and foresight of the faith of the audience—we who, as a worshiping assembly, are "taking note" of Jesus (2:9), even though we do not now "see" all things subjected to him (2:8).

In keeping the Passover and the "applying" or "pouring" of the "blood," Moses demonstrated his faith in the future salvific effectiveness regarding the sacrificial blood of the Passover lamb, so that the one who was to destroy (Exod 12:23) the firstborn might not even touch them (11:28)—the firstborn sons of Israel (11:22). This serves as a model for the faith of the audience in the future salvific effectiveness regarding the sacrificial blood of the Christ, namely, that the "blood" of the Christ, who through the eternal Spirit "offered" himself unblemished to God, *will* cleanse our conscience from sinful dead works to offer worship to the living God (9:14). Moses' faith in God regarding the firstborn sons of

---

8. Koester, *Hebrews*, 504: "This implies that Moses did not actually see God. It is difficult to identify this passage with God's revelation in the burning bush, in the pillar of cloud and fire, or in visions. Instead, the text underscores the nature of faith itself."

Israel—that God would not allow the one who was to destroy the "firstborn" so much as touch them—bolsters the faith of the audience regarding the firstborn divine Son. God leads the "firstborn" into the heavenly world to be worshiped by God's angels (1:6) along with the audience as among those assisted by these angelic spirits (1:14).[9]

That, by faith in the promises of God, the sons of Israel, led by Moses (3:16), went through the Red "Sea" "as" if they were going through dry land (11:29a; cf. Exod 14:21–22) resonates with another comparison involving the sea in God's promise that Abraham's descendants would be "as" the innumerable sand beyond the shore of the "sea" (11:12). In contrast to the faith of the patriarchs, who died without "receiving" or "taking" hold of the promises (11:13), by their lack of faith, the Egyptians were drowned, "taking" an attempt to go through that same Red Sea (11:29b). Those who did go through the Red Sea thus underscore for the audience the life-giving dimension of faith.

Just as "the corpses fell" in the wilderness of those who had sinned (3:17), in accord with God's promise that they would not enter into his rest (3:11, 18; 4:5), so by faith "the walls of Jericho fell," having been encircled on seven days (11:30), in accord with God's promise that they would do so (Josh 6:1–17). This serves as a model of faith for the audience, for whom God's promise to enter into his heavenly rest still remains (4:1), to strive to enter into that rest and worship, so that not anyone of them may "fall" in the same pattern of disobedience (4:11). That by faith Jacob worshiped "on" the top of his "staff" (11:21) anticipates the heavenly worship promised by God (1:6, 14). Similarly, that by faith the walls of Jericho were encircled "on" seven days anticipates their fall, as promised by God (11:30; cf. Josh 6:15–17). And that by faith "Rahab" (*Rhaab*, an alliterative chiastic parallel with *rhabdou*, "staff," in 11:21) the harlot welcomed the Israelite spies with peace anticipates her not perishing together with those who disobeyed (11:31; cf. Josh 2:1–21; 6:22–25), as sworn to her by God (Josh 2:12).[10] This further emphasizes for the audience the life-giving dimension of faith.

---

9. MacDonald, "By Faith Moses."

10. Lane, *Hebrews 9–13*, 379: "The traditional description of Rahab as *hē pornē*, 'the prostitute,' has its source in Scripture (Josh 2:1; 6:17, 22, 25). She was, nevertheless, a recognized member of her family group (Josh 2:12–13, 18; 6:23), and this was a status not normally enjoyed by a prostitute."

The faith of Rahab that resulted in her not perishing with "those who disobeyed" (11:31a) serves as a model for the life-giving faith of the audience so that they do not perish (3:17) with "those who disobeyed" and did not enter into God's rest (3:18). Rather, the audience are to enter into God's own heavenly rest and worship as those who believed (4:3). In view of those who did not enter into God's rest because of "disobedience" (4:6), Rahab's faith further reinforces the exhortation for the audience to strive to enter into that rest and worship, so that not anyone of them may fall in the same pattern of "disobedience" (4:11). And that by faith Rahab welcomed the spies with "peace" (11:31b) adds to her appeal as a model of faith for the audience, as it associates her with the venerable Melchizedek, king of "peace" (7:2).[11]

II. 11:32–40

A [32a] And *what* still may I say?

    B [32b] For the time will fail me giving an account *concerning* Gideon, Barak, Samson, Jephthah, David, as well as Samuel and the prophets,

        C [33a] who *through faith* conquered kingdoms, worked righteousness, obtained *promises*,

            D [33b] shut the mouths of lions, [34] quenched the power of fire, fled the mouths of the *sword*, they were empowered from weakness, they became strong *in* battle, they laid low the camps of others.

                E [35a] Women *received*

                    F [35b] their dead from *resurrection*.

                        G [35c] But some were tortured, not accepting deliverance,

                    F′ [35d] that they might obtain a better *resurrection*.

                E′ [36] But others *received* a trial of scorns and scourgings, and even of chains and imprisonment.

---

11. Koester, *Hebrews*, 505–6: "Peace characterizes God (Heb 13:20–21) and Melchizedek, who foreshadows Christ (7:2)." See also Mosser, "Rahab."

D′ ³⁷ They were stoned, they were sawed in two, they died *in* murder by a *sword*; they went about *in* sheepskins, *in* goatskins, being in need, being afflicted, being maltreated. ³⁸ The world was not worthy of them; they were wandering over deserts and mountains and caves and the crevices of the earth.

C′ ³⁹ And these all, testified *through the faith*, did not acquire the *promise*.

B′ ⁴⁰ᵃ God *concerning* us,

A′ ⁴⁰ᵇ providing *something* better, that they would not be made perfect without us.

At the conclusion of the preceding unit in 11:20–31 is a reference to "faith"—"by *faith* Rahab the harlot did not perish together with those who disobeyed, having welcomed the spies with peace" (11:31). The reference to "faith" provides the transitional word connecting this unit to the next one in 11:32–40, which begins with a reference to the "faith" through which noteworthy individuals accomplished remarkable deeds (11:33). The transition thus moves the focus from the faith modeled by Rahab to the faith modeled by a group of significant individuals.

With regard to the second macrochiastic level, after the central and pivotal unit in 11:20–31 the audience experience a chiastic relationship between this unit in 11:32–40 and the unit in 11:8–19 provided by the terms "promise," "better," "dead," and "acquire." "By faith he [Abraham] sojourned in the land of the *promise* as [land] of another, having dwelt in tents with Isaac and Jacob, the fellow heirs of the same *promise*" (11:9) . . . not receiving the *promises*" (11:13) . . . and the one who accepted the *promises*" (11:17) in the unit in 11:8–19. They "obtained *promises*" (11:33) and they "did not acquire the *promise*" (11:39) in 11:32–40. "But now they long for a *better* one [fatherland]" (11:16) in the unit in 11:8–19. And "that they might obtain a *better* resurrection" (11:35) and "providing something *better*" (11:40) in 11:32–40. Abraham "reasoning that God is able to raise even from the *dead*, whence him, indeed in a parable, he *acquired*" (11:19) in the unit in 11:8–19. And "women received their *dead* from resurrection" (11:35), as well as "they did not *acquire* the promise" (11:39) in 11:32–40.

In addition, at the second macrochiastic level, the audience experience a chiastic relationship between the unit in 2:10–18 and this unit in 11:32–40 provided by the expression "made perfect." Whereas 2:10–18 declares, "to make the initiator of their salvation, through suffering, *perfect*" (2:10), 11:32–40 indicates that "they would not be made *perfect* without us" (11:40).

After all of the preceding models of faith, the author poses a rhetorical question to the audience: "and what still may I say?" (11:32a). This question functions in an ambivalent manner. On the one hand, it asks what the author can "still say" in view of all that has been said by the preceding models of faith, epitomized by Abel, who, even though having died, is "still speaking" as a model of faith (11:4) for the audience as a worshiping assembly. But, on the other hand, it alerts the audience to what the author still has to say regarding further demonstrations of faith.[12] More models of faith are then mentioned: "For the time will fail me giving an account concerning Gideon, Barak, Samson, Jephthah, David, as well as Samuel and the prophets" (11:32b).[13] The audience have had a long amount of "time" in which to become teachers (5:12). After so long a "time" David said in Ps 94:7–8, "Today if you hear his voice, do not harden your hearts" (4:7). But the "time" will fail the author to give a full account concerning additional models of faith, including David, as well as Samuel and the "prophets," recalling God's having spoken much time ago to the fathers in the "prophets" (1:1).

The remarkable accomplishments of these additional models of faith are noted: "who through faith conquered kingdoms, worked righteousness, obtained promises" (11:33a). That "through faith" they "obtained" "promises," associating them with Abraham, who "obtained" the "promise" (6:15), reinforces the exhortation for the audience to become

---

12. The ambivalence of the question is facilitated by the fact that the verbal form *legō* can be taken as either in the subjunctive ("what may/can I say") or indicative ("what may/shall I say") mood. Lane, *Hebrews 9–13*, 382: "This is a common homiletical and literary idiom for indicating that time and space are limited. . . . The rhetorical flourish commonly announces an intention of abbreviating the matter under discussion."

13. Johnson, *Hebrews*, 306: "The author does not say why he selects these names, or why he arranges them in this sequence. The biblical order would be Barak (Judg 4–5), Gideon (Judg 6–8), Jepththah (Judg 11–12), Samson (Judg 13–16), Samuel (1 Sam 1), and David (1 Sam 16). No single aspect of their stories is singled out, because they are meant to stand as representative of the faith that moved and directed all those who spoke and acted for God and through whom God spoke and acted."

imitators of those who "through faith" and patience are inheriting the "promises" (6:12). That they conquered earthly "kingdoms" associates them with Jesus, as it resonates with his heavenly "kingdom" as the enthroned divine Son of God (1:8). And that they worked "righteousness" further commends them as models of faith. It associates them with Noah, who became an heir of "righteousness" according to faith (11:7), with Melchizedek, king of "righteousness" (7:2), with the audience, who are to be experienced in the word of "righteousness" (5:13), and with Jesus, who loved "righteousness" and hated lawlessness (1:9).

That they quenched the "power" of "fire" (11:34a) indicates to the audience the divine strength they gained through faith, as both "power" and "fire" have been closely associated with God. By faith Abraham received divine "power" for the founding of descendants (11:11). Jesus arose as a different priest (7:15) according to the divine "power" of an indestructible life (7:16). And, as the Son of God, Jesus bears up all things by the pronouncement of the "power" of God (1:3). A zeal of "fire" about to devour the adversaries is part of divine judgment (10:27). And the angelic ministers of God have been described as a flame of "fire" (1:7).

Through faith in God these exemplary figures not only shut the "mouths" of lions able to devour humans (11:33b), but fled the "mouths" of the sword wielded by humans against humans (11:34). They gained the divine strength to do this since, as the audience recall, living is the word of the God in whom they believe and effective and sharper than every "two-edged" sword, that is, a sword with a deadly "double mouth" (4:12). In contrast to the Levitical high priests, who themselves have and are surrounded by human "weakness" (5:2; 7:28), these exemplary figures, through faith, were empowered by God (divine passive) from their human "weakness" (11:34). That they were divinely "empowered" from their human weakness further associates them with Jesus. It deepens the audience's appreciation for Jesus as the divine and heavenly high priest "able" or "having the power" to sympathize with our human "weaknesses" (4:15).

Further associated with Jesus, who in the days of his flesh offered both prayers and supplications with "strong" outcrying and tears to the God "able" to save him from death (5:7), these models of faith became by the power of God (divine passive) "strong" in battle (11:34). This reinforces the exhortation for the audience to have a "strong" encouragement to hold fast to the hope, represented by Jesus as the heavenly high priest

(6:19–20), lying ahead for them (6:18). That these models of faith laid low the camps of "others" on earth (11:34) deepens the audience's appreciation for what lies ahead for them in heaven. It resonates with Abraham merely sojourning on earth as on land of "another" (11:9), and with the blood that is not of "another" but of the high priest Jesus himself by which he entered into the heavenly holy things (9:25) on behalf of us (9:24).

These models of faith were tortured rather than accepting deliverance (11:35c) from death on earth that they might obtain a "better" resurrection (11:35d), that is, not a resurrection that is a resuscitation to earthly life (11:35b), but a resurrection to eternal life in heaven.[14] They have in view a heavenly resurrection, just as the patriarchs long for a "better" fatherland, that is, a heavenly one (11:16). This further commends them as models of faith for the audience, who accepted the confiscation of their earthly possessions with joy, knowing that they have a "better" possession that remains in heaven (10:34). The audience know that these noteworthy figures may hope that through faith they might "obtain" a better, heavenly resurrection, since Jesus has "obtained" a more excellent, heavenly ministry of worship, to the degree that he is guarantor of a "better" covenant, which on the basis of "better" promises was given law (8:6). The hope for a "better" resurrection to eternal life in heaven thus takes its place in the series of "better" things previously presented to the audience (1:4; 6:9; 7:7, 19, 22; 9:23).

In contrast to the women who through faith "received" their dead from resurrection (11:35), these other models of faith "received" a trial of scorns and scourgings (11:36a). Whereas the faithless Egyptians drowned, rashly "taking an attempt" (*peiran labontes*) to go through the Red Sea as if on dry ground (11:29), these other models of faith patiently "received a trial" (*peiran elabon*) of scorns and scourgings. That they received a trial even of "chains" (*desmōn*) and imprisonment (11:36b) further commends them as models for the audience, who even suffered with the "prisoners" (*desmiois*, 10:34).

Whereas some of these models of faith were able to flee the mouths of the "sword" (11:34), others were not only stoned and sawed in two, but died in murder by a "sword" (11:37). Whereas some became strong "in" battle (11:34), others not only died "in" murder by a sword, but went about "in" sheepskins and "in" goatskins (11:37). That they "died" in

---

14. Cockerill, "Better Resurrection."

murder by a sword associates them with the patriarchs, who in accord with faith all "died," not receiving the promises but from afar seeing them and greeting and confessing that they are strangers and sojourners on the earth (11:13). That through faith they were not only being afflicted and maltreated but "being in need" (11:37) ironically but poignantly reinforces the warning for the audience to make sure none of them seem to "have been lacking" in faith (4:1). Those who through faith experienced suffering and humiliation (11:37) thus complement those who through faith experienced power and strength (11:33b–34).

The "world" was not worthy of these models of faith (11:38a), recalling that by faith Noah condemned the faithless "world" of his day (11:7). In contrast to those who are ignorant and "wandering" in sinfulness (5:2), and to the faithless ancestors who were always "wandering" in heart, not knowing God's ways (3:10), these exemplary figures, through faith, were "wandering" over deserts and mountains and caves and the crevices of the earth (11:38b). That they were wandering over the crevices of "the earth" further associates them, as models of faith for the audience, with the faithful patriarchs who, as strangers and sojourners on "the earth" (11:13), are seeking a fatherland in heaven (11:14–16), the place of rest and worship of God.

That "these all," testified through the faith, did not acquire the "promise" (11:39) was epitomized by the patriarchs: in accord with faith "these all" died, not receiving the "promises" (11:13). That these all were "testified" through the faith likens them to Enoch, who was "testified" to have pleased God (11:5), and to Abel, who was "testified" to be just, God "testifying" on the basis of his sacrificial gifts (11:4). As among the elders who were "testified" in faith (11:2), they are commended as models for the audience.

With a noteworthy progression from the more general "through faith," by which "promises" in general were obtained (11:33), to the more particular "through *the* faith," all these figures did not acquire "*the* promise," the fulfillment of the more particular promise of final salvation in heaven (11:39). As prefigured by Abraham, who "acquired" Isaac in accord with God's promise (11:19), these did not yet "acquire the promise." This reinforces the exhortation for the audience to have endurance so that, doing the will of God, "you may acquire the promise" (10:36), "the promise" of an eternal inheritance (9:15) in heaven, which includes entrance into the rest and worship of God.[15]

The something "better" that God has provided for us (11:40) includes the "better" resurrection to eternal life in heaven that those who were tortured, not accepting deliverance from death on earth, might obtain (11:35), as well as the "better," heavenly fatherland for which the patriarchs of old longed (11:16). It accords with the "better" possession that the audience know they have remaining eternally in heaven for them, so that they accepted the confiscation of their earthly possessions with joy (10:34). That God has "provided" or "foreseen" something better for us resonates with the opening description of faith as a demonstration of divine things not being "noticed" or "seen" (11:1). By faith we understand that from divine things not apparent what is being "noticed" or "seen" came to be (11:3).[16]

That these venerable models of faith would not be made "perfect" without us (11:40) means that they would not be made worthy or fit for participation in the heavenly worship without us who have the benefit of the self-sacrifice of Jesus as our heavenly high priest. This is confirmed by the theme of "making perfect," first with regard to Jesus and then with regard to the audience, which has developed throughout the letter.

With regard to Jesus, it was fitting for God, in leading many sons into heavenly glory, to make the initiator of their salvation, Jesus, through sufferings, "perfect" for his role in heavenly worship (2:10). Having been made "perfect," Jesus became for all those who obey him a source of eternal salvation (5:9), having been designated by God high priest according to the order of Melchizedek (5:10). Although the law made nothing "perfect" (7:19), Jesus, as the Son of God, has been made "perfect" forever (7:28).

With regard to the audience, the gifts and sacrifices being offered in the earthly tabernacle are not able according to conscience to make "perfect" the one offering worship (9:9). Indeed, the law never is able to make "perfect" those who approach for the worship of God (10:1). But, by one offering of himself, Jesus, the heavenly high priest, has made "per-

---

15. Attridge, *Hebrews*, 352: "The plural is customary in connection with figures from the Old Testament, while the singular is common for the ultimate promise realized in Christ."

16. Koester, *Hebrews*, 516: "The verb *problepein* means both 'foresee' and 'make provision.' Through faith (11:1) one can confess that God makes provision for things that transcend human vision."

fect" for all time those who are being made holy (10:14), so that they may worthily participate in the heavenly worship. Thus, the audience are to appreciate that God has provided something better in heaven for us, so that we may participate in heavenly worship along with these venerable models of faith, as those who would be made "perfect" together with us (11:40b). It is all the more incumbent, then, for the audience to imitate these past exemplary heroes of faith whom they look forward to joining in the heavenly liturgy.[17]

III. 12:1–11

A [12:1] Consequently, we also, having such a cloud of witnesses surrounding us, taking off every burden and easily ensnaring sin, through endurance let us traverse the struggle lying ahead for us, [2] fixing our eyes on the initiator and perfecter of the faith, Jesus, who, for the sake of the *joy* lying ahead of him, endured the cross, despising its shame, and took his seat on the right of the throne of God (Ps 109:1). [3] For reflect on the one who has endured such disputing against himself from sinners, that you may not become fatigued, growing weary in your souls. [4] You have not yet resisted to the point of blood, struggling *with* (*pros*) sin.

B [5] And you have forgotten the encouragement, which is addressed *to you as sons*, "My son, do not disdain the discipline of the Lord and do not grow weary, being reproved by him, [6] for *whom* the Lord loves he disciplines, and scourges every *son whom* he accepts" (Prov 3:11–12).

C [7a] For discipline endure;

B′ [7b] God is being offered *to you as sons*. For what *son* is there *whom* a father does not discipline? [8] If you are without discipline, in which all have become partners, then you are illegitimate ones and not *sons*. [9] Furthermore, we had our fathers of flesh as disciplinarians and we respected them. Shall we not much more then be subjected to the Father of spirits and live?

---

17. Lane, *Hebrews 9–13*, 394: "The privileged status of Christians as those who have shared in the fulfillment of God's promise should motivate them to be more willing and equipped to endure the testing of faith than were their predecessors, all of whom received attestation from God through their faith." Motyer, "Not Apart from Us"; Alexander, "Prophets."

A′ ¹⁰ For they disciplined *for* (*pros*) a few days according to what seemed fit to them, but he on the basis of what is beneficial in order that we may share his holiness. ¹¹ All discipline, *when* (*pros*) it is present, does not seem to be of *joy* but of sorrow, but later it gives back the peaceful fruit of righteousness to those who have been trained through it.

Toward the conclusion of the preceding unit in 11:32–40 is a reference to all of these past models of faith who were "testified" (*martyrēthentes*) through the faith (11:39). At the beginning of the next unit in 12:1–11 is a reference to this same group as a cloud of "witnesses" (*martyrōn*) surrounding us (12:1). These occurrences of expressions for "testify/witness" thus serve as the transitional words connecting these units as they retain a focus on the exemplary figures of faith from the past.

With regard to the second macrochiastic level, the audience experience a chiastic relationship between the unit in 11:1–7 and the one in 12:1–11 provided by the term "righteousness." The unit in 11:1–7 declares that Noah became an heir of "righteousness" according to faith (11:7). And the unit in 12:1–11 asserts that all discipline later gives back the peaceful fruit of "righteousness" to those who have been trained through it (12:11). In addition, at the second macrochiastic level, the audience experience a chiastic relationship between the unit in 2:5–9 and the one in 12:1–11 provided by the only occurrences in Hebrews of the verb "to subject." In 2:5–9 are the statements, "not to angels did he *subject* the heavenly world" (2:5), "all things you *subjected* under his feet" (2:8), "in *subjecting* to him all things he left nothing to him unsubjected" (2:8), and "we do not see all things *subjected* to him" (2:8). And in 12:1–11 is the question, "shall we not much more then be *subjected* to the Father of spirits and live?" (12:9).

The author's application of the significance of all of these past models of faith for the audience, "consequently, we also, *having* such a cloud of witnesses surrounding us" (12:1a), introduces another strong exhortation for the audience, as it resonates with introductions to previous exhortations. As those "having" a great high priest who has passed through the heavens, Jesus the Son of God, the audience were exhorted to hold fast to the confession as a worshiping assembly (4:14). As those "having" a need of "milk" and not "solid food," the audience were exhorted to allow the author to teach them again the elements of the beginning of the sayings of God (5:12). The audience, as those "having" boldness for entrance into the heavenly holy things in the blood of Jesus (10:19), were exhorted to approach God for worship with a true heart in assurance of faith (10:22). And now, "having" such a cloud of witnesses, the audience are exhorted, "through endurance let us traverse the struggle lying ahead for us" (12:1b).

In contrast to every high priest being "surrounded" by weakness (5:2), the audience are "surrounded" by a cloud of strong witnesses (12:1a). This cloud of "witnesses" refers to all of the exemplary figures of the past who were "testified" through the faith (11:39). As witnesses to a faith that includes a strong belief in an eternal life in heaven, they stand in contrast to the "witnesses" whose testimony leads to death (10:28). Moses, a preeminent figure among this cloud of surrounding witnesses, chose rather to be mistreated with the people of God than to have a temporary enjoyment of "sin" (11:25). He thus provides a stellar model for the audience, who are to be taking off every burden and easily ensnaring "sin" that prevents worship (12:1a).

That the audience, through "endurance," are to traverse (12:1b) the struggle lying ahead for us (12:1c) reinforces the exhortation for them to have the "endurance" they need to do the will of God and acquire the promise (10:36), the promise of the eternal inheritance in heaven (9:15).[18] Through endurance the audience are to traverse the struggle lying ahead for them (12:1) by keeping their eyes fixed on the "initiator" (*archēgon*) and "perfecter" (*teleiōtēn*) of the faith, Jesus (12:2).[19] They are enabled to do this because it was fitting for God, in leading many sons into heavenly glory, to make Jesus, as the "initiator" of their salvation, through sufferings, "perfect" (2:10). Jesus, who for the sake of the "joy" "lying ahead" of him (12:2c), as the embodiment of the hope "lying ahead" for us in heaven (6:18), "endured" the cross, despising its shame (12:2d). This is

---

18. For the suggestion that the "struggle" lying ahead for the audience to "traverse" in 12:1 is better understood as portraying a pilgrimage rather than an athletic race to the presence of God, see Sims, "Hebrews 12:1," 54–88. While the pilgrimage theme seems to be primary, it is presented with athletic connotations. Johnson, "Scriptural World," 241: "The image of the race is drawn from the Greek culture of competitive games. But because of this marvelous intertwining of textual allusion, the hearers know that this race is one of pilgrimage begun by Abraham as he looked for a lasting city (Heb 11:13–16)."

19. According to Attridge, *Hebrews*, 356, the juxtaposition of *archēgos* with *teleiōtēs*, "with its obvious play on *arch-* and *tel-* stems, suggests that *archēgos* also carries connotations of 'founder' or 'initiator.'" Croy, "Hebrews 12:2."

to empower the audience, through "endurance," to traverse the struggle "lying ahead" for us (12:1). And this is what makes Jesus so relevant for the audience, as "you" who "*endured* much conflict of sufferings" (10:32), and "accepted the confiscation of your possessions with *joy*" (10:34).

The audience have heard a series of allusions to Ps 109:1 as an expression of the heavenly enthronement of Jesus as the divine Son of God. Having made a cleansing for sins, Jesus "sat at the right of the Majesty in the heights" (1:3). To Jesus, in contrast to the angels, God issued the privilege, "Sit at my right, until I place your enemies as a footstool for your feet" (1:13). The audience have been assured that in Jesus we have a high priest who "sat at the right of the throne of the Majesty in the heavens" (8:1). Jesus, having offered himself for all time on behalf of sins, "sat at the right of God," henceforth waiting until his enemies are placed as a footstool for his feet (10:12–13). Jesus, after enduring the cross, "took his seat on the right of the throne of God" (12:2), thus completing the course of the pilgrimage to heaven as "forerunner" on behalf of us (6:20). This provides the audience with a desirable goal to keep before them in their struggle to endure the grueling course lying ahead of them before they complete their pilgrimage to the heavenly city promised by God to participate in the heavenly liturgy.

That Jesus, who "endured" the cross (12:2), provides the audience with an empowering model to follow in taking off every burden and easily ensnaring "sin," in order, through "endurance," to traverse the "struggle" lying ahead for them (12:1) is then confirmed. They are invited to reflect upon Jesus, the high priest who is separated from "sinners" (7:26), as the one who has "endured" such disputing against himself from "sinners" (12:3a). Such reflection will enable the audience not to become fatigued, growing weary in their souls (12:3). For, as the audience are pointedly reminded, in their "struggling" with "sin," they have not yet resisted to the point of "blood" (12:4).[20] This deepens their appreciation for Jesus, who did resist to the point of blood, so that through his own "blood" he entered once for all into the heavenly holy things as high priest, finding eternal redemption (9:12). Jesus thus serves as an inspiring model that can motivate the audience to resist opposition to sinfulness, even to the point of shedding their own blood, if necessary.

---

20. The close connection between the expressions, "you have not yet resisted to the point of blood (*haimatos antikatestēte*)" and "struggling with sin (*hamartian antagōnizomenoi*)," is underscored by the rhythm of their artful alliteration.

Not only have the audience not resisted to the point of blood in their struggling with sin (12:4), but, having been exhorted to have a strong "encouragement" to hold fast to the hope lying ahead (6:18), they have forgotten the "encouragement" addressed to them as sons (12:5a). The forgotten encouragement addressed to the audience as "sons," recalling that they are among the many "sons" God is leading into the glory of heavenly worship through Jesus (2:10), is that given by a father to his son in Prov 3:11–12. The opening address of this scriptural encouragement, "my son" (12:5a), resonates with the scriptural voice of God from the combination of Ps 2:7 and 2 Sam 7:14 that has addressed Jesus as "*son of mine* are you, I today have begotten you" (1:5; 5:5) and "I will be to him as a Father, and he will be to *me* as a *son*" (1:5). This invites the audience, as "sons" of God, to consider Jesus, whose scriptural voice from Ps 21:23 declared to God the Father, "I will proclaim your name to *my brothers*" (2:12), as the model for the scriptural encouragement that a father addresses to "my son" (12:5a).

The audience, having forgotten the encouragement addressed to them as sons, are not to disdain the discipline of the Lord God and not to grow "weary" (*eklyou*)—alliteratively linked to "you have forgotten" (*eklelēsthe*), being reproved by him (12:5). They are not to disdain the "discipline" of the "Lord," because the son whom the "Lord" loves he "disciplines" (12:6a).[21] The Lord disciplines the one whom he "loves" and scourges every "son" whom he accepts (12:6). This applies to the audience as "sons" of God, who have been addressed as "beloved" (6:9) and as "my son" (12:5a). It also applies to Jesus as the divine Son of God, to whom the scriptural voice of God acknowledged, "You *loved* righteousness and hated lawlessness; therefore God, your God, anointed you with the oil of gladness beyond your partners (Ps 44:8)" (1:9). Jesus thus presents the audience with a model of how a "son" whom God loves, in turn loves the righteousness of God and thus God himself.

That the audience are to endure for the sake of God's "discipline" (12:7a) reinforces the exhortation for them as "sons" not to disdain the "discipline" of the Lord God (12:5). The audience, previously acknowl-

---

21. Lane, *Hebrews 9–13*, 420: "The biblical concept of discipline (*paideia*) combines the nuances of training, instruction, and firm guidance with those of reproof, correction, and punishment. The notion of God as disciplinarian was derived from the parent-child relationship: 'As a man disciplines his son, so the Lord your God disciplines you' (Deut 8:5)." See also Allen, *Deuteronomy*, 79–82.

edged as "you who *endured* much conflict of sufferings" (10:32), are now to "endure" for the sake of divine discipline, inspired by the example of Jesus, who has "endured" such disputing against himself from sinners (12:3), who indeed "endured" the cross, despising its shame (12:2).[22]

In the scriptural encouragement from Prov 3:11–12, which is addressed to the audience—"to you as sons" (12:5), God himself, with his paternal discipline, is being offered "to you as sons" (12:7b). The audience, whom the scriptural encouragement addresses as "my *son*" (12:5), are to consider what "son" there is "whom" a father does not "discipline" (12:7b), which resonates with the scriptural assertion that "whom" the Lord God loves he "disciplines" (12:6). Of Jesus it was said that, although being a "son," he learned from the things he suffered obedience (5:8). And Jesus is the divine Son to whom the scriptural voice of God from 2 Sam 7:14 declared, "I will be to him as a *Father*, and he will be to me as a *son*" (1:5). The audience are thus invited to consider not only themselves but Jesus as the "son" whom God as a "father" disciplines (12:7b). The Jesus who endured suffering as divine discipline, then, serves as an empowering model for the audience, who have already endured and are still to endure suffering as divine discipline.

The audience are not to be without "discipline" (12:8a), the divine "discipline" for the sake of which they are to endure (12:7a), the "discipline" of the Lord they are not to disdain (12:5). The audience, who have become "partners" of the Holy Spirit (6:4) and "partners" of the Christ (3:14), and who are "partners" of a heavenly calling (3:1), have all also become "partners" in divine discipline (12:8b). If they would be without divine discipline, then they would be illegitimate ones and not true "sons" (12:8c), the "sons" to whom God the Father is being offered (12:7b), and the "sons" to whom the scriptural encouragement for divine discipline from Prov 3:11–12 is addressed (12:5).[23]

Since the audience respected their physical fathers, their "fathers" of flesh, as disciplinarians (12:9a), with each "father" disciplining his son (12:7b), they should much more then be subjected to God as the "Father" of spirits and live (12:9b). All the more shall we be "subjected" to God as the Father of spirits, since we do not yet see all things "subjected" to him (2:8b), who "subjected" the heavenly world not to angels (2:5) but to

---

22. Hengel, *Crucifixion*; Neyrey, "Shame of the Cross"; DeSilva, "Despising Shame"; idem, *Despising Shame*.

23. Guthrie, "Hebrews," 987: "[T]he difficulties that the hearers face are actually a sign that they are true children of the Father."

Jesus. This is in accord with the scriptural declaration from Ps 8:7 that "all things you *subjected* under his feet." And in "subjecting" to him all things, which includes the audience, God left nothing to him unsubjected (2:8a). That the audience are to be subjected to God as the Father of "spirits" and live (12:9) contributes to the worship associations of this exhortation. The audience have heard the scriptural proclamation from Ps 103:4 that God makes his angels "spirits" and his ministers a flame of fire (1:7). God sent these angelic ministering "spirits" to assist the audience as among those who are going to inherit eternal salvation (1:14), and thus participate in the heavenly worship.

That we will "live" by being subjected to God as the Father of spirits (12:9), means that we will live the eternal life provided by the "living" God into whose hands it is fearful to fall (10:31), the "living" God from whom no one in the audience is to fall away with an evil heart of unfaithfulness (3:12). This resonates with the scriptural declaration from Hab 2:4 that "my just one from faith *will live*" (10:38), that is, will live presently as well as eternally to participate in the heavenly worship of the ever living God.

With its movement from what is "fleshly" to what is "spiritual," the exhortation that, since we had our fathers of "flesh" as disciplinarians and we respected them, we shall "much more" be subjected to the Father of "spirits" and "live" further contributes to the worship associations of this exhortation (12:9). It reminds the audience of a similar movement: For if the blood of goats and bulls and the sprinkling of a heifer's ashes makes holy those defiled for the cleansing of the "flesh," "how much more" will the blood of the Christ, who through the eternal "Spirit" offered himself unblemished to God, cleanse our conscience from dead works to offer worship to the "living" God (9:13–14). Hence, Christ, as the divinely disciplined Son of God, provides the audience not only with the example but the empowerment to endure their sufferings as the divine discipline that prepares and qualifies them for participation in the heavenly worship of the living God, the God whose eternal life we are to live.

Every father "disciplines" a son (12:7), even God the Father, who "disciplines" every son he loves (12:6). Their earthly fathers thus "disciplined" the audience, who are still struggling "with" (*pros*) sin (12:4), "for" (*pros*) a few days according to what seemed fit to them (12:10a). Whereas they disciplined according "to what seemed fit" to them, God the Father disciplines on the basis of "what is beneficial" for us in order that we may share his holiness (12:10). Whereas the earth that drinks the rain coming upon it repeatedly and produces useful vegetation for those on account of whom it is cultivated "shares" a blessing from God (6:7), God the Father disciplines the audience in order that they may "share" his holiness as participants in heavenly worship.

That God the Father disciplines in order that the audience may share his "holiness" (12:10) adds to the worship associations of this exhortation. Jesus "makes holy" the audience as among those who are being "made holy" as his brothers (2:11). We have been "made holy" through the offering of the body of Jesus Christ once for all (10:10). For by one offering Jesus has made perfect for all time those who are being "made holy" (10:14). Every member of the audience was "made holy" in the blood of Jesus, the Son of God (10:29). As the divinely disciplined Son of God, then, Jesus serves as not only the preeminent model but the encouraging empowerment for the audience "made holy" by him to share in the divine "holiness" needed to worship God in the heavenly "holy things" (8:2; 9:3, 8, 12, 24; 10:19). For if the blood of goats and bulls and the sprinkling of a heifer's ashes "makes holy" those defiled for the cleansing of the flesh (9:13), how much more will the blood of the Christ cleanse our conscience from sinful dead works to offer worship to the living God (9:14).

The exhortations for the audience not to disdain the "discipline" of the Lord (12:5), for the sake of "discipline" to endure (12:7), and not to be without "discipline" in order to be true sons of God (12:8) are reinforced by further explanation of discipline. All "discipline," "when" (*pros*) it is present, even "for" (*pros*) a few days, in contrast to what "seemed" fit to fathers who discipline (12:10), does not "seem" to be of joy but of sorrow (12:11a). That discipline does not presently seem to be of "joy" sharpens the focus of the audience upon the example of the disciplined Jesus, who, for the sake of the future "joy" lying ahead of him, endured the cross (12:2). That future joy results from discipline is confirmed by the assertion that later it gives back the peaceful fruit of righteousness to those who have been trained through it (12:11b).

That divine discipline gives back the "peaceful" fruit of God's "righteousness" to those who are "trained" through it (12:11) reinforces the exhortation for the audience to be experienced of the word of God's "righteousness" (5:13). They are to be those who because of their maturity have faculties "trained" for distinguishing of the beneficent and of the baneful (5:14). It adds to the relevance for the audience of the models presented to them—of those who through faith worked God's "righteousness" (11:33), of Rahab who by faith welcomed the spies with "peace" (11:31), of Noah who became an heir of God's "righteousness" according to faith (11:7). It deepens the appreciation of the audience for Melchizedek as king of "righteousness" and king of "peace" (7:2). Finally, it underscores the significance of the model and motivation provided by Jesus, the divinely disciplined Son of God, who loved God's "righteousness," so that God anointed him with the oil of gladness (1:9) as an object of the heavenly worship (1:6) in which he has enabled the audience to participate (9:14; 10:19–22).[24]

IV. 12:12–29

A [12] *Therefore* restore the hands that have become weakened and the knees that have become *paralyzed* ([*paralelymena*], Isa 35:3), [13] and make straight paths for your feet (Prov 4:26), that what is lame may not be dislocated, but rather may be healed. [14] Peace pursue with all, and the holiness without which no one will see the Lord, [15] seeing to it lest anyone be lacking of the *grace* of God, lest any root of bitterness springing up may cause trouble (Deut 29:17) and through it many may become defiled, [16] lest anyone be immoral or profane like Esau, who for a single meal gave back his own rights as firstborn. [17] For you know that also afterwards, wanting to inherit the blessing, he was rejected, for he did not find a place for repentance, although with tears he sought it.

    B [18] For you have not *approached* what is to be felt—a blazing fire and darkness and gloom and a whirlwind [19] and a blast of a trumpet and *voice* of pronouncements, which those who heard *refused*, lest a word be added for them, [20] for they could not bear what was ordered, "If even an animal touch the *mountain*, it shall be stoned" (Exod 19:12–13).

    C [21a] Indeed, so *fearful* (*phoberon*) was what was appearing,

---

24. According to Attridge, *Hebrews*, 364, "of righteousness" (*dikaiosynēs*) here "recalls common expressions from the Old Testament linking peace and righteousness or referring to the fruit of righteousness. Its position at the end of the verse is emphatic, but like *eirēnikon*, it functions evocatively. Righteousness has been associated with the exalted Christ and was seen to be a result of faith." Mitchell, *Hebrews*, 273: "In the LXX the expression 'fruit of righteousness' occurs in Amos 6:12 and Prov 11:30." See also, as more generally relevant to this unit, Sisson, "Fear of Death," 670–78; Thiessen, "Hebrews 12.5–13."

  D²¹ᵇ Moses said,

 C′²¹ᶜ "I am *terrified* (*ekphobos*) and trembling" (Deut 9:19).

B′ ²² Rather you have *approached Mount* Zion, and the city of the living God, the heavenly Jerusalem, and myriads of angels in full festal gathering, ²³ and the assembly of the firstborn enrolled in heaven, and God, the judge of all, and the spirits of just ones having been made perfect, ²⁴ and Jesus, guarantor of a new covenant, and the blood of the sprinkling that speaks better beyond Abel. ²⁵ Take note that you do not *refuse* the one who is speaking! For if they, *refusing* the one warning on earth, did not escape, much more we who turn away the one from heaven, ²⁶ whose *voice* shook the earth then, but now he has promised, saying, "Once more I will stir up not only the earth but also the heaven" (Hag 2:6). ²⁷ The "once more" indicates the change of the things being shaken as things that have been made, so that the things not being shaken may remain.

A′ ²⁸ *Therefore, acquiring* (*paralambanontes*) an unshakable kingdom, let us have *grace*, through which we may offer worship pleasing to God with reverence and awe. ²⁹ For indeed our God is a consuming fire! (Deut 4:24).

At the conclusion of the preceding unit in 12:1–11 is a reference to the "peaceful" fruit of righteousness (12:11). Near the beginning of the next unit in 12:12–29 is an exhortation to pursue "peace" with all (12:14). These occurrences of expressions regarding "peace" thus serve as the transitional words connecting these units as they move the focus from what is peaceful to peace itself.

 With regard to the second macrochiastic level, the audience experience a chiastic relationship between the unit in 10:31–39 and the one in 12:12–29 provided by the terms "fearful," "hand," "remain," and "living God." In 10:31–39 is the declaration that it is "fearful" to fall into the "hands" of the "living God" (10:31) and the notice that the audience have a better possession that "remains" (10:34). And in 12:12–29 is the exhortation to restore the "hands" that have become weakened (12:12), the declaration that so "fearful" was what was appearing (12:21), the reference to the city of the "living God" (12:22), and the statement that the things not being shaken may "remain" (12:27). In addition, at the second macrochiastic level, the audience experience a chiastic relationship between the unit in 2:1-4 and the one in 12:12-29 provided by the only occurrences in Hebrews of the verb "to escape." In 2:1-4 is the question of "how will we *escape*, neglecting so great a salvation" (2:3). And in 12:12-29 is the statement that those "refusing the one warning on earth, did not *escape*" (12:25).

Extending the athletic/pilgrimage imagery with an allusion to Isa 35:3 (cf. Sir 25:23), the author continues his exhortation for the audience to be trained through divine discipline (12:11): "Therefore restore the hands that have become weakened and the knees that have become paralyzed" (12:12).[25] The hands that have become "weakened" (*pareimenas*) are closely coupled through alliteration with the knees that have become "paralyzed" (*paralelymena*), highlighting the need for the audience to be those who have been trained through divine discipline. The "hands" (*cheiras*) that have become weakened point, by way of an alliterative wordplay, to the need for the divine discipline that does not presently seem to be of "joy" (*charas*), but later gives back the peaceful fruit of God's righteousness to those who have been trained through it (12:11). Restoring their own hands that have become weakened will thus prepare the audience for the fearful prospect of falling into the divine "hands" of the living God (10:31).

With a continuation of alliterative wordplays, the audience are not only to "restore" (*anorthōsate*) their "hands" (*cheiras*) and knees (12:12), but to make "straight" (*orthas*) "paths" (*trochias*) for their feet (12:13a), alluding to Prov 4:26. This accords with the exhortation that through endurance we are to traverse the struggle lying ahead for us (12:1), fixing our eyes on the initiator and perfecter of the faith, Jesus, who for the sake of the joy lying ahead of him, endured the cross (12:2). The audience are to make straight paths for their feet, that what is lame may not be dislocated, but "rather" may be healed by God (12:13), the Father of spirits to whom we shall all the more or "rather" be subjected and live (12:9).[26]

This very artful collocation of "hands," "knees," and "feet" (12:12-13) serves not only the athletic/pilgrimage imagery but also the worshiping

---

25. Johnson, *Hebrews*, 323: The author returns here "to the physical imagery of the race or athletic competition, which stands for their pilgrimage toward God."

26. Attridge, *Hebrews*, 365: "The 'lameness' . . . likely refers to the general situation of lassitude and spiritual 'flabbiness' that the author detects in his addressees. . . . The exhortation to faithful endurance built on athletic imagery and the proverbial understanding of suffering as educative discipline thus closes on a positive note."

context that pervades Hebrews. The audience are exhorted to restore the weakened "hands" (*cheiras*) that are often used in various gestures (praying, blessing, etc.) associated with worship, including the laying on of "hands" (6:2).[27] They are to restore the weakened "knees" (*gonata*) that they bow and fall upon in worship.[28] That they are to make straight paths for their "feet" suggests that they avoid deviating from the ways of God, as it accords with the exhortations that they not abandon their own gathering for worship (10:25), nor fall away in unfaithfulness from the living God (3:12).[29] Making such straight paths for their "feet" will thus prepare the audience to participate in the angelic worship of Jesus (1:6), enthroned at the right of God in heaven, waiting for all things, including his enemies, to be subjected under his "feet" (1:13; 2:8; 10:13).

Rahab by faith welcomed the Israelite spies "with peace," and thus did not perish with those who disobeyed (11:31). This inspires the audience to pursue "peace" as a divine gift together "with" all other members of the community (12:14a), as part of their divine discipline which gives back the "peaceful" fruit of God's righteousness to those trained through it (12:11).[30] As those trained through the divine discipline that enables them to share in God's own "holiness" (*hagiotētos*, 12:10), the audience, as "holy ones" (3:1; 6:10) "made holy" by Christ (2:11; 10:10, 14, 29), are to pursue the "holiness" without which no one "will see" the Lord (12:14b). This recalls that Christ, the Lord (1:10; 2:3; 7:14), "will be seen," by those eagerly awaiting him, for final salvation (9:28).[31]

---

27. Radl, "*cheir*," 463.

28. Nützel, "*gony*," 258. Ellingworth, *Hebrews*, 658: "Elsewhere in the NT, knees are mentioned only in connection with kneeling in worship."

29. Koester, *Hebrews*, 530–31: "Metaphorically, folllowing a straight path means adhering to the will of God (Prov 3:6; 4:11, 26–27). . . . In Hebrews the danger focused on is turning away from the faith and the community (Heb 3:12; 6:4–8; 10:25)."

30. Lane, *Hebrews 9–13*, 449: "The stress falls on active Christian effort in response to divine gifts. . . . 'Peace' denotes the objective basis of the solidarity of the community. It is an expression of the reality of Christ's accomplishment. 'Peace' is to be actively pursued because this gift of Christ is given visibility in the solidarity of the community."

31. Ibid., 425, 450: "The rare term *hagiotētos* denotes the holiness that is the essential attribute of God's character, which Christians are to share. The expression came into use only late in hellenistic Judaism; it occurs only here in the NT. In v 10 the stress is placed not on human endeavor (as in v 14) but upon the fact that God bestows as a gift a share in his holiness through divine discipline. . . . The basis for a practical holiness of life is *ton hagiasmon*, 'the holiness,' which is the gift of Christ."

The audience were previously exhorted to be afraid "lest," while the promise to enter into God's own heavenly rest is left, "anyone" of them seem to have been "lacking" (4:1). And now they are similarly exhorted to see to it "lest anyone" of them be "lacking" of the "grace" of God (12:15a), the "grace" by which Christ tasted death on behalf of all (2:9). This resonates with the warning that not anyone of them should insult the Spirit of "grace" (10:29) by abandoning the worshiping assembly. And this concern for each member of the community reinforces the exhortation for the entire audience as worshipers to approach with boldness the throne of "grace" to receive mercy and find "grace" for timely help (4:16).

With an allusion to Deut 29:17, the audience are exhorted also to see to it lest any root of bitterness springing up may cause trouble and through it many may become defiled (12:15b). They are thus to make sure that none of them introduces into the community the "bitterness" of hardening their hearts to the voice of God as in the "rebellion" (*parapikrasmō*)—alliteratively linked to "bitterness" (*pikrias*)—during the day of testing in the wilderness (3:8, 15), when all of those who came out of Egypt through Moses heard but "rebelled" (*parepikranan*) against God (3:16). For many of them to become "defiled" (*mianthōsin*) would be inappropriate for them as those whose conscience the blood of Christ, the "undefiled" (*amiantos*) high priest (7:26), will cleanse from sinful dead works to offer worship to the living God (9:14).[32]

The audience are also to see to it lest anyone be immoral or profane like Esau (12:16a), whom, with his brother Jacob, their father Isaac, by faith concerning things to come, blessed (11:20).[33] In contrast to the undisciplined son Esau, who for a single meal "gave back" his own rights as firstborn (12:16b; cf. Gen 25:31–34), the divine discipline the audience, as sons of God, are to endure "gives back" the peaceful fruit of God's righteousness for those trained through it (12:11). Whereas by faith Moses demonstrated his deep regard for the firstborn by keeping the Passover

---

32. Ibid., 454: "This dual aspect of cultic and moral overtones in *mianthōsin* in 15b is sharpened by the prior reference to *hagiasmos*, 'holiness,' in v 14."

33. According to Ellingworth, *Hebrews*, 665, that Esau was "immoral" (*pornos*) has overtones of his "unfaithfulness to God, which is the author of Hebrews' ultimate concern." Koester, *Hebrews*, 532: "The term *pornos* commonly meant sexual immorality. In choosing food over his rights as firstborn Esau was said to have sought immediate physical gratification rather than abiding benefit. His marriage to two Hittite women (Gen 26:34–35) came to be considered immoral. Sexual immorality was associated with idolatry."

and the applying of the blood, so that the one who was to destroy the "firstborn" might not touch them (11:28), Esau demonstrated his unfaithful disregard for his own rights as "firstborn" by giving them back. Indeed, Esau failed to appreciate his own rights as "firstborn" by giving them back for an emphatically "single meal"—merely one part of the earthly "foods" that foreshadow heavenly worship (9:10).[34] This sharpens the audience's appreciation for Jesus as the divine Son whom God leads as the "firstborn" into the heavenly world for them, together with the angels, to worship (1:6).

The reminder that also afterwards, wanting to inherit the blessing, Esau was rejected, for he did not find a place for repentance, although with tears he sought it (12:17; cf. Gen 27:31–38), underlines the relevance of Esau as a negative model for the audience. The audience are to be imitators of those who through faith and patience are "inheriting" the promises of God (6:12), as those who are going to "inherit" salvation (1:14) from the Jesus (9:28) who has "inherited" a name beyond the angels (1:4). In contrast, Esau was rejected by God (divine passive) in wanting to "inherit" the blessing. That in his desire to inherit the "blessing" Esau did not find a place for "repentance" reinforces the exhortation for the audience to bear forward toward the perfection, not again laying down a foundation of "repentance" from dead works and of faith in God (6:1). For it is impossible for those having fallen away again to renew to "repentance" (6:6) and share a "blessing" from God (6:7).

In contrast to the "place" that was found for a new covenant (8:7), and to Abraham, who by faith obeyed to go out to a "place" which he was about to receive as an inheritance (11:8), the unfaithful Esau did not find a "place" for repentance (12:17). In contrast to Enoch, who by faith was not "found" because God changed him (11:5), and to the high priest Jesus, who "found" eternal redemption (9:12), the unfaithful Esau did not "find" a place for repentance. His negative example thus bolsters the exhortation for the audience as worshipers to approach with boldness the throne of grace to receive mercy that we may "find" grace for timely help (4:16).

In contrast to Jesus, who in the days of his flesh offered both prayers and supplications with strong outcrying and "tears" to the God able to save him from death, and he was heard from his reverence (5:7), Esau was

---

34. Koester, *Hebrews*, 532: Hebrews here "implies that a pre-occupation with food binds one to the transient realm."

rejected by God, although with "tears" he sought the blessing (12:17).[35] That Esau was rejected by God despite having "sought" God's blessing highlights his lack of faith, as it confirms that without faith it is impossible to please God (11:6). That the unfaithful Esau "sought" (*ekzētēsas*) the blessing but was rejected by God illustrates, with the aid of alliteration, how one may become "dislocated" (*ektrapē*, 12:13). That Esau individualistically sought, "with" tears, God's blessing underlines the need for the audience to pursue God's peace together "with" all their fellow members within the worshiping community (12:14).

The audience have been informed about the necessity of faith for "approaching" God in worship: "Without faith it is impossible to please, for it is necessary that the one *approaching* God believe that he exists" (11:6). With the faith that they have, the audience were exhorted: "Let us approach" God for worship with a true heart in assurance of faith (10:22). This echoes the exhortation: "Let us approach" with boldness the heavenly throne of grace to receive divine assistance (4:16) through the intercession of Jesus as the eternal high priest, who is able to save completely those who "approach" God through him, always living to intercede on behalf of them (7:25). On the other hand, the Mosaic law never is able to make perfect those who "approach" God for worship (10:1). Mindful of this inability, the audience are assured that in their worship of God, "you have not *approached*" (*proselēlythate*) a tangible and earthly Mount Sinai where that law was given through Moses (12:18). This reinforces, with the aid of alliteration, the exhortation for the audience to restore the knees that have become "paralyzed" (*paralelymena*) in "approaching" for worship (12:12).

As a worshiping assembly, the audience have not approached "what is to be felt" (12:18a), that is, Mount Sinai described as foreboding, by means of an allusion to Deut 4:11–12, with all of its dreadful and deadly aspects. That what is to be felt on Mount Sinai includes a blazing "fire" and darkness and "gloom" and a whirlwind (12:18b) associates it with the death-bringing aura of divine judgment, as it resonates with the fearful expectation of God's judgment and "zeal of fire" about to devour

---

35. Ibid., 533: "God responded to Jesus' 'reverence' not to his tears alone." Lane, *Hebrews 9–13*, 458: "The identification of the antecedent of *autēn*, 'it,' in v 17c as the independent articular noun *tēn eulogian*, 'the blessing,' in v 17a demonstrates that the writer has conformed his statement to the detail of the account in Gen 27:30–40. There, it is the blessing, not repentance, that Esau sought with tears."

the adversaries (10:27). The "blazing" fire recalls that the end of what is rejected by God is the "burning" of divine judgment (6:8). What is to be felt on Mount Sinai (12:18) included a blast of a trumpet and voice of "pronouncements" that are divine (12:19a). This has been indicated by the "pronouncement" of God by which the ages have been provided (11:3), by the beneficent "pronouncement" of God that the audience have already tasted (6:5), and by the "pronouncement" of the power of God by which the divine Son is bearing up all things (1:3).

That those who "heard" the "voice" of God's pronouncements refused it, lest a word be added for them (12:19b), associates them with the unfaithful and disobedient wilderness generation, who failed to heed the divine scriptural proclamation from Ps 94:7–8 that "today if you *hear* his *voice*, do not harden your hearts" (3:7, 15; 4:7). The word of God for "hearing" did not benefit them, who were not united in faith with those who "heard" (4:2). For all of those who came out of Egypt through Moses "heard" but rebelled (3:16). That those who approached Mount Sinai heard the voice of God's pronouncements but refused it thus serves as a foil to reinforce the warning for the audience all the more to attend to the things that have been "heard" (2:1) regarding the great salvation that was confirmed by those who "heard" (2:3) and that they are not to neglect as a worshiping assembly.

Those who approached Mount Sinai "heard" the voice of God's pronouncements but refused it, lest a "word" be added for them (12:19), for they could not "bear" what was ordered in accord with Exod 19:12–13, "If even an animal touch the mountain, it shall be stoned" (12:20). This serves as a negative example for the warning that the audience have become sluggish in "hearing" (5:11) and are inexperienced of the "word" of righteousness (5:13). Therefore, departing from the "word" at the beginning about the Christ, the author exhorted his audience, in contrast to those who approached Mount Sinai, "let us *bear* forward toward the perfection" (6:1). The faithless inability to bear the divine order regarding a deadly "touch"—that if even an animal "touch" "the mountain," "the mountain" on which Moses was shown the model for the heavenly tabernacle (8:5), it shall be stoned, stands in sharp contrast to the life-giving faith of Moses that triumphed over a death-bringing "touch." By faith Moses kept the Passover and the applying of the blood, so that the one who was to destroy the firstborn might not "touch" them (11:28).

The audience have heard how Moses has been associated with significant acts of "speaking." Moses was faithful in all God's house as an attendant for testimony of the things that would be "spoken" (3:5). Moses "spoke" nothing concerning priests about the tribe of Judah from which our Lord sprang up (7:14). After every commandment was "spoken" according to the law to all the people by Moses (9:19), he "said," "This is the blood of the covenant which God has commanded to you (Exod 24:8)" (9:20). By faith Moses, having become great, refused to be "said" to be a son of the daughter of Pharaoh (11:24). And now Moses "said" (12:21b), introducing another noteworthy instance of Mosaic speaking. The declaration that "so *fearful* [*phoberon*] was what was appearing" (12:21a) to the assembly that approached Mount Sinai is intensified by the direct quotation of Moses who said "I am *terrified* [*ekphobos*] and trembling."[36] The audience are to appreciate that the encounter with Mount Sinai was fearful and terrifying not only for the people but for Moses himself.[37]

Told that "you have not *approached*" for worship at the ominous scene as at Mount Sinai (12:18), "the *mountain*" not even an animal may touch without dying (12:20), the audience are now made aware that rather "you have *approached*" for worship at "Mount" Zion, its heavenly counterpart (12:22). The audience are to appreciate that they, as a worshiping assembly, have been privileged to approach also the "city" of the living God, the "heavenly" Jerusalem (12:22), that is, the "heavenly" fatherland the patriarchs longed for and the "city" God has made ready for them (11:16), the "city" having foundations, whose architect and builder is God (11:10). The audience, who are partners of a "heavenly" calling (3:1), and who have tasted of the "heavenly" gift (6:4), have now approached for worship at the "heavenly" city.

The audience were warned lest there be in anyone of them an evil heart of unfaithfulness in falling away from the "living God" (3:12). This was reinforced by the declaration that it is fearful to fall into the hands of the "living God" for judgment (10:31). But that they have now approached for worship at the heavenly city of the "living God" (12:22) fortifies the

---

36. For a discussion of the use of Deut 9:19 here, see Allen, *Deuteronomy*, 62–66.

37. Johnson, *Hebrews*, 330: "By ascribing to Moses the term *ekphobos* and by adding to it the term *entromos* ('trembling'; see Ps 17:8; Acts 7:32; 16:29), Hebrews signals that Moses indeed confronts the living God and that he shared the fear of the people." Lane, *Hebrews 9–13*, 464: "The emphasis falls on the sense of immense distance that separates the worshiper from God under the Sinai covenant."

assurance that the blood of Christ will cleanse our conscience from sinful dead works to offer worship to the "living God" (9:14).

The audience have heard the scriptural voice of God, who leads his firstborn divine Son into the heavenly world, proclaim, "And let all the *angels* of God worship him" (1:6). And of the "angels" the divine scriptural voice declares that God makes his "angels" spirits who are ministers of heavenly worship (1:7), that is, ministering spirits sent to assist (1:14) those participating in heavenly worship. In accord with this, the audience are now informed that they have approached to participate in heavenly worship along with myriads of "angels" in "full festal gathering" (*panēgyrei*, 12:22), that is, "all" (*pantes*) of the angels God has invited to worship the divine Son (1:6).[38]

In addition to the heavenly Jerusalem and myriads of angels in full festal gathering for worship (12:22), the audience have approached the assembly of the firstborn enrolled in heaven (12:23), with the alliteration underlining the close association of the "angels" (*aggelōn*) gathered for worship in heaven with the firstborn "enrolled" (*apogegrammenōn*) in heaven. That the audience have approached the "assembly" of the firstborn to join them in heavenly worship is underscored by the recall of the scriptural announcement of Jesus from Ps 21:23 regarding an assembly for worship: "I will proclaim your name to my brothers, in the midst of the *assembly* I will praise you" (2:12). This assembly of the "firstborn" is associated not only with Jesus, God's "firstborn" Son (1:6), as a worshiping assembly of his "brothers," but also with the "firstborn" saved from destruction by Moses (11:28). It is an assembly "in heaven," that is, "in the heavens" that provide the patterns for worship on earth (9:23), "in the heavens" where our high priest Jesus sat at the right of the throne of the divine Majesty (8:1).

The audience have approached for worship not only the city of the living "God" (12:22) but "God" himself, the "judge" of all (12:23), the Lord who will "judge" his people (10:30). And they have approached the "spirits" of the just ones having been made perfect (12:23), those who

---

38. "Full festal gathering" (*panēgyris*) is a compound of "all" (*pas*) and "gathering" (*agyris* = *agora*); see BDAG, 753–54. Lane, *Hebrews 9–13*, 467: "The term *panēgyris*, which occurs only here in the NT, has reference to a joyful gathering in order to celebrate a festival." Mitchell, *Hebrews*, 283: "In contrast to the terrifying sights associated with the Sinai phenomenon, the heavenly Jerusalem will be a place of festivity, filled with angels beyond counting."

have been subjected to the divine discipline of the heavenly Father of "spirits" in order to live (12:9) the eternal life offered by the living God. These spirits of the "just ones" include Abel, whom God testified as "just" (11:4), an example of God's "just one" who from faith will live (10:38). These just ones having been made "perfect" for heavenly worship (12:23) include the ancient models of faith, who would not be made "perfect" without us (11:40). They were made perfect by the heavenly high priest Jesus, who by one offering of himself in heaven made "perfect" for all time those who are being made holy (10:14). Earthly sacrifices were not able to make "perfect" the one offering worship (9:9; 10:1), for the law made nothing "perfect" (7:19). But Jesus, the divine Son, has been made "perfect" forever (7:28), since it was fitting for God to make the initiator of our salvation "perfect" through sufferings (2:10). Having been made "perfect," he became for all those who obey him a source of eternal salvation (5:9).

The audience have also approached for worship Jesus himself, the "guarantor of a new covenant" (12:24). This recalls that Jesus "is guarantor of a better covenant " (8:6). Indeed, he "is guarantor of a new covenant," so that those who have been called, among whom are the audience, might receive the promise of the eternal inheritance (9:15). The audience have also approached for worship the "blood" of the "sprinkling" associated with the new covenant of which Jesus is the guarantor (12:24). As part of the old covenant, Moses took the "blood" of animals and "sprinkled" both the book of the covenant and all the people (9:19). The tabernacle and all the vessels of the ministry for worship he likewise "sprinkled" with "blood" (9:21). But if the "blood" of goats and bulls and the "sprinkling" of a heifer's ashes makes holy those defiled for the cleansing of the flesh (9:13), how much more will the "blood" of the Christ cleanse our conscience from dead works to offer worship to the living God (9:14). That they have approached the "blood" of the "sprinkling," then, reinforces the exhortation for the audience, who have boldness for the entrance into the heavenly holy things in the "blood" of Jesus (10:19), to approach for worship with a true heart in assurance of faith, "sprinkled" with regard to the hearts from an evil conscience (10:22).

The blood of the sprinkling that the audience have approached "speaks" better beyond Abel (12:24), who by faith offered to God a greater sacrifice beyond Cain, through which he was testified to be just, God testifying on the basis of his gifts, and through this, having died, he is still "speaking" (11:4). That Abel is still speaking through faith means that he is still indicating that it is by faith that he "offered" to God a greater "sacrifice" "beyond" Cain. But the sacrificial blood of Jesus speaks "beyond" Abel and his faith, because the faithful Jesus (2:17; 3:2, 5–6) offered himself, and the blood of that self-offering speaks better beyond Abel. The scriptural voice of Jesus from Ps 39:7–9 says that "sacrifice" of animals God did not want (10:5). But Jesus said, "Behold I have come to do, O God, your will" (10:7, 9). The Jesus who thus "offered" himself unblemished to God (9:14), one "sacrifice" having "offered" for all time, sat at the right of God (10:12). It is the blood of this self-sacrifice of Jesus that "speaks" better beyond Abel, who did not offer himself as a sacrifice to God.

Those who approached Mount Sinai "refused" the voice of divine pronouncements they heard (12:19). But the audience, having been exhorted not to abandon their gathering for worship as "you take note" of the day drawing near (10:25), and that "you take note" lest there be in anyone an evil heart of unfaithfulness in falling away from the living God (3:12), are to "take note" that you do not "refuse" the one who is speaking (12:25). The one who is "speaking" refers to the divine voice "speaking" through the self-sacrificial blood of Jesus (12:24). This is the divine voice of the Lord through whom our great salvation received a beginning of being "spoken" (2:3), and the divine voice of the God who, having "spoken" to the fathers in the prophets (1:1), at the end of these days has "spoken" to us in a divine Son (1:2), a divine speaking that invites a response of worship.

What this divine voice is "speaking" includes preeminently the scriptural voice of Jesus that the audience have heard. From Ps 21:23 they have heard Jesus "saying" that he will proclaim God's name to his brothers, in the midst of the worshiping assembly they will hear him praise God (2:12). From Ps 39:7–9 they have heard the Jesus who is "saying" (10:5, 8) that God does not want sacrifices of animals (10:5–6, 8). Instead, as Jesus emphatically "said" (10:7, 9), he has come to do God's will (10:7, 9). By doing the will of God in offering his own God-given body once for all (10:10) and his blood in an unblemished self-sacrifice to God, Jesus has made it possible for the audience to offer worship in heaven to the living God (9:14; 10:19). The audience are thus to take note not to refuse this divine "speaking" they have already heard, as well as that which they are still to hear as a worshiping assembly (12:25).[39]

The warning to take note that "you do not refuse" the one who is speaking is reinforced by a comparison with those at the event on Mount Sinai. Those "refusing" the one "warning" on earth (12:25) at Mount Sinai recalls that Noah was divinely "warned" about things not yet being noticed (11:7), and that Moses was divinely "warned" regarding the heavenly model for worship (8:5). When those at Mount Sinai "refused" the voice of the divine pronouncements they heard (12:19), they did not "escape" the terrifying threat of death (12:20). Through the comparison it is all the more certain, then, that we who turn away the one from "heaven," recalling that the assembly of the firstborn are enrolled in "heaven" (12:23), the "heavenly" Jerusalem (12:22), will likewise not "escape" the terrifying threat of death (12:25). This intensifies the warning of how "we will escape," if we neglect so great a salvation that began to be spoken through the Lord (2:3). The warning that we not "turn away the one from heaven" resonates with the warning that there not be in anyone in the audience an evil heart of unfaithfulness in "falling away from the living God" (3:12). The assertion that "much more" we who turn away the one from heaven will not escape the threat of death bolsters the exhortation that we "much more" be subjected to the heavenly Father of spirits and live (12:9).

The one warning on "earth," the one from heaven (12:25), is further identified as the one whose "voice" shook the "earth" then, that is, when those at Mount Sinai heard the "voice" of divine pronouncements (12:19). The scriptural voice of God from Hag 2:6, the faithful God who once "promised" Abraham (6:13; 10:23; 11:11), has now "promised," saying, "Once more I will stir up not only the earth but also the heaven" (12:26).[40] The divine scriptural voice that has now promised by "saying" further identifies the divine voice of the one who is "speaking," whom the audience as a worshiping assembly are to take note not to refuse (12:25).

The promise that God once more will stir up not only the "earth" (12:26) refers to his warning on "earth" (12:25) at the terrifying and stirring event on Mount Sinai (12:18–20). But now he will also stir up the "heaven" (12:26), that is, the "heavenly" Jerusalem (12:22), the "heaven" in which the firstborn are enrolled (12:23), and the "heaven" from which

---

39. Smillie, "Hebrews 12:25."
40. For a discussion of the use of Hag 2:6 here, see Guthrie, "Hebrews," 988–91.

is speaking this divine voice the audience are not to refuse (12:25). The all-embracing divine power over both earth and heaven expressed in this scriptural promise resonates with the scriptural voice of God from Ps 101:26 addressed to the heavenly enthroned divine Son, asserting that "you at the beginnings, Lord, founded the *earth*, and the *heavens* are the works of your hands" (1:10).

The promise that "once more" God will stir up not only the earth but also the heaven (12:26) receives elaboration from the author. The "once more" "indicates," resonating with the Holy Spirit "indicating" that the way to the heavenly holy things had not appeared while the first, earthly tabernacle had standing (9:8), the change of the things being shaken as earthly things that have been made, so that the heavenly things not being shaken may remain (12:27). This divine "change" from what is earthly to what is heavenly accords with the divine "change" of Enoch from an earthly to a heavenly being. Enoch was "changed" so that he did not see death, and he was not found because God "changed" him, for before the "change" he was testified to have pleased God (11:5). It also accords with the divine "change" from an earthly to a heavenly priesthood. For the priesthood being "changed" by God from that according to Aaron (earthly) to that according to Melchizedek (heavenly), of necessity a divine "change" of law regarding worship also comes about (7:12).

The "once more" indicates the divine change of things being "shaken," recalling the event on Mount Sinai when the divine voice "shook" the earth (12:26), as things made on earth, so that the things not being "shaken" may remain in heaven (12:27). That the things not being shaken may "remain" in heaven resonates with the better possession the audience know they have that "remains" in heaven (10:34), with the priesthood of Jesus that is permanent, because he "remains" forever in heaven (7:24), and with Melchizedek who "remains" a priest for all time in heaven (7:3).

In an alliterative contrast with the exhortation to "therefore" restore the hands that have become weakened and the knees that have become "paralyzed" (*paralelymena*, 12:12), the audience are described as those "therefore" "acquiring" (*paralambanontes*) an "unshakable" heavenly kingdom (12:28). This accords with the things "not being shaken" that remain in heaven (12:27). In contrast to the heroes of old who through faith conquered earthly "kingdoms" (11:33), and in accord with the heavenly "kingdom" of the enthroned divine Son (1:8), the audience are acquiring a heavenly "kingdom" that is unshakable. Having been warned lest anyone be lacking of the "grace" of God (12:15), and not to insult the Spirit of "grace" (10:29), the audience, as those acquiring an unshakable heavenly kingdom, are exhorted, "let us have *grace*" (12:28). This reinforces the exhortation for us to approach for worship then with boldness the throne of "grace," so that we may receive mercy and may find "grace" for timely help (4:16) from the Jesus who, by the "grace" of God, tasted death on behalf of all (2:9). "Let us have" grace reaffirms the exhortation that we who have taken refuge "may have" a strong encouragement to hold fast to the hope lying ahead (6:18).

Acquiring an unshakable heavenly kingdom, with divine grace we may "offer worship" pleasing "to God" with reverence and awe (12:28). This bolsters again the assurance that the blood of Christ will cleanse our conscience from dead works to "offer worship" "to God" who is ever living (9:14). The exhortation for us to offer worship "pleasing" to God presupposes that we have the faith necessary to "please" God (11:6), like Enoch, who was testified to have the faith that "pleased God" (11:5). That we may offer worship pleasing to God with "reverence" and awe likens us to Noah, who became "reverent" toward God (11:7). It also likens us to the worshiping Jesus, who in the days of his flesh offered both prayers and supplications with strong outcrying and tears to the God able to save him from death, and he was heard from his "reverence" (5:7).

The exhortation for us to have divine grace through which we may offer worship pleasing to God with reverence and awe (12:28) is emphatically punctuated with an allusion to Deut 4:24: "For indeed our God is a consuming fire!" (12:29). That our God is a "consuming fire" resonates with the "blazing fire" of God's ominous judgment at the terrifying event on Mount Sinai (12:18; cf. 6:8). It recalls the warning of a certain fearful expectation of divine judgment and "zeal of fire to devour" the adversaries (10:27), if we deliberately go on sinning (10:26).[41] But the audience have also been reminded that through faith the exemplary heroes of old quenched the power of "fire" (11:34). In addition, the audience have been assured that God made the angels, his spirits who minister in heavenly

---

41. Lane, *Hebrews 9–13*, 487: "The reference to fire evokes the theme of the judgment of God which is expressed through the symbol of fire in each of the prior warnings concerning apostasy (6:8; 10:27)." Ellingworth, *Hebrews*, 692: "To speak of God as fire is to draw attention to one aspect of his being."

worship, a flame of "fire" (1:7) sent to assist those who are going to inherit eternal salvation as worshipers in the heavenly liturgy (1:14).[42]

V. 13:1–16

A [13:1] Let the brotherly love remain. [2] Hospitality *do not neglect*, for through it some have unknowingly entertained as strangers angels. [3] Remember the prisoners as fellow-imprisoned, the maltreated as you yourselves are also in the body. [4] Marriage is to be honored among all and the marriage bed undefiled, for *God* will judge the immoral and adulterers. [5] Your manner is to be without the love of money, being content with things present, for he has said, "You never will I leave and you never will I abandon" (Deut 31:6), [6] so that we may have courage to say, "The Lord is my helper, I will not be afraid, what will a man do to me" (Ps 117:6)? [7] Remember your leaders, who spoke to you the word of *God*; observing the outcome of their conduct, imitate their faith. [8] Jesus Christ yesterday and today is the same and for the ages. [9a] Do not be carried away by various and strange teachings.

> **B** [9b] For it is beneficent for the heart to be confirmed by grace, not by foods in which those conducting themselves have not benefited. [10] *We have* an altar from which those offering worship in the tabernacle do not have a right to eat.
>
>> **C** [11] For the *blood* of the animals as a sin offering is *borne* into "the *holy things*" through the high priest; their bodies are burned *outside of the camp*.
>>
>>> **D** [12a] Therefore also Jesus,
>>
>> **C'** [12b] that he might *make holy* the people through his own *blood*, suffered outside of the gate. [13] Hence let us go out to him *outside of the camp, bearing* his reproach.
>
> **B'** [14] For *we have* not here a city that remains, but we are seeking the one that is to come.

A' [15] Through him then let us offer up a sacrifice of praise continually to *God*, that is, the fruit of lips confessing his name. [16] The doing of good and fellowship *do not neglect*, for with such sacrifices *God* is pleased.

---

42. Rhee, "Chiasm."

At the conclusion of the preceding unit in 12:12–29 is a reference to "God" in the warning that "indeed our *God* is a consuming fire" (12:29). Near the beginning of the next unit in 13:1–16 is the next reference to "God" in the warning that "*God* will judge the immoral and adulterers" (13:4). These consecutive occurrences of "God" thus serve as the transitional words connecting these units as they retain a focus on divine judgment.

With regard to the second macrochiastic level, the audience experience a chiastic relationship between the unit in 10:15–30 and the one in 13:1–16 provided by expressions for "heart," "remember," "abandon," "make holy," and "will judge." Noteworthy is that these are the only occurrences in Hebrews of the verbal forms for "abandon" and "will judge." In 10:15–30 are references to "giving my laws upon their *hearts*" (10:16) and to approaching "with a true *heart* in assurance of faith, sprinkled with regard to the *hearts*" (10:22). And in 13:1–16 is a statement that "it is beneficent for the *heart* to be confirmed by grace" (13:9). In 10:15–30 is the promise that "their sins and lawless deeds I certainly will *remember* no longer" (10:17). And in 13:1–16 are the commands to "*remember* the prisoners" (13:3) and to "*remember* your leaders" (13:7). In 10:15–30 is a reference to "not *abandoning* our own gathering" (10:25). And in 13:1–16 is God's promise that "you never will I *abandon*" (13:5). In 10:15–30 is a reference to "the blood of the covenant in which he was *made holy*" (10:29). And in 13:1–16 is a reference to "the holy things" (13:11) and the statement that Jesus "might *make holy*" (13:12). In 10:15–30 is the warning that "the Lord *will judge* his people" (10:30). And in 13:1–16 is the warning that "God *will judge* the immoral and adulterers" (13:4).

In addition, at the second macrochiastic level, the audience experience a chiastic relationship between the unit in 1:5–14 and the one in 13:1–16 provided by the expression "the same." In 1:5–14 is the statement directed to the divine Son that "you are *the same* and your years will not cease" (1:12). And in 13:1–16 is the statement that "Jesus Christ yesterday and today is *the same* and for the ages" (13:8).

And with regard to the third macrochiastic level, the unit in 13:1–16 exhibits a parallel relationship with the unit in 12:1–11. The parallels are indicated by the only occurrences in Hebrews of the term "fruit." After the central and pivotal unit in 12:12–29 with its assurance that the audience have approached for worship at the heavenly city of the living God, "the peaceful *fruit* of righteousness" (12:11) is paralleled by "the *fruit* of lips confessing his name" (13:15).

The audience, who are among those designated as "brothers" of Jesus (2:11-12, 17) and who have been addressed as "brothers" several times (3:1, 12; 10:19), are now exhorted to let "brotherly love" remain (13:1). That they are to let brotherly love "remain" gives it a permanent character of continuing forever. It resonates with the unshakable heavenly things that may "remain" forever (12:27), with the better possession of the audience that "remains" forever (10:34), with the permanent priesthood of Jesus who "remains" forever (7:24), and with Melchizedek who "remains" a priest for all time (7:3).

"Hospitality," literally "love of strangers" (*philoxenias*), alliteratively conjoined to "brotherly love" (*philadelphia*, 13:1), the audience are not to neglect, for through it some have unknowingly "entertained as strangers" angels sent as messengers from God (13:2).[43] That they are not to "neglect" hospitality to strangers strengthens the assurance that God is not unjust so as to "neglect" their work and the love which they demonstrated for his name, having assisted the holy ones, and continuing to assist them (6:10). In resonance with the God who, according to Ps 8:5, "remembers" human beings (2:6), and who promises, according to Jer 38:34, that their sins "I will certainly *remember* no longer" (8:12), indeed their sins and their lawless deeds "I certainly will *remember* no longer" (10:17), the audience are to "remember" the prisoners as fellow-imprisoned (13:3). That they are to remember with a compassionate concern the "prisoners" as those who are "fellow-imprisoned" recalls that they suffered with the "prisoners" and accepted the confiscation of their possessions with joy, knowing that they have a better possession that remains (10:34).

They are also to remember the "maltreated," those who were "maltreated" like the ancient models of faith (11:37), as they themselves are also in the body (13:3). For the audience to remember with compassionate concern the maltreated who share the same kind of physical "body" is appropriate for them as those washed with regard to the "body" by

---

43. Lane, *Hebrews 9–13*, 511: "[H]ospitality to strangers (*philoxenia*) is the corollary of brotherly love (*philadelphia*). The extension of hospitality provided a practical measure for identifying with brothers and sisters, including many who were as yet unknown (6:10)." Koester, *Hebrews*, 558: "Abraham and Sarah provided food, water, and a place to rest for the three strangers who proved to be messengers of God (Gen 18:1–8; cf. 19:1–14; Judg 6:11–18; 13:3–22; Tob 12:1–20). Encountering a divine messenger in disguise was also a Greco-Roman motif." Johnson, *Hebrews*, 340: "The point for the hearers of this discourse is clear: they must be willing to extend hospitality to all strangers, for they can never know what manner of visitation from God the strangers might bring."

clean water (10:22). They also have been made holy through the offering of the "body" of Jesus Christ once for all (10:10), the Jesus Christ whose scriptural voice from Ps 39:7 declared to God that "a *body* you provided for me" (10:5). Remembering those maltreated thus presents the audience with an opportunity to use their own physical bodies, likewise provided for them by God, in a self-sacrificial way similar to that of Jesus Christ.

Marriage is to be honored among "all," as is appropriate for "all" those who obey Jesus as their source of eternal salvation (5:9), and the marriage bed is to be "undefiled" (13:4a), in accord with Jesus being our "undefiled" high priest (7:26). For, as the audience are warned, God will judge adulterers and the "immoral" (13:4b), like the "immoral" Esau, who for a single meal gave back his own rights as firstborn (12:16). That God himself, with the term "God" in an emphatic position at the end of the sentence, "will judge" the immoral and adulterers intensifies the scriptural warning from Deut 32:36 that the Lord "will judge" his people (10:30).

In alliterative accord but in contrast with their "brotherly love" (*philadelphia*, 13:1) and "love of strangers" (*philoxenias*, 13:2), the manner or way of life of the audience is to be "without the love of money" (*aphilargyros*, 13:5). In correlation with the notice that all discipline, when it is "present," does not seem to be of joy but of sorrow, but later it gives back the peaceful fruit of righteousness to those who have been trained through it (12:11), the audience are to be content with things "present" (13:5).

This exhortation regarding the conduct of the audience (13:1–5), especially their being content with things "present," is given added motivation by the scriptural voice of God himself in the assuring divine promise from Deut 31:6.[44] For "he" (*autos*) himself, intensifying the emphasis upon God himself (13:4), has definitively "said" (*eirēken* in perfect tense; cf. 1:13; 4:3–4; 10:9) to his people, addressed as a whole in the communal singular with a most definite form of negation, "*You never* will I leave."[45] In other words, God emphatically and decidedly promises never to leave or desert, but to be always appropriately "present" to every individual in the audience as those content with things "present" (13:5). The deter-

---

44. For the argument that Deut 31:6 is the most likely source for Heb 13:5, see Allen, *Deuteronomy*, 68–71.

45. Ibid., 69–70: "[C]oupled with the emphatic *autos*, the use of the 1st person adds extra significance to an already weighty promise. . . .The completed sense of the perfect *eirēken* may also increase the surety of the promise" (n. 154).

mined intensification of this divine scriptural promise, "and *you never will I abandon*" (13:5), reinforces the exhortation for the audience not to be "abandoning" their own gathering for communal worship (10:25).

In response to the divine scriptural promise that God will never leave nor abandon "you" in the singular (13:5), the audience as a whole are exhorted to have the courage to pronounce Ps 117:6 with its corresponding communal singular, "The Lord is *my* helper, I will not be afraid, what will a man do to me?" (13:6).[46] This scriptural affirmation that the "Lord" is "my" helper reverberates with the scriptural proclamation by God himself from Deut 32:35–36, "*Mine* is vengeance, I will repay" and again, "The *Lord* will judge his people" (10:30). That the Lord is my "helper" reinforces the exhortation for the audience to approach with boldness the throne of grace in worship, so that we may receive mercy and may find grace for timely "help" (4:16). It also bolsters the assurance that the Lord Jesus is able to "help" those who are being tested (2:18).

The scriptural resolve that "I will not be afraid " (13:6) resonates with the model of faith provided by Moses not being "afraid" of the fury of the king (11:27), just as his parents by faith were not "afraid" of the edict of the king (11:23). This lack of fear based on the powerful promise of divine presence reinforces the need for fear with regard to God in the exhortation for us to be "afraid" lest, while the promise to enter into God's own heavenly rest is left, anyone seem to have been lacking (4:1). The scriptural resolve that "I will not be afraid" is completed by the rhetorical query, "what will a man do to me?" (13:6), underlining the elimination of the fear of what is merely human in light of the overwhelming superiority of the divine promise. This expression of the total transcendence of God above mere human beings thus resonates with the similar rhetorical query addressed directly to God from Ps 8:5, "*what is man* that you remember him?" (2:6).

Whereas the audience are to "remember" with compassionate concern the prisoners (13:3), they are to "remember" the model provided them by their leaders (13:7). They spoke to the audience the word of "the God," "the God" who will judge the immoral and adulterers (13:4). "The word of God" their leaders spoken to them (13:7) is "the word of God" that is living and effective and sharper than every two-edged sword and penetrating as far as a division of soul and spirit, as well as of joints and

---

46. Steyn, "Hebrews 13:6."

marrow, and able to scrutinize deliberations and thoughts of the heart (4:12). Such a "word of God" demands in return a "word" of response from the audience as worshipers (4:13). By observing the outcome of their conduct, the audience are not only to "remember" (*mnēmoneuete*) their leaders but to "imitate" (*mimeisthe*) their faith (13:7), with the close connection between "remembering" and "imitating" enhanced by their alliteration. The audience are to imitate the "faith" of their leaders who, together with the stellar OT models of faith (11:1–40), exemplify the scriptural dictum from Hab 2:4 that God's just one from "faith" will live (10:38).[47]

The scriptural promise of God's abiding presence with the audience, emphatically introduced with the intensive pronoun "he" (*autos*) has said (13:5), is reinforced by the reassuring affirmation that Jesus Christ yesterday and today is the "same" (*autos*) and for the ages (13:8). That "Jesus Christ" is the same from the past to the present and for the ages to come reminds the audience that we have been and still are made holy for the worship of God through the past offering of the body of "Jesus Christ" once for all (10:10).[48] That Jesus Christ is the same "for the ages" strongly restates the eternal character of Jesus Christ, who is the divine Son and our heavenly high priest "forever" (1:8; 5:6; 6:20; 7:17, 21, 24, 28), the one through whom God made "the ages" (1:2; 11:3).

Already given an initial foundation of "teaching" about baptisms, of laying on of hands, of resurrection of the dead, and of eternal judgment (6:2), the audience are not to be carried away by various and strange "teachings" (13:9a). In contrast to the "various" acts of power and distributions of the Holy Spirit by which God testified to our great salvation (2:4), the audience are not to be carried away by "various" teachings. Whereas the audience are not to neglect hospitality, that is, the "love of strangers," since through it some have unknowingly "entertained as strangers" angels (13:2), they are not to be carried away by "strange" teachings. Such "strange" teachings are not in accord with the heavenly calling of those who are "strangers" and sojourners on earth (11:13).

The audience are those whose faculties have been trained for distinguishing of the "beneficent" and of the baneful (5:14), who have tasted the "beneficent" pronouncement of God (6:5), and who have been ex-

---

47. Allen, "Heb 13,1–8."
48. This is the only previous instance in Hebrews of the designation "Jesus Christ."

horted to stir up love and "beneficent" works (10:24). For them it is "beneficent" for the heart to be confirmed by grace, not by foods in which those conducting themselves have not benefited (13:9b). It is beneficent for the heart to be "confirmed" by grace, just as our great salvation was "confirmed" by those who heard (2:3). And it is beneficent for the heart to be confirmed by "grace." This recalls the "grace" of God by which Jesus tasted death on behalf of all (2:9), the "grace" we may find for timely help in approaching the throne of "grace" (4:16), the "grace" whose Spirit is not to be insulted (10:29), the "grace" of God that none should be lacking (12:15). It especially recalls the "grace" we are to have, through which we may offer worship pleasing to God with reverence and awe (12:28).

It is beneficent for the heart of the audience to be confirmed by the grace of God rather than by "foods" in which those conducting themselves have not benefited (13:9b), the "foods" on the basis of which (9:10) gifts and sacrifices are offered in the earthly tabernacle that are not able according to conscience to make perfect the one offering worship (9:9).[49] The word for hearing did not "benefit" the disobedient and unfaithful ancestors in the wilderness (4:2). And the former commandment of the law that made nothing perfect (7:19) was removed because of its weakness and "uselessness" (7:18)—its failure to be of "benefit" for salvation. Similarly, those concerned with these foods have not "benefited" from them.

"We have" an altar from which those offering worship in the tabernacle do not have a right to eat (13:10). This resonates with the assertions that in Jesus "we have" a heavenly high priest able to sympathize with our weaknesses (4:15; cf. 4:14). Indeed, in Jesus "we have" an anchor of the soul, both sure and firm, which enters into the interior of the heavenly veil (6:19). And in Jesus "we have" a high priest who sat at the right of the throne of the Majesty in the heavens (8:1). Although Jesus sprang up from the tribe of Judah from which no one attended to an "altar" on earth (7:13), in him as our heavenly high priest we have an "altar" in heaven. Whereas those of the sons of Levi who receive the priesthood on earth

---

49. Lane, *Hebrews 9–13*, 535: "The terms *brōmasin*, '[prescribed] foods,' and *en hois . . . hoi peripatountes*, 'those who walk in them,' are appropriate to halakhic food regulations and to the connection between v 9 and v 10, with its reference to the possession of an altar and eating. The allusion is to the eating of prescribed foods within a Jewish cultic setting. Those who framed their conduct by such ceremonial meals, then, are Jewish. Such observances have not brought them the eschatological salvation, the writer insists."

"have" a commandment to tithe the people according to the law (7:5), those offering worship in the earthly tabernacle "have" no right to eat from the heavenly altar that "we have."

Those "offering worship" in the earthly "tabernacle" (13:10) are those who "offer worship" in a pattern and shadow of the heavenly things according to which Moses made the earthly "tabernacle" (8:5). While the first, earthly, "tabernacle" had standing (9:8), both gifts and sacrifices were offered that were not able according to conscience to make perfect the one "offering worship" (9:9; cf. 10:2). But we are privileged not only to have a heavenly altar from which those offering earthly worship have no right to eat, but to "have grace" (cf. 13:9), through which we may "offer worship" pleasing to the living God with reverence and awe in the heavenly tabernacle (12:28; cf. 9:14).[50]

That the "blood" of the animals as a "sin offering" is borne "into the holy things" on earth through the "high priest" (13:11) recalls that the "high priest" enters "into the holy things" each year with "blood" not his own (9:25). But it is impossible for the "blood" of bulls and goats to take away "sins" (10:4) that prevent worship. However, not through the "blood" of goats and calves but through his own "blood" Christ the high priest entered once for all "into the holy things" in heaven, finding eternal redemption (9:12), the great salvation (2:3) not to be neglected in worship. The "bodies" of these sacrificial animals are burned outside of the camp (13:11; cf. Lev 16:27).[51] But we have been made holy through the

---

50. Ibid., 539: "'Eating from the altar' is a figurative expression for participating in the sacrifice. The act of eating from the altar in Jerusalem gave those who participated in the meal a share in what had transpired on the altar. The declaration that the adherents of the old cultus have no right to eat from the altar asserts that they have no share in the sacrifice of Christ on Golgotha and are excluded from its benefits. Participation in the efficacy of Jesus' sacrifice is limited to those who recognize in the cross-event the source of the grace by which the heart is strengthened." With regard to a eucharistic allusion here, deSilva (*Perseverance*, 499–500) remarks: "For hearers accustomed to participating in this ritual [Eucharist], an allusion to it in 13:10 is unavoidable and has the potential to enrich their understanding of that meal and to safeguard them against an overly materialistic interpretation of its power and significance (as the author has laid ample stress on the once-for-all and unrepeatable quality of Jesus' sacrifice on the cross). Nevertheless, it is a resonance that the author will himself neither develop nor exclude."

51. Lane, *Hebrews 9–13*, 540: "In Lev 16:27 it is specified that both animals, whose blood has been brought into the sanctuary for the atonement ritual (Lev 16:11–19), may not be used as sacrificial food (cf. Lev 6:30); their remains must be taken outside the holy precinct of the camp for disposal in a region of cultic impurity by servants of the tabernacle (cf. Lev 16:28). The carcasses of the young bull and the goat were to be burned to prevent their remains from being eaten (cf. Exod 29:14; Ezek 43:21)."

offering of the "body" of Jesus Christ once for all (10:10), the "body" that God, who did not want sacrifice and offering of animals, provided him (10:5). He offered his own body as a sacrifice on behalf of the audience, who are also in their own "body" (13:3) provided to them by God, and who have been washed with regard to the "body" by clean water (10:22).

In contrast to the "blood" of the animals that is borne as a sin offering "into the holy things" on earth through the high priest (13:11), Jesus, as the heavenly high priest, was to "make holy" the people "through his own blood" (13:12). This fortifies the assurance for the audience that, because not through the "blood" of goats and calves "but through his own blood" Jesus entered once for all "into the holy things" in heaven, finding eternal redemption (9:12). Whereas the "blood" of goats and bulls and the sprinkling of a heifer's ashes makes holy those defiled for the cleansing of the flesh (9:13), how much more will the "blood" of the Christ, who through the eternal Spirit offered himself unblemished to God, cleanse our conscience from dead works to offer worship to the living God (9:14).

That Jesus might make holy "the people" through his own "blood" (13:12), "the people" of God whom the divine Lord will judge (10:30), underscores his status as a high priest, who not without "blood" offers on behalf of the inadvertent sins of "the people" (9:7; cf. 5:3). Jesus, however, is a heavenly high priest who does not have each day a necessity, in contrast to the earthly high priests, first on behalf of his own sins to offer up sacrifices then of "the people," for this he did once for all having offered up himself (7:27). Indeed, Jesus became a merciful and faithful high priest in things regarding God in order to expiate the sins of "the people" of God (2:17), thus enabling them to offer worship to God.

In order that he might make holy the people through his own blood, Jesus "suffered" outside of the gate of the city of Jerusalem (13:12). This recalls for the audience that it was not necessary for him repeatedly to "suffer" from the founding of the world, since he has now appeared at the completion of the ages for the removal of sin through his sacrifice (9:26). It reminds them that although being a son, he learned from the things he "suffered" obedience (5:8). Indeed, in what he himself "suffered" in being tested, those who are being tested he is able to help (2:18).

In contrast to all of those who "came out" of Egypt through Moses, but rebelled against God (3:16), and to the Levitical priests who tithe their own people, although they have "come out" from the loins of Abraham (7:5), the audience are now exhorted, "let us go out" to Jesus outside of the camp, bearing his reproach (13:13). A model for the faith they will need for this has been provided for them by the faith of Abraham who, being called by God, obeyed "to go out" to a place which he was about to receive as an inheritance, and he "went out" not knowing where he was going (11:8). They are to go out "to him" as the eternal high priest and divine Son of God. This means "to him" as the Jesus to whom the scriptural voice of God proclaimed, "The Lord has sworn and will not change, 'You are a priest forever (Ps 109:4)'" (7:21), and "to him" as the Jesus to whom the scriptural voice of God proclaimed, "Son of mine are you, I today have begotten you (Ps 2:7)" (5:5).

Whereas the bodies of the animals offered in sacrifice are burned "outside of the camp" (13:11), Jesus suffered the offering of his own body and blood "outside of the gate" (13:12).[52] The audience, then, are to go out to him "outside of the camp," that is, outside of the confines of their own sacred community, bearing his reproach (13:13).[53] A model for the audience to bear his "reproach" has been provided by Moses who considered greater wealth than the treasures of Egypt the "reproach" of the Christ, for he was looking away to the heavenly recompense (11:26). The audience, who have already been publicly exposed to "reproaches" and afflictions (10:33), are now exhorted to persevere in bearing the "reproach" of Jesus.

In contrast to those who could not "bear" what was ordered by the terrifying divine pronouncement on Mount Sinai (12:20), the audience are to go outside of the camp, "bearing" the reproach of Jesus (13:13). They are to "bear" the reproach of the Jesus whose death was "borne" by himself as the one who covenanted in the establishment of the new covenant (9:16). They are to "bear" this reproach as those exhorted that

---

52. Johnson, *Hebrews*, 348–49: "If Jesus had acted out a ritual imitation of the ancient cult, his blood would have been spilled in the temple and his body burned outside the gate. But here it is all one act: his despised rejection and death outside the gate is itself an entering into the heavenly sanctuary (through the veil of his flesh), and an eternal offering for the sanctification of the people."

53. Lane, *Hebrews 9–13*, 542–43: "The repetition of the phrase *exō tēs parembolēs*, 'outside the camp,' has the effect of tying v 13 narrowly to v 11 ('outside the camp') and to v 12 ('outside the gate'). It shows that the homiletical comparison in vv 11–12 was drawn in the service of this moving exhortation. The allusion to Lev 16:27 in v 11 serves to clarify the significance of the fact that Jesus suffered death by crucifixion 'outside the gate' (v 12) and furnishes the basis for the admonition to follow him 'outside the camp, bearing the shame he bore.' . . . The task of the community is to emulate Jesus, leaving behind the security, congeniality, and respectability of the sacred enclosure, risking the reproach that fell upon him."

"we bear" forward toward the "perfection" for heavenly worship (6:1) provided by Jesus, who is "bearing" up all things by the pronouncement of the power of God (1:3), the Jesus who, as the "perfecter" of the faith, and for the sake of the joy lying ahead of him, endured the cross, despising its shame (12:2).[54]

Although in Jesus "we have" a heavenly high priest (4:15; 8:1) and "we have" a heavenly anchor of the soul (6:19), and although "we have" a heavenly altar from which those offering worship in the tabernacle do not have a right to eat (13:10), "we have" not here on earth a city that remains (13:14a). Melchizedek "remains" a priest for all time (7:3). Jesus has the priesthood that is permanent because he "remains" forever (7:24). The audience have a better possession that "remains" forever in heaven (10:34). The heavenly things not being shaken may "remain" forever (12:27). The brotherly love is to "remain" forever (13:1). But we have not here on earth a city that "remains" forever.

That we have not here on earth a "city" that remains, but we are "seeking" the one that is to come (13:14), likens us to the patriarchs of old. For them, as those "seeking" a fatherland (11:14), a heavenly one, God has made ready a "city" in heaven (11:16). It also likens us to Abraham who was waiting for the heavenly "city" having foundations, whose architect and builder is God (11:10). That we are seeking the heavenly "city" that is to come makes even more relevant the bold assertion that the audience, as a worshiping community, have approached Mount Zion, and the "city" of the living God, the heavenly Jerusalem (12:22).

The close connection between the city that "remains" (*menousan*) and the city that is "to come" (*mellousan*) is underscored for the audience through the alliteration of these terms (13:14). The city that is "to come" that we are seeking reminds the audience of the future orientation of their faith, as it resonates with the fact that by faith concerning good things "to come" Isaac blessed Jacob and Esau (11:20; cf. 10:1). It reminds the audience that they have already been privileged to taste the beneficent pronouncement of God and the powers of the age "to come" (6:4). And it deepens their appreciation for the fact that it was not to angels but to the divine Son that God subjected the heavenly world, the one that is "coming" (2:5).

---

54. Young, "Bearing His Reproach."

Recalling that Jesus is able to save completely those who approach God for worship "through him," always living to intercede on behalf of them (7:25), the audience are exhorted, "*Through him* then let us offer up a sacrifice of praise continually to God" (13:15a; cf. Ps 49:14). We are to "offer up a sacrifice" of praise through the Jesus who does not have each day a necessity, like the earthly high priests, first on behalf of his own sins "to offer up sacrifices" then of the people, for this he did once for all having "offered up" himself (7:27). Through the intercession of the Jesus who offered himself to God, we are enabled to offer up as a "sacrifice of praise" our bearing the reproach of Jesus (13:13) as our ethical worship, our praise to God, with the close connection between "let us offer up" (*anapherōmen*) and "bearing" (*pherontes*) enhanced through the alliterative wordplay. In contrast to the Levitical priests who complete the offerings of worship by going "continually" into the earthly tabernacle (9:6), we, who are "continually" held in slavery by the fear of death (2:15), are to offer up a sacrifice of praise "continually" to the God living in heaven.

That our offering up a "sacrifice of praise" includes our bearing the reproach of Jesus (13:13) as our behavioral worship is confirmed by its explanation as the "fruit" of lips (cf. Hos 14:3) confessing his name (13:15). This resonates with the peaceful "fruit" of righteousness that all discipline, including especially the discipline involved in bearing the reproach of Jesus, gives back to those who have been trained through it (12:11).[55] In continuity with the patriarchs of old who, in accord with their faith in God, "confessed" that they are strangers and sojourners on the earth (11:13), our offering up a sacrifice of praise continually to God is the fruit of lips "confessing" the name of God. By such a confessing of the name of God as worshipers, we may hold to the "confession" of the hope unwaveringly, for faithful is the God who promised (10:23), and we may hold fast to the "confession" of Jesus as our heavenly high priest and divine Son of God (3:1; 4:14).

The offering up of a sacrifice of praise continually to God, which is the fruit of lips confessing "his name" (13:15), further endorses the conduct of the audience as an integral part of their worship of God, indeed the ethical or moral worship that complements their liturgical worship. The audience have already been assured that God is not unjust so as to

---

55. Johnson, *Hebrews*, 350: "Just as the result of training/discipline is a 'peaceful fruit (*karpos*) of righteousness,' so does the confession of God's name in the robust sense meant by Hebrews yield the 'fruit' (*karpos*) that is a sacrifice of praise."

neglect their work and the love which they demonstrated for "his name," having assisted the holy ones, and continuing to assist (6:10). Thus, such loving assistance amounts to "confessing his name," worshiping the name of God by their behavior and offering up a sacrifice of praise continually to "God," as those observing the outcome of the conduct and imitating the faith of their leaders who spoke to them the word of "God" (13:7). Such worship enables the audience to emulate the worship of Jesus himself whose scriptural voice from Ps 21:23 declared, "I will proclaim *your name* to my brothers, in the midst of the assembly I will praise you" (2:12).

The audience, who are "not to neglect" hospitality extended to strangers (13:2), are also "not to neglect" the doing of good and fellowship of sharing within their community (13:16a). This reinforces the exhortation for them to turn attention to one another for stirring up love and beneficent works (10:24), "not abandoning their own gathering," a "gathering" that connotes communal worship (10:25). That their doing of good and generous fellowship are designated as such "sacrifices" with which "God" is pleased (13:16b) further confirms how offering up a "sacrifice" of praise continually to "God" (13:15) includes especially their moral or ethical worship, the worship they render by their communal conduct.[56]

That with such sacrifices as the doing of good and communal fellowship God is "pleased" (13:16) recalls that by his faith Enoch was testified to have "pleased" God (11:5). Without faith it is impossible to "please," for it is necessary that the one approaching God for worship believe that he exists and that for those seeking him he becomes a "rewarder" (11:6). It reinforces the exhortation for the audience to have grace, through which they may offer worship "pleasing" to God with reverence and awe (12:28). The warning that "God" will judge the immoral and adulterers (13:4) is now complemented by the assurance that such sacrifices, which consist of the audience's upright moral conduct, amount to a worship with which "God" is "pleased" (*euaresteitai*).[57]

---

56. On not neglecting the "doing of good" (*eupoiias*) and "fellowship" (*koinōnias*), Lane (*Hebrews 9–13*, 552) notes: "The term *eupoiia* occurs only here in the Greek Bible. Hellenistic parallels show that it denotes 'acts of kindness' that give tangible expression to concern for others. This relatively rare term is clarified by the parallel concept *koinōnia*, which in this context carries the nuance of 'generosity.' Both terms are oriented toward shared life in the community of faith."

57. Ellingworth, *Hebrews*, 722: "*Euaresteō* in the Greek Bible is not, however, used of sacrifices, but almost always of people, who are pleasing, generally to God... God, as the subject of the passive verb, is mentioned emphatically at the end of the sentence."

VI. 13:17–25

A ^{17a} Be confident in *your leaders* and submit to them, for they are keeping watch on behalf of *your* souls,

    B ^{17b} as giving back a *word*, that with joy they may do this and not be groaning, for this would be unprofitable for *you*. ¹⁸ Pray for us, for we are confident that we have a beneficent conscience, among all wanting to be beneficently treated. ¹⁹ All the more I *encourage* to do this, that *soon* I may be restored to *you*.

        C ^{20a} May the God of peace, who led up from the dead the shepherd of the sheep, the one great in the blood of the *eternal* covenant,

            D ^{20b} our Lord *Jesus*,

                E ^{21a} provide you with every good thing in order to do the will of *him*,

                E' ^{21b} doing among us what is pleasing before *him*

            D' ^{21c} through *Jesus* Christ,

        C' ^{21d} to whom be glory for the *ages* of the *ages*, amen.

    B' ²² I *encourage* you, brothers, hold on to the *word* of the *encouragement*, for indeed through brief things I have written by letter to *you*. ²³ Know that our brother Timothy has been released, with him, if he comes *soon*, I will see you.

A' ²⁴ Greet all *your leaders* and all the holy ones. Those from Italy greet you. ²⁵ The grace be with all of *you*!

At the conclusion of the preceding unit in 13:1–16 is a reference to the "doing of good" that is not to be neglected (13:16). Toward the beginning of the next unit in 13:17–25 is the statement that the leaders may "do" this (13:17). These occurrences of expressions for "doing" thus serve as the transitional words connecting these units as they move the focus from what the audience are to do to what their leaders may do.

With regard to the second macrochiastic level, the audience experience a chiastic relationship between the unit in 10:1–14 and the one in 13:17–25 provided by expressions for "good," "provide," "to do," "will," and "Jesus Christ." In 10:1–14 is a reference to "the *good* things to come"

(10:1), and in 13:17–25 to "every *good* thing" (13:21). In 10:1–14 is a reference to "a body you *provided* for me" (10:5), and in 13:17–25 to "*provide* you with every good thing" (13:21). In 10:1–14 are references to "*to do*, O God, your *will*" (10:7) as well as to "I have come *to do* your *will*" (10:9), and in 13:17–25 to "I encourage *to do* this" (13:19) as well as to "in order *to do* the *will* of him" (13:21). Finally, in 10:1–14 is a reference to "the offering of the body of *Jesus Christ* once for all" (10:10), and in 13:17–25 to "doing among us what is pleasing before him through *Jesus Christ*" (13:21).

In addition, at the second macrochiastic level, the audience experience a chiastic relationship between the unit in 1:1–4 and the one in 13:17–25 provided by the expression "the ages." In 1:1–4 is a reference to "through whom also he made *the ages*" (1:2), and in 13:17–25 to "whom be glory for *the ages*" (13:21).

With regard to the third macrochiastic level, the unit in 13:17–25 exhibits a parallel relationship with the unit in 11:32–40. The parallels are indicated by occurrences of the expression "dead." In 11:32–40 is the statement that "women received their *dead* from resurrection" (11:35). And in 13:17–25 is the reference to "the God of peace, who led up from the *dead* the shepherd of the sheep" (13:20).

Speaking as one of their leaders, the author has assured the audience that "we are *confident* concerning you, beloved, of better things, indeed those having to do with salvation" (6:9). The audience are now to reciprocate this confidence as they are exhorted, "Be *confident* in your leaders and submit to them" (13:17a). Motivation for this has been provided by the confidence Jesus promised to place in God himself through his scriptural voice from Isa 8:17b, "I will be *confident* in him" (2:13). That the audience are to be confident in "your leaders" reinforces the exhortation for them to remember "your leaders" as those who spoke to them the word of God; by observing the outcome of their conduct, they are to imitate their faith (13:7). That the leaders of the audience are keeping watch on behalf of "your souls" resonates with the author's concern for the audience not growing weary in "your souls" by reflecting in their worship on Jesus who has endured such disputing against himself from sinners (12:3).

That the leaders are keeping watch on behalf of the souls of the audience, as giving back a "word " (13:17b), complements their speaking to the audience the "word" of God (13:7). It stands in contrast to those on Mount Sinai, who refused the voice of divine pronouncements, lest a "word" be added for them (12:19). And it contributes to the audience's bearing forward toward the perfection, as they depart from the "word" at the beginning about the Christ (6:1). Their giving back a "word" resonates with the accountability connoted in the assertion that no creature is invisible before God, whose "word" is living (4:12), but all things are naked and laid bare to the eyes of him, regarding whom there is upon us the "word" (4:13), which includes the "word" of our response to the living "word" of God. But in accord with the divine discipline that "gives back" the peaceful fruit of righteousness to those who have been trained through it (12:11), the leaders are "giving back" a word as an appropriate response to the word of God. "With joy" the leaders are to be able to do this and not be groaning, for this would be unprofitable for the audience (13:17b). And this may be especially appreciated by the audience as those who accepted the confiscation of their possessions "with joy," knowing that they have a better possession that remains forever in heaven (10:34).

The exhortation for the audience to pray "for us" (*peri hēmōn*), that is, for the author as one of their leaders (13:18a), has been facilitated by the author's previous assertion that God has provided something better "concerning us" (*peri hēmōn*), that is, the author and his audience (11:40). Having exhorted his audience to "be confident" in their leaders, one of whom is the author himself, the author provides further motivation for that exhortation as he declares that "we are confident" that we have a beneficent conscience (13:18a). That we have a "beneficent conscience" draws the author more closely to his audience, as it resonates with the exhortation for us—author and audience—to approach God for worship with a true heart in assurance of faith, sprinkled with regard to the hearts from an "evil conscience" (10:22).

Having exhorted the audience that marriage is to be honored "among all" of them (13:4), the author, as "among all" in the audience, wants to be beneficently treated (13:18b). In correspondence to his having a "beneficent" conscience (13:18a), the author wants to be "beneficently" treated among all. In contrast to Esau who, "wanting" to inherit the blessing, was rejected by God (12:17), the author "wants" to be beneficently treated among all. That the author wants to be beneficently "treated" among all may be especially appreciated by his audience whom he has acknowledged as having endured much conflict of sufferings (10:32), on the one hand publicly exposed to reproaches and afflictions, on the other hand becoming partners of those so "treated" (10:33).

The author included himself in the exhortation that it is necessary for us "all the more" to attend to the things that have been heard, lest we drift away (2:1). Now, in a transition in self-reference from the first person plural (13:18) to the first person singular, the author poignantly singles himself out as a leader of the audience in the exhortation that "all the more" I encourage to do this, that soon I may be restored to you (13:19). That I "encourage" to do this reinforces the exhortations for the audience not to be abandoning our own gathering for communal worship, but "encouraging" (10:25) one another to love and beneficent works (10:24), and to "encourage" one another each day, that not anyone of them may become hardened by the deceit of sin (3:13). And that I encourage to "do this" reinforces the exhortation for the audience to be confident in their leaders, that they may "do this," that is, keep watch on behalf of their souls (13:17). Whereas it would be unprofitable "for you" to cause the leaders to be groaning (13:17), by the audience's praying for the author (13:18), he may be restored "to you."

Having exhorted the audience to pray for him as one of their leaders (13:18–19), the author reciprocates in advance by commencing his own prayer for the audience: "May the God of peace, who led up from the dead the shepherd of the sheep, the one great in the blood of the eternal covenant" (13:20a). The prayer invokes the God of "peace," that is, God as the ultimate source and giver of the "peace" that the audience are to pursue with all (12:14). God is also the source of the "peaceful" fruit of righteousness that divine discipline gives back to those trained through it (12:11), of the "peace" with which Rahab, by her faith in God, welcomed the spies (11:31), and the "peace" of which Melchizedek, priest of the God Most High (7:1), is king (7:2).

God took hold of the hand of the ancestral fathers of Israel to "lead" them out of the land of Egypt with its threat of death (8:9). God is "leading" many sons, among whom are the audience, from slavery to the fear of death (2:15) to heavenly glory (2:10). God "leads" the firstborn divine Son into the heavenly world (1:6). This same God "led up" from the dead the divine Son as the shepherd of the sheep (13:20a). That God led up from the "dead" the shepherd of the sheep (cf. Isa 63:11) represents the resurrection that is better than that experienced by the women who received their "dead" from resurrection (11:35). It confirms the faith of Abraham, who reasoned that God is able to raise even from the "dead" (11:19). And it forms the basis for the fundamental teaching of the resurrection of the "dead" (6:2).

That "the shepherd of the sheep" is further described as the one "great" in the blood of the eternal covenant (13:20a) links the metaphor of the "shepherd" to the priesthood of Jesus, who is a "great" priest over the house of God (10:21). It reinforces the exhortation that, having a "great" high priest who has passed through the heavens, Jesus the Son of God, let us hold fast to the confession (4:14).[58] In contrast to the "blood" of the old "covenant" (9:20) that is near to disappearing (8:13), the shepherd of the sheep whom God led up from the dead is the one great in the "blood" of the eternal "covenant." That this covenant is "eternal," that is, divine and everlasting, resonates with the divine heavenly inheritance that is "eternal" (9:15), the divine "eternal" Spirit through whom Christ offered himself unblemished to God (9:14), the divine "eternal" redemption found in heaven by Christ the high priest (9:12). It also resonates with the divine judgment that is "eternal" (6:2), and the "eternal" salvation of which the divine Son and high priest is the source (5:9).

Although Jesus has been referred to as "our Lord" in discussing his heavenly priesthood (7:14), this is the first occurrence of the more specific designation "our Lord Jesus" (13:20b). That Jesus is referred to as "our" Lord unites the author to the audience as among the "sheep" of the "shepherd" who is the Lord Jesus, the one who is great as the heavenly high priest in the blood of the eternal covenant.

The God by whose pronouncement the ages have been "provided" (11:3) is asked to "provide" the audience with every "good" thing (13:21a), resonating with the "good" things to come of which the law has only a shadow (10:1), and with the "good" things that have come to be of which Christ has come as high priest (9:11). The provision of every good thing

---

58. Attridge, *Hebrews*, 406: "The use of the metaphor of the shepherd at this point may in fact best be understood as a substitution for or transformation of the christological image of the priest that dominated most of Hebrews. The effect of the substitution is to emphasize one of the qualities that was traditionally associated with the title of High Priest, Christ's heavenly intercessory function. The one whom God exalted from the dead is the one who ever remains as guide of God's flock." Ellingworth, *Hebrews*, 729: "*Ton megan* ['the one great']is emphatic by position: Christ is the great shepherd, as he is the great (high) priest (4:14; 10:21) by contrast with lesser levitical high priests, and perhaps with subordinate leaders of the Christian community, such as the *hēgoumenoi* of vv. 7, 17; also of Moses, mentioned in Is. 63:11, and who is traditionally known as 'the shepherd of Israel.' Yet the relationship is one of dependence, not only one of contrast."

will enable the audience "to do the will of him," the will of God himself. This request for God to "provide" the audience with every good thing resonates with the scriptural voice of Jesus from Ps 39:7–9, which declares to God that a body you "provided" for me (10:5), and, "Behold I have come, as in the scroll of the book it is written concerning me, *to do*, O God, *your will*" (10:7, 9). In the doing of this "will" of God we have been made holy through the offering of the body of Jesus Christ once for all (10:10). This prayer request reinforces the exhortation that the audience have need of endurance so that, "doing the will of God," they may acquire the promise of the eternal rest and worship of the living God in heaven (10:36).

The prayer for God to provide the audience with every "good" thing in order "to do" his will (13:21a) aims to contribute to the fulfillment of the exhortation that they not neglect the "doing of good" and fellowship, for with such sacrifices God is pleased (13:16). Indeed, with such sacrifices the audience may offer up a "sacrifice of praise" as their ethical worship continually to God, that is, the fruit of lips confessing his name (13:15). The author's prayer here thus functions as a speech act, that is, an utterance whose purpose begins to be accomplished in and through its very performance.[59] In praying that God provide the audience with every good thing they need to do the divine will, the author is making the audience aware that in their very hearing of the oral performance of this letter God has already begun to provide them with every good thing they need to do his will in what they have heard about the doing of that will through the self-sacrifice of Jesus. In addition, hearing the prayer assures the audience that God will continue to provide them with every good thing they need in the future to do his will, as a way of worshiping God not only liturgically but by the way they conduct themselves ethically in their doing of good.

The focus of the prayer shifts from the request for God to provide the audience with every good thing for them to "do" the divine will of "him" (13:21a) to what God himself is "doing" among us that is pleasing before "himself" (13:21b). The audience have already heard what God has done and still is doing among "us": God has surrounded "us" with a cloud of witnesses, the past models of faith (11:1–40), that we may traverse the struggle lying ahead for "us" (12:1). In the blood of Jesus a fresh and living way into the heavenly holy things was divinely inaugurated for

---

59. On speech act theory, see Austin, *How to Do Things with Words*.

"us" (10:20). The divine Holy Spirit testifies to "us" regarding the divine promise of a new covenant (10:15). In Jesus God provided a high priest fitting for "us" in every way (7:26). There is upon "us" the word (4:13), the word of God that is ever living (4:12). And God has spoken to "us" in his divine Son (1:2). All of this good that the audience have heard that God has done and is doing among us thus confirms that, in their very hearing of the oral performance of the letter, the audience realize that God has already begun to provide them with every good thing they need to do his will as their act of ethical worship.

That God is "doing" among us what is "pleasing" before himself (13:21b) reaffirms for the audience that God himself indeed is providing every good thing they need "to do" his divine will (13:21a). God himself is making possible the audience's "doing of good" that amounts to a sacrifice, a sacrifice consisting of their ethical worship, with which God is "pleased" (13:16).[60] This further reinforces the exhortation for the audience to avail themselves of divine grace, through which they may offer worship "pleasing" to God with reverence and awe (12:28). This also means that God himself gives the faith without which it is impossible to "please" him (11:6), as exemplified by Enoch, who was testified to have "pleased" God by his faith (11:5). That God is doing what is pleasing "before him" recalls that no creature is invisible "before him" (4:13), as the God of the word that is ever living (4:12). Hence, it is all the more incumbent upon the audience to respond to this word as worshipers with sacrifices of doing good that are pleasing before God.

The prepositional phrase, "*through* Jesus Christ" (13:21c), emphasizes that "our Lord Jesus," the shepherd of the sheep as our great high priest in the blood of the eternal covenant (13:20), is the "Jesus Christ" who yesterday and today is the same and for the ages (13:8). He is the one "through" whom we may offer up a sacrifice of praise continually to God (13:15), that is, the doing of good and communal fellowship as sacrifices pleasing to God (13:16). That God is doing among us what is pleasing before him "through Jesus Christ" (13:21c) recalls that it is "through" the offering of the body of "Jesus Christ" once for all that we have been made holy for the worship of God (10:10). It reminds the audience that, because he is a priest forever, Jesus Christ is able to save completely those who

---

60. Alliteration underscores the close connection between the "doing of good" (*eupoiias*) and "is pleased" (*euaresteitai*).

approach God for worship "through" him, always living to intercede on behalf of them (7:25).

A stimulating doxology concludes the author's prayer for his audience, drawing them into his own worshipful praise: "to whom be glory for the ages of the ages, amen" (13:21d). The prayer's acknowledgement of the divine "glory" that belongs to Jesus Christ through whom God is doing what is pleasing before him, as he provides the audience with every good thing they need to do the divine will (13:21), reaffirms the divine status of Jesus Christ as an object of heavenly worship (1:6). He is worthy of the divine heavenly "glory" associated with the cherubim among the holy things in the tabernacle (9:5). And he is worthy of greater "glory" beyond Moses (3:3), the divine heavenly "glory" to which God is leading his many sons (2:10) by means of his divine Son whom he crowned with heavenly "glory" and honor (2:7, 9), and who is the radiance of the divine "glory" (1:3). That glory be to Jesus Christ "for the ages" of "the ages," amen, emphatically extends the assertion that Jesus Christ yesterday and today is the same and "for the ages" (13:8). It bolsters the declaration that now once at the completion of "the ages" Jesus Christ has appeared for the removal of sin through his sacrifice, the sacrifice he offered with his own blood, the blood of the "eternal" covenant (13:20a).

In addressing his audience as one of their leaders, the author declared, "all the more I *encourage* to do this" (13:19a), that is, to treat him beneficently by praying for him so that he may soon be restored to them (13:18, 19b). Now he addresses them as a fellow brother, declaring, "I *encourage* you, *brothers*" (13:22). This recalls that as "brothers" having boldness for the entrance to the heavenly holy things in the blood of Jesus (10:19), they are to approach God for worship with a true heart in assurance of faith (10:22). It reinforces the exhortation for the audience as "brothers" to take note lest there be in anyone of them an evil heart of unfaithfulness in falling away from the living God (3:12), and to "encourage" one another each day, so that not anyone of them may become hardened by the deceit of sin (3:13; 10:25). And it resonates with the exhortation for them as holy "brothers," who are partners with one another and with the author of a heavenly calling to participate in heavenly worship, to turn attention to the apostle and high priest of our confession, Jesus (3:1).

The declaration that "I encourage" you as brothers to hold on to the word of the "encouragement" emphatically underscores that what the author has composed in this letter is indeed a homiletic word aimed at encouraging his audience (13:22).⁶¹ That the audience are to "hold on to" the author's word of the encouragement resonates with and climactically reinforces the exhortations for both author and audience that, as worshipers, "we hold to" the confession of the hope unwaveringly, for faithful is the one who promised (10:23). "We are to hold" the beginning of the reality firm until the end (3:14). And "we are to hold to" the boldness and to the boast of the hope (3:6) as a worshiping assembly.

That the author designates his letter as the "word" of the encouragement (13:22) associates him with the other leaders of the audience, as giving back a "word" for the benefit of the audience (13:17)—his own particular "word" of worshipful response (4:13) to the living "word" of God (4:12). The author through brief things has written by letter "to you" (13:22), as he hopes soon to be restored "to you" (13:19), that is, to his audience for whom it would be unprofitable "for you" not to submit to and be confident in "your leaders" (13:17).⁶²

The audience, as "brothers" who suffered with prisoners and accepted the confiscation of their possessions with joy, "knowing" that they have a better possession that remains forever in heaven (10:34), are now to "know" that our "brother" Timothy has been released, by implication, from prison (13:23a; cf. 13:3).⁶³ The hope that the author "soon" may be restored to "you" (13:19), the audience as the "you" he is encouraging with this letter (13:22), is bolstered by his hope that with the released Timothy, if he comes "soon," I will see "you" (13:23b). This mutual concern by the author and audience for a fellow individual "brother" bolsters

---

61. On "the word of the encouragement" here, Lane (*Hebrews 9–13*, 568) remarks: "The expression appears to have been an idiomatic designation for the homily or edifying discourse that followed the public reading from the designated portions of Scripture in the hellenistic synagogues." For an example, see Acts 13:15; and for similar language, see 1 Macc 10:24; 2 Macc 7:24; 15:8–11.

62. On the phrase "through brief things" (*dia bracheōn*), Ellingworth (*Hebrews*, 733) comments that this "expression of the author's modesty does not require more detailed explanation, but 'relatively brief for the greatness of the theme' may be implied; less probably 'relatively brief, considering the readers' dangerous situation.'" Lane, *Hebrews 9–13*, 568: "The reference to brevity, however, is simply a polite literary convention."

63. On the implication that it is from prison that Timothy "has been released" (*apolelymenon*), Lane (*Hebrews 9–13*, 569) points out: "The assumption that Timothy has been in custody is supported by the common meaning of *apolyein* in the NT, especially when it is used absolutely, as here, and by the writer's concern for those Christians who remain in custody in the near context (13:3)."

the exhortations for the audience's concern for each one of their members as a worshiping assembly (3:12; 4:1, 11; 12:15, 16).

The audience have been persuaded to imitate their ancestral leaders in faith, all of whom died, not receiving the heavenly promises but from afar seeing them and "greeting" and confessing that they are strangers and sojourners on the earth (11:13). Now they are not only to be confident in and submit to "your leaders" (13:17), whose faith they are to imitate (13:7), but also to "greet" all of those who are "your leaders" presently (13:24).

That the audience are to greet all the "holy ones" (13:24) reminds them that they are united to their fellow believers as those who have been made holy by Jesus. Indeed, he who "makes holy" and those who are being "made holy" are all from one, for which reason he is not ashamed to call them brothers (2:11). It is through the offering of the body of Jesus Christ once for all that we have been "made holy" (10:10). By this one offering he has made perfect for heavenly worship for all time those who are being "made holy" (10:14). It is through the blood of Jesus as the blood of the new covenant that each believer was "made holy" (10:29). As "holy ones," we have boldness for entrance into the heavenly "holy things" in the blood of Jesus to participate in the worship of God (10:19). For if the blood of animals "makes holy" those defiled for the cleansing of the flesh (9:13), how much more will the blood of the Christ cleanse our conscience from dead works to offer worship to the living God (9:14).

In reciprocation for the author's request that the audience "greet" all their leaders and all the holy ones, he assures them that those from Italy, those who are their fellow strangers and sojourners on the earth (11:13), "greet" you (13:24). That those from Italy greet "you" bolsters the concern for the audience on the part of the author, who prays that God provide "you" with every good thing to do his will (13:21), who encourages "you" to hold on to the word of the encouragement he has written for them (13:22), and who hopes that he will see "you" soon (13:23).[64]

The author's final greeting, "the *grace* be with all of you" (13:25), resonates with and climactically sums up all of the previous exhortations

---

64. Koester, *Hebrews*, 581: "[T]he reference to Italy shows that the circle in which Hebrews originated included Christians who lived outside Palestine in the Greco-Roman world." Lane, *Hebrews 9–13*, 571: "The significance of the greeting lies in the allusion to a larger group of persons who care, as does the writer, about what is happening on the home base."

regarding divine "grace" in this word of the encouragement. The audience have been exhorted not to be carried away by various and strange teachings, for it is beneficent for the heart to be confirmed by the "grace" of God (13:9). They are to take advantage of the "grace" of God available to them, through which they may offer worship pleasing to God with reverence and awe (12:28). They are to see to it that none of them be lacking of this "grace" of God (12:15). They are not to insult the divine Spirit of this "grace" of God (10:29). They have been exhorted to approach with boldness the heavenly throne of "grace," so that they may receive mercy and may find divine "grace" for timely help (4:16). And as worshipers they are to take note of the Jesus who tasted death on behalf of all by the "grace" of God (2:9).

The author, as one of the leaders of the audience, has exhorted them to be confident in their leaders and submit to them, for they are keeping watch on behalf of "your" souls (13:17). And now the author adds his own personal concern for his audience as their preeminent leader with his final greeting that the grace be with all of "you" (13:25). This declaration about grace "with all" of you thus reinforces the exhortation for the audience, who are to greet all their fellow "holy ones" (13:24), to pursue peace "with all," and the "holiness" without which no one will see the Lord (12:14).

Noteworthy is that the author's final and climactic greeting contains no explicit verb. Literally, it is heard as "the grace with all of you!" (13:25). This facilitates its multiple functions as a speech act whose purpose begins to be accomplished in the very hearing of it. First, it affirms that "the grace *has been* with all of you," thus reminding the audience that they have already received the grace of God in the past, in accord with the fact that Jesus tasted death on behalf of all by the grace of God (2:9). Secondly, it asserts that "the grace *is now* with all of you," thus indicating to the audience that the grace of God is now presently being given to them in and through their hearing and heeding of the letter itself as the author's word of the encouragement (13:22). Finally, it prays that "the grace *will be* with all of you," thus assuring the audience that the grace of God will continue to be available to them in the future. This accords with the encouraging exhortation, "Let us approach then with boldness the throne of grace, so that we may receive mercy and may find grace for timely help" (4:16).

Conclusion

I. By faith concerning things to come, that is, concerning the promised good things to come regarding the heavenly worship of which the law concerning earthly worship has only a shadow (10:1), Isaac blessed both of his sons, Jacob and Esau (11:20). That the dying Jacob worshiped on the top of his staff (11:21) provides the audience with a model of faith that includes the hope of participating in the heavenly worship of the heavenly fatherland. That Joseph reminded the sons of Israel concerning the "exodus" or "way out" of an earthly land (11:22) anticipates the fresh and living "way" into the heavenly holy things as the place of worship that Jesus inaugurated for us (9:8; 10:20).

That Moses chose to be mistreated with the people of God than to have a temporary enjoyment of sin (11:25) commends him as a model of faith for the audience, as among the people of God for whom the heavenly Sabbath rest and worship of God still remains (4:9). That Moses endured the reproach of the Christ, for he was looking away to the recompense from God (11:26), reinforces the exhortation for the audience as a worshiping assembly not to throw away their boldness, which has great recompense from God (10:35). The foresight and insight of the faith of Moses who persevered as if seeing the God who is invisible (11:27) serves as a model for the audience, who, as a worshiping assembly, are taking note of Jesus (2:9), without yet seeing all things subjected to him (2:8). Moses' faith that God would not allow the one who was to destroy the firstborn so much as touch them (11:28) bolsters the faith of the audience regarding the firstborn divine Son as an object of heavenly worship (1:6). Those who went through the Red Sea without drowning (11:29) and Rahab, who welcomed the Israelite spies with peace so that she did not perish together with those who disobeyed (11:30–31), underscore the life-giving dimension of the faith by which the audience are to worship God.

II. In contrast to the Levitical high priests, who themselves have and are surrounded by human weakness (5:2; 7:28), the additional exemplary figures (11:32–33), through faith, were empowered by God from their human weakness (11:34). This deepens the audience's appreciation for Jesus as the divine and heavenly high priest who has the power to sympathize with our human weaknesses (4:15). That these models of faith became by the power of God strong in battle (11:34) reinforces the exhortation for the audience to have a strong encouragement to hold fast to the hope, represented by Jesus as the heavenly high priest (6:19–20), lying ahead for them (6:18). And that these models of faith laid low the camps of others on earth (11:34) deepens the audience's appreciation for what lies ahead for them in heaven. It resonates with Abraham merely sojourning on earth as on land of another (11:9), and with the blood that is not of another but of the high priest Jesus himself by which he entered into the heavenly holy things (9:25) on behalf of us (9:24).

These noteworthy figures may hope that through faith they might obtain a better, heavenly resurrection (11:35), since Jesus has obtained a more excellent, heavenly ministry of worship (8:6). That through faith they were not only being afflicted and maltreated but being in need (11:37) reinforces the warning for the audience to make sure none of them seem to have been lacking in faith (4:1). That they were wandering over the crevices of the earth (11:38) further associates them with the faithful patriarchs who, as strangers and sojourners on the earth (11:13), are seeking a fatherland in heaven (11:14–16), the place of rest and worship of God. As prefigured by Abraham, who acquired Isaac in accord with God's promise (11:19), these did not yet acquire the promise. This reinforces the exhortation for the audience to have endurance so that, doing the will of God, they may acquire the promise (10:36), the promise of an eternal inheritance (9:15) in heaven, which includes entrance into the rest and worship of God. That these venerable models of faith would not be made perfect without us (11:40) means that they would not be made worthy or fit for participation in the heavenly worship without us who have the benefit of the self-sacrifice of Jesus as our heavenly high priest.

III. Through endurance the audience are to traverse the struggle lying ahead for them (12:1) by keeping their eyes fixed on Jesus as the initiator and perfecter of the faith (12:2). Jesus, who for the sake of the joy lying ahead of him, as the embodiment of the hope lying ahead for us in heaven (6:18), endured the cross, despising its shame (12:2). And that Jesus, after enduring the cross, took his seat on the right of the throne of God (12:2) provides the audience with a desirable goal to keep before them in their struggle to endure the grueling course lying ahead of them before they complete their pilgrimage to the heavenly city promised by God and participate in the heavenly liturgy. Jesus serves as an inspiring model that can motivate the audience to resist opposition to sinfulness, even to the point of shedding their own blood, if necessary (12:3-4).

The audience are invited to consider not only themselves but Jesus as the "son" whom God as a "father" disciplines (12:5-7). Since we had our fathers of flesh as disciplinarians and we respected them, we should much more be subjected to the Father of spirits and live (12:8-10). Christ, as the divinely disciplined Son of God, provides the audience not only with the example but the empowerment to endure their sufferings as the divine discipline that prepares and qualifies them for participation in the heavenly worship of the living God, the God whose eternal life we shall live. That divine discipline gives back the peaceful fruit of God's righteousness to those who are trained through it (12:11) underscores the significance of the model and motivation provided by Jesus. He loved God's righteousness so that God anointed him with the oil of gladness (1:9) as an object of the heavenly worship (1:6) in which he has enabled the audience to participate (9:14; 10:19-22).

IV. The collocation of "hands," "knees," and "feet" (12:12-13) contributes to the worshiping context that pervades Hebrews. The audience are exhorted to restore the weakened hands that are often used in various gestures (praying, blessing, etc.) associated with worship. They are to restore the weakened knees that they bow and fall upon in worship. That they are to make straight paths for their feet suggests that they avoid deviating from the ways of God, as it accords with the exhortations that they not abandon their own gathering for worship (10:25).

That the audience are exhorted to see to it lest anyone of them be lacking of the grace of God (12:15a) resonates with the warning that not anyone of them should insult the Spirit of grace (10:29) by abandoning the worshiping assembly. And this concern for each member of the community reinforces the exhortation for the entire audience as worshipers to approach with boldness the throne of grace to receive mercy and find grace for timely help (4:16). For many of them to become defiled through a root of bitterness springing up among them (12:15b) would be inappropriate for them as those whose conscience the blood of Christ, the undefiled high priest (7:26), will cleanse from sinful dead works to offer worship to the living God (9:14).

Told that they have not approached for worship at the ominous scene as at Mount Sinai (12:18-21), the audience are now made aware that they have rather approached for worship at Mount Zion, its heavenly counterpart (12:22). The audience are to appreciate that they, as a worshiping assembly, have been privileged to approach also the city of the living God, the heavenly Jerusalem (12:22). They have approached to participate in heavenly worship along with myriads of angels in full festal gathering (12:22), that is, all of the angels God has invited to worship, and assist the audience to worship, the divine Son (1:6, 14). They have approached not only the assembly of the firstborn enrolled in heaven but God himself, the judge of all, and the spirits of the just ones having been made perfect (12:23), which include the ancient models of faith, who would not be made perfect without us (11:40).

That the audience have also approached for worship Jesus himself and the blood of the sprinkling associated with the new covenant of which Jesus is the guarantor (12:24) reinforces the exhortation for the audience to approach for worship with a true heart in assurance of faith, sprinkled with regard to the hearts from an evil conscience (10:22). This blood of the self-sacrifice of Jesus speaks better beyond Abel (12:24), who offered to God a greater sacrifice beyond Cain (11:4), but, unlike Jesus, did not offer his very self. The audience are to take note that they do not refuse the one who is speaking to them as worshipers (12:25). What this divine voice is speaking includes what the audience have heard Jesus "saying" (10:5, 8)— that God does not want sacrifices of animals (10:5–6, 8). Instead, as Jesus emphatically "said" (10:7, 9), he has come to do God's will (10:7, 9). By doing the will of God in offering his own God-given body once for all (10:10) and his blood in an unblemished self-sacrifice to God, Jesus has made it possible for the audience to offer worship in heaven to the living God (9:14; 10:19). The audience are thus to take note not to refuse this divine speaking they have already heard, as well as that which they are still to hear as a worshiping assembly (12:25).

The audience, as those acquiring an unshakable heavenly kingdom (12:26–27), are exhorted, "let us have grace" (12:28). This further reinforces the exhortation for us to approach for worship with boldness the throne of grace, so that we may receive mercy and may find grace for timely help (4:16). Acquiring an unshakable heavenly kingdom, with divine grace we may offer worship pleasing to God with reverence and awe (12:28). This likens us to the worshiping Jesus, who in the days of his flesh offered both prayers and supplications with strong outcrying and tears to the God able to save him from death, and he was heard from his reverence (5:7).

V. Remembering those maltreated presents the audience with an opportunity to use their own physical bodies (13:3), provided for them by God, in a self-sacrificial way similar to that of Jesus Christ (10:5, 10). The determined intensification of God's scriptural promise, "and you never will I abandon" (13:5), reinforces the exhortation for the audience not to be abandoning their own gathering for communal worship (10:25). In response to the divine scriptural promise that God will never leave nor abandon them (13:5), the audience are exhorted to have the courage to pronounce Ps 117:6, "The Lord is my helper, I will not be afraid, what will a man do to me?" (13:6). That Jesus Christ is the same from the past to the present and for the ages to come (13:8) reminds the audience that we have been and still are made holy for the worship of God through the past offering of the body of Jesus Christ once for all (10:10).

Those offering worship in the earthly tabernacle (13:10) are those who offer worship in a pattern and shadow of the heavenly things according to which Moses made the earthly tabernacle (8:5). While the first, earthly, tabernacle had standing (9:8), both gifts and sacrifices were offered that were not able according to conscience to make perfect the one offering worship (9:9; cf. 10:2). But we are privileged not only to have a heavenly altar from which those offering earthly worship have no right to eat, but to have grace (cf. 13:9), through which we may offer worship pleasing to the living God with reverence and awe in the heavenly tabernacle (12:28; cf. 9:14).

That we are seeking the heavenly city that is to come (13:14) makes even more relevant the bold assertion that the audience, as a worshiping community, have approached Mount Zion, and the city of the living God, the heavenly Jerusalem (12:22). Recalling that Jesus is able to save completely those who approach God for worship through him, always living to intercede on behalf of them (7:25), the audience are exhorted, "*Through him* then let us offer up a sacrifice of praise continually to God" (13:15a; cf. Ps 49:14). Through the intercession of the Jesus who offered himself to God, we are enabled to offer up as a "sacrifice of praise" our bearing the reproach of Jesus (13:13) as our ethical worship, our praise to God. The offering up of a sacrifice of praise continually to God, which is the fruit of lips confessing his name (13:15), further endorses the conduct of the audience as an integral part of their worship of God, indeed the ethical or moral worship that complements their liturgical worship. Such sacrifices, which consist of the audience's upright moral conduct, amount to a worship with which God is pleased (13:16).

VI. Having exhorted the audience to pray for him as one of their leaders (13:18-19), the author reciprocates in advance by expressing his own prayer for the audience: "May the God of peace, who led up from the dead the shepherd of the sheep, the one great in the blood of the eternal covenant, our Lord Jesus, provide you with every good thing in order to do the will of him, doing among us what is pleasing before him through Jesus Christ, to whom be glory for the ages of the ages. Amen" (13:20-21). That "the shepherd of the sheep" is further described as the one "great" in the blood of the eternal covenant (13:20a) links the metaphor of the "shepherd" to the priesthood of Jesus, who is a "great" priest over the house of God (10:21). It reinforces the exhortation that, having a "great" high priest who has passed through the heavens, Jesus the Son of God, let us, as worshipers, hold fast to the confession (4:14). This prayer reinforces the exhortation that the audience have need of endurance so that, "doing the will of God," they may acquire the promise of the eternal rest and worship of the living God in heaven (10:36).

The author's prayer here thus functions as a speech act, that is, an utterance whose purpose begins to be accomplished in and through its very performance. In praying that God provide the audience with every good thing they need to do the divine will, the author is making the audience aware that in their very hearing of the oral performance of this letter God has already begun to provide them with every good thing they need to do his will in what they have heard about the doing of that will through the self-sacrifice of Jesus. In addition, hearing the prayer assures the audience that God will continue to provide them with every good thing they need in the future to do his will, as a way of worshiping God not only liturgically but by the way they conduct themselves ethically in their doing of good.

That God is doing among us what is pleasing before himself (13:21b) reaffirms for the audience that God himself indeed is providing every good thing they need to do his divine will (13:21a). God himself is making possible the audience's doing of good that amounts to a sacrifice, a sacrifice consisting of their ethical worship, with which God is pleased (13:16). The prayer's acknowledgement of the divine glory that belongs to Jesus Christ through whom God is doing what is pleasing before him reaffirms the divine status of Jesus Christ as an object of heavenly worship (1:6).

The declaration that "I encourage" you as brothers to hold on to the word of the "encouragement" emphatically underscores that what the author has composed in this letter is indeed a homiletic word aimed at encouraging his audience (13:22). Noteworthy is that the author's final and climactic greeting, "the grace with all of you!" (13:25), contains no explicit verb. This facilitates its multiple functions as a speech act whose purpose begins to be accomplished in the very hearing of it. First, it affirms that "the grace *has been* with all of you," thus reminding the audience that they have already received the grace of God in the past, in accord with the fact that Jesus tasted death on behalf of all by the grace of God (2:9). Secondly, it asserts that "the grace *is now* with all of you," thus indicating to the audience that the grace of God is now presently being given to them in and through their hearing and heeding of the letter itself as the author's word of the encouragement (13:22). Finally, it prays that "the grace *will be* with all of you," thus assuring the audience that the grace of God will continue to be available to them in the future. This accords with the encouraging exhortation, "Let us approach then with boldness the throne of grace, so that we may receive mercy and may find grace for timely help" (4:16).

Conclusion: Worship in Hebrews

SUMMARIES OF THE THEME of worship within the progression of the chiastic units comprising the letter to the Hebrews have been provided at the conclusion of each of the previous six chapters. This final chapter, therefore, will focus primarily on drawing out the implications and ramifications of the theme of worship in Hebrews for Christian worship today. The guiding question will be: As we listen today to how the theme of worship progresses throughout the letter to the Hebrews, how does it deepen, enrich, and inspire our own worship?

Through a hymnic call to worship that opens the letter (Heb 1:1–4) we are invited to respond with a worshipful awe and reverence to the marvelous way God has definitively spoken to us in a Son. Thanks to the Son's having made a cultic cleansing to remove the sins that prevent worship, we are able to offer true worship. Because of this act of expiatory worship on the part of the Son, he was divinely enthroned in heaven at the right of God and became, along with God, an object of worship. That this Son projects divine glory motivates us in turn to glorify both God and God's divine Son in and through our worship.

Not only are the angels themselves to worship the firstborn Son whom God leads into the heavenly realm (1:6), but, as ministers of God they also are to assist us in this heavenly worship (1:7). We are to appreciate that through our worship on earth we can also be participants, along with and through the assistance of the angels, in the heavenly worship of God's divine Son. God's scriptural pronouncement that the earth and the heavens will be transformed (1:11–12) contributes to the future focus of our worship. As worshipers we have the hope of inheriting the salvation (1:14) resulting from God's scriptural pledge to place enemies in utter subjugation to his divine royal Son (1:13).

We will not be able to escape the just penalty of a recompense from God (2:2) if we neglect "so great a salvation" (2:3). We are thus to pay close attention to the salvific realities God has spoken to us in addressing his divine royal Son through the chain of scriptural quotations (1:5–14) heard by us as worshipers (2:1). The confirmation given us by those believers who heard of this great salvation previously (2:3), as well as God's further testifying (2:4), provide us with a firm footing that prevents our "drifting away" (2:1) and neglecting this great salvation that is to inspire and motivate our worship.

As we hear the quotation from Psalm 8 that "all things you (God) subjected under his (the Son's) feet" (2:8), we are drawn to participate in this hymnic act of worship by praising God for what he has done for his Son on behalf of all human beings. Along with the identification of the divine royal Son, who is also a son of man (2:6), a human being, as Jesus (2:9), we receive further delineation of the great salvation we are not to neglect as worshipers (2:3). This salvation is so great because it includes salvation from the power of death (2:9), implicitly among the enemies God will place in total subjection to his heavenly enthroned Son (1:13). This salvation is for all human beings, on behalf of whom Jesus, himself a human being, fully experienced the death all human beings must experience, before he was exalted from this death to a seat at God's right (1:3), crowned with heavenly glory and honor (2:7, 9). This deepens our appreciation for the relevance and worthiness of Jesus to be an object of our heavenly worship.

As among the many sons God is leading into the glory of heavenly worship (2:10), we are being made holy by Jesus (2:11) and thus being perfected to approach and worship God, as well as Jesus. With his scriptural voice Jesus promises God an act of worship in which he will proclaim God's name to us, his brothers, in the midst of our worshiping assembly (2:12). As a speech act, this promise begins to be fulfilled in our very hearing of it. Jesus freed us, as among the children God gave him, his fellow human brothers, from the slavery of our life-long fear of death (2:11–15). This further specifies the salvation that is so great that we ought not to neglect it as the basis and motivation for our communal worship (2:3). As a merciful and faithful high priest who performed an act of worship in expiating the sins that prevent worship, Jesus is able to help us as a worshiping assembly. In what he himself suffered in being tested, Jesus is able to help us who are also being tested with sufferings (2:17–18).

We are to direct our attention to Jesus as the apostle and high priest of our confession (3:1), the object of our public confession of faith, allegiance, and homage that takes place preeminently in our communal worship, but extends as well to the domain of daily living in the society outside of our liturgical assembly. Jesus has been considered worthy of greater glory beyond Moses (3:3), underscoring his worthiness to be glorified by both the angels and by us in heavenly worship. We are to hold to the boldness and the boast of the hope (3:6), the hope of inheriting (1:14) so great a salvation (2:3), if we are to remain identified as the familial "house" of worship of the divine royal Son.

As worshipers we are to hear the scriptural voice of God that implores us, "Do not harden your hearts" (3:7–8). We are rather to open our hearts, our inner persons, the very center or core of our beings, which are determinative for our lives and for our worship, to the voice of God. We are not to harden our hearts in resistance to God's will, but open them to listen to and learn God's ways from the divine royal Son, who promises that he will proclaim God's name to us as his brothers in the midst of our worshiping assembly (2:12). We will then be able to enter into God's own rest (3:11), the rest of God's heavenly sanctuary where we will be able to worship God and his Son.

If we would have an evil heart of unfaithfulness, we risk falling away from the living God (3:12). We are thus to encourage one another during each liturgical "today," so that not anyone of our worshiping community may become hardened by the deceit of sin (3:13). For us to be partners of the Christ in heavenly worship, we must hold the beginning of the divine reality of the word of God's great salvation firm until the end (3:14) by persevering in our response to this reality as a worshiping assembly. We are to respond with obedience and faithfulness when, as a worshiping assembly, we hear the voice of the living God. This is the God who invites us to enter into the heavenly rest of his eternal living to participate in heavenly worship (3:15–19).

We who have received the good news (4:2), with its still remaining promise to enter into God's rest (4:1), have begun to realize the fulfillment of that promise, as we are already entering into that rest as those who have believed (4:3). This means that, although not yet complete, the process of our entering into the heavenly glory of the eternal rest of the living God has begun and is underway. That a Sabbath rest remains for the people of God (4:9) confirms that the "other day" about which God has spoken (4:8) refers both to the seventh day, the day for observance of God's Sabbath rest (4:4), and to the liturgical "today" for hearing the voice of God during worship (4:7). Each of us has been urged to avoid not only unfaithfulness, the deceit of sin, and being deficient, but also the disobedience of a heart hardened to the salvific voice of God that prevents final entrance into the eternal and heavenly Sabbath rest of the living God to participate in heavenly worship (4:10–11).

The word of God that is emphatically "living" (4:12) is the word for us to hear during our liturgical worship. It is the living word that not only promises but can produce for each of us a living beyond this mortal life entangled in slavery to the fear of death (2:15), a living of the eternal life and heavenly rest that includes worship of the living God himself (3:12). That all things are naked and laid bare to the eyes of the living God (4:13) bolsters our hope that God sees our vulnerability to the fear of a death preventing our entrance into the heavenly rest and worship of God's eternal life. And that regarding God there is upon us the word (4:13) refers, first of all, to the word from God that is living (4:12) and that is now directed to or upon us, with its innerly effective, powerfully penetrating, and sharply double-edged message of both warning and encouragement. Secondly, it refers to the word that we, as a worshiping assembly, are to return to God in response to God's word to us. We are expected to respond with the word of our communal confession of faithful obedience to the living word of the ever-living God.

We are to hold fast to our communal confession, because we have a great high priest who has passed through the heavens, Jesus the Son of God (4:14). Jesus has passed through the heavens in a celestial, ceremonial procession preliminary not only to his role as the great high priest in the heavenly worship but to his exaltation as the royally enthroned Son of God and object of heavenly worship by the angels and by us (1:6). We are to approach with boldness the throne of grace available to us as worshipers, in order to receive mercy and find grace for timely help (4:16) from the great high priest able to sympathize with our weaknesses (4:15). That the prayers and supplications Jesus offered as high priest on behalf of human beings to the God able to save him from death were answered (5:7) deepens our appreciation for the significance of Jesus suffering death on behalf of all. Jesus was made perfect as a Son who learned from the things he suffered obedience (5:8), so that he became for all those who obey him a source of eternal salvation (5:9). To gain this eternal salvation we are thus to obey the Son who learned from the things he suffered obedience to the God whom he prayerfully worshiped.

We are invited to bear forward with the help of our homilist author toward becoming perfected (6:1) as spiritually mature adults made fit for proper liturgical and ethical worship (5:14). As a liturgical assembly, we have not only "tasted" and thus fully experienced the pronouncement of God (6:5) by listening to the word of God proclaimed in worship, but we have also "tasted" of the heavenly gift (6:4), which includes our partaking of the eucharistic meal. We are thus warned that in the event of our falling away as worshipers, it will be impossible for us, whose faith has already been founded on our repentance (6:1), to again renew to repentance (6:6). God will surely not restore us to repentance, if we should fail to appreciate what is involved in our worship. We are thus to assist our fellow worshipers as part of our ethical worship (6:10). Since God will surely not neglect our work and the love demonstrated for his name (6:10), our perseverance will facilitate our bearing forward with the author toward the perfection (6:1) needed for our participation in heavenly worship. Rather than becoming spiritually sluggish (5:11; 6:12), we are to become imitators of those who through faith and patience are inheriting the promises (6:12), which include the promised blessing from God (6:7), calling for our response of the blessing and praise of God in and through our worship.

The entrance of Jesus as the hope that is a sure and firm anchor of the soul into the heavenly sanctuary (6:19–20) encourages us to strive to enter into the heavenly Sabbath rest of God to participate in heavenly worship (4:11), the rest we are even now entering into as those who believed and those who now worship within the liturgical assembly (4:3). The Jesus who entered into the heavenly sanctuary is an eternal high priest, since he became according to the order of Melchizedek high priest *forever* (6:20).

We are to consider how great this Melchizedek truly must be, if even Abraham, *the* patriarch, freely gave him a tenth from the choice spoils of his victory over the kings (7:1–2). In being made eternal like the Son of God, Melchizedek remains a priest for all time (7:3). Whereas the sons of Levi who receive the priesthood tithe those who come from the loins of Abraham (7:5), Levi himself was still in the loins of his father Abraham when he was tithed by Melchizedek, the eternal priest of the God Most High. It is according to the order of this eternal priest Melchizedek that

Jesus became high priest forever (6:20) for our benefit as a worshiping assembly.

There was a need for a different priest to arise according to the order of Melchizedek, that is, not only to appear but to be raised from the dead to heavenly exaltation, and not said to be according to the order of Aaron, since there was no perfection for heavenly worship through the Levitical priesthood (7:11). Jesus is a different priest because he partook in a tribe different from that of Levi. That from this different tribe no one attended to the altar (7:13) indicates the non-priestly nature of his human lineage. We are thus to appreciate not only his difference from Levitical priests but also his likeness to both Melchizedek and to ourselves. That Jesus has come about as a priest according to the power of an indestructible life (7:16) further specifies his likeness to Melchizedek (7:15), who does not have end of life, but remains a priest for all time (7:3), as he goes on living forever (7:8). This empowers Jesus to remain a priest forever (7:17) on behalf of us as a worshiping assembly.

In contrast to the Levitical priests who were many because they were prevented by death from remaining on (7:23), Jesus, because he remains a priest forever, possesses the priesthood that is permanent (7:24). We are to realize that Jesus is able to save us completely and forever (7:25) as those who, as a worshiping assembly drawing near to God (7:19), approach God through him. That Jesus is always living to intercede on behalf of us is a consequence of his entrance into the interior of the heavenly veil (6:19) as forerunner on behalf of us (6:20). Jesus is a high priest who became higher than the heavens (7:26), the heavens through which he has passed as our great high priest to make possible our heavenly worship (4:14). The Levitical high priests have a necessity each day to offer up sacrifices for their own sins before offering for the sins of the people. In contrast, Jesus did this once for all, that is, a completely effective "once" at his sacrificial death and a singularly definitive "for all time," having offered up himself (7:27). Jesus forever has been made permanently, absolutely, and enduringly perfect (7:28). He is thus completely and fully fit for his role in the heavenly worship on our behalf.

Jesus' divinely authoritative seat as high priest at the right of the Majesty in the heavens (8:1) positions and empowers him for his high priestly role as cultic minister of the holy things, the things involved in the heavenly worship. Jesus is a minister of the tent or tabernacle, the true one, that is, the place of heavenly worship (8:2). That those on earth offer worship only in a pattern and shadow of the heavenly things (8:5) deepens our appreciation that we are those who have already tasted of the heavenly gift (6:4), and who are partners of a heavenly calling (3:1), those who are called to participate in this heavenly worship.

We are among the people regarding whom God now promises in a new covenant that "I will be to them as God, and they will be to me as people" (8:10). We will be God's own people as a consequence of God's promise to Jesus that "he will be to me as Son" (1:5), since, as the heavenly enthroned divine Son, Jesus is also the eternal high priest of the people of God (7:28—8:6), who makes possible our participation in heavenly worship. We are to appreciate how the covenantal promise of God that "the sins of them I will certainly remember no longer" (8:12) is based on the definitive self-sacrifice of Jesus, his act of heavenly worship as the divinely enthroned Son and eternal high priest. And we are to deepen our appreciation for what this new covenant, which supplants the old and aging one that is near to disappearing (8:13), promises for us as a worshiping assembly.

That the way to the heavenly holy things had not appeared while the earthly tabernacle had standing (9:8) resonates with the fact that the first covenant was not faultless, so that for a second one God sought a place (8:7). The gifts and sacrifices being offered under the first covenant were not able according to conscience to make perfect for heavenly worship the one offering worship (9:9), since they are offered only on the basis of foods and drinks and various baptisms. These are regulations of the flesh imposed until the time of correction or setting things right (9:10). That time has arrived when the first covenant and its first tabernacle are becoming old, aging, and near to disappearing, because of the arrival of the new covenant promised by God (8:13), the new covenant with its regulations not for earthly but for the heavenly worship of which we are to be participants.

Not through the blood of goats and calves but through his own blood Jesus entered once for all into the heavenly holy things, finding eternal redemption (9:12). His finding of an eternal redemption further motivates us, as a worshiping assembly, to approach with boldness the throne of grace, so that we may receive mercy and may find grace for timely help (4:16). We may "find" that grace precisely because Jesus, in his act of worship as heavenly high priest, "found" eternal redemption. The blood of the Christ, who through the eternal Spirit offered himself unblemished to God, will cleanse our consciences from the dead works of sinfulness to offer worship to the living God (9:14).

That Jesus, the heavenly divine Son and high priest, bore his own death as the one who covenanted (9:16) explicates how he is guarantor of a new covenant as a will or testament, so that those called, among whom are we, might receive the eternal inheritance (9:15) and thus take their place in the heavenly worship of God. The blood of the covenant with which Moses sprinkled the earthly tabernacle and the vessels for the ministry of worship (9:21) is the sacrificial blood of the calves and the goats (9:19). It sharply contrasts Jesus' own blood through which he entered once for all into the heavenly tabernacle (9:12) to perform his act of self-sacrificial worship as the heavenly high priest. This is the blood of the new covenant of which we partake in our eucharistic celebrations.

Instead of repeatedly offering himself (9:25) and repeatedly suffering from the founding of the world, Christ once at the completion of the ages for the removal of sin has appeared (9:26). This appearance of Christ indicates that the way to the heavenly holy things has now appeared on earth for our benefit as a worshiping assembly. Christ will be seen a second time on earth without sin, that is, not only without his own sin but without the sins of all sinners, by those eagerly awaiting him for salvation (9:28). This is the future and final salvation that we anticipate in and through our worship.

In contrast to the offerings God did not want (10:5, 8), it is through the offering of the body of Jesus Christ once for all, the body God provided for him (10:5) and that he provided for us to share in our eucharistic celebrations, that we have been made holy (10:10). In contrast to every Levitical priest offering repeatedly the same sacrifices, which are never able to cast off the sins that prevent worship (10:11), Jesus Christ offered one sacrifice on behalf of sins for all time (10:12). That the heavenly enthroned Jesus Christ is still waiting until his enemies are placed as a footstool for his feet (10:13) reminds us that the great salvation we are not to neglect (2:3) as a worshiping assembly is still to be consummated. Although the law never is able to make perfect those who approach for worship (10:1), because those offering worship still have consciousness of sins (10:2), by one offering of himself, Jesus Christ has made us perfect for all time as those who are being made holy (10:14) for their role in heavenly worship.

Conclusion: Worship in Hebrews

That our entrance to the heavenly "holy things" is in the blood and through the flesh of Jesus (10:19–20), the blood and flesh of which we partake in the Eucharist, leads us to appreciate that the self-offering of Jesus as the eternal high priest was accomplished in and through the blood and flesh he shared with us as our fellow and fraternal human being (2:14). Since we have boldness for entrance to the heavenly holy things and a great priest over the house of God (10:19–21), we are to approach for the worship of God with a true heart in assurance of faith. It is as a consequence of the better sacrificial self-offering of the body of Jesus (10:5, 10) that we have been washed with regard to the body by the clean water (10:22) of our baptism and thus enabled to participate fully in the worship of God. We are urged never to abandon our gathering for communal worship, but rather to encourage one another to prepare for the decisive day of final salvation at each day set as the "today" for listening during our communal worship to the voice of God inviting us to enter into God's own eternal Sabbath rest and worship that remains for us in heaven (4:7–11).

When we encounter sufferings and losses, we are to know that we have a better possession that remains forever (10:34). We are not to throw away the boldness we have for entrance into the heavenly holy things in and through the blood of Jesus (10:19), which we share in the Eucharist, as it has great recompense from God (10:35). We have need of endurance so that, doing the will of God as part of our ethical worship, we may acquire the promise (10:36) of an eternal inheritance for those who have been called by God for entrance into the liturgy of heaven (9:15; 3:1).

The divine realities that we are now noticing by faith (11:3) include the taking note of Jesus as the divine Son crowned by God with heavenly glory and honor (2:9) to be the object of heavenly worship. The exemplary faith of both Enoch (11:5) and Abel (11:4) demonstrates how without faith it is impossible for anyone to please God through worship, for it is necessary that the one approaching God in worship believe that God exists and that for those seeking him he becomes a rewarder (11:6). That God rewarded both Abel and Enoch with a significant status beyond death inspires us to seek him as the God who can reward us with a heavenly existence beyond death.

Abraham and his fellow patriarchs, who were seeing the fulfillment of the promises from afar and greeting them and confessing (11:13), serve as models for us. That the patriarchs manifested that they were seeking a heavenly fatherland (11:14) exemplifies the kind of faith we need to please God as we approach him in worship. With regard to the faith of Abraham, who was waiting for the city having foundations, whose architect and builder is God (11:10), God has made ready for the patriarchs and for us a city, indeed, a heavenly one (11:16) with a heavenly worship. That by faith Abraham acquired Isaac encourages us to have endurance so that, doing the will of God as part of our ethical worship, we may acquire the promise of final salvation that includes entrance into the Sabbath rest and liturgy of heaven (10:36).

That Moses endured the reproach of the Christ, for he was looking away to the recompense from God (11:26), encourages us not to throw away our boldness as believers and to likewise endure reproach, since this has great recompense from God (10:35). Those who went through the Red Sea without drowning (11:29) as well as Rahab, who welcomed the Israelite spies with peace so that she did not perish together with those who disobeyed (11:30–31), underscore the life-giving dimension of the faith by which we are to worship God.

That exemplary figures of the past, through their faith, became by the power of God strong in battle (11:34) encourages us to hold fast to the hope, represented by Jesus as the heavenly high priest (6:19–20), lying ahead for us (6:18). That these venerable models of faith would not be made perfect without us (11:40) means that they would not be made worthy or fit for participation in the heavenly worship without us who have the benefit, as a worshiping community, of the self-sacrifice of Jesus, our heavenly high priest.

That Jesus, after enduring the cross, took his seat on the right of the throne of God (12:2) provides us with a desirable goal to keep before us in our struggle to endure the grueling course lying ahead of us before we complete our pilgrimage to the heavenly city promised by God and participate in the heavenly liturgy. Christ, as the divinely disciplined Son of God, provides us not only with the example but the empowerment to endure our sufferings as the divine discipline that prepares and qualifies us for participation in the heavenly worship of the living God, the God whose eternal life we are to live (12:5–10). That divine discipline gives back the peaceful fruit of God's righteousness to those who are trained through it (12:11) underscores the significance of the model and motivation provided by Jesus. He loved God's righteousness so that God anointed him with the oil of gladness (1:9) as an object of the heavenly worship (1:6) in which he has enabled us to participate (9:14; 10:19–22).

We are to appreciate that in our liturgy we have been privileged to approach Mount Zion, the city of the living God, the heavenly Jerusalem (12:22). We approach to participate in heavenly worship along with myriads of angels in full festal gathering (12:22), that is, all of the angels God has invited to worship, and assist us to worship, the divine Son (1:6, 14). We approach not only the assembly of the firstborn enrolled in heaven but God himself, the judge of all, and the spirits of the just ones having been made perfect for heavenly worship (12:23).

That we also approach for worship Jesus himself and the blood of the sprinkling associated with the new covenant of which Jesus is the guarantor (12:24), the blood of which we partake in the Eucharist, encourages us to worship with a true heart in assurance of faith, sprinkled with regard to our hearts from an evil conscience (10:22). This blood of the self-sacrifice of Jesus speaks better beyond Abel (12:24), who offered to God a greater sacrifice beyond Cain (11:4), but, unlike Jesus, did not offer his very self.

We are to take note that we do not refuse the one who is speaking to us as worshipers (12:25). What this divine voice is speaking includes what we have heard Jesus "saying" (10:5, 8)—that God does not want sacrifices of animals (10:5–6, 8). Instead, as Jesus emphatically "said" (10:7, 9), he has come to do God's will (10:7, 9). By doing the will of God in offering his own God-given body once for all (10:10) and his blood in an unblemished self-sacrifice to God—the body and blood we share in the Eucharist—Jesus has made it possible for us to offer worship in heaven to the living God (9:14; 10:19). As those who are acquiring an unshakable heavenly kingdom, with divine grace we may offer heavenly worship pleasing to God with reverence and awe (12:28).

Remembering those maltreated presents us with an opportunity to use our own physical bodies (13:3), provided for us by God, in a self-sacrificial way similar to that of Jesus (10:5, 10). In response to the scriptural promise that God will never leave nor abandon us (13:5), we are encouraged as worshipers to pronounce Ps 117:6, "The Lord is my helper, I will not be afraid, what will a man do to me?" (13:6). As worshipers we are privileged to have a heavenly altar from which those offering earthly worship have no right to eat (13:10), an altar available to us in the Eucharist.

Recalling that Jesus is able to save completely those who approach God for worship through him, always living to intercede on behalf of them (7:25), we are exhorted, "*Through him* then let us offer up a sacrifice of praise continually to God" (13:15). Through the intercession of the Jesus who offered himself to God, we are enabled to offer up as a "sacrifice of praise" our bearing the reproach of Jesus (13:13) as our ethical worship, our praise to God. The offering up of a sacrifice of praise continually to God, which is the fruit of lips confessing his name (13:15), further endorses our conduct as an integral part of our worship of God, indeed the ethical or moral worship that complements our liturgical worship. Such sacrifices, which consist of our upright moral conduct, amount to a worship with which God is pleased (13:16).

Our author's climactic closing prayer functions as a speech act, that is, an utterance whose purpose begins to be accomplished in and through its very performance: "May the God of peace, who led up from the dead the shepherd of the sheep, the one great in the blood of the eternal covenant, our Lord Jesus, provide you with every good thing in order to do the will of him, doing among us what is pleasing before him through Jesus Christ, to whom be glory for the ages of the ages. Amen" (13:20–21). In praying that God provide us with every good thing we need to do the divine will, the author is making us aware that in our very hearing of this letter God has already begun to provide us with every good thing we need to do his will in what we have heard about the doing of that will through the self-sacrifice of Jesus. In addition, hearing the prayer assures us that God will continue to provide us with every good thing we need in the future to do his will, as a way of worshiping God not only liturgically but by the way we conduct ourselves ethically in our doing of good.

The declaration that "I encourage" you as brothers to hold on to the word of the "encouragement" emphatically underscores that what the author has composed in this letter is indeed a homiletic word aimed at encouraging us (13:22). Noteworthy is that the author's final and climactic greeting, "the grace with all of you!" (13:25), contains no explicit verb. This facilitates its multiple functions as a speech act whose purpose begins to be accomplished in the very hearing of it. First, it affirms that "the grace *has been* with all of you," thus reminding us that we have already received the grace of God in the past, in accord with the fact that Jesus tasted death on behalf of all by the grace of God (2:9). Secondly, it asserts that "the grace *is now* with all of you," thus indicating that the grace of God is now presently being given to us in and through our hearing and heeding of the letter itself as the author's word of the encouragement

(13:22). Finally, it prays that "the grace *will be* with all of you," thus assuring us that the grace of God will continue to be available to us in the future. This accords with the encouraging exhortation to us as a worshiping community: "Let us approach then with boldness the throne of grace, so that we may receive mercy and may find grace for timely help" (4:16).

Bibliography

Adams, Edward. "The Cosmology of Hebrews." In *The Epistle to the Hebrews and Christian Theology*, edited by Richard J. Bauckham et al., 122-39. Grand Rapids: Eerdmans, 2009.

Aitken, Ellen Bradshaw. *Jesus' Death in Early Christian Memory: The Poetics of the Passion*. NTOA 53. Göttingen: Vandenhoeck & Ruprecht, 2004.

———. "Portraying the Temple in Stone and Text: The Arch of Titus and the Epistle to the Hebrews." In *Hebrews: Contemporary Methods, New Insights*, edited by Gabriella Gelardini, 131-48. BIS 75. Leiden: Brill, 2005.

Alexander, Loveday C. A. "Prophets and Martyrs and Exemplars of Faith." In *The Epistle to the Hebrews and Christian Theology*, edited by Richard J. Bauckham et al., 405-21. Grand Rapids: Eerdmans, 2009.

Allen, David M. "Constructing 'Janus-Faced' Exhortations: The Use of Old Testament Narratives in Heb 13,1-8." *Bib* 89 (2008) 401-9.

———. *Deuteronomy and Exhortation in Hebrews: A Study in Narrative Re-Presentation*. WUNT 238. Tübingen: Mohr Siebeck, 2008.

———. "The Holy Spirit as Gift or Giver?: Retaining the Pentecostal Dimension of Hebrews 2.4." *BT* 59 (2008) 151-58.

———. "More Than Just Numbers: Deuteronomic Influence in Hebrews 3:7-4:11." *TynBul* 58 (2007) 129-49.

Andriessen, Paul. "L'Eucharistie dans l'Épître aux Hébreux." *NRTh* 94 (1972) 269-77.

Attridge, Harold W. *The Epistle to the Hebrews*. Hermeneia. Philadelphia: Fortress, 1989.

———. "Paraenesis in a Homily (*Logos Parakleseos*): The Possible Location of, and Socialization in, the 'Epistle to the Hebrews.'" In *Paraenesis: Act and Form*, edited by Leo G. Perdue and John G. Gammie, 211-26. Semeia 50. Atlanta: Scholars Press, 1990.

———. "The Psalms in Hebrews." In *The Psalms in the New Testament*, edited by Steve Moyise and Maarten J. J. Menken, 197-212. London: T. & T. Clark, 2004.

Aune, David E. "Worship, Early Christian." In *ABD* 6:973-89.

Austin, John Langshaw. *How to Do Things with Words*. Cambridge: Harvard University Press, 1962.

Backhaus, Knut. *Der Neue Bund und das Werden der Kirche: Die Diatheke-Deutung des Hebräerbriefs im Rahmen der frühchristlichen Theologiegeschichte*. NTAbh 29. Münster: Aschendorff, 1996.

Balz, Horst. "*hagios*." In *EDNT* 1:16-20.

———. "*entygchanō*." In *EDNT* 1:461-62.

———. "*oikoumenē*." In *EDNT* 2:503-4.

Bateman, Herbert W. "Psalm 45:6-7 and Its Christological Contributions to Hebrews." *TJ* 22 (2001) 3-21.

Bauckham, Richard J. "The Divinity of Jesus Christ in the Epistle to the Hebrews." In *The Epistle to the Hebrews and Christian Theology*, edited by Richard J. Bauckham et al., 15-36. Grand Rapids: Eerdmans, 2009.

Becker, Eve-Marie. "'Gottes Wort' und 'Unser Wort': Bemerkungen zu Heb 4,12-13." *BZ* 44 (2000) 254-62.

Bénétreau, Samuel. "Le repos du pèlerin (Hébreux 3,7-4,11)." *ETR* 78 (2003) 203-23.

Bergh, R. H. van der. "A Textual Comparison of Hebrews 10:5b-7 and LXX Psalm 39:7-9." *Neot* 42 (2008) 353-82.

Blomberg, Craig L. "'But We See Jesus': The Relationship Between the Son of Man in Hebrews 2.6 and 2.9 and the Implications for English Translations." In *A Cloud of Witnesses: The Theology of Hebrews in Its Ancient Contexts*, edited by Richard Bauckham et al., 88-99. LNTS 387. London: T. & T. Clark, 2008.

Böcher, Otto. "*diabolos*." In *EDNT* 1:297-98.

Bockmuehl, Markus N. A. "Abraham's Faith in Hebrews 11." In *The Epistle to the Hebrews and Christian Theology*, edited by Richard J. Bauckham et al., 364-73. Grand Rapids: Eerdmans, 2009.

Bradshaw, Paul F. *Eucharistic Origins*. London: SPCK, 2004.

Brawley, Robert Lawson. "Discoursive Structure and the Unseen in Hebrews 2:8 and 11:1: A Neglected Aspect of the Context." *CBQ* 55 (1993) 81-98.

Bruce, Frederick Fyvie. *The Epistle to the Hebrews*. NICNT. Grand Rapids: Eerdmans, 1990.

Bühner, Jan-Adolf. "*apostolos*." In *EDNT* 1:142-46.

Cahill, Michael. "The Implications of *episynagōgē* in Hebrews 10,25: The First Eucharistic Homily?" *Questions liturgiques et paroissiales* 74 (1993) 198-207.

Campbell, Alastair. "Worship in the New Testament." In *In Praise of Worship: An Exploration of Text and Practice*, edited by David J. Cohen and Michael Parsons, 70-83. Eugene, OR: Wipf and Stock, 2010.

Caneday, Ardel B. "The Eschatological World Already Subjected to the Son: The *Oikoumenē* of Hebrews 1.6 and the Son's Enthronement." In *A Cloud of Witnesses: The Theology of Hebrews in Its Ancient Contexts*, edited by Richard Bauckham et al., 28-39. LNTS 387. London: T. & T. Clark, 2008.

Clivaz, Claire. "Hebrews 5.7, Jesus' Prayer on the Mount of Olives and Jewish Christianity: Hearing Early Christian Voices in Canonical and Apocryphal Texts." In *A Cloud of Witnesses: The Theology of Hebrews in Its Ancient Contexts*, edited by Richard Bauckham et al., 188-209. LNTS 387. London: T. & T. Clark, 2008.

Cockerill, Gareth Lee. "The Better Resurrection (Heb 11:35): A Key to the Structure and Rhetorical Purpose of Hebrews 11." *TynBul* 51 (2000) 215-34.

———. *Hebrews: A Bible Commentary in the Wesleyan Tradition*. Indianapolis: Wesleyan Publishing House, 1999.

———. "Hebrews 1:6: Source and Significance." *BBR* 9 (1999) 51-64.

———. "Melchizedek Without Speculation: Hebrews 7.1-25 and Genesis 14.17-24." In *A Cloud of Witnesses: The Theology of Hebrews in Its Ancient Contexts*, edited by Richard Bauckham et al., 128-44. LNTS 387. London: T. & T. Clark, 2008.

Cortez, Felix H. "From the Holy to the Most Holy Place: The Period of Hebrews 9:6-10 and the Day of Atonement as a Metaphor of Transition." *JBL* 125 (2006) 527-47.

Cosaert, C. P. "The Use of *Hagios* for the Sanctuary in the Old Testament Pseudepigrapha, Philo, and Josephus." *AUSS* 42 (2004) 91-103.

Croy, N. Clayton. "A Note on Hebrews 12:2." *JBL* 114 (1995) 117-19.
D'Angelo, Mary R. *Moses in the Letter to the Hebrews*. SBLDS 42. Missoula, MT: Scholars, 1979.
Davidson, R. M. "Christ's Entry 'Within the Veil' in Hebrews 6:19-20: The Old Testament Background." *AUSS* 39 (2001) 175-90.
Davis, Casey Wayne. "Hebrews 6:4-6 from an Oral Critical Perspective." *JETS* 51 (2008) 753-67.
DeSilva, David A. "Despising Shame: A Cultural-Anthropological Investigation of the Epistle to the Hebrews." *JBL* 113 (1994) 439-61.
———. *Despising Shame: Honor Discourse and Community Maintenance in the Epistle to the Hebrews*. SBLDS 152. Atlanta: Scholars, 1995.
———. "Entering God's Rest: Eschatology and the Socio-Rhetorical Strategy of Hebrews." *TJ* 21 (2000) 25-43.
———. "Hebrews 6:4-8: A Socio-Rhetorical Investigation (Part 1)." *TynBul* 50 (1999) 33-57.
———. "Hebrews 6:4-8: A Socio-Rhetorical Investigation (Part 2)." *TynBul* 50 (1999) 225-35.
———. *Perseverance in Gratitude: A Socio-Rhetorical Commentary on the Epistle "to the Hebrews."* Grand Rapids: Eerdmans, 2000.
DeYoung, Kevin. "Divine Impassibility and the Passion of Christ in the Book of Hebrews." *WTJ* 68 (2006) 41-50.
Docherty, Susan E. *The Use of the Old Testament in Hebrews: A Case Study in Early Jewish Bible Interpretation*. WUNT 2/260. Tübingen: Mohr/Siebeck, 2009.
Eberhart, Christian A. "Characteristics of Sacrificial Metaphors in Hebrews." In *Hebrews: Contemporary Methods, New Insights*, edited by Gabriella Gelardini, 37-64. BIS 75. Leiden: Brill, 2005.
Ellingworth, Paul. *The Epistle to the Hebrews: A Commentary on the Greek Text*. NIGTC. Grand Rapids: Eerdmans, 1993.
Emmrich, Martin. "'Amtscharisma': Through the Eternal Spirit (Hebrews 9:14)." *BBR* 12 (2002) 17-32.
———. "Hebrews 6:4-6—Again! (A Pneumatological Inquiry)." *WTJ* 65 (2003) 83-95.
———. *Pneumatological Concepts in the Epistle to the Hebrews: Amtscharisma, Prophet, & Guide of the Eschatological Exodus*. Lanham, MD: University Press of America, 2003.
Farkasfalvy, Denis. "The Eucharistic Provenance of New Testament Texts." In *Rediscovering the Eucharist: Ecumenical Conversations*, edited by Roch A. Kereszty, 27-51. Mahwah, NJ: Paulist, 2003.
Farris, Stephen. "Hymns, NT." In *The New Interpreter's Dictionary of the Bible* 2:923. Nashville: Abingdon, 2007.
Farrow, Douglas. "Melchizedek and Modernity." In *The Epistle to the Hebrews and Christian Theology*, edited by Richard J. Bauckham et al., 281-301. Grand Rapids: Eerdmans, 2009.
Fitzmyer, Joseph A. *The Acts of the Apostles: A New Translation with Introduction and Commentary*. AB 31. New York: Doubleday, 1998.
———. "Melchizedek in the MT, LXX, and the NT." *Bib* 81 (2000) 63-69.
Friedrich, Johannes H. "*klēronomeō*." In *EDNT* 2:298-99.
Fuchs, Albert. "*bebaios*." In *EDNT* 1:210-11.
Fuhrmann, Sebastian. "Christ Grown into Perfection: Hebrews 9,11 from a Christological Point of View." *Bib* 89 (2008) 92-100.

———. "Failures Forgotten: The Soteriology in Hebrews Revisited in the Light of Its Quotation of Jeremiah 38:31–34 [LXX]." *Neot* 41 (2007) 295–316.

Gane, R. E. "Re-Opening *Katapetasma* ('Veil') in Hebrews 6:19." *AUSS* 38 (2000) 5–8.

Gelardini, Gabriella. "Hebrews, an Ancient Synagogue Homily for *Tisha be-Av*: Its Function, Its Basis, Its Theological Interpretation." In *Hebrews: Contemporary Methods, New Insights*, edited by Gabriella Gelardini, 107–27. BIS 75. Leiden: Brill, 2005.

Gheorghita, Radu. *The Role of the Septuagint in Hebrews: An Investigation of Its Influence with Special Consideration to the Use of Hab 2:3–4 in Heb 10:37–38*. WUNT 2/160. Tübingen: Mohr/Siebeck, 2003.

Gleason, Randall C. "The Eschatology of the Warning in Hebrews 10:26–31." *TynBul* 53 (2002) 97–120.

———. "The Old Testament Background of Rest in Hebrews 3:7–4:11." *BSac* 157 (2000) 281–303.

———. "The Old Testament Background of the Warning in Hebrews 6:4–8." *BSac* 155 (1998) 62–91.

Granerø, Gard. "Melchizedek in Hebrews 7." *Bib* 90 (2009) 188–202.

Gray, Patrick. *Godly Fear: The Epistle to the Hebrews and Greco-Roman Critiques of Superstition*. SBLAbib 16. Atlanta: Society of Biblical Literature, 2003.

Greenlee, J. Harold. "Hebrews 11:11—'By Faith Sarah Received Ability.'" *AsTJ* 54 (1999) 67–72.

———. "Hebrews 11:11—Sarah's Faith or Abraham's?" *Notes* 4 (1990) 37–42.

Gräbe, Peter. "The New Covenant and Christian Identity in Hebrews." In *A Cloud of Witnesses: The Theology of Hebrews in Its Ancient Contexts*, edited by Richard Bauckham et al., 118–27. LNTS 387. London: T. & T. Clark, 2008.

Guthrie, George H. "The Case for Apollos as the Author of Hebrews." *Faith and Mission* 18 (2001) 41–56.

———. "Hebrews." In *Commentary on the New Testament Use of the Old Testament*, edited by Gregory K. Beale and Donald A. Carson, 919–95. Grand Rapids: Baker, 2007.

Guthrie, George H., and R. D. Quinn. "A Discourse Analysis of the Use of Psalm 8:4–6 in Hebrews 2:5–9." *JETS* 49 (2006) 235–46.

Hagner, Donald A. *Encountering the Book of Hebrews: An Exposition*. Encountering Biblical Studies. Grand Rapids: Baker, 2002.

Hahn, Scott W. "A Broken Covenant and the Curse of Death: A Study of Hebrews 9:15–22." *CBQ* 66 (2004) 416–36.

———. "Covenant, Cult, and the Curse-of-Death: *Diathēkē* in Heb 9:15–22." In *Hebrews: Contemporary Methods, New Insights*, edited by Gabriella Gelardini, 65–68. BIS 75. Leiden: Brill, 2005.

Hamm, Dennis. "Praying 'Regularly' (not 'Constantly'): A Note on the Cultic Background of *dia pantos* in Luke 24:53, Acts 10:2 and Hebrews 9:6, 13:15." *ExpTim* 116 (2004) 50–52.

Hartley, Donald E. "Heb 11:6—A Reassessment of the Translation 'God Exists.'" *TJ* 27 (2006) 289–307.

Hartman, Lars. "*onoma*." In *EDNT* 2:519–22.

Heil, John Paul. *Hebrews: Chiastic Structures and Audience Response*. CBQMS 46. Washington, DC: Catholic Biblical Association, 2010.

———. *The Meal Scenes in Luke-Acts: An Audience-Oriented Approach*. SBLMS 52. Atlanta: Society of Biblical Literature, 1999.

Hengel, Martin. *Crucifixion: In the Ancient World and the Folly of the Message of the Cross*. Philadelphia: Fortress, 1977.
Hoerber, R. G. "On the Translation of Hebrews 11:1." *Concordia Journal* 21 (1995) 77–79.
Hofius, Otfried. *Katapausis: Die Vorstellung von endzeitlichen Ruheort im Hebräerbrief*. WUNT 11. Tübingen: Mohr Siebeck, 1970.
———. "*katapausis*." In *EDNT* 2:265–66.
———. "*katapetasma*." In *EDNT* 2:266.
———. "*sabbatismos*." In *EDNT* 3:219.
Horst, Pieter Willem van der. "Did Sarah Have a Seminal Emission?" *BRev* 1 (1992) 34–39.
———. "Sarah's Seminal Emission: Hebrews 11:11 in the Light of Ancient Embryology." In *Greeks, Romans, and Christians: Essays in Honor of Abraham J. Malherbe*, edited by David L. Balch et al., 287–302. Minneapolis: Fortress, 1990.
Hübner, Hans. "*teleioō*." In *EDNT* 3:344–45.
Hurtado, Larry W. *At the Origins of Christian Worship: The Context and Character of Earliest Christian Devotion*. Grand Rapids: Eerdmans, 1999.
———. *How on Earth Did Jesus Become a God?: Historical Questions about Earliest Devotion to Jesus*. Grand Rapids: Eerdmans, 2005.
———. *Lord Jesus Christ: Devotion to Jesus in Earliest Christianity*. Grand Rapids: Eerdmans, 2003.
———. "Worship, NT Christian." In *The New Interpreter's Dictionary of the Bible*, 5:910–23. Nashville: Abingdon, 2009.
Jobes, Karen H. "The Function of Paronomasia in Hebrews 10:5–7." *TJ* 13 (1992) 181–91.
———. "Rhetorical Achievement in the Hebrews 10 'Misquote' of Psalm 40." *Bib* 72 (1991) 387–96.
Johnson, Luke Timothy. *Hebrews: A Commentary*. NTL. Louisville: Westminster John Knox, 2006.
———. "The Scriptural World of Hebrews." *Int* 73 (2003) 237–50.
Joslin, Barry C. "Christ Bore the Sins of Many: Substitution and the Atonement in Hebrews." *Southern Baptist Journal of Theology* 11 (2007) 74–103.
———. *Hebrews, Christ, and the Law: The Theology of the Mosaic Law in Hebrews 7:1—10:18*. Paternoster Biblical Monographs. Milton Keynes, UK: Paternoster, 2008.
———. "Hebrews 7–10 and the Transformation of the Law." In *A Cloud of Witnesses: The Theology of Hebrews in Its Ancient Contexts*, edited by Richard Bauckham et al., 100–117. LNTS 387. London: T. & T. Clark, 2008.
Just, Arthur A. "Entering Holiness: Christology and Eucharist in Hebrews." *CTQ* 69 (2005) 75–95.
Kistemaker, Simon J. "The Authorship of Hebrews." *Faith and Mission* 18 (2001) 57–69.
Klauck, Hans-Josef. "Lord's Supper." In *ABD* 4:362–72.
Koenig, John. *The Feast of the World's Redemption: Eucharistic Origins and Christian Mission*. Harrisburg: Trinity, 2000.
Koester, Craig R. *Hebrews: A New Translation with Introduction and Commentary*. AB 36. New York: Doubleday, 2001.
Koosed, Jennifer L., and Robert P. Seesengood. "Constructions and Collusions: The Making and Unmaking of Identity in Qoheleth and Hebrews." In *Hebrews: Contemporary Methods, New Insights*, edited by Gabriella Gelardini, 265–80. BIS 75. Leiden: Brill, 2005.

Kruijf, Th. C. de. "The Priest-King Melchizedek: The Reception of Gen 14,18–20 in Hebrews Mediated by Psalm 110." *Bijdragen* 54 (1993) 393–406.
Laansma, Jon. "Hidden Stories in Hebrews: Cosmology and Theology." In *A Cloud of Witnesses: The Theology of Hebrews in Its Ancient Contexts*, edited by Richard Bauckham et al., 9–18. LNTS 387. London: T. & T. Clark, 2008.
Lane, William L. *Hebrews 1–8*. WBC 47a. Dallas: Word, 1991.
———. *Hebrews 9–13*. WBC 47b. Dallas: Word, 1991.
Lee, J. A. L. "Hebrews 5:14 and *Hexis*: A History of Misunderstanding." *NovT* 39 (1997) 151–76.
Leithart, Peter J. "Womb of the World: Baptism and the Priesthood of the New Covenant in Hebrews 10.19–22." *JSNT* 78 (2000) 49–65.
Limbeck, Meinrad. "*anomia*." In *EDNT* 1:106.
Lincoln, Andrew T. *Hebrews: A Guide*. London: T. & T. Clark, 2006.
Lincoln, L. "Translating Hebrews 9:15–22 in Its Hebraic Context." *JOTT* 12 (1999) 1–29.
Lohr, Joel N. "Righteous Abel, Wicked Cain: Genesis 4:1–16 in the Masoretic Text, the Septuagint, and the New Testament." *CBQ* 71 (2009) 485–96.
MacDonald, Nathan. "By Faith Moses." In *The Epistle to the Hebrews and Christian Theology*, edited by Richard J. Bauckham et al., 374–82. Grand Rapids: Eerdmans, 2009.
Mackie, Scott D. "Confession of the Son of God in the Exordium of Hebrews." *JSNT* 30 (2008) 437–53.
MacLeod, D. J. "Christ, the Believer's High Priest: An Exposition of Hebrews 7:26–28." *BSac* 162 (2005) 331–43.
Marshall, I. Howard. "Soteriology in Hebrews." In *The Epistle to the Hebrews and Christian Theology*, edited by Richard J. Bauckham et al., 253–77. Grand Rapids: Eerdmans, 2009.
Mason, Eric F. "Hebrews 7:3 and the Relationship Between Melchizedek and Jesus." *BR* 50 (2005) 41–62.
———. *'You Are a Priest Forever': Second Temple Jewish Messianism and the Priestly Christology of the Epistle to the Hebrews*. STDJ 74. Leiden: Brill, 2008.
Mathewson, David. "Reading Heb 6:4–6 in Light of the Old Testament." *WTJ* 61 (1999) 209–25.
Matthews, Victor H. "House." In *The New Interpreter's Dictionary of the Bible* 2:902–3. Nashville: Abingdon, 2007.
McBride, S. Dean. "Bless." In *The New Interpreter's Dictionary of the Bible* 1:476–77. Nashville: Abingdon, 2006.
McCormick, Bruce L. "'With Loud Cries and Tears': The Humanity of the Son in the Epistle to the Hebrews." In *The Epistle to the Hebrews and Christian Theology*, edited by Richard J. Bauckham et al., 37–68. Grand Rapids: Eerdmans, 2009.
McCruden, Kevin B. "Christ's Perfection in Hebrews: Divine Beneficence as an Exegetical Key to Hebrews 2:10." *BR* 47 (2002) 40–62.
McGowan, Andrew B. "Is There a Liturgical Text in This Gospel?: The Institution Narratives and Their Early Interpretive Communities." *JBL* 118 (1999) 73–87.
McLay, R. Timothy. "Biblical Texts and the Scriptures for the New Testament Church." In *Hearing the Old Testament in the New Testament*, edited by Stanley E. Porter, 38–58. McMaster New Testament Studies. Grand Rapids: Eerdmans, 2006.
———. *The Use of the Septuagint in New Testament Research*. Grand Rapids: Eerdmans, 2003.
Milavec, Aaron. *The Didache: Text, Translation, Analysis, and Commentary*. Collegeville, MN: Liturgical 2004.

Miller, James C. "Paul and Hebrews: A Comparison of Narrative Worlds." In *Hebrews: Contemporary Methods, New Insights*, edited by Gabriella Gelardini, 245–64. BIS 75. Leiden: Brill, 2005.
Mitchell, Alan C. *Hebrews*. SP 13. Collegeville, MN: Liturgical, 2007.
———. "Holding on to Confidence: *Parrēsia* in Hebrews." In *Friendship, Flattery, and Frankness of Speech*, edited by John T. Fitzgerald, 203–26. NovTSup 82. Leiden: Brill, 1996.
Moberly, R. Walter L. "Exemplars of Faith in Hebrews 11: Abel." In *The Epistle to the Hebrews and Christian Theology*, edited by Richard J. Bauckham et al., 252–63. Grand Rapids: Eerdmans, 2009.
Moffitt, David M. "'If Another Priest Arises': Jesus' Resurrection and the High Priestly Christology of Hebrews." In *A Cloud of Witnesses: The Theology of Hebrews in Its Ancient Contexts*, edited by Richard Bauckham et al., 68–79. LNTS 378. London: T. & T. Clark, 2008.
Mosser, Carl. "Rahab Outside the Camp." In *The Epistle to the Hebrews and Christian Theology*, edited by Richard J. Bauckham et al., 383–404. Grand Rapids: Eerdmans, 2009.
Motyer, Steve. "'Not Apart from Us' (Hebrews 11:40): Physical Community in the Letter to the Hebrews." *EvQ* 77 (2005) 235–47.
Müller, Paul Gerd. "*blepō*." In *EDNT* 1:221–22.
Murray, Scott R. "The Concept of *diathēkē* in the Letter to the Hebrews." *CTQ* 66 (2002) 41–60.
Nardoni, Enrique. "Partakers in Christ (Hebrews 3.14)." *NTS* 37 (1991) 456–72.
Newman, Carey C. "Glory, Glorify." In *The New Interpreter's Dictionary of the Bible* 2:576–80. Nashville: Abingdon, 2007.
Neyrey, Jerome H. "Despising the Shame of the Cross." *Semeia* 68 (1994) 113–37.
———. "'Without Beginning of Days or End of Life' (Hebrews 7:3): Topos for a True Deity." *CBQ* 53 (1991) 439–55.
Niederwimmer, Kurt. *The Didache: A Commentary*. Hermeneia. Minneapolis: Fortress, 1998.
Nongbri, Brent. "A Touch of Condemnation in a Word of Exhortation: Apocalyptic Language and Graeco-Roman Rhetoric in Hebrews 6:4–12." *NovT* 45 (2003) 265–79.
Nützel, Johannes M. "*gony*." In *EDNT* 1:257–58.
O'Brien, Peter Thomas. *The Letter to the Hebrews*. Pillar New Testament Commentary. Grand Rapids: Eerdmans, 2010.
Peterson, David G. *The Acts of the Apostles*. Pillar New Testament Commentary. Grand Rapids: Eerdmans, 2009.
———. *Engaging with God: A Biblical Theology of Worship*. Downers Grove, IL: InterVarsity, 1992.
———. *Hebrews and Perfection: An Examination of the Concept of Perfection in the "Epistle to the Hebrews."* SNTSMS 47. Cambridge: Cambridge University Press, 1982.
Portalatín, Antonio. *Temporal Oppositions as Hermeneutical Categories in the Epistle to the Hebrews*. European University Studies 23: Theology 833. Frankfurt: Lang, 2006.
Powell, Mark Allan. "Worship, New Testament." In *Eerdmans Dictionary of the Bible*, edited by David Noel Freedman, 1391–92. Grand Rapids: Eerdmans, 2000.
Proctor, John. "Judgement or Vindication?: Deuteronomy 32 in Hebrews 10:30." *TynBul* 55 (2004) 65–80.

Radl, Walter. "*rhēma*." In *EDNT* 3:210–11.
———. "*cheir*." In *EDNT* 3:462–63.
Rascher, Angela. *Schriftauslegung und Christologie im Hebräerbrief*. BZNW 153. Berlin: de Gruyter, 2007.
Rhee, Victor. "Chiasm and the Concept of Faith in Hebrews 12:1–29." *WTJ* 63 (2001) 269–84.
———. "Christology, Chiasm, and the Concept of Faith in Hebrews 10:19–39." *Filología Neotestamentaria* 16 (2003) 33–48.
Richardson, Christopher. "The Passion: Reconsidering Hebrews 5.7–8." In *A Cloud of Witnesses: The Theology of Hebrews in Its Ancient Contexts*, edited by Richard Bauckham et al., 51–67. LNTS 387. London: T. & T. Clark, 2008.
Roloff, Jürgen. "*hilastērion*." In *EDNT* 2:185–86.
Rutenfranz, Monika. "*hymneō*." In *EDNT* 3:392–93.
Salevao, Iutisone. *Legitimation in the Letter to the Hebrews: The Construction and Maintenance of a Symbolic Universe*. JSNTSup 219. London: Sheffield Academic, 2002.
Sand, Alexander. "*kardia*." In *EDNT* 2:249–51.
Sänger, Dieter. "*mesitēs*." In *EDNT* 2:410–11.
Schenck, Kenneth L. *Cosmology and Eschatology in Hebrews: The Settings of the Sacrifice*. SNTSMS 143. Cambridge: Cambridge University Press, 2007.
———. "Keeping His Appointment: Creation and Enthronement in Hebrews." *JSNT* 66 (1997) 91–117.
———. *Understanding the Book of Hebrews: The Story Behind the Sermon*. Louisville: Westminster John Knox, 2003.
Schmitt, Mary. "Restructuring Views on Law in Hebrews 7:12." *JBL* 128 (2009) 189–201.
Schnabel, Eckhard J. *Paul the Missionary: Realities, Strategies and Methods*. Downers Grove, IL: InterVarsity, 2008.
Schröger, Friedrich. "*Melchisedek*." In *EDNT* 2:405.
Sims, C. "Rethinking Hebrews 12:1." *IBS* 27 (2008) 54–88.
Sisson, R. B. "Overcoming the Fear of Death: Physical Body and Community in Hebrews." *Scriptura* 90 (2005) 670–78.
Smillie, Gene R. "Contrast or Continuity in Hebrews 1.1–2?" *NTS* 51 (2005) 543–60.
———. "'*ho logos tou theou*' in Hebrews 4:12–13." *NovT* 46 (2004) 338–59.
———. "'The One Who Is Speaking' in Hebrews 12:25." *TynBul* 55 (2004) 275–94.
———. "'The Other *logos*' at the End of Heb. 4:13." *NovT* 47 (2005) 19–25.
Smith, Dennis E. *From Symposium to Eucharist: The Banquet in the Early Christian World*. Minneapolis: Fortress, 2003.
Snyman, Andreas H. "Hebrews 6:4–6: From a Semiotic Discourse Perspective." In *Discourse Analysis and the New Testament: Approaches & Results*, edited by Jeffrey T. Reed and Stanley E. Porter, 354–68. JSNTSup 170. Sheffield: Sheffield Academic, 1999.
Son, Kiwoong. *Zion Symbolism in Hebrews: Hebrews 12:18–24 as a Hermeneutical Key to the Epistle*. Paternoster Biblical Monographs. Milton Keynes, UK: Paternoster, 2005.
Spicq, Ceslas. *Theological Lexicon of the New Testament*. Translated and edited by James D. Ernest. 3 vols. Peabody, MA: Hendrickson, 1994.
Stanley, Steve. "Hebrews 9:6–10: The 'Parable' of the Tabernacle." *NovT* 37 (1995) 385–99.
Steyn, Gert Jacobus. "The Occurrence of Psalm 118(117):6 in Hebrews 13:6: Possible Liturgical Origins?" *Neot* 40 (2006) 119–34.

———. "Some Observations about the *Vorlage* of Ps 8:5–7 in Heb 2:6–8." *Verbum et Ecclesia* 24 (2003) 493–514.

———. "The *Vorlage* of the Melchizedek Phrases in Heb 7.1–4." *Acta Patristica et Byzantina* 13 (2002) 207–23.

———. "The *Vorlage* of Psalm 45:6–7 (44:7–8) in Hebrews 1:8–9." *HTS* 60 (2004) 1085–1103.

Stringer, Martin D. *Rethinking the Origins of the Eucharist*. SCM Studies in Worship and Liturgy. London: SCM, 2010.

Swetnam, James. "Another Note on *Logos* as Christ in Hebrews 4,12–13." *Filología Neotestamentaria* 18 (2005) 129–33.

———. "*ho apostolos* in Hebrews 3,1." *Bib* 89 (2008) 252–62.

———. "Christology and the Eucharist in the Epistle to the Hebrews." *Bib* 70 (1989) 74–95.

———. "The Context of the Crux at Hebrews 5,7–8." *Filología Neotestamentaria* 14 (2001) 101–20.

———. "The Crux at Hebrews 5,7–8." *Bib* 81 (2000) 347–61.

———. "*Ex Henos* in Hebrews 2:11." *Bib* 88 (2007) 517–25.

———. "Hebrews 9,2: Some Suggestions about Text and Context." *Melita Theologica* 51 (2000) 163–85.

———. "Hebrews 10,30–31: A Suggestion." *Bib* 75 (1994) 388–94.

———. "Jesus as *logos* in Hebrews 4:12–13." *Bib* 62 (1981) 214–24.

———. "A Liturgical Approach to Hebrews 13." *Letter & Spirit* 2 (2006) 159–73.

———. "A Merciful and Trustworthy High Priest: Interpreting Hebrews 2:17." *Pacific Journal of Theology* 21 (1999) 6–25.

———. "On the Literary Genre of the 'Epistle' to the Hebrews." *NovT* 11 (1969) 261–69.

———. "*Tōn lalēthēsomenō* in Hebrews 3,5." *Bib* 90 (2009) 93–100.

Swinson, L. T. "'Wind' and 'Fire' in Hebrews 1:7: A Reflection Upon the Use of Psalm 104 (103)." *TJ* 28 (2007) 215–28.

Tanner, J. P. "For Whom Does Hebrews 10:26–31 Teach a 'Punishment Worse Than Death'?" *Journal of the Grace Evangelical Society* 19 (2006) 57–77.

Thiessen, Matthew. "Hebrews and the End of the Exodus." *NovT* 49 (2007) 353–69.

———. "Hebrews 12.5–13, the Wilderness Period, and Israel's Discipline." *NTS* 55 (2009) 366–79.

Thomas, Gordon J. "The Perfection of Christ and the Perfecting of Believers in Hebrews." In *Holiness and Ecclesiology in the New Testament*, edited by Kent E. Brower and Andy Johnson, 293–310. Grand Rapids: Eerdmans, 2007.

Thompson, James W. "EPHAPAX: The One and the Many in Hebrews." *NTS* 53 (2007) 566–81.

Tipei, John Fleter. *The Laying on of Hands in the New Testament: Its Significance, Techniques, and Effects*. Lanham, MD: University Press of America, 2009.

Towner, Philip H. *The Letters to Timothy and Titus*. NICNT. Grand Rapids: Eerdmans, 2006.

Van der Minde, Hans-Jügen. "*geuomai*." In *EDNT* 1:245–46.

Walker, Peter. "A Place for Hebrews?: Contexts for a First-Century Sermon." In *The New Testament in Its First Century Setting: Essays on Context and Background in Honour of B. W. Winter*, edited by P. J. Williams et al., 231–49. Grand Rapids: Eerdmans, 2004.

Webster, John. "One Who Is Son: Theological Reflections on the Exordium to the Epistle to the Hebrews." In *The Epistle to the Hebrews and Christian Theology*, edited by Richard J. Bauckham et al., 69–94. Grand Rapids: Eerdmans, 2009.

Wedderburn, Alexander J. M. "The 'Letter' to the Hebrews and Its Thirteenth Chapter." *NTS* 50 (2004) 390–405.

Weiser, Alfons. "*agalliaō*." In *EDNT* 1:7–8.

Weiss, H. "*Sabbatismos* in the Epistle to the Hebrews." *CBQ* 58 (1996) 674–89.

Westcott, Brooke Foss. *The Epistle to the Hebrews: The Greek Text with Notes and Essays*. Grand Rapids: Eerdmans, 1977.

Whitfield, Bryan J. "Pioneer and Perfecter: Joshua Traditions and the Christology of Hebrews." In *A Cloud of Witnesses: The Theology of Hebrews in Its Ancient Contexts*, edited by Richard Bauckham et al., 80–87. LNTS 387. London: T. & T. Clark, 2008.

Wiid, J. S. "The Testamental Significance of *diathēkē* in Hebrews 9:15–22." *Neot* 26 (1992) 149–56.

Witherington, Ben. *Letters and Homilies for Jewish Christians: A Socio-Rhetorical Commentary on Hebrews, James and Jude*. Downers Grove, IL: InterVarsity, 2007.

Worley, D. R. "Fleeing to Two Immutable Things, God's Oath-Taking and Oath-Witnessing: The Use of Litigant Oath in Hebrews 6:12–20." *ResQ* 36 (1994) 223–36.

Wray, Judith H. *Rest as a Theological Metaphor in the Epistle to the Hebrews and the Gospel of Truth: Early Christian Homiletics of Rest*. SBLDS 166. Atlanta: Scholars, 1998.

Wright, Terry J. "The Seal of Approval: The Interpretation of the Son's Sustaining Action in Hebrews 1:3." In *The Epistle to the Hebrews and Christian Theology*, edited by Richard J. Bauckham et al., 140–48. Grand Rapids: Eerdmans, 2009.

Young, Norman H. "'Bearing His Reproach' (Heb 13.9–14)." *NTS* 48 (2002) 243–61.

———. "The Day of Dedication or the Day of Atonement?: The Old Testament Background to Hebrews 6:19–20 Revisited." *AUSS* 40 (2002) 61–68.

———. "Where Jesus Has Gone as a Forerunner on Our Behalf (Hebrews 6:20)." *AUSS* 39 (2001) 165–73.

Scripture Index

Old Testament (LXX numbering)

Genesis
2:2	65, 67, 84
3:17–18	94
5:24	192
6:13	195
7:22–23	195
14:17–20	100
21:12	196, 201, 208
22:17	95, 96, 100, 196, 199, 208
25:31–34	233
27:31–38	234
47:31	207, 209
50:24–25	207, 210

Exodus
1:15–22	210
2:2	210
3:16–17	66
4:22–23	24
4:22	23, 23n20
4:27–31	66
6:1–9	66
12:7	207
12:13	207
12:23	212
13:5	23n20
13:11	23n20
14:21–22	213
19:12–13	229, 236
23:20	23n20
24:1–11	5
24:8	143, 149–50, 150n44, 161, 210, 237
25:23–30	131
25:30	131
25:31–39	131
25:40	119, 122, 131, 150, 157

Leviticus
6:10	131
6:18	131
6:22	131
7:1	131
7:6	131
10:12	131
10:17	131
14:13	131
16:27	251

Numbers
12:7	50, 51, 54
12:8	54
14:26–30	66
14:29	64
14:32	64

Deuteronomy
4:11–12	235
4:24	230, 243

Deuteronomy (*cont.*)

6:10	23n20
6:23	23n20
7:1	23n20
9:19	230, 237n36
11:29	23n20
12:9	59
17:6	171, 179
29:17	229, 233
31:6	244, 247, 247n44
32:35–36	248
32:35	171, 181
32:36	171, 181, 247
32:43	21, 24, 24n21, 71n28, 166, 209
32:47	71n28

Joshua

2:1–21	213
2:12	213
6:1–17	208, 213
6:15–17	213
6:22–25	213
21:43	68
22:4	68

2 Samuel (2 Kingdoms)

7:14	21, 22, 23, 24, 42, 46, 200, 225, 226
7:24	23
22:3	39

3 Kingdoms

8:56	59

1 Chronicles

17:13	22
17:22	23
23:13	131

2 Chronicles

13:11	131

1 Maccabees

10:24	265n61

2 Maccabees

7:24	265n61
15:8–11	265n51

Psalms

2:6	22
2:7	21, 22, 28, 46, 76, 80, 82, 86, 199, 225, 253
2:8	16, 22, 37
8:5–7	33, 35, 36, 37, 47
8:5	41, 79, 246, 248
8:7	36, 227
21:23	39, 42, 48, 101, 225, 238, 240, 256
39:7–9	163, 165, 166, 186, 202, 240, 262
39:7	173, 189, 247
39:9	184
44:7–8	21, 25
44:7	133
44:8	54, 173, 225
49:14	255, 272
88:27	24
88:28	24
88:51–52	211n7
94:6	56n14
94:7–11	55, 71, 126, 166, 172, 203
94:7–8	60, 63, 65, 68, 90, 92, 191, 216, 236
94:7	56, 66
94:8	57, 83
94:10	128
94:11	64, 65, 67, 96, 110
96:7	21, 24, 24n21, 166, 209

Psalms (cont.)

101:26–28	21
101:26	26, 106, 182, 242
101:27	26, 27, 27n28
101:28	27
103:4	21, 24, 227
109:1	15, 19, 22, 28, 37, 120, 163–64, 169, 172, 179, 221, 224
109:4	76, 80, 83, 86, 87, 89, 98, 104, 105, 107, 108, 110, 114, 172, 189, 253
117:6	244, 248, 272, 285
131:14	59

Proverbs

3:11–12	221, 225, 226
4:26	229, 231

Job

7:21	15, 18

Wisdom

7:25–26	15, 18
11:7	210n6

Sirach

25:23	231

Hosea

11:1	23
14:3	255

Habakkuk

2:3–4	182
2:3	184, 185
2:4	185, 186, 190, 191, 193, 195, 227, 249

Zephaniah

1:18	171, 179

Haggai

2:6	230, 241, 241n40

Zechariah

8:8	23n19

Isaiah

8:17	39, 43, 258
8:18	39, 43, 166
26:11	171, 179
26:20	181, 184
35:3	229, 231
53:10–12	5
53:12	152, 153, 156, 162, 165, 170, 184–85
63:11	260
66:1	59

Jeremiah

7:23	23n19
11:4	23n19
24:7	23n19
38:1	23n19
38:31–34	5, 124, 125, 144, 158, 166
38:31	124
38:33–34	183, 189
38:33	23, 171, 172, 173, 180, 203, 204
38:34	128, 153, 156, 171, 172, 173, 203, 246
39:38	23n19

Baruch

2:35	23n19

Ezekiel

11:20	23n19
14:11	23n19
36:28	23n19
37:33	23n19
43:12	131

New Testament

Matthew

26:26–29	5
26:28	151n45

Mark

14:22–25	5
14:24	151n45

Luke

22:19–20	5
22:20	151n45

Acts of the Apostles

2:42	3
7:30	30
7:38	30
7:53	30
13:15	6, 265n61
14:1–3	33n35
18:24	6n15
19:22	7

1 Corinthians

11:23–26	5
11:24–25	150n44
12:4–11	33n35
16:8	6n15, 7
16:10	6n15
16:12	6n15

Galatians

3:19	30

1 Timothy

1:3	7
4:13	4

2 Timothy

1:18	7
3:16	4
4:12	7

Hebrews

1:1—5:10	8, 9
1:1—2:18	11, 13, 15–49
1:1–4	9, 11, 13, 15–21, 36, 46, 258, 275
1:1–2	20, 22, 24, 29, 35, 53, 76
1:1	15, 15n1, 16, 30, 45, 47, 54, 56n9, 57, 125, 191, 216, 240
1:2	15, 16, 17, 18, 19, 20, 22, 23, 23n20, 24, 25, 26, 28, 29, 30, 32, 35, 36, 40, 41, 45, 46, 47, 54, 56n9, 74, 76, 80, 82, 125, 136, 146, 155, 178, 190, 191, 195, 197, 240, 249, 258, 263
1:3	15, 17, 18, 19, 20, 22, 25, 26, 28, 29, 31, 36, 38, 40, 41, 45, 46, 47, 48, 52, 53, 62, 63, 69, 76, 77, 78, 79, 80, 85, 93, 113, 113n40, 114, 120, 122, 128, 134, 147, 151, 161, 169, 188, 190, 217, 224, 236, 254, 264, 276
1:4–7	44
1:4–5	24, 26

Hebrews (cont.)

1:4   15, 19, 20, 22, 23n20, 24, 26, 29, 36, 40, 42, 46, 52, 76, 83, 95, 109, 113, 122, 146, 151, 183, 200, 211, 218, 234

1:5–14   9, 11, 13, 21–29, 30, 32, 34, 47, 70, 245, 276

1:5–13   28, 35, 42

1:5–10   26

1:5   21, 22, 23, 24, 25, 26, 27, 28, 32, 34, 35, 40, 41, 42, 43, 46, 52, 56, 56n9, 57, 67, 80, 82, 86, 127, 128, 158, 199, 200, 225, 226, 281

1:6–7   29, 47, 78

1:6   21, 23n20, 24, 24n21, 25, 28, 29, 33, 34, 36, 40, 41, 42, 43, 45, 46, 48, 51, 53, 54, 56, 56n9, 59, 61, 62, 67, 72, 77, 83, 84, 86, 106, 109, 120, 122, 145, 166, 209, 213, 229, 232, 234, 238, 260, 264, 268, 270, 271, 274, 275, 278, 285

1:7   21, 25, 28, 33, 36, 46, 51, 53, 56, 56n9, 70, 72, 121, 179, 217, 227, 238, 243–44, 275

1:8–12   41, 48

1:8–9   25, 26, 46

1:8   21, 25, 26, 27, 28, 32, 32n34, 35, 40, 41, 46, 52, 78, 81, 82, 100, 111, 120, 133, 209, 217, 242, 249

1:9   21, 25, 26, 31, 46, 51, 52, 54, 62, 83, 90, 100, 173, 195, 217, 225, 229, 270, 284–85

1:10   21, 26, 27, 32, 32n34, 46, 67, 106, 113, 120, 153, 182, 232, 242

1:11–12   27, 47, 275

1:11   21, 27, 27n28, 73, 129

1:12   21, 27, 27n28, 245

1:13–14   28, 78

1:13   22, 28, 29, 32, 34, 37, 38, 41, 43, 44, 47, 48, 52, 56, 56n9, 74, 77, 78, 170, 179, 224, 232, 247, 275, 276

1:14   22, 28, 29, 31, 33, 34, 36, 38, 40, 41, 42, 43, 44, 45, 47, 48, 49, 51, 53, 54, 55, 59, 66, 70, 72, 82, 83, 87, 93, 95, 114, 120, 121, 122, 145, 146, 157, 195, 213, 227, 234, 238, 244, 271, 275, 277, 285

2:1–4   9, 11, 13, 29–33, 34, 66, 231

2:1   29, 30, 31, 32, 33, 47, 57, 58, 59, 62, 66, 68, 90, 93, 98, 236, 260, 276

2:2–3   71, 72, 92, 93

2:2   20, 29, 30, 31, 32, 47, 54, 56n9, 63, 66, 97, 145, 148, 184, 193, 212, 275

2:3–4   34

2:3   29, 31, 32, 34, 35, 38, 40, 41, 44, 47, 48, 49, 53, 54, 55, 56, 56n9, 57, 59, 63, 66, 68, 82, 83, 87, 90, 95, 106, 111, 126, 139, 146, 148, 157, 162, 170, 203, 231, 232, 236, 240, 241, 250, 251, 275, 276, 277, 282

2:4   29, 33, 35, 47, 53, 56, 70, 72, 92, 93, 106, 135, 249, 276

2:5–9   9, 11, 13, 33–38, 39, 40n44, 60, 222

2:5   33, 34, 35, 36, 37, 44, 47, 54, 93, 164, 222, 226, 254

Hebrews (cont.)

2:6–8	47
2:6	33, 35, 36, 37, 38, 40, 41, 48, 56, 56n9, 67, 79, 128, 246, 248, 276
2:7	33, 35, 36, 37, 38, 44, 48, 52, 80, 134, 264, 276
2:8–9	93
2:8	33, 34, 36, 38, 38n42, 47, 58, 74, 189, 212, 222, 227, 232, 268, 276
2:9–15	53
2:9–10	77
2:9	5, 33, 37, 38, 38n42, 39, 40, 41, 43, 44, 48, 51, 52, 58, 60, 64, 68, 79, 80, 81, 92, 98, 111, 134, 145, 156, 168, 180, 183, 189, 190, 193, 205, 212, 233, 243, 250, 264, 267, 268, 274, 276, 283, 286
2:10–18	9, 11, 13, 39–45, 50, 56, 216
2:10–15	55
2:10–12	43, 45, 49
2:10–11	45, 53
2:10	39, 40, 41, 42, 43, 44, 45, 48, 49, 51, 52, 59, 61, 64, 66, 74, 80, 82, 84, 87, 91, 93, 94, 104, 112, 113, 115, 122, 134, 137, 139, 146, 156, 157, 170, 183, 216, 220, 223, 225, 239, 260, 264, 276
2:11–17	198, 206
2:11–15	276
2:11–14	44, 49
2:11–12	43, 44, 49, 101, 246
2:11	39, 41, 44, 48, 51, 61, 91, 95, 116, 141, 145, 168, 170, 201, 228, 232, 266, 276
2:12–13	141
2:12	39, 40, 42, 43, 44, 48, 56, 56n9, 59, 61, 84, 95, 116, 225, 238, 240, 256, 276, 277
2:13–14	44, 45, 49
2:13	39, 43, 44, 49, 61, 67, 105, 166, 167, 210, 258
2:14–18	93, 166
2:14–16	50
2:14–15	61, 79, 81, 82, 87, 92, 107, 111, 145
2:14	39, 43, 44, 49, 72, 74, 81, 106, 138, 140, 141, 141n34, 175, 192, 203, 210, 283
2:15	39, 44, 49, 62, 66, 71, 73, 74, 85, 106, 112, 125, 141, 148, 179, 185, 192–93, 255, 260, 278
2:16	39, 44, 96, 100, 125, 198, 199, 201, 206
2:17–18	58, 276
2:17	39, 40, 44, 45, 49, 50, 51, 53, 61, 62, 69, 74, 78, 79, 80, 85, 86, 95, 101, 105, 114, 116, 117, 127, 128–29, 177, 240, 246, 252
2:18	39, 44, 45, 49, 56, 57, 74, 77, 79, 81, 82, 137, 155, 201, 248, 252
3:1—5:10	50–87
3:1–6	9, 11, 13, 50–55, 56, 61, 208
3:1–3	52
3:1–2	61
3:1	50, 51, 52, 53, 55, 60, 62, 68, 75, 77, 78, 83, 92, 95, 101, 116, 122, 145, 157, 168, 174, 177, 184, 198, 199, 200, 205, 206, 226, 232, 237, 246, 255, 264, 277, 281, 283

Hebrews (cont.)

3:2	50, 51, 63, 75, 83, 122, 158, 177, 210n4, 240
3:3–4	83
3:3	50, 52, 63, 80, 83, 110, 131, 134, 169, 180, 190, 195, 210n4, 264, 277
3:4	50, 52, 54, 131
3:5–6	61, 240
3:5	50, 53, 54, 55, 63, 83, 106, 122, 158, 177, 210n4, 237
3:6	50, 54, 55, 58, 62, 63, 78, 82, 92, 95, 97, 110, 122, 158, 168, 174, 175, 177, 180, 184, 188, 195, 265, 277
3:7—5:10	11, 13
3:7–11	9, 11, 13, 55–59, 60, 67, 76
3:7–8	63, 68, 92, 172, 203, 277
3:7	22n18, 55, 56, 57, 58, 62, 63, 66, 70, 71, 72, 74, 83, 84, 90, 93, 115, 135, 236
3:8–9	56
3:8	55, 57, 58, 60, 62, 64, 72, 73, 74, 77, 83, 84, 126, 176, 178, 233
3:9–10	59, 83
3:9	55, 57, 58, 62, 67, 77
3:10	55, 58, 59, 60, 61, 62, 72, 73, 74, 79, 83, 98, 127, 128, 166, 176, 183, 219
3:11–12	66
3:11	55, 59, 61, 64, 67, 84, 96, 98, 110, 122, 140, 213, 277
3:12–19	9, 11, 13, 60–65, 70
3:12	60, 61, 62, 64, 69, 71, 72, 73, 74, 84, 85, 93, 98, 101, 107, 112, 127, 143, 149, 158, 174, 175, 176, 178, 182–83, 185, 189, 227, 232, 237, 240, 241, 246, 264, 266, 277, 278
3:13	22n18, 60, 62, 63, 69, 74, 78, 80, 84, 129, 178, 260, 264, 277
3:14	60, 62, 63, 84, 92, 95, 98, 148, 168, 177, 188, 209, 211, 226, 265, 277
3:15–19	84, 277
3:15–16	68
3:15	22n18, 60, 63, 66, 71, 72, 73, 74, 90, 127, 176, 233, 236
3:16–19	67, 72, 93, 98
3:16–17	68
3:16	60, 63, 66, 90, 122, 125, 158, 210n4, 211, 213, 233, 236, 252
3:17	60, 63, 69, 178, 182, 213, 214
3:18	60, 64, 66, 67, 69, 82, 93, 96, 98, 110, 115, 122, 140, 182, 213, 214
3:19	60, 64, 65, 66, 68, 69, 98, 137, 140, 189
4:1–11	9, 11, 13, 65–70
4:1	65, 66, 67, 69, 84, 95, 96, 102, 123, 140, 146, 179, 198, 206, 210, 212, 213, 219, 233, 248, 266, 269, 277
4:2	65, 66, 67, 68, 71, 84, 90, 185, 236, 250, 277
4:3–4	67, 85, 247
4:3	65, 66, 67, 68, 84, 93, 96, 98, 110, 115, 116, 122, 140, 143, 155, 185, 198, 214, 277, 279
4:4	65, 67, 68, 69, 85, 143, 278
4:5	65, 67, 93, 98, 115, 122, 140, 213

Hebrews (cont.)

Ref	Pages
4:6–11	174
4:6	65, 67, 68, 69, 82, 85, 93, 98, 140, 179, 182, 218
4:7–11	204, 283
4:7	22n18, 65, 68, 69, 71, 72, 73, 74, 85, 90, 127, 176, 178, 216, 236, 278
4:8	65, 68, 69, 85, 178, 191, 277–78
4:9–11	73, 74, 85, 178, 182
4:9	65, 69, 71, 80, 85, 101, 105, 117, 127, 179, 181, 204, 211, 268, 277
4:10–11	85, 278
4:10	65, 69, 70, 71, 140, 143
4:11	65, 69, 82, 93, 98, 116, 122, 140, 143, 182, 213, 214, 266, 279
4:12–13	9, 11, 70–75, 76
4:12	70, 71, 71n28, 72, 73, 73n32, 74, 77, 85, 86, 89, 97, 112, 127, 149, 185, 186, 205, 217, 249, 259, 263, 265, 278
4:13	70, 73, 73n32, 74, 75, 76, 77, 85, 86, 89, 107, 140, 249, 259, 263, 265, 278
4:14—5:10	9, 11, 13, 75–83, 89
4:14	75, 76, 77, 78, 80, 82, 86, 94, 97, 113, 118, 120, 153, 168, 173, 175, 177, 199, 206, 211, 222, 250, 255, 261, 273, 278, 280
4:15	75, 76, 77, 78, 79, 80, 81, 86, 107, 113, 114, 120, 129, 137, 142, 157, 165, 183, 201, 211, 217, 250, 254, 268, 278
4:16	75, 78, 79, 80, 86, 112, 120, 141, 146, 160, 165, 174, 175, 180, 184, 193, 233, 234, 235, 243, 248, 250, 267, 270, 271, 274, 278, 281, 287
5:1	5, 75, 76, 79, 81, 86, 98, 113, 114, 121, 129, 135, 136, 137, 151, 155, 168–69, 179, 190
5:2	75, 79, 81, 86, 114, 137, 217, 219, 223, 268
5:3	75, 76, 79, 81, 86, 101, 105, 113, 117, 127, 129, 135, 166, 252
5:4–5	86
5:4	75, 76, 80, 105, 130n11, 133, 145, 159, 197
5:5	22n18, 76, 80, 82, 89, 114, 139, 154, 168, 199, 225, 253
5:6	76, 80, 83, 86, 87, 89, 98, 100, 103, 105, 111, 117, 156, 249
5:7	76, 81, 86, 97, 111, 112, 121, 137, 138, 145, 148, 175, 192, 194, 195, 217, 234, 243, 272, 278
5:8	76, 82, 87, 115, 154, 197, 205, 226, 252, 278
5:9	76, 82, 87, 91, 94, 104, 112, 115, 137, 139, 141, 146, 157, 170, 197, 205, 220, 239, 247, 261, 278
5:10	76, 82, 87, 98, 103, 117, 220
5:11—9:28	8, 9
5:11—7:28	11, 13, 88–118
5:11—6:12	9, 11, 14, 88–95, 96, 109, 152
5:11	88, 89, 90, 95, 109, 115, 116, 236, 279
5:12	88, 90, 91, 105, 115, 128, 174, 184, 216, 222–23

Hebrews (*cont.*)

5:13	88, 90, 91, 92, 100, 109, 115, 195, 217, 228, 236
5:14—6:1	100
5:14	88, 90, 91, 93, 94, 104, 115, 140, 228, 249, 279
6:1	88, 91, 93, 94, 95, 104, 105, 109, 115, 116, 137, 140, 142, 147, 148, 168, 177, 185, 198, 211, 234, 236, 254, 259, 279
6:2	3, 88, 91, 137, 141, 148, 156, 182, 201, 232, 249, 260–61
6:3	88, 91
6:4–5	94
6:4	88, 92, 93, 97, 115, 116, 122, 135, 157, 165, 182, 183, 190, 200, 206, 226, 237, 254, 279, 281
6:5	88, 93, 115, 136, 164, 190, 236, 249, 279
6:6	89, 93, 94, 97, 115, 116, 165, 234, 279
6:7	89, 94, 95, 96, 97, 116, 154, 227–28, 234, 279
6:8	89, 94, 95, 116, 129, 236, 243
6:9	89, 94, 109, 116, 122, 139, 152, 157, 183, 200, 218, 225, 258
6:10	89, 95, 116, 177, 232, 246, 256, 279
6:11	89, 95, 97, 110, 116, 128, 176, 177, 188, 209
6:12	89, 95, 96, 97, 102, 116, 123, 146, 176, 185, 198, 201, 206, 209, 217, 234, 279
6:13–20	9, 11, 14, 95–99, 104, 144
6:13	95, 96, 97, 100, 110, 139, 177, 199, 241
6:14	95, 96, 100, 199, 208
6:15	95, 97, 102, 116, 123, 146, 198, 205–6, 216
6:16	96, 97, 111, 139
6:17–20	177
6:17	96, 97, 102, 107, 111, 123, 144, 146, 195, 197, 205
6:18–20	178
6:18–19	97
6:18	96, 97, 110, 111, 116, 148, 164, 165, 177, 186, 188, 189, 218, 223, 225, 243, 269, 284
6:19–20	110, 116, 122, 148, 166, 188, 217–18, 268–69, 279, 284
6:19	96, 97, 98, 99, 113, 118, 120, 131, 140, 144, 148, 153, 161, 175, 186, 250, 254, 280
6:20	5, 96, 98, 100, 103, 104, 110, 111, 111n36, 113, 116, 117, 118, 120, 131, 140, 148, 154, 156, 161, 168, 211, 224, 249, 279, 280
7:1–10	9, 11, 14, 99–103, 104, 139
7:1–2	116, 210, 279
7:1	99, 100, 102, 103, 117, 169, 208, 260
7:2	99, 100, 101, 102, 195, 214, 217, 229, 260
7:3	99, 100, 103, 107, 111, 112, 117, 118, 164, 169, 172, 184, 242, 246, 254, 279, 280
7:4	99, 101, 102, 169
7:5	99, 101, 102, 103, 104, 107, 110, 117, 123, 127, 250–51, 252, 279
7:6	99, 102, 117, 123, 201, 206, 208

Hebrews (cont.)

7:7	99, 102, 109, 117, 122, 183, 200, 208, 218
7:8	99, 102, 103, 107, 112, 117, 118, 139, 148, 156, 172, 180, 185, 189, 191, 280
7:9	99, 103, 117
7:10	99, 103, 104, 117
7:11–17	9, 11, 14, 103–8, 130
7:11–12	109
7:11	103, 104, 105, 106, 107, 108, 112, 115, 117, 120, 123, 127, 130, 133, 137, 139, 158, 159, 280
7:12	103, 105, 107, 112, 113, 123, 147, 192, 242
7:13	103, 105, 106, 117, 120, 131, 250, 280
7:14	103, 104, 106, 117, 122, 125, 210n4, 232, 237, 261
7:15–16	109
7:15	104, 106, 107, 118, 123, 217, 280
7:16	104, 107, 108, 112, 118, 122, 123, 138, 167, 192, 198, 217, 280
7:17	104, 107, 111, 118, 156, 172, 189, 192, 249, 280
7:18–28	9, 11, 14, 108–15, 120, 124
7:18–19	109, 118
7:18	108, 109, 112, 114, 155, 250
7:19	108, 109, 110, 111, 112, 114, 115, 118, 122, 123, 126, 137, 139, 151, 169, 170, 178, 183, 188, 200, 219, 220, 239, 250, 280
7:20	108, 110, 111, 114
7:21	108, 110, 111, 114, 118, 120, 121, 249, 253
7:22	108, 111, 111n36, 118, 123, 134, 139, 144, 151, 168, 183–84, 200, 218
7:23	108, 111, 118, 145, 192, 280
7:24	108, 111, 112, 113, 118, 154, 184, 192, 242, 246, 249, 254, 280
7:25	5, 108, 112, 113, 114, 118, 137, 149, 154, 165, 174, 175, 185, 235, 255, 263–64, 272, 280, 285–86
7:26	108, 113, 113n40, 114, 118, 120, 135, 142, 153, 156, 211, 224, 233, 247, 263, 270, 280
7:27	5, 108, 113, 114, 118, 120, 124, 127, 129, 135, 140, 142, 147, 152, 154, 155, 156, 168, 169, 179, 252, 255, 280
7:28—8:6	128, 158, 281
7:28	108, 109, 114, 115, 118, 120, 123, 126, 137, 139, 164, 169, 170, 217, 220, 239, 249, 268, 280
8:1—9:28	119–62
8:1–6	9, 11, 12, 13, 14, 119–23, 124, 208
8:1–2	122, 136
8:1	119, 120, 121, 122, 135, 136, 151, 153, 157, 169, 200, 224, 238, 250, 254, 280
8:2	119, 121, 122, 132, 136, 140, 153, 157, 175, 228, 280
8:3	119, 121, 135, 136, 142, 151, 155, 157, 168, 190
8:4	119, 121, 130, 137, 157, 167, 190, 200
8:5	119, 122, 130, 131, 132, 135, 137, 150, 151, 153, 157, 158, 164, 194, 200, 210n4, 236, 241, 251, 272, 280–81

Scripture Index

Hebrews (cont.)

8:6	119, 122, 123, 124, 126, 134, 139, 144, 150, 151, 158, 183–84, 200, 218, 239, 269
8:7—9:28	12, 13
8:7–13	10, 12, 14, 124–29, 130, 153
8:7	124, 125, 126, 129, 131, 135, 136, 145, 158, 159, 167–68, 234, 281
8:8	124, 125, 126, 128, 129, 134, 144, 158, 166, 166n1, 167, 209
8:9	124, 125, 126, 127, 128, 134, 158, 166, 166n1, 182, 211, 260
8:10	23, 124, 126, 127, 128, 134, 147, 158, 166, 166n1, 172, 175, 176, 181, 183, 209, 281
8:11	124, 128, 129, 159, 183
8:12	124, 128, 129, 153, 156, 159, 173, 183, 246, 281
8:13	124, 129, 130, 131, 132, 133, 136, 138, 144, 145, 159, 160, 168, 202, 261, 281
8:8–12	5
9:1–10	10, 12, 14, 129–38, 139, 144
9:1–3	133, 134
9:1	129, 130, 131, 135, 136, 138, 145, 159
9:2	4, 129, 131, 132, 135, 136, 159, 194
9:3	129, 131, 135, 136, 159, 175, 228
9:4–5	159
9:4	129, 130, 132, 133, 144, 194, 209
9:5	130, 134, 264
9:6	130, 135, 136, 159, 194, 255
9:7	5, 130, 135, 136, 137, 140, 149, 150, 154, 155, 159, 252
9:8	130, 136, 139, 140, 141, 142, 159, 160, 174, 202, 210, 228, 242, 251, 268, 272, 281
9:9	130, 136, 137, 138, 139, 141, 142, 151, 155, 156, 160, 164, 165, 170, 176, 190, 198, 202, 220, 239, 250, 251, 272, 281
9:10	130, 137, 138, 141, 160, 198, 234, 250, 281
9:11–14	10, 12, 14, 138–43, 144, 148
9:11	138, 139, 140, 142, 153, 160, 164, 168, 261
9:12	138, 140, 141, 142, 144, 145, 146, 149, 150, 153, 160, 161, 166, 168, 193, 224, 228, 234, 251, 252, 261, 281, 282
9:13–14	227
9:13	138, 141, 141n34, 142, 149, 151, 160, 161, 165, 168, 170, 176, 228, 239, 252, 266
9:14–15	5
9:14	138, 139, 141, 142, 144, 145, 146, 148, 149, 151, 154, 160, 161, 165, 168, 170, 174, 176, 178, 180, 183, 185, 190, 191, 204, 210, 211, 212, 228, 229, 233, 237–38, 239, 240, 243, 251, 252, 261, 266, 270, 271, 272, 282, 285
9:15–23	10, 12, 14, 143–52
9:15–17	149
9:15	143, 144, 145, 146, 147, 148, 149, 160, 161, 184, 192, 197, 198, 205, 219–20, 223, 239, 261, 269, 282, 283

Hebrews (cont.)

Ref	Pages
9:16	143, 144, 146, 147, 148, 160, 161, 192, 253, 282
9:17	143, 144, 147, 148, 161, 185
9:18	143, 149, 150, 161, 174
9:19–21	151
9:19	143, 149, 150, 161, 167, 176, 179, 181, 210n4, 237, 239, 282
9:20	5, 143, 144, 150, 150n44, 161, 180, 210, 237, 261
9:21	143, 150, 161, 176, 239, 282
9:22	5, 143, 150, 151, 161, 169, 173, 176
9:23	144, 151, 152, 153, 155, 161, 162, 176, 184, 200, 218, 238
9:24–28	10, 12, 14, 152–57, 164
9:24	5, 152, 153, 154, 154n49, 155, 156, 161, 166, 168, 174, 175, 199, 200, 218, 228, 269
9:25	152, 154, 155, 156, 161, 162, 164, 165, 168, 174, 197, 218, 251, 269, 282
9:26	152, 153, 154, 155, 156, 157, 162, 164, 165, 168, 179, 198, 252, 282
9:27	152, 156, 162, 179, 180, 191
9:28	5, 152, 153, 156, 157, 162, 165, 168, 170, 185, 195, 203, 211, 232, 234, 282
10:1—13:25	8, 10
10:1—11:19	12, 13, 163–206
10:1–14	10, 12, 14, 163–70, 171, 197, 257, 258
10:1	163, 164, 165, 166, 167, 169, 170, 175, 188, 202, 203, 208, 220, 235, 239, 254, 257–58, 261, 268, 282
10:2	163, 165, 167, 170, 176, 202, 203, 251, 272, 282
10:3	163, 165, 202
10:4	163, 165, 166, 168, 202, 251
10:5–10	194
10:5–6	167, 240, 271, 285
10:5	5, 163, 165, 166, 166n1, 168, 169, 173, 176, 190, 195, 202, 203, 240, 247, 252, 262, 271, 272, 282, 283, 285
10:6–10	190
10:6–9	202
10:6	163, 166, 186, 194
10:7	163, 167, 168, 184, 186, 195, 240, 258, 262, 271, 285
10:8	163, 167, 168, 173, 186, 194, 203, 240, 271, 282, 285
10:9	163, 167, 168, 184, 186, 195, 202, 240, 247, 258, 262, 271, 285
10:10	5, 163, 168, 169, 170, 173, 176, 184, 203, 228, 232, 240, 247, 249, 251–52, 258, 262, 263, 266, 271, 272, 282, 283, 285
10:11	163, 169, 203, 282
10:12–13	172, 224
10:12	5, 163, 169, 170, 171, 190, 203, 240, 282
10:13	163, 169, 170, 179, 197, 198, 203, 232, 282
10:14	164, 170, 173, 203, 220–21, 228, 232, 239, 266, 282

Hebrews (cont.)

10:15–30	10, 12, 14, 171–81, 182, 187, 245
10:15–16	173, 203
10:15	171, 172, 172n8, 179, 180, 187, 189, 263
10:16–17	5
10:16	171, 172, 173, 175, 176, 179, 180, 181, 183, 204, 245
10:17	171, 172, 173, 179, 183, 203, 245, 246
10:18	5, 171, 173, 179, 203
10:19–22	229, 270, 285
10:19–21	175, 203, 283
10:19–20	175, 203, 283
10:19	171, 174, 175, 180, 184, 204, 223, 228, 239, 240, 246, 264, 266, 271, 283, 285
10:20	171, 174, 175, 185, 210, 262–63, 268
10:21	171, 175, 211, 261, 273
10:22	171, 175, 176–77, 185, 187, 194, 203, 223, 235, 239, 245, 246–47, 252, 259, 264, 271, 283, 285
10:23	171, 177, 199, 203, 206, 241, 255, 265
10:24	171, 177, 178, 204, 249–50, 256, 260
10:25	6, 171, 178, 180, 189, 190, 204, 232, 240, 245, 248, 256, 260, 264, 270, 272
10:26	171, 178–79, 180, 181, 204, 243
10:27–30	204
10:27	171, 179, 181, 182, 204, 217, 235–36, 243
10:28	171, 179, 180, 191, 210n4, 223
10:29	5, 171, 180, 182, 198–99, 204, 211, 228, 232, 233, 243, 245, 250, 266, 267, 270
10:30	171, 181, 238, 245, 247, 248, 252
10:31–39	10, 12, 14, 181–86, 187, 230
10:31	181, 182, 185, 186, 204, 227, 230, 231, 237
10:32	181, 183, 204, 224, 225–26, 259
10:33	181, 183, 204, 211, 253, 259
10:34	181, 183, 186, 200, 204, 205, 218, 220, 224, 230, 242, 246, 254, 259, 265, 283
10:35	181, 184, 193, 204, 212, 268, 283, 284
10:36	181, 184, 186, 198, 202, 204, 206, 219, 223, 262, 269, 273, 283, 284
10:37–38	186
10:37	181, 184, 185, 197
10:38–39	189
10:38	182, 185, 186, 190, 191, 193, 195, 205, 227, 239, 249
10:39	182, 186, 187, 205
11:1–40	249, 262
11:1–7	10, 12, 14, 187–95, 196, 222
11:1	187, 188, 189, 190, 194, 205, 212, 220
11:2	187, 189, 190, 219
11:3	187, 189, 190, 194, 205, 220, 236, 249, 261, 283
11:4	187, 190, 191, 191n31, 192, 193, 195, 199, 201, 205, 209, 216, 219, 239–40, 271, 283, 285

Hebrews (cont.)

11:5	187, 192, 193, 195, 205, 219, 234, 242, 243, 256, 263, 283
11:6	187, 193, 194, 200, 205, 212, 235, 243, 256, 263, 283
11:7	187, 194, 195, 196, 197, 205, 217, 219, 222, 229, 241, 243
11:8–19	10, 12, 14, 196–202, 208, 215
11:8–9	199
11:8	196, 197, 201, 205, 234, 253
11:9	196, 197, 199, 200, 201, 205, 206, 208, 209, 215, 218, 269
11:10	196, 198, 201, 206, 237, 254, 284
11:11	196, 198, 199, 200, 201, 202, 206, 211, 217, 241
11:12	196, 199, 201, 202, 206, 210, 213
11:13	196, 199, 200, 201, 206, 208–9, 213, 215, 219, 249, 255, 266, 269, 283
11:14–16	219, 269
11:14	196, 200, 206, 254, 283–84
11:15–16	206
11:15	196, 200, 209
11:16	196, 200, 201, 206, 215, 218, 220, 237, 254, 284
11:17–18	206
11:17	196, 201, 215
11:18	196, 201, 208
11:19	196, 201, 202, 206, 215, 219, 260, 269
11:20—13:25	207–74
11:20–31	10, 11, 12, 13, 14, 207–14, 215
11:20	207, 208, 209, 233, 254, 268
11:21	207, 208, 209, 213, 268
11:22	207, 209, 210, 211, 212, 268
11:23	207, 210, 212, 248
11:24	207, 211, 237
11:25	207, 211, 223, 268
11:26	207, 211, 212, 253, 268, 284
11:27	207, 212, 248, 268
11:28	207, 212, 233–34, 236, 238, 268
11:29	207, 213, 218, 268, 284
11:30–31	268, 284
11:30	207–8, 213
11:31	208, 213, 214, 215, 229, 232, 260
11:32—13:25	12, 13
11:32–40	10, 12, 14, 214–21, 222, 258
11:32–33	268
11:32	6, 214, 216
11:33–34	219
11:33	214, 215, 216, 217, 219, 228, 242
11:34	214, 217, 218, 243, 268, 269, 284
11:35	214, 215, 218, 220, 258, 260, 269
11:36	214, 218
11:37	215, 218, 219, 246, 269
11:38	215, 219, 269
11:39	215, 219, 222, 223
11:40	215, 216, 220, 221, 239, 259, 269, 271, 284
12:1–11	10, 12, 14, 221–29, 230, 245
12:1	221, 222, 223, 223n18, 224, 231, 262, 269
12:2	221, 223, 224, 226, 228, 231, 254, 269, 284
12:3–4	270
12:3	221, 224, 226, 258

Hebrews (*cont.*)

12:4	221, 224, 225, 227
12:5–10	284
12:5–7	270
12:5	221, 225, 226, 228
12:6	221, 225, 226, 227
12:7	221, 225, 226, 227, 228
12:8–10	270
12:8	221, 226, 228
12:9	221, 222, 226, 227, 231, 239, 241
12:10	222, 227, 228, 232
12:11	222, 228, 230, 231, 232, 233, 245, 247, 255, 259, 260, 270, 284
12:12–29	10, 12, 14, 229–44, 245
12:12–13	231, 270
12:12	229, 230, 231, 235, 242
12:13	229, 231, 235
12:14	229, 230, 232, 235, 260, 267
12:15	229, 233, 242–43, 250, 266, 267, 270
12:16	229, 233, 247, 266
12:17	229, 234–35, 259
12:18–21	270
12:18–20	241
12:18	229, 235, 236, 237, 243
12:19	229, 236, 240, 241, 258–59
12:20	229, 236, 237, 241, 253
12:21	229, 230, 237
12:22	230, 237, 238, 241, 254, 271, 272, 285
12:23	230, 238, 239, 241, 271, 285
12:24	5, 230, 239, 240, 271, 285
12:25	230, 231, 240, 241, 242, 271, 285
12:26–27	271
12:26	230, 241, 242
12:27	230, 242, 246, 254
12:28	230, 242, 243, 250, 251, 256, 263, 267, 271, 272, 285
12:29	230, 243, 245
13:1–16	10, 12, 14, 244–56, 257
13:1–5	247
13:1	244, 246, 247, 254
13:2	244, 246, 247, 249, 256
13:3	244, 245, 246, 248, 252, 265, 272, 285
13:4	244, 245, 247, 248, 256, 259
13:5	244, 245, 247, 247n44, 248, 249, 272, 285
13:6	3, 244, 248, 272, 285
13:7	244, 245, 248, 249, 256, 258, 266
13:8	244, 245, 249, 263, 264, 272
13:9	244, 245, 249, 250, 251, 267, 272
13:10	4, 244, 250, 251, 254, 272, 285
13:11	244, 245, 251, 252, 253
13:12	244, 245, 252, 253
13:13	244, 252–53, 255, 272, 286
13:14	244, 254, 272
13:15–16	3
13:15	244, 245, 255, 256, 262, 263, 272, 286
13:16	244, 256, 257, 262, 263, 273–74, 286
13:17–25	10, 12, 14, 257–67
13:17	257, 258, 259, 260, 265, 266, 267
13:18–19	260, 273
13:18	3, 257, 259, 260, 264
13:19	6, 257, 258, 260, 264, 265
13:20–21	273, 286
13:20	5, 257, 258, 260, 261, 263, 264, 273

Hebrews (cont.)

13:21	257, 258, 261, 262, 263, 264, 266, 273
13:22	1, 6, 257, 264–65, 266, 267, 274, 286–87
13:23	6, 7, 257, 265, 266
13:24	7, 257, 266, 267
13:25	257, 266, 267, 274, 286

Author Index

Adams, Edward, 17n6
Aitken, Ellen Bradshaw, 5n13, 7n19
Alexander, Loveday C. A., 221n17
Allen, David M., 23n20, 24n21, 33n36, 70n27, 71n28, 92n6, 94n9, 147n41, 225n21, 237n36, 247n44, 247n45, 249n47
Andriessen, Paul, 2n2
Attridge, Harold W., 6n15, 6n17, 7n20, 19n14, 21n17, 55n7, 56n10, 56n14, 77n34, 94n7, 101n21, 112n37, 113n40, 114n41, 125n4, 125n5, 137n28, 150n43, 150n44, 151n47, 156n52, 170n7, 178n15, 178n16, 182n19, 211n7, 220n15, 223n19, 229n24, 231n26, 261n58
Aune, David E., 3n6, 4n9
Austin, John Langshaw, 262n59

Backhaus, Knut, 2n2
Balz, Horst, 23n20, 41n46, 113n39, 121n1
Bateman, Herbert W., 25n24
Bauckham, Richard J., 21n17
Becker, Eve-Marie, 75n33
Blomberg, Craig L., 38n43
Bockmuehl, Markus N. A., 202n42
Bradshaw, Paul F., 5n12

Brawley, Robert Lawson, 189n29
Bruce, Frederick Fyvie, 6n15
Bénétreau, Samuel, 70n27
Böcher, Otto, 43n49
Bühner, Jan-Adolf, 51n1

Cahill, Michael, 178n15
Campbell, Alastair, 3n6
Caneday, Ardel B., 23n20
Clivaz, Claire, 81n40
Cockerill, Gareth Lee, 24n21, 25n23, 100n16, 218n14
Cortez, Felix H., 138n31
Cosaert, C. P., 98n14
Croy, N. Clayton, 223n19

Davidson, R. M., 98n14
Davis, Casey Wayne, 94n8
De Kruijf, T. C., 100n16
DeSilva, David A., 6n15, 70n27, 94n10, 226n22, 251n50
DeYoung, K., 45n51
Docherty, Susan E., 4n10, 22n18, 24n21, 24n22, 25n23, 25n24
D'Angelo, Mary R., 210n4

Eberhart, Christian A., 114n43
Ellingworth, Paul, 6n15, 38n42, 53n5, 66n24, 78n38, 92n5, 92n6, 97n12, 101n20, 102n23, 103n26, 104n27, 121n2, 123n3, 125n5, 126n6, 131n15,

Ellingworth, Paul (*cont.*)
    134n24, 136n27, 137n28,
    142n35, 150n44, 150n45,
    155n51, 156n52, 156n53,
    157n54, 166n2, 167n3,
    168n5, 172n10, 183n20,
    184n22, 194n35, 195n36,
    210n6, 232n28, 233n33,
    243n41, 256n57, 261n58,
    265n62
Emmrich, Martin, 33n36, 94n8,
    142n35

Farkasfalvy, Denis, 2n2
Farris, Stephen, 20n16
Farrow, Douglas, 81n39
Fitzmyer, Joseph A., 4n8,
    100n16
Friedrich, Johannes H., 20n15
Fuchs, Albert, 30n32
Fuhrmann, Sebastian, 129n10,
    139n32

Gane, R. E., 98n14
Gelardini, Gabriella, 6n17
Gheorghita, Radu, 18n10, 24n21
Gleason, Randall C., 59n20,
    94n10, 181n18
Granerød, Gard, 103n25
Gray, Patrick, 44n50, 55n7,
    73n31
Greenlee, J. Harold, 198n42
Gräbe, Peter, 111n36
Guthrie, George H., 6n15, 16n5,
    35n38, 35n39, 56n12,
    166n1, 173n11, 185n23,
    226n23, 241n40

Hagner, Donald A., 6n16
Hahn, Scott W., 151n46
Hamm, Dennis, 135n25
Hartley, Donald E., 193n33
Hartman, Lars, 20n15
Heil, John Paul, 4n8, 7n21,
    40n44

Hengel, Martin, 226n22
Hoerber, R. G., 188n26
Hofius, Otfried, 59n19, 69n25,
    98n14
Hurtado, Larry W., 2n3, 2n4,
    3n5, 4n11, 5n12
Hübner, Hans, 41n45

Jobes, Karen H., 167n4
Johnson, Luke Timothy, 6n15,
    16n2, 17n6, 55n7, 58n18,
    62n21, 73n31, 77n35,
    77n36, 97n12, 100n17,
    102n22, 106n30, 110n35,
    111n36, 127n9, 131n15,
    135n26, 137n28, 137n29,
    141n33, 143n37, 144n38,
    147n41, 150n43, 172n9,
    177n14, 183n21, 188n26,
    189n28, 191n31, 202n43,
    211n7, 216n13, 223n18,
    231n25, 237n37, 246n43,
    253n52, 255n55
Joslin, Barry C., 105n29,
    111n36, 114n43, 125n5,
    126n7, 126n8, 209n3
Just, Arthur A., 2n2

Kistemaker, Simon J., 6n15
Klauck, Hans-Josef, 5n14
Koenig, John, 5n12
Koester, Craig R., 6n15, 7n18,
    35n38, 53n5, 55n7,
    57n16, 58n18, 59n19,
    62n21, 66n23, 66n24,
    71n29, 77n35, 78n37,
    81n41, 94n9, 95n11,
    97n12, 100n17, 100n18,
    101n20, 105n28, 106n30,
    106n31, 109n34, 114n42,
    121n2, 123n3, 125n4,
    126n6, 126n8, 127n9,
    131n15, 132n18, 133n21,
    134n22, 137n28, 137n29,
    147n42, 149n43, 153n48,

Koester, Craig R. (*cont.*)
    154n50, 155n51, 167n3,
    168n5, 170n6, 172n10,
    173n12, 197n40, 208n1,
    210n6, 212n8, 214n11,
    220n16, 232n29, 233n33,
    234n34, 235n35, 246n43,
    266n64
Koosed, Jennifer L., 6n15

Laansma, Jon, 57n15
Lane, William L., 6n15, 16n2,
    18n11, 101n20, 106n30,
    112n38, 113n39, 115n44,
    121n1, 131n15, 132n17,
    137n28, 142n36, 144n38,
    146n39, 150n45, 172n9,
    188n26, 189n28, 190n30,
    191n31, 193n32, 195n38,
    197n39, 208n1, 209n2,
    210n5, 211n7, 213n10,
    216n12, 221n17, 225n21,
    232n30, 232n31, 233n32,
    235n35, 237n37, 238n38,
    243n41, 246n43, 250n49,
    251n50, 251n51, 253n53,
    256n56, 265n61, 265n62,
    265n63, 266n64
Lee, J. A. L., 88n1
Leithart, Peter J., 176n13
Limbeck, Meinrad, 26n26
Lincoln, Andrew T., 6n17
Lincoln, L., 151n46
Lohr, Joel N., 191n31

MacDonald, Nathan, 213n9
MacLeod, D. J., 115n44
Mackie, Scott D., 21n17
Marshall, I. Howard, 29n30
Mason, Eric F., 45n51, 100n19
Mathewson, David, 94n8
Matthews, Victor H., 52n3
McBride, S. Dean, 95n11
McCormick, Bruce L., 81n40

McCruden, Kevin B., 41n45
McGowan, Andrew B., 5n13
McLay, R. Timothy, 24n21
Milavec, Aaron, 5n13
Miller, James C., 113n39
Mitchell, Alan C., 6n15, 18n9,
    55n7, 102n22, 102n24,
    109n34, 111n36, 112n37,
    131n12, 131n15, 133n20,
    134n22, 138n30, 154n50,
    172n10, 178n15, 186n24,
    188n26, 188n27, 193n34,
    195n37, 197n40, 198n41,
    229n24, 238n38
Moberly, R. Walter L., 191n31
Moffitt, David M., 108n32
Mosser, Carl, 214n11
Motyer, Steve, 221n17
Murray, Scott R., 147n41
Müller, Paul Gerd, 38n42

Nardoni, Enrique, 62n22
Newman, Carey C., 17n7
Neyrey, Jerome H., 100n19,
    226n22
Niederwimmer, Kurt, 5n12
Nongbri, Brent, 95n11
Nützel, Johannes M., 232n28

O'Brien, Peter Thomas, 6n15,
    16n2, 17n8, 19n12,
    19n13, 20n16, 30n31,
    32n33, 35n38, 36n41,
    51n2, 78n38, 81n40,
    90n3, 92n6, 98n13,
    113n39

Peterson, David G., 1n1, 3n7,
    41n45
Portalatín, Antonio, 6n17
Powell, Mark Allan, 2n4
Proctor, John, 181n17

Quinn, R. D., 35n39

Radl, Walter, 18n9, 232n27
Rascher, Angela, 35n40, 56n10
Rhee, Victor, 186n25, 244n42
Richardson, Christopher, 82n42
Roloff, Jürgen, 134n23
Rutenfranz, Monika, 42n48

Salevao, Iutisone, 6n15
Sand, Alexander, 57n17
Sänger, Dieter, 123n3
Schenck, Kenneth L., 6n17, 7n19, 17n6, 21n17
Schmitt, Mary, 105n29
Schnabel, Eckhard J., 62n21
Schröger, Friedrich, 100n16
Seesengood, Robert P., 6n15
Sims, C., 223n18
Sisson, R. B., 229n24
Smillie, Gene R., 16n3, 72n30, 75n33, 241n39
Smith, Dennis E., 5n12
Snyman, Andreas H., 94n8
Son, Kiwoong, 59n19
Spicq, Ceslas, 25n23
Stanley, Steve, 131n13
Steyn, Gert Jacobus, 25n24, 35n39, 100n16, 248n46
Stringer, Martin D., 5n12
Swetnam, James, 2n2, 42n47, 45n51, 51n1, 54n6, 71n29, 82n42, 131n14, 183n20
Swinson, L. T., 25n23

Tanner, J. P., 181n18
Thiessen, Matthew, 24n20, 56n13, 229n24
Thomas, Gordon J., 41n45
Thompson, James W., 114n42
Tipei, John Fleter, 91n4
Towner, Philip H., 4n9

van der Bergh, R. H., 167n4
van der Horst, Pieter Willem, 198n42
van der Minde, Hans-Jügen, 38n43

Walker, Peter, 6n17
Webster, John, 21n17
Wedderburn, Alexander J. M., 6n16
Weiser, Alfons, 26n25
Weiss, H., 69n26
Westcott, Brooke Foss, 18n11, 38n42, 132n16, 133n19, 154n49, 172n8
Whitfield, Bryan J., 55n8
Wiid, J. S., 151n46
Witherington, Ben, 6n15
Worley, D. R., 99n15
Wray, Judith H., 6n17, 59n19
Wright, Terry J., 17n8

Young, Norman H., 98n14, 254n54

www.ingramcontent.com/pod-product-compliance
Lightning Source LLC
Chambersburg PA
CBHW021344300426
44114CB00012B/1078